LEADERS

AND

LEADERSHIP

IN CANADA

Edited by

Maureen Mancuso

Richard G. Price

Ronald Wagenberg

Toronto   OXFORD UNIVERSITY PRESS   1994

Oxford University Press
70 Wynford Drive, Don Mills, Ontario M3C 1J9

Toronto   Oxford   New York
Delhi   Bombay   Calcutta   Madras   Karachi
Kuala Lumpur   Singapore   Hong Kong   Tokyo
Nairobi   Dar es Salaam   Cape Town
Melbourne   Auckland   Madrid

and associated companies in
Berlin   Ibadan

Oxford is a trademark of Oxford University Press

Canadian Cataloguing in Publication Data
Main entry under title:

Leaders and leadership in Canada

Includes bibliographical references and index.
ISBN 0–19–540922–1

1. Political leadership – Canada.   I. Mancuso, Maureen.   II. Price, Richard G.
III. Wagenberg, R. H., 1939–

JL196.L43 1994   324.271   C94–930026–8

Design: Heather Delfino
This book is printed on permanent (acid-free) paper ⊗.
Printed in Canada

TABLE OF CONTENTS

LIST OF CONTRIBUTORS

Keith Archer
University of Calgary

Peter Aucoin
Dalhousie University

Herman Bakvis
Dalhousie University

Joan Price Boase
University of Windsor

Kathy Brock
University of Manitoba

Janine Brodie
York University

David C. Docherty
University of Toronto

Ian Greene
York University

Lawrence LeDuc
University of Toronto

Heather MacIvor
University of Windsor

Maureen Mancuso
University of Guelph

Howard R. Pawley
University of Windsor

Richard G. Price
University of Windsor

Andrew Sancton
University of Western Ontario

Ian Stewart
Acadia University

Ronald Wagenberg
University of Windsor

Alan Whitehorn
Royal Military College of Canada

In Canada the importance of leadership is more often acknowledged than studied. Biographies of prime ministers and premiers are plentiful, and the machinations of Cabinet government have received their share of scrutiny, but political leadership — a multi-faceted function, practised in a wide variety of environments — has attracted more sporadic attention. We became aware of this void in the process of discussing and developing a seminar course on the topic of leadership in Canada. What we really wanted was a single volume that dealt with leadership in different institutional settings.

At the same time we felt that a survey of various types of leadership would provide only a static and incomplete perspective on a dynamic phenomenon: we seem to pay particular attention to our leaders when we are in the process of changing them. We have sought, therefore, to organize our discussion of leadership thematically. Beginning with the acquisition of leadership positions, we then turn to the exercise of leadership roles, and conclude with the relinquishment, graceful or otherwise, of a leadership career.

The contributors to this book examine leaders and leadership in the context of political parties and their relationship to the electorate; in the executive, legislative, and judicial branches of government; and in the federal, provincial, and municipal jurisdictions. Encompassing a wide range of approaches, the following chapters should foster a broader understanding of the scope of Canadian political leadership.

Students of government will, we hope, learn that leadership is more than a party convention or a first ministers' conference. Rather, it is a widespread and continual process engaged in by elected politicians at all levels, as well as non-elected leaders such as judges and senior bureaucrats. A better appreciation of leaders can only help to improve the quality of the leadership they provide.

We wish to thank each of our authors for their original contributions to this volume. We are pleased they considered this topic as important as we do, and appreciate their co-operation in all phases of production. At Oxford University Press we would like to thank Sally Livingston and Phyllis Wilson, and especially Brian Henderson, for encouraging this undertaking and for patiently awaiting its completion. Barbara Faria of the Department of Political Science at the University of Windsor has provided invaluable assistance from start to finish. Lucia Brown and her staff in the Word Processing Centre produced a high-quality manuscript with good humour despite seemingly endless revisions. With the assistance of so many, it is only fair that the co-editors assume responsibility for any mistakes. The value of the book, however, derives directly from the contributions of our colleagues.

M.M.
R.P.
R.W.
October 1993

LEADERS AND LEADERSHIP IN CANADA

An Introduction

—

Maureen Mancuso, Richard G. Price, and Ronald Wagenberg

In the past decade, Canadians have become increasingly cynical about their political leaders. Fuelled by an economic recession, the constitutional débâcle, high unemployment, and political scandals, attacks on leadership have come from all parts of the country. Public confidence in both political institutions and office-holders has waned, and what support there is for decision-makers is tenuous at best. Is there a crisis in Canadian leadership? For the members of the Spicer Commission, after hearing the testimony, opinions, and complaints of thousands of Canadians across the country, the answer was definitely 'yes'.[1]

Part of the problem may stem from the mystery that surrounds the concept of leadership. For many citizens the processes of leadership selection appear puzzling, complex and alien. For example, while Canadians have a fairly good idea of how individuals become members of Parliament, the elevation of members to Cabinet remains somewhat blurry; the most popular image is the photograph of the new Cabinet, following the official swearing-in ceremony at Rideau Hall. Party leadership conventions have received increasingly detailed coverage, but the ins and outs of delegate selection and voting procedures are generally familiar only to partisan activists.

The exercise of leadership is easier for the public to observe. The media cover closely the day-to-day activities of the prime minister and provincial premiers. We can actually see political leaders in action in the House of Commons and the provincial legislatures, and we live with the results of their legislative decision-making. Nevertheless, if the policy-making and symbolic functions of office-holders make for good press, the burdens of public office remain private. And while biographies of various leaders have succeeded in filling in the details of the administration of power and in illuminating leadership styles, these accounts have tended to be biased in the direction of federal politics, central Canada, and party leaders.

The process of relinquishing a leadership role can be either a full public spectacle or a personal decision taken in private, behind closed doors. Leaders who are publicly trounced at the polls have the decision to resign taken away from them. Others determine that they have devoted enough of their time and energy to public service and simply call it quits. For all, the act of leaving a leadership position is difficult. Yet the public is not always sympathetic to the pressures, demands, obligations, and stresses that leaders face.

If the current expressions of public cynicism toward leaders in Canada can be attributed in some degree to a lack of understanding about leadership, this book provides information and analysis that may help to alleviate some of the misperceptions and criticism that colour our opinions of the performance of our various political leaders. Instead of focusing on the perquisites that accrue to leaders, whether they be the much-vilified pensions of MPs, or ministers' chauffeur-driven limousines, this collection of essays attempts to reveal the machinery of leadership selection, the rigours of governing, and the frustration of career termination.

In Canada leaders are those persons who, by virtue of occupying a particular public position, engage in activities that attract the support of citizens who permit them to make decisions on their behalf. In this sense, the public become followers. A wide range of individuals and institutions attempt to entrain the public will. Although leadership is most obviously exercised by elected politicians, in fact the potential leadership system also includes non-elected office-holders, such as bureaucrats and judges, at the federal, provincial, municipal, and community levels of government. Nor is political leadership restricted to members of this system. Interest groups, the media, even citizen activists can play a strong leadership role in the shaping of public opinion. Ultimately, however, their efforts are directed at those invested with decision-making authority.

For the purposes of this book, therefore, we consider Canada's pool of leaders to include all those men and women who hold positions of authority in governing organizations, most of which are state institutions, but some of which involve the governance of private communities, such as aboriginal Canadians. Given the degree to which, to paraphrase Kenneth Prewitt, 'governing bodies flourish in Canada',[2] the number of positions occupied by potential political leaders is clearly substantial. From an organizational perspective, however, potential leaders can be distinguished by two criteria: level of government (federal, provincial, municipal, community) and type of office (elected or appointed). Such a classification only hints at the thousands of Canadians who have had leadership opportunities as Cabinet ministers, members of Parliament or provincial legislatures, mayors, senior bureaucrats, judges, or chiefs.

The role of followers is vital in a democratic state, for leaders need their support. Loyalty can be withheld or transferred; leaders can be replaced. The need to maintain support is reflected in the various techniques employed in the exercise of leadership. The relationship of political leaders to their followers is conditioned by the political culture of a society.

In Canada, that relationship has been influenced by the particular circumstances of the history and development of the country. Confederation was born not through revolution but rather through the compromises of politicians representing diverse ethnic and linguistic populations in the United Province of Canada and the Maritime colonies that had developed with little connection to what was to become central Canada. These realities created a need for the leader as broker rather than as visionary or hero. The political circumstances did not provide the material for myth-making, and Canadians have never managed to revere Sir John A. Macdonald in the way that Americans do George Washington.

Instead, biographers and historians, with some exceptions, have generally depicted leaders not as demi-gods but as ordinary, flawed human beings who occupy important societal positions. Canadians have focused less on the leadership qualities of the person and more on the leadership activities and accomplishments of the office-holder. This concept of the political career is an important theme in this book (and the literature on leadership). Max Weber differentiated between 'avocation' and 'vocation' politicians:

> Politics, just as economic pursuits, may be a man's avocation or his vocation. One may engage in politics, and hence seek to influence the distribution of power within and between political structures as an 'occasional' politician. We are all 'occasional' politicians when we cast our ballot or consummate a similar expression of intention, such as applauding or protesting in a 'political' meeting, or delivering a 'political speech,' etc.[3]

Vocational politicians, on the other hand, live either 'for politics or off politics'. They are, like avocational politicians, committed to a political party, ideology, or belief in community, but they also make politics their main source of income. As Anthony King has observed, the modern political office-holder has become almost entirely professionalized — our current politicians are for the most part vocational.[4] While the image of the politician-as-amateur is still alive, especially in the rhetoric used by the term-limitation movement in the United States, the reality is that political leaders overwhelmingly view their positions as jobs, not hobbies.

Some may still be born leaders, but no longer do any have leadership thrust upon them unwillingly, though many try to cultivate that impression. Political leadership is for the most part restricted to those ambitious men and women who desire a life-style permanently influenced, or even driven, by the holding of public office. Accordingly, this book is organized around three inter-related career stages:

- recruitment—gaining entrance to the leadership pool;
- governing—exercising a leadership role; and
- leaving—retiring from leadership and returning to private life.

As with any career, each of these three stages features unique obstacles and challenges that a leader must overcome.

GETTING THERE
Recruiting Political Leaders

Robert Putnam has neatly defined political recruitment as 'the processes that select from among the several million socially favoured and motivated citizens comprising the political stratum, those several thousand who reach positions of significant national influence.'[5] These processes vary according to the position involved, but are a critical step in transforming an ordinary, albeit ambitious, citizen into a leader. The incentives and barriers they present to potential leaders are the initial phases of the continual socialization process that separates the governing élite from the mass of the governed.

Seligman has reported that recruitment systems consist of four stages: eligibility, selection, role assignment, and role behaviour.[6] Political eligibility is influenced by both formal and informal 'opportunity structures'—requirements (such as citizenship or residency) and conventions (such as ethnic and geographical balance) that may attract certain individuals to leadership positions or exclude them—as well as the risks inherent in seeking office. Elected positions in particular demand the sacrifice of significant personal resources for an uncertain and volatile gain. Personal ambitions and motivations also affect eligibility—some people seem almost desperate to achieve office, and will surmount or circumvent obstacles that deter otherwise equally qualified candidates.

Selection processes winnow the pool of eligible candidates for any position down to the ultimately chosen leader. These processes can be 'open'—as in a general election, where the public has the final decision, based (at least in theory) on full disclosure of qualifications, intentions, and motivations—or 'closed'—as in Cabinet selection or judicial appointments, where the choice devolves to an existing leader of 'superior' authority with little or no public input, and need not be defended or justified. Open processes such as elections involve the entrusting of power upward, from people to representative, while closed processes typify the delegation of authority downward to subordinate leaders.

In Chapter 1 Heather MacIvor reports that early in this century, Canada's major political parties moved from a relatively closed process—leaders were chosen by caucus—to the more open process of the leadership convention. The convention system is only partly open, however, as the mediating mechanism of delegate selection insulates the choice from the public. Recently some provincial parties have tried out a 'direct vote' system that obviates the need for a formal convention, but the federal parties have been reluctant to follow suit. MacIvor suggests that leadership conventions, while still valuable to party élites, are under stress. The extraordinary amount of money involved in running a long leadership campaign, abuse of delegate-selection and voting rules, and high costs to delegates continue to threaten the viability of leadership conventions.

Alan Whitehorn and Keith Archer in Chapter 2 examine the case of the New Democratic Party, which has consciously tried to lower the barriers between the leaders and the led. Unlike other parties, the NDP constitutionally grants ultimate authority to its convention delegates, not only in choosing a leader, but also in setting party policy and positions on various issues. Drawing on survey data about NDP convention delegates compiled between 1971 and 1989, Whitehorn and Archer examine two aspects of political leadership in Canada—the socio-demographic and attitudinal profile of party activists, and the issue of leadership selection within a national party. Their findings reveal that activists hold a number of characteristics in common, and that the active membership of the party certainly supports the populist and more democratic operations of the party machinery.

Political parties select leaders who appear to possess 'the right stuff' to win a general election. In all parties political experience has ceased to be an important credential for selection, and the elusive aura of 'winnability' has increased in value. Voters, especially flexible partisans and those with relatively low interest in politics (the largest single groups in the Canadian electorate) tend to place particular emphasis on the 'images' of leaders. In Chapter 3, Lawrence Leduc notes that parties have come to rely on the images of their leaders, often choosing to give the party as a whole a quick face-lift by simply changing the person at the top. Of course, new leaders can also drag their parties down. Given the importance of the image of the party leader, LeDuc argues that televised leadership debates serve to reinforce the images of leaders that voters already have, not necessarily to change their perceptions. Ultimately, the images of the leaders, like the images of the parties they lead, are shaped by performance over a period of time, and once established in the public eye they are not easily changed.

One facet of the image of political leaders has remained remarkably consistent despite many other changes: most are men. Janine Brodie, in Chapter 4, addresses the unique hurdles that women face in both the eligibility and selection processes. During the constitutional negotiations of 1992, the concept of gender parity appeared more inconsistent with fundamental principles of democratic responsibility than either cultural or regional guarantees. And it seems that public consensus on the goal of increasing women's political representation is fragile and incomplete; no one is certain of how best to accomplish this goal. Recent marginal gains in the numbers of female MPs, party leaders, provincial leaders, even the selection of a female prime minister, should not be interpreted as the beginning of an inevitable progression toward gender parity in political leadership in Canada. Rather, Brodie makes a cogent assessment of the rationales for, and the effectiveness of, different strategies for affirmative action, which she considers to be a necessary tactic in women's struggle for political power.

Once a leader has survived a selection process, Seligman's next two phases become applicable. 'Role assignment' refers to the position that a leader has been recruited to;

'role behaviour', to how a leader carries out his or her responsibilities. The challenges of recruitment give way to the challenges of administering and maintaining governmental authority. The second section of this book examines how different types of leaders in Canada govern, how they cope with the burdens of public responsibility, and how they respond to the institutional constraints that influence their decision-making ability.

BEING THERE
Governing in Canada

Leaders govern in different decisional contexts: cultural, institutional, legal, and situational. In this volume eight essays examine the environments in which leaders of various kinds exercise their particular responsibilities as first ministers, Cabinet ministers, MPs or MLAs, mayors, civil servants, judges, or Grand Chiefs. In most cases, leaders have considerable latitude in the way they choose to operate. While the legal and perhaps cultural contexts may remain relatively stable, position-holders may have an opportunity to select, among different styles or modes of decision-making, those they find most comfortable or effective.

Some leaders, usually executive leaders, even have the ability to reorganize the machinery of government to suit their preferences. But such reorganization is a luxury in which no leader can indulge very often. In general, the work environment of Canada's leaders tends to remain relatively stable. However, choices about 'how to govern' or 'what part of the job to emphasize' are inherent in any position of leadership, and it is these choices that constitute the main theme of this second section of the book.

For example, while prime ministers must govern in conjunction with the Cabinet, they may do so in various ways. In Chapter 5, Peter Aucoin suggests that there are four modes of Cabinet decision-making that a prime minister can adopt. In the 'command' mode the prime minister exercises her or his own constitutional powers or intervenes in a policy area to impose the outcome of her or his choice. In the 'collegial' mode the prime minister attempts to integrate decision-making in order to co-ordinate the interdependent aspects of different policy areas. The 'corporate' mode of decision-making is an extension of the chief executive's primary responsibilities and involves an attempt to co-ordinate public policy along horizontal lines. Finally, in the 'conglomerate' mode a prime minister makes individual ministers responsible for the management of specialized departments that provide for various public services and regulation.

Howard Pawley is the only contributor who has experience both in the world of politics and in academic life. In Chapter 6 he identifies three factors that bear upon the leadership skill and success of a first minister: previous political experience, the multiple responsibilities of an executive leader, and the powerful influence of circumstances over which the leader has little control. The premier is leader of the party, chair of caucus and Cabinet, employer and office manager, supervisor of the public service, architect of government organization, chief communicator with the media and interest groups, and representative of the province in matters concerning federal-provincial relations. Succeeding at such diverse tasks requires competence, persistence, and good judgement. Finally, from Premier Pawley's perspective, successful leadership requires that a leader's personal style and policy agenda fit comfortably with society's economic, social, and political circumstances.

Successful Cabinet leadership in the twentieth century requires that ministers be well-rounded generalists. In Chapter 7, Herman Bakvis's assessment of Cabinet ministers is that they are more frequently followers than leaders. Ministers, like prime ministers and premiers, have multiple responsibilities, which require quite different competencies and skills. They are expected to provide leadership for their particular department (for example, Transportation or National Revenue), leadership in Cabinet, party leadership (for example, in national, regional, or provincial caucus), and public leadership. Given the often contradictory expectations and demands imposed on Cabinet ministers, it is unrealistic to expect high levels of effectiveness in any single area of ministerial responsibility. Bluntly stated, this means that criteria other than ministerial competence loom large when a prime minister puts together a Cabinet—for example, home province, language, ethnicity, and gender. To increase the collective competence of a Cabinet, it seems, would require changes to the electoral system, if not Canadian history.

It has become conventional wisdom that legislative assemblies everywhere have declined in power and influence, and Canada's legislatures are no exception. In Chapter 8, Ian Stewart acknowledges this decline in power and identifies the relationships between declining legislative authority and the exercise of parliamentary leadership. As legislatures have declined in importance, so have the opportunities for leadership. This decline in power has followed the rise of mass parties, the development of the positive state, the growing complexity of public policy, the changing nature of the parliamentary process, and the relatively recent appearance of corporatist forms of policy-making. To a large extent, modern parliamentarians are casualties of these changes in society and politics. Concomitantly, MPs and MLAs face continuous pressures to conform to the demands of first ministers, Cabinet ministers, and even local electorates, which have typically been unsympathetic to mavericks and independent candidates.

As local executive leaders, Canada's mayors are weak in comparison with first ministers because their power bases (legal and partisan) are substantially restricted. Nonetheless, municipal power bases do vary, and thus mayors have role options as well. Andrew Sancton, in Chapter 9, notes that mayors select styles of leadership compatible with their own personal resources and skills, their municipal power bases, and their roles as community leaders, leaders of municipal organizations, and, occasionally, leaders of local political parties. Mayors in Canada are expected to provide leadership without possessing power and authority. Drawing on recent examples, Sancton shows that some mayors are more successful than others at meeting this most difficult of political challenges.

In Chapter 10, Joan Boase begins by asserting that the contemporary public service must respond to the challenges presented by an era of fiscal restraint. To meet these challenges, effective management must become a priority. And to have effective management, there must be strong leadership from within the public service. The task, as Boase sees it, is for senior managers to find a way to transcend the perception of hierarchical, top-down direction and motivate their employees to be self-leaders. Effective leadership that can successfully tap this self-leadership capability will give employees a sense of 'owning' their jobs, thereby enhancing the principle of public-service autonomy, and possibly diminishing the need for elaborate external account-ability controls.

Ian Greene discusses judges as leaders in Chapter 11. Canadians have traditionally perceived judges as playing a leadership role, and this perception has been reinforced since the enactment of the Charter of Rights and Freedoms in 1982. But Greene maintains that the required leadership skills of judges must necessarily be somewhat different from those of leaders in the political arena. He illustrates the nature of these skills by examining judicial leadership from three perspectives: judges as leaders in the legal-judicial community; judges as administrative leaders; and public expecta-tions about judicial leadership and judicial response to these expectations. Successful judicial leaders have demonstrated that the key to their success is to resist the temptation of trying to become 'political' leaders in the usual sense, and to turn their leadership ambitions and skills to the writing of their decisions and the administra-tion of justice.

Chapter 12 explores the concept of leadership in the context of the aboriginal community. Kathy Brock explains that the processes of decision-making in aboriginal communities are dominated by the principle of consensus. This principle is in direct conflict with the adversarial style of decision-making that characterizes the federal Parliament and most provincial legislatures. The challenge to aboriginal leaders, therefore, is to preserve their consensual style of governing while at the same time developing the institutional arrangements that are necessary if they are to provide effective political representation in their interactions with federal and provincial governments.

Fundamentally, the exercise of leadership is about making choices. The chapters in this section illustrate that, across a wide variety of leadership roles, leaders must choose not only the direction in which to lead their followers, but also the means by which they go about the business of leading them. This is not an easy task. Making the 'right' decision in the 'wrong' way can be just as harmful to a leadership career as making a skilful but misguided choice. Such failures in leadership, and the stress that accompanies the possibility of failure, can be important determinants of a leader's longevity.

LEAVING THERE
Relinquishing a Leadership Role

The final phase in a leader's career—leaving public office—is an under-examined subject. Biographies and leadership studies dwell at length on the rise of leaders and the years of leadership, but since retirement is anticlimactic, and sometimes tainted by negative circumstances, this subject is often glossed over with a 'they lived happily (or obscurely) ever after'. Yet understanding political leadership necessarily involves understanding changes in the composition of leading institutions as existing leaders give way to new ones. Although government positions have a tendency to multiply, most recruitment opportunities are still precipitated by a retirement.

This turnover in leadership is triggered by voluntary as well as involuntary departures. Some leaders simply choose to leave, having either achieved their goals, become too frustrated to continue, exhausted their personal resources, taken ill, or grown weary of public life. Others have the choice made for them, whether by the public in an election, by the prime minister in a Cabinet shuffle, or by the damaging consequences of their own mistakes. Of course, office-holders forced out of office by scandal always seem to try to portray their departure—to 'spend more time with the family'—as voluntary. What research is available suggests that voluntary retirement is increasing in Canada. Apparently, while the professionalization of politics has made public office into a full-time career, it has become a less permanent vocation. Whereas once a business or legal career might have been viewed as a stepping-stone to public leadership, now, for some, public office can be valuable preparation for private-sector success.

Since voluntary retirement from leadership remains essentially a private decision, most of the available information focuses on parliamentarians, the leaders whose careers attract the most public attention. This section offers two chapters that discuss the exit patterns of MPs and ministers. The trends in involuntary and voluntary retirement are examined by David Docherty in Chapter 13. Docherty analyses the reasons why parliamentary leaders choose to leave, and posits a relationship between the manner in which a member leaves—voluntary or involuntary—and the nature of the career given up: amateur or careerist. He provides answers to the basic question 'Which members are likely to leave and which are likely to stay?' with some interesting results.

A specific type of involuntary retirement is the subject of the final chapter. Maureen Mancuso scrutinizes political careers that have been brought to an explosive halt by scandal. While media coverage might suggest that scandal rages uncontrolled and uncontrollable, leaders have at least the opportunity to manage the scandals in which they are embroiled. Their degree of success will depend on the type and 'temperature' of the scandal. No one who pockets public funds can hope to recuperate, but less heinous breaches of the public trust have occasionally proven to be 'forgivable'. Misdeeds and missteps in public office are usually punished, and often entail a period of solitary repentance, but in the right circumstances a skilful leader can maximize his or her chances for rehabilitation and return to a leadership role.

CONCLUSION

Like many aspects of politics in a democratic society, the concept of leadership is subject to a paradox. On the one hand, members of a democratic polity value the opportunity to have a personal impact on their political destinies, free from coercion and manipulation. On the other hand, in pluralistic societies with representative institutions, the public expects to give certain individuals a primary role in decision-making, and is usually satisfied if the results are what it considers to be sound public policy. Specific policy initiatives and priorities are openly bandied about, but ulti-mately most political debate revolves around the set of people who occupy leadership positions — whether they should be retained or thrown out, and who should replace them. Periods of severe dislocation — economic, social, and sometimes political — can occasion a different kind of debate in which the nature and institutions of leadership are challenged and calls are heard to 'get government back into the hands of the people'. The Reform movement draws much of its strength from this type of senti-ment. In the democratic context of Canada, therefore, the concept of leadership must be related to the existence of a satisfied followership.

Obviously leaders themselves and the choices they make must bear most of the responsibility for the satisfaction or dissatisfaction engendered in their followers. But the virtue of democracy is that our leaders are not imposed on us by an external force, and are drawn from the ranks of the citizenry. It is our hope that a better understand-ing of the ways in which we recruit, maintain, and eventually discard our leaders will improve the quality of leadership we ultimately fashion for ourselves. If a society gets the leaders it deserves, then it is important to appreciate and if possible improve the processes that govern leadership, so that we can learn either to accept the leaders we give ourselves, or to deserve better.

NOTES

[1] *Citizen's Forum on Canada's Future*, 27 June 1991.

[2] Kenneth Prewitt, *The Recruitment of Political Leaders: A Study of Citizen Politicians* (Indianapo-lis: Bobbs-Merrill, 1970), 3.

[3] H.H. Gerth and C. Wright Mills, eds, *From Max Weber: Essays in Sociology* (New York: Oxford University Press, 1958); see 'Politics as Vocation', 77-128.

[4] Anthony King, 'The Rise of the Career Politician in Britain — and its Consequences', *British Journal of Political Science* 11 (1981): 249-85.

[5] Robert D. Putnam, *The Comparative Study of Political Elites* (Englewood Cliffs, NJ: Prentice Hall, 1976), 46.

[6] See Lester Seligman, 'Political Parties and the Recruitment of Political Leaders', Chapter 10 in Lewis J. Edinger, ed., *Political Leadership in Industrialized Societies* (New York: John Wiley, 1967), 294-315; Lester Seligman et al., *Patterns of Recruitment: A State Chooses its Lawmakers* (Chicago: Rand McNally, 1974) and William A. Welsh, *Leaders and Elites* (New York: Holt, Rinehart and Winston, 1979).

GETTING THERE

—■—

Recruiting Political Leaders

CHAPTER ONE

THE LEADERSHIP CONVENTION

An Institution Under Stress

———

Heather MacIvor

INTRODUCTION

A party leadership convention is a gathering of delegates[1] for the purpose of selecting a new party leader. The delegates assemble in one place and cast successive
ballots, with the field narrowing each time until one candidate receives a majority of
the votes cast. The delegates are chosen in several different ways: some are elected
by constituency associations; others are *ex officio*; still others are chosen by the
members of special party organizations, to represent women, young people, or
aboriginal Canadians.

Over the past seventy years the leadership convention has become one of the most
visible and dramatic of Canadian political events. The campaign to win delegates
provides months of 'horse-race' material for the news media to cover. The convention
itself generates exciting and suspenseful television viewing, which arouses public
interest in the party and its new leader. The candidates, particularly the front-runners,
receive a great deal of attention from reporters, and their campaigning skills are tested

before the entire electorate, so that the delegates can judge which candidate will perform best in an election campaign. At the same time, the candidates benefit from the process of building national campaign structures in the months before the convention: structures that will provide a ready-made support and organization network for the eventual winner. The convention system even provides a mechanism for removing a leader who has overstayed his or her welcome: delegates to national (non-leadership) conventions can vote on whether to hold a leadership election, a process called 'leadership review'.[2]

In recent years, however, the institution of the leadership convention has come under increasing stress. Its disadvantages — in particular, the prohibitive costs of campaigning and the frequent abuse of delegate selection procedures — have become the focus of sustained public criticism. Moreover, Canadian political culture appears to be changing. Today there are growing demands for more direct participation in politics, including direct election of party leaders by all party members.

This chapter sketches the history of Canadian leadership conventions. It then offers an analysis of the current stresses on the institution, and concludes that the Canadian party leadership convention is headed the way of the dinosaur.

A BRIEF HISTORY OF LEADERSHIP CONVENTIONS IN CANADA

The first national leadership convention in Canada was held by the Liberal party in Ottawa in August 1919. Until then, national leaders of both the Liberal and Conservative parties had been chosen by the caucus, if the party was in opposition, or by a small party élite, in consultation with the governor general, when it was in government.[3] The involvement of the governor general arose from the British tradition of the royal prerogative: the prime minister had to have the confidence of the Crown as well as that of a majority in the House of Commons. The Crown did not play a role in the selection of opposition leaders. Only sitting MPs could be considered for the leadership, although the Conservative party was led briefly by two senators in the years immediately following the death of Sir John A. Macdonald. (For a list of the leaders of all three major parties, see Table 1.1.)

By the end of the First World War there were growing pressures on the parties to abandon their traditional leadership selection systems.[4] These pressures arose for three reasons. First, a number of provincial parties had already held leadership conventions, and many of the leaders so chosen had gone on to smashing electoral victories. Second, the American parties had held presidential nominating conventions since 1832. (The proximity of the American model has always influenced Canadian parties, especially in the western provinces and Ontario, and indeed provincial leadership conventions had been held most regularly and frequently in those provinces.)

Third, the war had created (or revealed) a change in Canadian political culture. There was a new spirit of progressivism, of challenge to established authority, which led to demands for more direct democracy in political decision-making. The strongest demands were made by the Progressives, who emerged as a political force in

---

TABLE 1.1   **CANADIAN PARTY LEADERS 1867-1993**[1]

Leaders chosen by caucus are marked with an asterisk (*).

1. **Conservative Party**[2]

Sir John A. Macdonald	1867-1891*
Sir John Abbott (senator)	1891-1892*
Sir John Thompson	1892-1894*
Sir Mackenzie Bowell (senator)	1894-1896*
Sir Charles Tupper	1896-1900*
Sir Robert Borden	1900-1920*
Arthur Meighen	1920-1927*
R.B. Bennett	1927-1938
R.J. Manion	1938-1940
Arthur Meighen	1940-1942*[3]
John Bracken	1942-1948
George Drew	1948-1956
John Diefenbaker	1956-1967
Robert Stanfield	1967-1976
Joe Clark	1976-1983
Brian Mulroney	1983-1993
Kim Campbell	1993

2. **Liberal Party**

Sir Alexander MacKenzie	1872-1880*
Edward Blake	1880-1887*
Sir Wilfrid Laurier	1887-1919[4]
Mackenzie King	1919-1948
Louis St Laurent	1948-1958
Lester Pearson	1958-1968
Pierre Trudeau	1968-1984
John Turner	1984-1990
Jean Chrétien	1990-

3. **New Democratic Party**

Tommy Douglas	1961-1971
David Lewis	1971-1975
Ed Broadbent	1975-1989
Audrey McLaughlin	1989-

[1] The CCF is not included in this and following tables because of irregularities in its leadership. See Alan Whitehorn, *Canadian Socialism: Essays on the CCF-NDP* (Toronto: Oxford University Press, 1992).

[2] The Conservative party did not become the Progressive Conservative party until 1942, when John Bracken requested the name change as a condition for accepting the leadership.

[3] Arthur Meighen temporarily resumed the leadership of the Conservative Party in 1940 at the request of the caucus, after the resignation of Manion, because the party could not hold a national leadership convention under wartime emergency conditions. A convention was eventually held in 1942.

the west and Ontario in the 1921 election. The Progressives' attacks on the political parties, with their secret back rooms and their lack of concern for the 'little man', struck a chord with many voters. Given this change in the political climate, it made sense for the national parties — especially a party in opposition, as the Liberals were — to seek an electoral advantage by adopting a more 'democratic' leadership selection system.

In addition to these general factors, there were two more specific reasons for the Liberal party to select Laurier's successor at a convention.[5] First, the party had held a national convention in 1893 to discuss policy and to strengthen the party organization. A motion to approve Laurier's leadership had been put forward at that meeting and had passed unanimously. This was favourably regarded in some quarters as a first step towards a leadership vote by the extra-parliamentary party. So the idea of a leadership convention in 1919 was not completely without precedent.

The second specific factor that moved the party towards a convention was political. The Liberal party had been shattered by the conscription issue during the First World War. The Liberal alliance of anglophones and francophones broke apart as most of the anglophone MPs joined the Union government under Borden and the francophones remained with Laurier. In 1919 the Liberal caucus was still lopsided: 62 of the 82 Liberal MPs were Québec francophones. The party knew that a leader chosen by such an unrepresentative caucus would be a political liability in English Canada, where it desperately needed to rebuild its organization. Had none of the other pressures for a leadership convention existed, the regionally and linguistically unbalanced caucus might have provided a sufficient reason to broaden the selectorate.

All of these factors — the provincial and American examples, the change in the political culture, the 1893 precedent, and the impracticability of caucus selection — combined to produce the first national party leadership convention in the British Empire. It was won on the fifth ballot (though only the third completed ballot) by William Lyon Mackenzie King, who went on to win the 1921 general election, against a Conservative leader chosen by caucus, and remained the Liberal leader until 1948. The Liberal party was reunited and its organization rebuilt, although the return to power did as much to rebuild the party as any new leader could have done. The first national leadership convention in Canadian history had clearly been a success.

By 1927 the Conservatives had decided to copy that success, holding their first leadership convention in that year. The winner was R.B. Bennett, who went on to win a majority in the 1930 general election. After 1927 the leadership convention became a fixture of Canadian political life, and the effects on Canadian politics have been debated ever since.

Central to these debates has been the question of the successful candidates' qualifications. It has been argued that candidates with less political experience are at an advantage in a leadership convention.[6] Under the pre-1919 caucus system, only parliamentarians could rise to the leadership and only those with considerable experience and proven skills would be seriously considered. With the move to conventions came a striking change in the type of candidates who began to seek party leaderships.[7] Men without a great deal of political experience became credible candidates for a position that could propel them into the prime minister's office.

Of the nine leadership conventions held before 1967,[8] six were won by men with either the least parliamentary experience of the candidates or no parliamentary experience at all.[9] Of the nine conventions since 1967, five were won by candidates with less than five years' parliamentary experience (although one of those, Robert Stanfield, had been a provincial premier for over a decade). In the British caucus system, by contrast, it is customary for a successful leadership candidate to have served at least a decade in Parliament and to have held one or more of the key Cabinet portfolios.[10] Some observers have argued that the amount of experience required of a Canadian leadership candidate has diminished because of the convention system itself.[11] Others have argued that a party in government will tend to prefer a more experienced candidate than a party in opposition, no matter what the selection system used.[12] Whatever the reason, most of the successful candidates at leadership conventions have had less legislative and Cabinet experience than their competitors. This fact has suggested to some observers that Canada should return to a caucus selection system, where a lengthy apprenticeship is a prerequisite and not a liability. However, in view of the greater democratic legitimacy of conventions, and the advantages of conventions for the parties, this is not a practical idea.

The history of Canadian leadership conventions falls into two periods.[13] The conventions in the first period, from 1919 to 1958, were small and dominated by the caucuses. In each case only a few serious candidates presented themselves, and competitiveness was low; there was usually a clear front-runner, sometimes with the overt endorsement of the retiring leader. The candidates did not usually conduct lengthy campaigns or travel widely, and the media paid relatively little attention. The second period, from 1967 to 1990, saw larger conventions with less influence from the parliamentary wing of the party, greater numbers of serious candidates, and a greater degree of competition and unpredictability. Unprecedented numbers of people turned out to vote or to run for delegate positions. The candidates campaigned across the country for several weeks or even months, and the news media followed events with intense interest. We will discuss each period separately.

1919-1958

There were nine national leadership conventions in Canada between 1919 and 1958 (see Table 1.2). The average number of delegates was 1,317; the average number of serious candidates was three. Leadership contests were low-key affairs, dominated by the *ex officio* delegates.[14] Constituency delegates were fewer in number than they would be after 1967, and many of them were chosen by MPs or provincial executives rather than elected by party members.[15] The Liberal conventions of 1948 and 1958 were dominated by the outgoing leaders, who made it clear that they expected the delegates merely to confirm their own choice of successors.[16] Meanwhile, the Progressive Conservative conventions of the period were dominated by cliques of insiders

TABLE 1.2 PARTY CONVENTIONS IN CANADA, 1919-1990
(Based on First-Ballot Vote Totals)[1]

Year	Party	Total Delegates	Candidates
1919	Liberal	947	4
1927	Conservative	1,564	5
1938	Conservative	1,565	5
1942	Conservative	870	3
1948	Liberal	1,227	3
1948	Conservative	1,242	3
1956	Conservative	1,284	3
1958	Liberal	1,380	2
1961	NDP	1,771	2
1967	Conservative	2,231	8
1968	Liberal	2,366	8
1971	NDP	1,698	5
1975	NDP	1,618	4
1976	Conservative	2,372	8
1983	Conservative	2,991	6
1984	Liberal	3,435	5
1989	NDP	2,400	6
1990	Liberal	4,600	6
1993	Conservative	3,550	5

[1] Only candidates who received more than 100 votes on the first ballot are included.

SOURCES: John C. Courtney, *The Selection of National Party Leaders in Canada* (Toronto: Macmillan, 1973); R. Kenneth Carty, 'Choosing New Party Leaders: The Progressive Conservatives in 1983, the Liberals in 1984', in Howard R. Penniman, ed., *Canada at the Polls, 1984: A Study of the Federal General Elections* (Washington, DC: AEIPPR, 1988); George C. Perlin, *The Tory Syndrome: Leadership Politics in the Progressive Conservative Party* (Montreal: McGill-Queens University Press, 1980); Perlin, *Party Democracy in Canada: The Politics of National Party Conventions* (Scarborough, Ont.: Prentice-Hall, 1988); Alan Whitehorn, *Canadian Socialism* (Toronto: Oxford University Press, 1992); Robert Krause and Lawrence LeDuc; 'Voting Behaviour and Electoral Strategies in the Progressive Conservative Leadership Convention of 1976', *Canadian Journal of Political Science*, XII; news reports.

who would decide on the best person to restore the electoral fortunes of the party, and then persuade the delegates to support that candidate.[17] Unfortunately for the party, these cliques were more successful at selling their candidates to the delegates than to the electorate at large.

For the most part, these leadership contests were treated as internal party matters. The press paid little attention, perhaps because there was little for them to cover.

Candidates did not travel across the country meeting with delegates; there were no national campaign organizations fighting it out in the constituencies. As late as 1958, Lester Pearson campaigned for the Liberal leadership by meeting with delegates in his Château Laurier hotel suite during the convention.[18] The drama and the intense media scrutiny that characterize modern conventions did not exist during this period. The conventions were small and predictable, in part because many of the serious contestants were already well-known party figures with years of experience in Parliament and (for Liberals) in Cabinet.[19]

1967-1990

Why did the nature of leadership conventions change? Why did they become huge, competitive national contests with intense media scrutiny and multi-million-dollar campaigns? The answers are not entirely clear, but a few can be suggested. The most important factor was the growth of the mass media, particularly television, in the 1960s.[20] As Canadians began watching their politicians on television, they became more interested in political events. The result was greater involvement in delegate-selection meetings. In addition, the leaders became the focal points of party activity because the television cameras focused on them; as a result, the selection of a leader assumed greater importance. Finally, because the conventions attract such intense media attention, they have become central to the relationship between Canadians and their political parties: a leadership race is usually the only occasion, between general elections, when most voters become aware of the parties.

A second reason for the change was the decision of the parties to open up their leadership conventions, by electing more delegates from each constituency. This was partly a response to greater demands for participation in the 1960s, and partly an attempt to raise more revenue from delegate fees. A third reason for the increased participation in the delegate-selection process, apart from the interest generated by the media coverage, was that the increased competitiveness of the leadership races mobilized people to become involved in the process for the first time.[21] It is estimated that between 75,000 and 100,000 people participated in delegate-selection meetings for the 1990 Liberal leadership convention; some constituency meetings attracted as many as 2,000 people.[22]

As we have seen, leadership conventions after 1967 have been characterized by greater numbers both of delegates (2,635, on average) and of serious candidates (an average of six) than earlier conventions. Starting as small, closed, internal party contests, leadership conventions have become huge, open races in which candidates criss-cross the country and thousands of delegates converge to cast their ballots in an emotionally charged marathon of horse-trading, triumph, and humiliation, capped by a public ceremony of healing and reconciliation in which the second-place finisher moves for the unanimous election of the winner. Because of the larger number of candidates, post-1967 conventions have generally required more ballots than earlier contests. Eight of the nine pre-1967 conventions required one or two ballots to produce a winner (1919 was the only exception); seven of the nine post-1967 conventions have lasted for four or five ballots (the Liberal conventions of 1984 and 1990 lasted for only two).

Leadership conventions have offered parties a number of advantages. First, they bring the constituency activists together, strengthening the grassroots organization and building the personal networks that are the heart and soul of political parties. Second, the campaigns give the candidates a chance to demonstrate their electoral skills to the party delegates — skills that go far beyond mere hand-shaking and public speaking. To succeed in an election campaign, the winner has to be a good fund-raiser, a shrewd judge of organizational and public-relations talent, and an adequate media performer. Third, it was long assumed that a party that held a convention shortly before a general election received an electoral boost; the media attention, the novelty of a new leader, and the reinvigorated party organization were believed to provide an advantage over rivals. This belief is no longer supported by the evidence.[23]

Fourth, conventions have allowed the parties to manipulate the composition of the selectorate in order to achieve particular representational goals: gender parity, inclusion of young people, integration of aboriginal Canadians into the party system. Finally, conventions have given party leaders some national legitimacy, even when the parties themselves have been regionally skewed. For example, when John Turner was elected leader there were only two Liberal MPs from west of Ontario in 1984; but there were as many delegates from each western constituency as from each Ontario or Québec constituency at the leadership convention. These advantages are not to be taken lightly by any national party in a country as large and diverse as Canada.

CURRENT ISSUES IN CANADIAN LEADERSHIP SELECTION

The greater 'openness' that has developed since 1967 has created a set of problems that threaten the survival of the leadership convention as a Canadian political institution. I will discuss four of these: the cost of running lengthy national campaigns; the abuse of delegate-selection rules; the problem of multiple voting for delegates; and the cost to delegates of attending the conventions.[24]

The cost of leadership campaigns has grown to alarming proportions. The front-runners in the last two national Liberal contests raised and spent two million dollars each.[25] This money was spent on travel for the candidates and their advisers; on telephones, fax machines, computers, regular mail, and other communications; on literature, buttons, posters, and other candidate paraphernalia; and, most controversially, on full-time organizers in the constituencies whose job it was to ensure the selection of sympathetic delegates. Most of these expenses are legitimate parts of running a national campaign. The constituency associations want to meet the candidate face-to-face, and no candidate wants to risk losing votes by staying away from a particular province or major urban area. In a country as large as Canada, therefore, high travel costs are inevitable. Similarly, few people would question the need for communications links, for campaign literature and posters, or for expensive events to attract wavering delegates at the convention itself. But the total cost of a serious leadership campaign has attracted criticism because it virtually eliminates any candidate who cannot attract large sums from corporate donors or wealthy interest groups. Worthy candidates without personal fortunes or close ties to big business are at a profound disadvantage, and this strikes many Canadians as unfair.

The aspect of candidate spending that has attracted the most criticism, the hiring of full-time constituency organizers, is linked to the second major problem with modern leadership conventions: the abuse of delegate-selection rules. The Liberal and Progressive Conservative leadership conventions of recent years have seen delegate-selection meetings turned into contests between slates of contestants, some of whom have little or no previous involvement with the party, chosen by stacked meetings dominated by 'instant' party members. The most notorious of these abuses have involved the use of people who cannot vote in general elections, such as minors and recent immigrants, to stack delegate-selection meetings; other abuses include the exploitation of street vagrants and ethnic minority groups. Because of the intense media attention paid to party leadership selection, such practices have likely helped to turn voters against both the leadership-selection process and the parties themselves.[26]

The problem of multiple voting for delegates is a result of the parties' efforts to ensure fair representation of women, youth, and other social groups.[27] In theory, an 18-year-old aboriginal female university student in the Liberal party could vote for youth delegates, campus delegates, delegates from the Women's Federation, delegates from the Aboriginal Federation, and constituency delegates. This situation violates the democratic principle of one member, one vote.

The cost of attending conventions is a little-discussed problem, but it is a major reason for the unrepresentativeness of convention delegates. Every national leadership convention in Canada has been dominated, to a disproportionate extent, by middle-aged, middle-class white males. Working-class people, women, ethnic minorities, native peoples, and the physically handicapped have been under-represented. One of the primary reasons is that most *ex officio* delegates are wealthy middle-aged men.[28] It costs a great deal of money to attend a convention in another province, both directly (travel, registration, accommodation) and indirectly (loss of work income). Only those who can afford to attend the convention can cast a vote for the leadership.

These problems with the present leadership convention system have prompted calls for reform that fall into three categories:[29] abandoning the convention system in favour of a direct-vote system; public regulation of leadership candidates' contributions and spending; and public regulation of the entire leadership-selection process (e.g., legislation to govern delegate selection). Direct voting will be discussed in the next section. The other two reforms were suggested to the Royal Commission on Electoral Reform and Party Financing in 1991, which recommended that parties be required to set cut-off dates for party memberships well before the dates of delegate-selection meetings (to eliminate stacking), and that leadership candidates be required to report the amounts and sources of all contributions over $250, observe spending limits, and report their expenses on the day before the leadership vote. In addition, the Commission recommended amendments to the Canada Elections Act to reinforce

the new party rules and to regulate the issuing of tax credits for campaign contributions by leadership candidates.[30] As of the fall of 1993, the House of Commons
Special Committee on Electoral Reform had not studied those recommendations, and
no legislative action had been taken by the government.

CONCLUSION
The Future of Party Leadership Selection in Canada

The leadership convention has been the target of frequent and severe criticism for the
past decade. Its survival is now in serious doubt. Several provincial parties have
chosen leaders by various forms of direct vote. The first such vote was held by the
Parti Québécois in 1985. Since then, the Prince Edward Island Progressive Conservatives and the Ontario Liberals and Progressive Conservatives have used modified
direct-vote systems, the Nova Scotia Liberals have experimented with a phone-in
voting system (in 1992), and in December 1992 the Alberta Progressive Conservatives elected Ralph Klein as leader and premier through direct vote — the first time a
governing party had used such a system. What is this direct-vote system, and why is it
catching on?

In essence, direct-vote leadership selection means giving a vote for the leader to
every party member. Instead of electing delegates who then vote for the leader on
behalf of their constituency association or affiliated party club, every party member in
good standing has the right to vote directly for whichever candidate he or she prefers.
The process is similar to that in a general election. Polling stations are set up in every
constituency, monitored by representatives of each candidate, and the votes are
counted at a central location. The candidate who wins a majority of the votes cast
becomes the party leader. The announcement of the final result is made on live
television, and there is generally a rally of party members to provide enthusiastic
'visuals' for the cameras.

The principal advantage of direct-vote systems, in theory, is that they permit the
broadest possible participation in leadership selection. Such broad participation is
consistent with the demands for greater democracy in the political process that are
now being heard again in Canada, as they were in 1919.[31] Parties are attracted to the
idea of a direct vote because it offers a greater chance of political legitimacy than do
conventions, partly because it would eliminate delegate-selection abuses, multiple
voting, and the high cost of attending conventions, and partly because it appeals to a
public weary both of politicians and of traditional forms of political participation. In
other words, parties are beginning to think of direct-vote leadership selection as a
vote-winner in general elections.

The key organizational problem with direct voting is to ensure that all party
members can vote, no matter where they live — to decentralize the process geographi-
cally — but at the same time to keep everyone informed about the balloting results and
bring them back to the polls for second and subsequent ballots.[32] There is no such
problem at a leadership convention, because most delegates remain in the building

throughout the balloting process; it is relatively easy to inform them of the results of each ballot, and to begin the voting on the next ballot immediately.

There are several ways to solve this problem in direct voting, though none is perfect. One approach is to eliminate all but the top two candidates on the first ballot, and hold a run-off election a week later. Another is to gather party members at a single location in each riding, keep them there for successive ballots, and send their votes to the central counting office (usually by fax or computer). A third method is to allow party members to vote by telephone from their homes, while watching live coverage of the balloting on television. A fourth mechanism is a hybrid of a convention and a direct vote, in which delegates are elected according to a ballot by all party members, and committed to vote for a particular candidate on the first ballot, after which they are free to vote for whomever they wish. Each of these systems has been tried by a Canadian party, although few have been truly put to the test because most of the direct-vote elections so far have been won on the first ballot. It is still unclear exactly how these systems would work over the entire area of Canada, with several time zones and high communications costs.

Despite its attractiveness in theoretical and electoral terms, direct voting presents a number of serious drawbacks. First, none of the direct-vote systems used in Canada to date, except perhaps for the convention hybrid, lends itself to the exciting television coverage associated with conventions. This is a serious drawback, given the importance of free publicity for a party and its new leader.[33] Second, the cost to the parties of national direct-vote elections could be prohibitive; instead of mailing information to three or four thousand delegates, they would be forced to communicate with a few hundred thousand members.[34] Third, direct-vote systems provide no opportunity for constituency activists from across the country to gather in one place, build organizational networks, and form the friendships that sustain political campaigns.[35] Fourth, direct-vote systems do not require candidates to build strong campaign organizations on the ground, in all constituencies and provinces; as a result, the winner may lack the organizational foundations for a general election campaign on which party leaders have relied under the convention system.[36]

Fifth, the parties would no longer be able to boost the representation of women and other groups in the leadership selectorate, once the party membership at large replaces delegates from specific party sectors.[37] Sixth, the careful balancing of regional representation that was the principal *raison d'être* for national conventions would pose considerable problems in a direct-vote system.[38] Seventh, the costs of campaigning would likely increase dramatically, as candidates attempted to reach hundreds of thousands of delegates and tried to monitor their preferences through polling.[39]

Finally, the provincial experience with direct-vote systems has not substantiated the hopes that direct democracy would lead to greater participation in the leadership selection process. The turnout rate for the 1985 PQ leadership was only 64 per cent;[40] fewer than half of the eligible voters bothered to cast ballots in the 1990 Ontario PC contest;[41] only two-thirds of Ontario Liberals voted in 1992;[42] and the party members who participated in the Prince Edward Island PC leadership direct-vote in 1990 were actually 500 fewer than the delegates who had attended the party's most recent leadership convention.[43]

Despite these problems, there is a clear momentum toward direct-vote leadership selection in Canadian parties. There are a number of provincial precedents, as there were when the Liberals decided to switch selection systems in 1919. Public pressures for more direct democracy in party affairs are strong, as they were in 1919. All three of the major national parties have discussed moving to direct-vote systems. The 1989 NDP convention sent the issue to a party commission for study, and over half of the respondents to a delegate survey said that they would prefer a 'one member-one vote' system.[44] The 1989 national PC convention debated a change in leadership selection, and instructed the national executive to investigate putting a direct-vote system into operation.[45] In 1990 the federal Liberal party approved a resolution requiring that the next leader be chosen by direct vote, and a specific plan was adopted in 1992.[46]

The leadership convention, as a Canadian political institution, is probably on its way out; but no one can say for certain how Canadian politics will be affected by the change to national direct votes. In particular, relations between parties and their leaders would be profoundly affected.[47] The present leadership review process can consume a party's energy for months or years, but it is a picture of simplicity compared to the prospect of removing a leader elected by the entire party membership. The power of the caucus in the parties was already reduced by the move to conventions; it would be almost completely destroyed by a direct-vote system. It has also been suggested that party members at large are ill-equipped to choose national leaders, because they lack the political experience to understand the requirements of the prime minister's position. Nevertheless, the appeal of direct-vote leadership selection may be impossible for parties to resist. It is therefore necessary to conclude that the party leadership convention, a fixture of Canadian political life for nearly 75 years, is not only under stress; it is at the last extremity.

GLOSSARY

Caucus is the term for a party's legislators. At the national level, the MPs and Senators of a party collectively make up its caucus.

Delegate is the term for a person who is elected by a group of people to represent them at a larger gathering. Leadership conventions are gatherings of delegates, elected to represent party members in the constituencies or in affiliated party groups.

Direct vote is an election system in which all members of a party are entitled to vote for a new leader, instead of electing delegates to vote on their behalf.

Ex officio delegates are not elected to represent constituencies or special party groups (e.g., women, youth). They are automatically awarded delegate status because they are legislators, party executive members, or party candidates for office.

Extra-parliamentary party is the term for those sections of the party organization that are separate from the party caucus: i.e., the national executive, and the provincial and constituency associations.

Leadership review is the process by which delegates to a party convention vote on whether or not to hold a leadership convention. The vote is intended to measure the extent of delegates' loyalty to the leader. In theory, a leader must win only 50 per cent plus 1 of the votes cast; in practice, a leader whose position is under threat must win at least two-thirds of the votes. A review vote is held only at the first national meeting after a general election at which the party lost, in the Liberal and Progressive Conservative parties. Every national NDP convention includes a leadership vote, but this is largely a fiction because nobody has ever run against a sitting leader.

Run-off elections require two rounds of voting. In the first round, voters cast their ballots for three or more candidates. In the second round, only the top two finishers are on the ballot and whichever candidate receives a majority of the votes cast wins the leadership.

Selectorate is the term for the group of people who select a party leader.

Slates are lists of people who run for delegate positions from a particular constituency association or party club. In a leadership contest between candidates X and Y, an X slate will run against a Y slate; whichever slate wins the most votes will go to the convention committed to vote for its candidate. Between 1984 and 1990 the percentage of Liberal delegates elected on slates doubled from 40 per cent to 80 per cent.[48]

Stacking (also called 'packing') is the process by which a candidate's organization brings a large number of people to a delegate-selection meeting, with instructions to vote for that candidate's slate of delegates. Stacking is probably the most notorious aspect of leadership conventions.

NOTES

[1] See the Glossary (p. 25) for definitions of this and other terms.

[2] For a discussion of the leadership review mechanism see Joseph Wearing, *Strained Relations: Canadian Parties and Voters* (Toronto: McClelland and Stewart, 1988), 159 and 178; John C. Courtney, *The Selection of National Party Leaders in Canada* (Toronto: Macmillan, 1973), 99-104; and Courtney, 'Leadership Conventions and the Development of the National Political Community in Canada', in R. Kenneth Carty and Peter Ward, eds, *National Politics and Community in Canada* (Vancouver: University of British Columbia Press, 1986), 101.

[3] See Courtney, *Selection*, 31-4; R. Kenneth Carty, 'Choosing New Party Leaders: The Progressive Conservatives in 1983, the Liberals in 1984', in Howard R. Penniman, ed., *Canada at the Polls, 1984: A Study of the Federal General Elections* (Washington, DC: AEIPPR, 1988), 56.

[4] Courtney, *Selection*, chapter 6; Courtney, 'Leadership Conventions', 100, Carty, 'Choosing New Party Leaders', 56.

[5] Courtney, *Selection*.

[6] Ibid.; Courtney, 'Leadership Conventions'; Carty, 'Choosing'.

[7] The first woman to seriously contest a national party leadership was Rosemary Brown of the NDP in 1975. She was followed by Flora MacDonald at the 1976 Progressive Conservative convention; Audrey McLaughlin, who won the 1989 NDP convention; and Sheila Copps, who placed third at the 1990 Liberal convention.

[8] 1919, 1942, 1948 (Liberal), 1948 (Progressive Conservative), 1958, 1961.

[9] Courtney, *Selection*, chapter 6.

[10] See MacIvor, 'Beyond the Greasy Pole: Party Leadership Selection in Four Parliamentary Systems' (unpublished PhD thesis, Queen's University), chapter 6.

[11] Courtney, *Selection*, chapter 6.

[12] R. Kenneth Carty and Peter James, 'Changing the Rules of the Game: Do Conventions and Caucuses Choose Different Leaders?', in R. Kenneth Carty, Lynda Erickson, and Donald E.

Blake, eds, *Leaders and Parties in Canadian Politics: Experiences of the Provinces* (Toronto: Harcourt Brace Jovanovich, 1992), 29-30.

[13] Donald V. Smiley 'The National Party Leadership Convention in Canada: A Preliminary Analysis', *Canadian Journal of Political Science* 1 (1968).

[14] Carty, 'Choosing', 57.

[15] Courtney, *Selection*, 91-92; Reginald Whitaker, *The Government Party: Organizing and Financing the Liberal Party of Canada 1930-1958*, (Toronto: University of Toronto Press, 1977), 172.

[16] Whitaker, *Government Party*, 176; Courtney, *Selection*, 214.

[17] John Williams, *The Conservative Party of Canada: 1920-1949* (Durham, NC: Duke University Press, 1956); Ian Stewart, 'The Brass Versus the Grass: Party Insiders and Outsiders at Canadian Leadership Conventions', in George C. Perlin, ed., *Party Democracy in Canada: The Politics of National Party Conventions* (Scarborough, Ont.: Prentice-Hall, 1988).

[18] See Peter C. Newman, *The Distemper of Our Times* (Toronto: McClelland and Stewart, 1968).

[19] Courtney, *Selection*; R. Kenneth Carty, 'Three Canadian Party Systems: An Interpretation of the Development of National Politics', in Perlin, ed., *Party Democracy*.

[20] George C. Perlin, 'Attitudes of Liberal Convention Delegates toward Proposals for Reform of the Process of Leadership Selection', in Herman Bakvis, ed., *Canadian Political Parties: Leaders, Candidates and Organization*, vol. 13 of the collected research studies for the Royal Commission on Electoral Reform and Party Financing (Ottawa and Toronto: RCERPF/Dundurn, 1991); Carty, 'Three Canadian Party Systems'.

[21] Smiley, 'National Party Leadership Convention', 377.

[22] Perlin, 'Attitudes', 59.

[23] David K. Stewart and R.K. Carty, 'Does Changing the Party Leader Provide an Electoral Boost? A Study of Canadian Provincial Parties: 1960-1992', *Canadian Journal of Political Science* XXVI, 2 (June 1993).

[24] These problems afflict the Liberal and Progressive Conservative parties more than the NDP, particularly the cost of campaigns, the abuse of delegate-selection procedures, and multiple voting. Campaign costs are strictly controlled by the NDP; its membership rules are stricter, which prevents most delegate-selection abuses; and there are fewer affiliated groups in the party (the New Democratic Youth and labour unions). See Alan Whitehorn, *Canadian Socialism: Essays on the CCF-NDP* (Toronto: Oxford University Press, 1992) and Keith Archer, 'Leadership Selection in the New Democratic Party', in Bakvis, ed., *Canadian Political Parties*.

[25] Perlin, 'Attitudes', 64.

[26] See George C. Perlin, 'Leadership Selection in the Progressive Conservative and Liberal Parties: Assessing the Need for Reform', in Hugh G. Thorburn, ed., *Party Politics in Canada*, 6th ed. (Scarborough, Ont.: Prentice-Hall, 1991), and Perlin, 'Attitudes'.

[27] Perlin, 'Attitudes', 62.

[28] Ibid., 61.

[29] Ibid., 65-7.

[30] See Royal Commission on Electoral Reform and Party Financing, *Final Report*, vol. 1, 'Reforming Electoral Democracy' (Ottawa: Minister of Supply and Services, 199), Recommendations 1.5.12 and 1.5.13.

[31] Perlin, 'Attitudes', 84-6.

[32] Suzanne Hayward and Alan Whitehorn, 'Leadership Selection: Which Method?', paper presented to the Douglas-Coldwell Foundation, 1991.

[33] See ibid.; Peter Woolstencroft, '"Tories Kick Machine to Bits": Leadership Selection and the Ontario Progressive Conservative Party', in Carty et al., eds, *Leaders and Parties*; Daniel Latouche, 'Universal Democracy and Effective Leadership: Lessons from the Parti Québécois

Experience', in Carty et al., eds, *Leaders and Parties*; MacIvor, 'Beyond the Greasy Pole', chapter 7.

[34] Hayward and Whitehorn, 'Leadership Selection'.

[35] Latouche, 'Universal Democracy'.

[36] Ibid.

[37] Hayward and Whitehorn, 'Leadership Selection'; MacIvor, 'Beyond the Greasy Pole'.

[38] See Woolstencroft, '"Tories"', for a description of the Ontario PC system.

[39] Hayward and Whitehorn, 'Leadership Selection'.

[40] Latouche, 'Universal Democracy', 183.

[41] Woolstencroft, '"Tories"', 216.

[42] MacIvor, 'Beyond the Greasy Pole'.

[43] Archer, 'Leadership Selection', 48.

[44] Ibid., 47.

[45] Woolstencroft, '"Tories"', 203-4.

[46] MacIvor, 'Beyond the Greasy Pole'.

[47] See Carty et al., 'Parties and Leaders: Experiences of the Provinces', in Carty et al., eds, *Leaders and Parties*, 13-14.

[48] Perlin, 'Attitudes'.

CHAPTER TWO

PARTY ACTIVISTS AND
POLITICAL LEADERSHIP

A Case Study of the NDP

—■—

Alan Whitehorn and Keith Archer

INTRODUCTION[1]

As the preceding chapter has shown, delegates to party conventions have for many years selected the leaders of all three of Canada's major political parties. Their role is particularly important, however, in the New Democratic Party, whose constitution vests ultimate authority in the biennial convention. Indeed, in addition to choosing who will fill crucial positions in the leadership structure (party president, vice-presidents, and some members of the federal council, as well as the leader), NDP delegates set party policy through the mechanism of convention resolutions. Thus NDP delegates themselves constitute a central element in their party's leadership.

The New Democratic Party traces its roots to the Great Depression of the 1930s. In Calgary on 1 August 1932, the Co-operative Commonwealth Federation (CCF) was born as a federation of farmers, labourers, and socialists. Twenty-nine years later in Ottawa on 4 August 1961, the New Democratic Party, a fusion of CCFers, unionists and the 'liberally minded', was given life.

According to Maurice Duverger's classification, the NDP belongs to the 'branch' type of mass party.[2] It relies on a large dues-paying membership base to provide organizational clout in the political arena. In contrast to both the Liberal and Progressive Conservative parties, which rely solely on individual members, the NDP has two types of members: those who have joined as individuals and those who belong to affiliated organizations. In the former category are members of riding associations, campus clubs, and recognized socialist study groups; these individuals pay dues directly to the party. In the latter category are individuals who belong to groups (e.g., trade unions) affiliated to the NDP; each of these people pays dues to the organization, which collectively has decided to affiliate with the NDP, and in turn the organization collectively forwards a certain monthly sum to the party. In 1987 there were 146,121 individual party members and 276,128 affiliated members.[3]

Its historic ties to the farm, labour, and socialist movements clearly mark the CCF-NDP as a newer type of party with strong extra-parliamentary roots and involvements. While conventional electoral politics is an important component of NDP activity, it is by no means the only one: education, both for members and for the broader public, and agitation are also important, and party manifestos and pamphlets abound.[4]

To explore the nature of the NDP and its activists, we have analysed available surveys of NDP convention delegates covering the period 1971 to 1989. As members of a mass party, NDP delegates differ dramatically from their counterparts in the cadre-style Liberal and Conservative parties.[5] For example, high proportions of NDP delegates in 1987 were members of unions (45.6%) or co-operatives (44.9%), almost all — 98.1% — indicated that they had signed petitions; and 90.4% had participated in a protest march. Just over half (57.7%) had been involved in a strike,[6] and more than one-third (34.7%) had engaged in a sit-in demonstration. Clearly, the NDP's extra-parliamentary involvement persists.

A DEMOGRAPHIC PROFILE OF NDP ACTIVISTS AND CONVENTIONS

In the early years of the CCF, conventions were annual assemblies, whereas today they are held every other year. Those early conventions were small, intimate affairs; for example, the founding convention of 1932 attracted only 131 persons. By contrast, at the 1987 NDP policy convention, 1,391 delegates gathered to debate policy and elect various officers of the party. Leadership conventions are usually even larger, involving over 1,600 voting delegates in 1971 and 1975, and 2,510 in 1989. In half a century, CCF-NDP conventions have grown approximately tenfold. What impact have the changes in frequency and size had? More people and perhaps a greater variety of groups now participate. However, it is also possible that decision-making has shifted away from conventions as they have become larger and less frequent. Certainly the type and amount of decision-making can be affected significantly by such changes.

Party activists attending conventions are selected by a number of means. The two most common methods are election by constituency association (based on one delegate per 50-100 individual members) or selection by union local (based on one delegate per 1,000-1,500 affiliated union members).[7] While the majority of delegates

(67% in 1987)[8] are elected by their riding associations, a significant minority (17.2% in 1987 and ranging from a low of 16.1% in 1983 to a high of 31.2% in 1971) are selected from affiliated organizations (both union locals and central labour bodies).[9] A still smaller number are *ex officio* delegates, such as members of Parliament or members of the federal council (the latter includes members of the party executive and table officers).

Most of the delegates in 1987 indicated that they had previously attended either a federal (64.2%) or provincial (82.0%) NDP convention. Almost half (43.1%) had attended the previous federal convention, two years earlier. In 1983 the average number of provincial or federal conventions previously attended was six. In terms of significant prior convention attendance, then, the delegates seem relatively experienced.

Party membership data also suggest substantial continuity and background experience, with most of the delegates (53.2% in 1983, 54.2% in 1987) having been party members for 6 to 20 years. Many of the delegates also held executive posts in party riding associations (see Table 2.1). For example, about two-fifths (38.3% in 1983 and 39.7% in 1987) were on federal riding executives, and one-half (50.4% in 1983 and 51.2% in 1987) were members of provincial riding executives. In addition, 76.6% in 1987 indicated that they had been election canvassers. What is perhaps most interesting about these data on convention attendance and membership in riding executive posts is that the numbers are higher for the provincial level in both cases. Perhaps tellingly, when federal delegates were asked which level of the party they felt closest to, a convincing majority (63.2%) indicated the provincial level.

In the past, party politics, both within the NDP and elsewhere, has been largely a male domain.[10] While the most recent survey samples suggest that increasing proportions of delegates are women, men still outnumber women by about two to one (for a detailed breakdown, see Table 2.2).[11]

Conventions have usually attracted a disproportionate number of delegates in their thirties. What is perhaps most surprising about these data is how few young people (i.e., under 21)—only 4.9% in 1983 and 3.7% in 1987—were in attendance, given that the party prides itself on being 'new', 'progressive', and in tune with youth's problems. Recent Conservative and Liberal leadership conventions have attracted far larger percentages of young delegates.[12] To what degree this can be explained by youth's enthusiasm for leadership campaigns, party encouragement and subsidization of youth involvement,[13] or the relevance of the agenda to today's youth is uncertain.

In terms of convention location, the CCF-NDP has had a decided western tilt, with western provinces hosting 11 of 16 CCF federal conventions and 8 of 16 in the NDP era. Reflecting the growth in importance of Ontario as a party base, 3 of the CCF and 6 of the NDP conventions have been in Ontario. By contrast, Atlantic Canada had never been selected as a site for a federal CCF-NDP convention until 1991. This may be a factor in the party's continuing poor electoral record in the region, and is certainly another example of the political alienation of the Maritimes. Similarly, Québec, accounting for almost one-quarter of Canada's population, has been

TABLE 2.1 **SELECTED PARTY ACTIVITY CHARACTERISTICS, 1983, 1987, AND 1989**

| | Year | | |
	1983	1987	1989
A. Delegate type			
Constituency	74.1	64.7	68.6
Federal council	7.1	8.5	4.7
Caucus	1.7	1.7	1.4
Youth	1.0	2.7	2.3
Central labour	3.7	5.2	4.6
Affiliated unions	12.4	17.3	18.4
B. Years of NDP membership			
1-5	23.3	26.9	20.4
6-10	26.7	24.0	21.8
11-20	26.5	30.2	33.4
21-30	14.6	12.2	17.7
31-40	6.9	3.3	3.4
more than 40	2.9	2.0	3.4
C. Federal conventions previously attended			
0/no response	23.8	37.1	52.1
1	13.0	19.9	13.6
2	10.8	11.2	9.3
3	10.1	10.6	9.5
4	7.6	6.4	4.8
5	5.7	4.3	3.7
6-10	18.3	8.8	5.8
11-20	8.1	1.6	1.1
more than 20	3.3	0.0	0.0
D. Party positions			
federal riding executive	38.3	39.7	41.7
provincial/territorial riding executive	50.4	51.2	47.9
provincial/territorial council	19.9	22.6	20.0
provincial/territorial executive	10.3	10.3	9.1
federal council	5.7	8.6	7.0
federal executive	1.7	2.2	1.6

TABLE   2.1   *(continued)*

| | Year | | |
	1983	1987	1989
E. Election activities			
campaign manager	25.6	23.8	N/A
canvass organizer	37.8	31.5	
canvasser	28.0	76.6	
paid party worker	N/A	21.9	
F. Caucus attendance			
Youth	N/A	10.9	6.6
Women		21.6	14.6
Left		8.2	7.7
Gay/Lesbian		N/A	3.3
Environment		N/A	13.6
Labour		24.0	17.6
Provincial		58.0	48.8
Regional		8.4	8.3
Municipal		1.4	2.0

N/A: Data not available in similar question format.

SOURCE: Data on delegate type are based on actual convention attendance and are from the NDP, *Report of the Credentials Committee,* 1983, 1987 and 1989 conventions. Data on other activities are from the 1983, 1987 and 1989 NDP Convention Studies.

chosen only three times (twice in the CCF era and, remarkably, only once in the NDP period). This is hardly a pattern likely to entice Quebeckers to show more interest and involvement in the party. However, given the organizational weakness, and at times disarray, of the Québec CCF-NDP, the tendency to hold meetings elsewhere is perhaps understandable.

In substantial contrast to Liberal or Conservative conventions, the regional profiles of NDP conventions are skewed. In 1987 the largest percentage of NDP delegates came from Ontario (44.7%), followed by British Columbia (13.0%) and Saskatchewan (12.7%). Very few delegates came from Québec (7.7%) and the Atlantic region (7.0%). Clearly the NDP, like the CCF before it, still retains a distinctive western emphasis (38.8% in all); east of the Ottawa River remains largely untapped territory.[14] As was noted above, most of the delegates came from constituency or riding associations, and, not surprisingly, most (58.8% in 1987) attended a provincial caucus during convention.[15]

It is clear from Québec election results and the fact that the preponderance of delegates are anglophone (88.9% in 1987) that the NDP has not drawn adequately

TABLE 2.2 **SELECTED SOCIAL-BACKGROUND CHARACTERISTICS, 1983, 1987, AND 1989**

	Year		
	1983 Regina	1987 Montreal	1989 Winnipeg
A. Region			
BC, Yukon, and NWT	22.6%	14.5%	21.0%
Prairies	44.0	25.0	36.9
Ontario	30.3	44.7	33.8
Québec	0.7	7.7	2.1
Atlantic	2.1	7.0	6.2
B. Gender			
Male	69.1	67.0	63.4
Female	30.9	33.0	36.6
C. Education			
Less than grade 12	17.1	10.8	10.2
Grade 12/13	14.4	11.1	10.0
Some or complete college/university	68.3	78.1	79.9
D. Age			
21 or under	4.9	3.7	3.5
22-29	12.5	14.0	9.9
30-39	31.7	31.4	31.4
40-49	14.7	23.7	23.6
50-59	16.7	14.4	12.9
60 and over	19.4	12.1	18.6
E. Language spoken at home			
English	96.8	91.4	93.6
French	1.7	6.8	1.7
Both	0.9	1.5	4.7
Other	0.5	0.3	0.0
F. Community size			
Farm	8.4	5.7	7.4
Rural (less than 1,000)	4.9	6.4	6.8
Town (1,000-9,999)	12.8	6.1	11.4
Small city (10,000-99,999)	20.4	17.6	19.4
Medium city (100,000-499,999)	20.9	26.7	25.5
Metropolis (500,000 or more)	32.7	36.7	29.5

TABLE 2.2 (continued)

| | Year | | |
	1983 Regina	1987 Montreal	1989 Winnipeg
G. Family income[1]			
less than $40,000	68.7[2]	44.1	37.3
$40,000-$60,000	31.3	34.3	29.0
more than $60,000	—	21.5	33.7
H. Occupation			
Professional	10.6	9.2	N/A
Owner or senior executive	0.5	1.8	
Manager	3.5	2.7	
Educator	10.6	7.7	
Small proprietor	3.0	4.2	
Sales/clerical	3.5	3.1	
Skilled white collar	14.6	22.0	
Farmer	5.9	3.1	
Skilled blue collar	10.1	10.4	
Unskilled labour	4.0	4.2	
Student	7.2	7.2	
Homemaker	5.4	3.5	
Retired	11.4	6.0	
Unemployed	1.7	2.6	
Union administrator/Official	7.9	9.3	

N/A: Data not available in similar question format.

[1] does not account for inflation.

[2] includes $40,000

SOURCE: 1983, 1987, and 1989 NDP Convention Studies. For comparable data from earlier periods see Alan Whitehorn, *Canadian Socialism: Essays on the CCF-NDP* (Toronto: Oxford University Press, 1992).

from one of the key linguistic groups in Canada. Making a major breakthrough in Québec remains only a distant hope.

Any discussion of the NDP will at some point call for analysis of the class background of party activists.[16] Relatively few (14.7% in 1987) NDP convention delegates classified themselves as coming from either the upper or upper middle classes: by far the most common responses were middle (40.7%) or working class (24.7%). What is worth noting is that over the time periods surveyed, a declining percentage of delegates identified themselves as working class and an increasing percentage labelled themselves as middle class.[17] While the demographics in Canadian society at large are also shifting, there is consistent evidence to suggest that the party conventions today may not have as strong a working-class base as in the past.[18] These data fuel allegations by left-wing critics that the party has forsaken its primary audience, the proletariat, and has shifted allegiance to the middle class. While this allegation is not easily answered by one indicator, particularly a subjective one, it is also useful to contrast the NDP data with comparable measures suggesting the class profiles of Conservative and Liberal conventions. Comparative measures of delegates' family income reveal that Liberal and Conservative conventions are more heavily skewed to the upper strata. For example, the proportions of delegates with family incomes over $50,000 in 1983 were 14.3% for the NDP, 26.1% for the Liberals, and 42.2% for the Conservatives.[19] Clearly important socio-economic differences remain between the activists of the three parties.

The most common 'occupations' listed by NDP delegates in 1987 were skilled white-collar (22.0%), skilled blue-collar (10.4%), union administrator/official (9.3%), professional (9.2%), educator (7.7%), student (7.2%), retired (6.0%), unskilled labour (4.2%), small proprietor (4.2%), and homemaker (3.5%). The high cumulative percentage of skilled white-collar, educator, professional, and union administrator/official categories (48.2%) reinforces the middle-class profile of NDP convention delegates.[20]

It is clear from the survey data that a very high percentage (68.3% in 1983) of delegates have had at least some university or college education. This again suggests that delegates are more likely to be recruited from the more articulate 'haves' in the country than from the least skilled and educated strata.

Assessing the size of community in which delegates live is complicated by the fact that the conventions have been held in different regions of the country. In general, however, the rural/urban profile seems reasonably consistent over time, with the majority of delegates coming from medium-sized cities or metropoli. The relatively low percentage of delegates from farms or rural locations is another indication that the NDP, in sharp contrast to the early CCF, is to a very significant degree not a rural-based populist party.

IDEOLOGICAL COMPOSITION OF NDP CONVENTIONS

Ideologically, New Democratic activists tend to be more distinctive and more consistent than delegates of the other major parties.[21] Nevertheless, any large party is an aggregation of many and diverse interests, and the differences within a party are often as significant as those between parties.[22] In this the NDP is no exception. Like the CCF before it, the NDP today is a blend of colours of the political rainbow. Whereas in 1971 a plurality (45.7%) of party members saw themselves as 'socialists', in more recent years a decreasing number have opted for this label (38.9% in 1979, 29.6% in 1983, and 27.6% in 1987; see Table 2.3). Instead, a plurality have selected the label 'social democrat' as their preferred self-description (48.4% in 1987, 44.6% in 1983, 52.9% in 1979, and 40.6% in 1971).[23] To some scholars these data indicate a growing

TABLE 2.3 **SELECTED IDEOLOGICAL CHARACTERISTICS, 1983, 1987, AND 1989**

| | Year | | |
	1983	1987	1989
A. Subjective class			
Upper	0.5	0.3	0.7
Upper middle	11.1	14.6	20.5
Middle	45.1	40.7	47.3
Lower middle	14.2	14.5	12.1
Working	27.7	24.7	18.2
Lower	1.3	1.6	1.3
B. Ideological self-description			
Social democrat	44.6	48.4	N/A
Socialist	29.6	27.6	
Reformer	4.3	3.9	
Social gospel	3.5	2.6	
Marxist	3.0	2.0	
Liberal	1.5	0.9	
Ecologist	1.3	2.2	
Populist	1.0	0.7	
Progressive	0.0	2.6	
Multiple entry	8.9	3.8	
Other	2.3	6.0	
C. Placement on left-right scale (left = 1, right = 7) (mean scores)			
self	2.8	2.7	2.5
federal NDP	3.4	3.4	3.6
provincial/territorial NDP	N/A	3.5	3.6
federal Liberals		5.3	5.6
federal Progressive Conservatives		6.2	6.6
Communist Party of Canada		1.9	N/A
most Canadians		4.5	4.8
people in your province/territory		4.6	N/A
most Americans		5.9	6.2

N/A: Data not available in similar question format.

SOURCE: 1983, 1987, and 1989 NDP Convention Studies. For comparable data from earlier periods see Whitehorn, *Canadian Socialism*.

de-radicalization of the party and a significant shift away from commitment to socialist programs such as nationalization.[24] While a case can be made for this position, there is also evidence to the contrary. For example, an overwhelming majority (76% in 1983, 77.7% in 1987) of delegates reported that they saw the NDP as a socialist party. These findings, coupled with the fact that a third of the respondents described themselves as socialists or Marxists, suggest that it would be premature to dismiss the party, as some have done, as merely 'liberals in a hurry', or 'populists'.[25]

Many socialist parties have experienced ideological schisms, purges and defections. From the CCF's founding in 1932 to the present-day NDP, there has always been a 'ginger group' endeavouring to guide the party into a more radical or even revolutionary path. Policy debates, votes on resolutions, and leadership contests are often interpreted in left-versus-right terms by participants and scholars alike. Convention delegates continued to believe that there was a 'significant'/'big' difference (68.3% in 1983 and 63.3% in 1987) between left and right factions within the NDP. To what degree such extensive and often prolonged disagreements have hampered the party's growth in the past is not easily determined. Certainly many party members have asserted that the rhetoric of the minority at conventions has weakened efforts to woo potential new supporters into the party. Whatever the impact in the past, there seemed to be little support (only 11.8% in 1983 and 13.2% in 1987) within the party rank and file for expelling 'ultra-left elements'.

It is conventional wisdom within the NDP that most members feel they are politically to the left of the party, and survey data from the 1980s document such positioning. For example, on a 7-point left-right scale, while the NDP was placed left of centre on the political spectrum (mean = 3.4 in 1987 and 3.6 in 1989), the NDP convention delegates placed themselves even further to the left (2.7 in 1987 and 2.5 in 1989). The gap has increased in the most recent survey. Does this suggest a widespread desire among delegates to see the party shift to the more left-wing position for which many radicals have called? Survey data from the 1980s indicate that more delegates wished to see the party 'move more clearly to the left' (55.6% in 1983, 39.9% in 1987) and not 'present a more moderate image to the general public' (76.8%).

CONVENTIONS AND INTRA-PARTY DEMOCRACY

Most NDP members believe that their party is more open and democratic than the Conservative and the Liberal parties. Data from the surveys found that a majority of delegates (55.7% in 1983 and 57.7% in 1987) agreed with the statement that 'NDP conventions are extremely democratic'. In addition, majorities, albeit declining ones (83.0% in 1979 and 61.7% in 1987) indicated that they felt they were 'effective in influencing party policy' (see Table 2.4). Yet the fact that significant numbers (29.7% in 1983, 16.6% in 1987) did not believe that NDP conventions were 'extremely democratic' suggests that there remains a minority who felt that the party could be more democratic. Even in 1979, nearly half (46.7%) of delegates felt there was not enough 'rank and file participation in party decisions'.

No discussion of intra-party decision-making, influence levels, and group lobbying

TABLE   2.4   ATTITUDES   OF   CONVENTION   DELEGATES,   1987
(row   percentages)

Question	Agree[1]	Uncertain	Disagree
The NDP should become more of a social movement and less of a political party	15.9	12.2	71.8
Trade unions have too much influence in the NDP	14.8	11.1	74.1
The NDP should move more clearly to the left	39.9	22.2	37.9
There are significant differences between the left and right within the party	63.3	17.4	19.3
NDP conventions are extremely democratic	57.7	13.4	29.0
The NDP should ensure that a significant percentage of its candidates and Party officers are women	82.8	6.7	10.5
Women are discriminated against within the NDP	14.0	10.2	75.8
Fifty percent of the Federal Council should be composed of women	63.4	12.8	23.8
Resolutions passed at federal NDP conventions should be binding on the federal leader	65.4	14.3	20.3
I feel effective in influencing NDP policy	61.7	21.8	16.6
The party leader should have the right to reject a candidate nominated by a constituency association if that candidate does not accept party policies	64.1	12.3	23.5
Provincial sections of the NDP should have the right to develop policies on issues of fundamental importance independent of the federal party	54.3	15.9	29.8

[1] 5-point Likert scale collapsed into 3 categories.

SOURCE: 1987 NDP Convention Study

within the NDP would be complete without some analysis of the role of labour in general and unions specifically.[26] As was noted earlier, fewer than 20% of the delegates were selected as representatives of affiliated unions. The labour caucuses were second (24.0%) only to the provincial caucuses as those most likely to be attended by delegates. But how influential is labour at NDP conventions? At the sharply polarized Lewis versus Laxer leadership convention in 1971, almost two-thirds (63.3%) of the delegates responded that unions have too much influence within the NDP. By contrast, at recent conventions[27] the overwhelming majority (67.0% in 1983 and 74.1% in 1987) indicated that they did not believe that trade unions have wielded too much power in the party. Indeed, by a ratio of almost two to one, delegates called for 'closer ties between trade unions and the NDP'.

Delegates were also asked their views on the effectiveness of women's representation in the party. As was noted earlier, women's participation in the NDP has increased; indeed, at the 1989 leadership convention the women's caucus attracted the third highest number of participants (14.6%), no doubt in part because of the presence of a high-profile female candidate for the leadership. Although a substantial majority of delegates at the 1987 policy convention (75.8%) believed that women were not discriminated against in the NDP, a significant minority either were uncertain (10.2%) or agreed (14.0%) that women were discriminated against. Most delegates thought the party should take concrete steps to redress the historic imbalance in gender representation within the party. However, it also appeared that support for gender-based affirmative action within the party weakened when the proposal entailed specific quotas for gender equity, as opposed to a more generalized commitment to equity. For example, while an overwhelming 82.8% of delegates agreed that the party should ensure that a significant number of its candidates and party officers are women, the meaning of the phrase 'a significant number' appears ambiguous. Whereas some delegates may interpret this as a commitment to gender parity, others may see it simply as a move in that direction. When a clear target of gender parity was suggested — i.e., 'fifty percent of the federal council should be composed of women' — support dropped to 63.4%. Furthermore, almost one-quarter (23.8%) of respondents in 1987 opposed gender parity on the federal council. Thus any move towards complete gender parity in all aspects of party governance may meet some resistance.

A party that prides itself on working-class solidarity is perhaps more likely than others to impose constraints upon its leadership. Leadership review is one such mechanism. Another is the rule that policy resolutions passed at convention are binding on the leader and, presumably, any future premier/prime minister. Two-thirds (65.4%) of NDP delegates endorsed such a position.[28]

Data are available from the 1983 and 1979 surveys on members' perceptions of the party leadership's responsiveness to 'ordinary members'. In both cases, the leader was Ed Broadbent. In 1979, only a small percentage (17%) felt that the leader was 'cut off too much from the opinions of ordinary party members'. Four years later, with the party at only 16% in the Gallup polls and still straining from both intra-party differences over the 1981 constitutional amendments and the proposed new Regina manifesto, almost half the convention delegates (48.7%) believed 'the NDP leadership does not pay sufficient attention to ordinary party members'. An increasingly common criticism is that party leaders rely too often on pollsters and technical advisers. In 1979, almost three-quarters of the delegates did not agree with this suggestion, but by 1989, two-thirds (67.8%) of delegates agreed that 'the NDP paid too much attention to pollsters and not enough to principles in the 1988 election campaign'.

Delegates to the 1987 convention also believed that one of the responsibilities of the leader is to ensure that other representatives and spokespersons of the party 'toe the party line'. Almost two-thirds (64.1%) agreed that the leader has the right to reject a nominated candidate if that candidate does not accept party policies. Delegates were somewhat more evenly divided over the question of whether the provincial sections of the party should be able to develop policies independent of, and possibly in direct opposition to, those adopted by the national party. Whereas slightly more than half (54.3%) the delegates thought that provincial sections should have the right to develop independent positions, almost three in ten (29.8%) thought they should not.

LEADERSHIP SELECTION AT NDP CONVENTIONS

As one would expect with a mass party, the NDP has always invested its conventions with the powers of leadership review and selection,[29] and its leaders have been chosen at conventions.[30] In theory, each federal NDP convention tests the mandate of the leader, who is elected for only two years and needs to renew her/his term at each subsequent convention, should she/he choose to run again. While the specific details for nomination have varied over the years, the general principle has remained unchanged. Any party member can run for the leadership simply by gaining the required number of signatures of convention delegates. As of 1989, a would-be candidate needs to acquire the signatures of 50 delegates from at least 8 different ridings or affiliated organizations.[31] If two candidates are so nominated, a leadership contest ensues; if no rival is nominated, the incumbent leader wins by acclamation. In practice, few meaningful leadership contests have emerged in the history of the federal CCF-NDP.[32]

One possible explanation for the relative rarity of leadership contests is Robert Michels's 'iron law of oligarchy'. This theory suggests that despite democratic mechanisms, leaders still dominate party structure[33] through their greater access to party funds, staff, information, and media exposure. Together these resources constitute such a strong base that they can often deter any would-be rivals from even entering the fray.

Recent years have seen growing discussion of the possibility of changing the method of leadership selection, from a convention of several thousand delegates to a direct ballot of all party members.[34] In the case of the NDP, direct voting could involve some 400,000 individual and affiliated members. While the 1989 leadership convention passed a resolution to study the constitutional and procedural reforms necessary to alter the method of leadership selection,[35] at the 1991 federal convention, there seemed little urgency for such a move;[36] delegates seemed more concerned with debate and formulation of policy on matters such as the Canadian constitution and North American free trade.

In all, the NDP and its predecessor the CCF have had only seven leaders: J.S. Woodsworth (1932-42); M.J. Coldwell (1942-60); Hazen Argue (1960-61); T.C. Douglas (1961-71); David Lewis (1971-75); Ed Broadbent (1975-89); and Audrey McLaughlin (1989-present). Even though it has had a more formally democratic mechanism in place for a longer time than either the Liberals or Conservatives, the CCF-NDP has not shown a significantly greater penchant for changing its leaders. Here again Michels's observation regarding the strong oligarchic tendencies in socialist parties seems to be borne out.[37] Indeed, the first three leaders of the CCF were elected unanimously by convention. Only in the NDP era has the leadership contest become in practice a significant phenomenon.

Despite the party's working-class base, its leaders have come from decidedly white-collar and professional backgrounds. Two were religious ministers, two were teachers, one was a lawyer, one was a social worker, and only one was a farmer (and he was a university graduate). By the time of their election as party leader, each was a success-ful politician. Six were members of Parliament and one, T.C. Douglas, had been a provincial premier. Their average age at election as leader was 51.3. Clearly these were seasoned socialists.

Leaving the leadership at an average age of 60.7 at least two retired for reasons related to their health (Woodsworth and Coldwell) and two in part because of age (Douglas and Lewis). In three of these cases, the leader had also lost his seat in the House of Commons; given the paucity of safe CCF-NDP seats, such an occurrence should not be underestimated as a factor in the decision to step down. Hazen Argue was the only leader who was, in a sense, challenged and subsequently defeated, though technically he was never challenged as leader because his party — the CCF — no longer existed. Elected leader of the CCF only in its twilight year of 1960, during its unique transformation into the NDP, Argue was the youngest leader of the old and dwindling party, and was perhaps too young and politically immature to have been selected as first leader of the new one. The first-ballot landslide for T.C. Douglas at the NDP's founding convention suggested that the delegates felt as much.

All three federal CCF leaders came from the west, as did the NDP's first leader. The next two leaders (Lewis and Broadbent), by contrast, came from Ontario, giving strength to suggestions that the western farmer-based socialist CCF has been trans-formed over the years into a more eastern, labour-oriented, and pragmatic party.[38] Certainly the more pragmatic emphasis can be seen in the outcome of the four leadership contests. Between the final two candidates in each of the contests, left-versus-right labelling has been common, and it has usually been the so-called right candidate who has defeated the more left-oriented campaigner (e.g., Douglas over Argue, Lewis over Laxer, Broadbent over Brown).[39] In regional terms, the two final candidates in the first contest were westerners, in the second two easterners; the third contest was inter-regional, with the easterner winning. The 1989 leadership contest saw two westerners, or to be more precise one westerner and one north-westerner, on the final ballot, with the candidate from the sparsely populated Yukon victorious.

While only seven cases in leadership selection and only four involving leadership contests form a very small base on which to generalize, several observations can be made. The number of candidates (from one in 1933 to seven in 1989) and hence the level of competitiveness have been increasing.[40] Correspondingly, the percentage vote for the eventual winner on the first and final ballots has been declining. Some have speculated that this trend may also show increasing dissatisfaction with the final leadership choice. Given the number of candidates in recent contests, the number of ballots required for victory has been four. Nevertheless, in all four NDP leadership contests, those individuals leading on the first ballot have won, and the final margin of victory has been sufficient for a clear-cut decision.

TABLE   2.5   **VOTING   RESULTS   DURING   FOUR   BALLOTS,**
            1989   NDP   LEADERSHIP   CONVENTION

Candidate	1		2		3		4	
	N	%	N	%	N	%	N	%
McLaughlin	646	26.9	829	34.3	1,072	44.4	1,316	54.7
Barrett	566	23.6	780	32.3	947	39.2	1,072	44.6
Langdon	351	14.6	519	21.5	393	16.3		
de Jong	315	13.1	289	12.0				
McCurdy	256	10.7						
Waddell	213	8.9						
Lagassé	53	2.2						
Spoiled	3	0.1	0	0.0	3	0.1	18	0.7
Total	(2,403)		(2,417)		(2,415)		(2,406)	

SOURCE: NDP, *Report of the Credentials Committee*, 1989 NDP Convention.

In contrast to earlier NDP leadership conventions, which were largely male-dominated affairs, the past two contests (1975 and 1989) have included women and black candidates. In 1989, a woman finally won the federal leadership of a major national party in Canada. Audrey McLaughlin's victory was an important step in the long overdue shift in political power. The next section explores in greater detail that historic 1989 contest.[41]

THE 1989 LEADERSHIP CONTEST

Ed Broadbent's decision in March 1989 to step down as party leader after 14 years at the helm set in motion a full-fledged leadership contest, which was held in Winnipeg from 30 November to 3 December 1989. Of the seven candidates, all but one were members of caucus during the campaign and convention.[42] Table 2.5 maps the voting results over the four ballots. Audrey McLaughlin, the acknowledged front-runner, finished slightly ahead of Dave Barrett on the first ballot, with 26.9% versus 23.6% of the vote. The other major candidates were 10 percentage points or more behind the two front-runners. The convention rule requiring candidates with the lowest vote total and/or those with less than 75 votes to withdraw forced Lagassé off the ballot, and both Waddell and McCurdy withdrew voluntarily after the first ballot. Lagassé freed his delegates, McCurdy moved to support Langdon, and Waddell supported Barrett.

The second ballot saw McLaughlin maintain her lead with 34.3% of the vote, although the gap between her and Barrett narrowed to 2%. Langdon's support grew in step with that of the two front-runners, and de Jong was forced off the ballot. In a moment charged with excitement, and later with controversy, de Jong moved to support McLaughlin. Although a live wireless microphone had recorded de Jong, minutes earlier, pledging to move to Barrett in exchange for a valued appointment in caucus, he chose not to act on that commitment. McLaughlin was then able to make gains on Barrett on the third ballot and, after Langdon was forced off the next ballot, she secured victory by a comfortable 10-point margin.

Did the Most Preferred Candidate Win?[43]

It has been argued that the winner of a contest decided by ballot is not necessarily the person with the greatest support among the electors. Kenneth J. Arrow notes that there exists no set of rules for aggregating preferences in a democracy that will ensure that the most preferred candidate is elected.[44] Indeed, the selection of the winner may depend more on the rules used in counting preferences than on the actual preferences. The same voter preferences, under different election rules, may produce different results.[45]

For example, Terrence J. Levesque has argued that the reason Brian Mulroney won the 1983 Conservative leadership contest was that the method of selection eliminated the last-place candidate from each ballot.[46] Specifically, the elimination of John Crosbie after the third ballot led to a showdown between Joe Clark and Mulroney, and Mulroney was preferred to Clark. However, according to Levesque, when one estimates the first-, second-, and third-place rankings, Crosbie emerges as the most preferred candidate. Projecting that Crosbie would have won in two-man contests with both Mulroney and Clark, Levesque concluded that the convention rules prevented the selection of the most preferred candidate. Did the rules of leadership selection have a similar effect at the 1989 NDP convention?

To answer this question, information is required about delegates' relative ranking of the candidates, information that is not provided by the simple ballot used at NDP conventions. Even in a multi-candidate contest, the convention voting rules allow for only a binary choice: one candidate is preferred, the others are not. Furthermore, the voting rules do not enable delegates to state whether a particular candidate is preferred to *each* of the others. To overcome this lack of detailed information, the 1989 survey instrument was constructed to make a more comprehensive assessment of delegates' candidate preferences. Surveyed delegates were asked to rank-order their preferences of the seven candidates from most to least preferred.

A Condorcet winner is one who can defeat every other candidate in a series of two-party contests. Data from the candidate rankings in the 1989 survey indicate that McLaughlin was the clear Condorcet winner. She defeated Barrett 61.8:38.2,[47] she defeated Langdon 65.8:34.2, and she defeated every other candidate by at least a 3:1 margin. For Barrett, on the other hand, the margin of victory was large only in relation to Lagassé, and was less than 6:4 for all others. Furthermore, not only was Barrett preferred less than McLaughlin, but he was also preferred less than Langdon. In addition, Langdon's margin of victory over the remaining candidates (other than

McLaughlin) exceeded Barrett's. Thus these data suggest that, contrary to the results of ballot 3, which placed McLaughlin first, Barrett second, and Langdon third, in fact the delegates' preference ordering placed Langdon ahead of Barrett. However, since McLaughlin defeated Langdon by an even greater margin than she did Barrett, the final outcome would have remained unchanged. And in a winner-take-all system, the most preferred candidate won.

Why Did McLaughlin Win?

There are a number of ways of trying to assess why Audrey McLaughlin won the leadership contest in 1989. The preceding analysis showed that she was a Condorcet winner, and was preferred to every other candidate in the race for the leadership. Yet in many ways she was an unlikely winner. The first person to win the CCF-NDP leadership without having first performed many years of high-profile service to the party,[48] she was little known either within or outside the NDP when she was first elected in a Yukon by-election in 1987. When delegates to the 1987 convention were asked who they would like to see replace Ed Broadbent when he stepped down, not a single respondent mentioned McLaughlin as a possible successor.[49] However, whereas the relatively unknown Joe Clark seems to have won the Conservative party leadership in 1976 because he was the least objectionable candidate, McLaughlin's victory was apparently not a surprise: over 60% of NDP delegates recalled that, before balloting began, they expected her to win, and a further 10% thought that either McLaughlin or Barrett would win. Thus McLaughlin was able to move from relative obscurity in 1987 to become both the front-running candidate on the eve of the 1989 convention and the eventual victor. These accomplishments are perhaps even more striking when one recalls that the selection of delegates to NDP conventions is not characterized by the misuse of 'instant' party members that has been a feature of recent Liberal and Conservative conventions.[50] That is, McLaughlin's victory was not the result of a large influx of new supporters into the party. Instead, she rose to the leadership with the support of convention delegates, most of them long-standing party members. How was she able to accomplish this?

One key to McLaughlin's success may be found in the field of candidates contesting the leadership. Indeed, the field of potential candidates who decided not to seek the leadership was one of the most talked-about topics of the campaign. The 1989 survey found that more than half the respondents (51.8%) said they preferred someone else to any of the declared candidates. Among those respondents the alternative names most frequently mentioned were Stephen Lewis (57.6%), Bob Rae (28.5%), Lorne Nystrom (18.2%), Bob White (11.6%), and Nelson Riis (10.6%), names that also appeared frequently in the 1987 survey. Whether McLaughlin would have won the leadership in the face of a challenge from a high-profile non-candidate such as Stephen Lewis or Bob Rae is a question that cannot be fully resolved here. The fact that she entered the contest early[51] and defeated the late entry and high-profile former premier Dave Barrett suggests that her appeal may have been stronger than some have assumed. The above data do indicate, however, that the absence from the leadership contest of several prominent New Democrats provided McLaughlin with the opportunity to emerge as a front-runner. The question that follows is how she was able to take advantage of this opportunity and become the candidate preferred to all other declared candidates.

By most accounts, the ideological divide in the 1989 leadership contest was less dramatic than in 1971 and 1975. Nevertheless, it is worth asking whether McLaughlin's ideological stance helped her to win. As we have seen, NDP delegates tended to place themselves farther left (2.5 on a 7-point scale) than the party (3.6). They also placed themselves farther to the left than any of the declared candidates (2.9 to 3.7). Both Langdon (2.9) and Waddell (3.3) were closer to the mean score for delegates than were the front-runners. McLaughlin was located near the middle of the candidates (3.4) and Barrett was slightly to the right of her (3.7). If ideology alone were the factor in victory, then, Langdon or Waddell would have won. In any case, of the two front-runners, the delegates chose the one who was closer to their own leftist placement. Still, ideology alone is insufficient for a full explanation of McLaughlin's victory.

Given the growing importance of women in politics generally and in the NDP,[52] it seems reasonable to expect that gender would play a role in delegates' preferences. Of the seven candidates, McLaughlin was the only woman. Despite the gains for women in the party, men still constitute a significant majority of delegates, particularly in the affiliated organizations (unions). For McLaughlin to win the leadership, she required a reasonable level of support from men. The data indicate that she was in fact able to appeal to both sexes, though not equally. For example, whereas on the fourth and final ballot women supported McLaughlin by almost three to one (72.2% to 27.8%), among the male delegates opinion was more evenly divided (55.7% for McLaughlin, 44.3% for Barrett). The considerable support that McLaughlin received from male delegates mitigated, although it clearly did not eliminate, the effect of gender as a determinant of voting preferences.

A number of other characteristics boosted McLaughlin's support among delegates. The most important of these was her style of leadership. Respondents were given two statements about the role of party leader in developing and articulating party policies. When asked whether they would rather have a leader who 'will take strong stands on issues even if you often don't agree with her/him' or one who 'tries to find positions that reconcile different views on issues', delegates were almost evenly split, with 49.0% preferring a leader who would take strong stands and 51.0% preferring a more conciliatory approach. Furthermore, among those preferring a leader who takes strong stands, the delegates were again almost evenly split on the fourth ballot, with 48.6% and 51.4% voting for Barrett and McLaughlin respectively. However, among those preferring a leader who reconciles different points of view, fourth-ballot voting favoured McLaughlin over Barrett by a wide margin (71.8% versus 28.2%).

When asked whether they preferred a leader who 'gets out in front and tells you what to do' or one who 'stays back more and expects you to help him/her make decisions', the latter option was favoured by a two to one margin. Of the third of delegates who preferred a leader who gets out front and directs the party, Barrett was slightly preferred over McLaughlin (53.5% versus 46.5%). By contrast, among the two-thirds of delegates who favoured a more co-operative leadership style, McLaughlin was the overwhelming preference over Barrett (71.7% versus 28.3%).

The issue of leadership style is important within the NDP, as it is within all parties. Although Ed Broadbent remained personally popular both with the NDP and with the Canadian public generally throughout his tenure as party leader, there were growing concerns near the end of his term that his circle of close advisers was becoming increasingly closed off from both the party's rank and file and many party veterans. These concerns were voiced most loudly in the wake of the 1988 federal election, in which the party's gains, while substantial, were well below expectations.[53] There was a widely shared perception that the party had miscalculated in downplaying the free-trade issue in the election, and furthermore that the leadership of the party had insisted on following that strategy in the face of considerable concern and opposition among the rank and file. It is against this backdrop that one can best understand the importance of leadership style in 1989. Audrey McLaughlin was seen as the candidate who would try to reconcile different views on issues, and who would adopt a consensual approach to leadership. That leadership style clearly played a key role in her victory at the leadership convention, although how successful it would prove to be later, in her performance as party leader, was another question.

The importance of leadership style can also be seen in the delegates' rankings of the candidates according to their perceived characteristics (Table 2.6). Respondents were given a list of attributes and asked to rank the candidates on each of them. The list of attributes included personal likeability, appealing image on TV, sound views on policy, and ability to unite the party, make tough decisions, help win the next election, strengthen ties with organized labour, and earn respect from international leaders. The present analysis is limited to the first-place rankings on each item.[54]

Delegates to the 1989 convention viewed McLaughlin as the candidate best able to unite the party; more than 6 in 10 (61.9%) respondents ranked her first on this item. Furthermore, the difference between her and Barrett was greater on this than on any other item. McLaughlin was also ranked significantly higher than other candidates in her perceived ability to help win the next election. More than half (51.8%) the delegates thought she was the candidate best able to lead the party to electoral success (versus 27.9% for Barrett). With regard to the oft-stated theme of the distinction, in the CCF-NDP, between the social movement and the political party,[55] these data highlight the importance of winning Commons seats as one of the primary functions of a party leader, even in a party such as the CCF-NDP.

The conciliatory style of McLaughlin's leadership was also highlighted in several other characteristics. For example, she trailed Barrett (39.4% versus 31.2%) in perceived ability to 'make tough decisions', and she trailed Steven Langdon (26.5% versus 26.3%) on 'sound views on policy'. The former can be seen as the flip side of the leadership-style coin. McLaughlin ranked lower on the 'tough decision' question because an inclusive, conciliatory style avoids the direct confrontation or zero-sum approach to decision-making. Likewise, the fact that she did not place first on policy

TABLE 2.6 PERCEIVED CHARACTERISTICS OF
LEADERSHIP CANDIDATES[1]

(Cell entries are the percentages ranking each candidate first
on each characteristic: row percentages)

	Candidate		
	McLaughlin	Barrett	Langdon
Personally likeable	26.3	25.4	9.7
Appealing TV image	30.2	42.2	4.0
Sound views on policy	26.3	20.6	26.5
Unite the party	61.9	12.5	8.9
Make tough decisions	31.2	39.4	12.3
Help win next election	51.8	27.9	5.8
Strengthen ties to labour	20.3	37.0	21.6
Earn respect from international leaders	42.2	26.4	12.5

[1] Only the top three candidates are included in the table. Other candidates and non-responses are included in the percentages but excluded from the table.

SOURCE: 1989 NDP Convention Study

views reflects the fact that many delegates perceived her as aggregating and articulating their preferences rather than pursuing her own agenda.

One of the more curious findings in Table 2.6 is the contrast in rankings between the candidates perceived as helping to win the next election and those with an appealing image on TV. As was noted earlier, NDP convention delegates are experienced activists who are quite knowledgeable about politics. They understand perhaps too well that modern election campaigns are conducted primarily on television, a medium that emphasizes leaders and personalities over ideology and issues. Yet even though McLaughlin was not seen as having the most appealing TV image, she was seen as the one best able to help the party win the next election. That apparent inconsistency can be resolved in several ways. One explanation is that the only candidate with a more positive ranking on TV appeal—Dave Barrett—was perceived as too problematic in other areas (e.g., party unity and soundness of policy). A second possible interpretation is that delegates believed there was sufficient time for McLaughlin to improve her TV image before the next election.

CONCLUSION

This chapter has focused on delegates to NDP conventions to examine two aspects of political leadership in Canada: namely, the socio-demographic and attitudinal profiles of party activists and the issue of leadership selection within the party. Delegates were found to come disproportionately from the regions west of Québec; though most likely to be male, highly educated, middle-aged, urban anglophones, they showed significant diversity in occupations and incomes. In addition, delegates tended to be party members and activists of long standing, occupying positions on riding executives and taking an active part in election campaigns. The class profile of the activists consistently emphasized the middle class during the 1980s, and also indicated a trend away from the working class and towards the middle and upper middle classes. However, this sociological change should not be read as necessarily involving a de-radicalization of the party. Most delegates continue to describe themselves as social democrats or socialists, and continue to view themselves as more left-wing on the left-right ideological continuum than the party itself.

Data on the attitudes of convention delegates toward leadership structures within the party generally indicate high levels of support. For example, large majorities of delegates were satisfied with the NDP's emphasis on its role as a political party rather than a social movement, and with the trade-union links to the party; in addition, most agreed on the need to increase the role of women in the party. They showed less consensus over whether the party should move farther to the left. While there was significant support for holding the resolutions passed at conventions to be binding on the leader, many also believed that the leader should be able to reject nominated candidates who do not accept party policies. Overall, the data indicate that delegates believe the party's ideological and policy profile should be established more by the rank-and-file delegates attending conventions than by those in positions of formal leadership within the party. In a sense, they want a more populist and democratic mass party.

These attitudes were also found to contribute significantly to Audrey McLaughlin's victory in the 1989 leadership contest. Unlike previous leaders of the CCF-NDP, McLaughlin was a relative newcomer to the party, and her ascent was swifter than that of her male predecessors. In 1989 gender was seen as an important factor in the voting behaviour of delegates, with women more likely than men to support McLaughlin. Ideology appears to have played a less significant role than in previous contests. One of McLaughlin's strengths was her leadership style. Many delegates perceived her as possessing an ability to reconcile different points of view, and to foster co-operation and teamwork within the party. Because of these qualities, the majority of convention delegates saw her as the candidate best able to unite the party and help it win the next election. In a sense, McLaughlin's victory was that of the delegates themselves. Her consultative leadership style, offering a greater role for party activists, appealed to many who had felt excluded in the 1988 election planning. It is less certain whether the new style will have a similar attraction to political journalists and the Canadian electorate.

NOTES

1 The first part of this chapter draws heavily from Alan Whitehorn, *Canadian Socialism: Essays on the CCF-NDP* (Toronto: Oxford University Press, 1992).

2 Maurice Duverger, *Political Parties* (New York: John Wiley, 1963).

3 Whitehorn, *Canadian Socialism*, 6.

4 See ibid.

5 Duverger, *Political Parties*.

6 While this rate is certain to be significantly higher than for delegates at either Conservative or Liberal conventions, it is perhaps lower than might be expected for a labour-based party. The reason will become evident below, when the educational, income, and job profiles of NDP delegates are analysed.

7 The ratio of delegates to membership is skewed roughly ten to one in favour of the constituency associations.

8 The proportion of people in each delegate category attending the convention differs somewhat from the proportion in each category that responded to the various surveys. A comparison of these percentages with the percentages in Table 2.1 (based on survey respondents) indicates that the differences are modest.

9 Data provided through correspondence with the federal office of the NDP. It should be noted that these data do not include labour representatives already on the federal council. While much speculation has been offered about the role of labour unions within the NDP, on average only about one-quarter of convention delegates are officially labour-sponsored. Of course, the percentage is usually higher when a serious leadership challenge and contest are anticipated. We document elsewhere that the percentage of actual union delegates is significantly lower than the total possible (i.e., 21.5% in non-leadership contests and 47.9% in leadership struggles). See Keith Archer and Alan Whitehorn, *Canadian Trade Unions and the New Democratic Party* (Kingston: Industrial Relations Centre Press, 1993). It also should be noted that to be convention delegates from their affiliated organizations, trade unionists must also be individual members of the party, even though most of the persons they represent need not be. Thus the differences between riding delegates and union delegates should not be overstated. All are clearly individual members of the party, albeit with different roles, clients, and methods of selection. See also J. Lele, G. Perlin, and H. Thorburn, 'The National Party Convention', in Hugh G. Thorburn, ed., *Party Politics in Canada*, 4th ed. (Scarborough, Ont.: Prentice Hall, 1979), 84, for a discussion of the election vs. selection aspects of union representation at conventions.

10 Alan Whitehorn and Keith Archer, 'The Gender Gap Amongst Party Activists: A Case Study of Women and the New Democratic Party', in F.P. Gingras, ed., *Gender and Politics in Contemporary Canada* (forthcoming).

11 For further evidence and commentary see Sylvia Bashevkin, *Toeing the Lines: Women and Party Politics in Canada*, 2nd ed. (Toronto: Oxford University Press, 1993); Whitehorn, *Canadian Socialism*; and Keith Archer, 'Leadership Selection in the New Democratic Party', in Herman Bakvis, ed., *Canadian Political Parties: Leaders, Candidates and Organization*, vol. 13 of the Research Studies of the Royal Commission on Electoral Reform and Party Financing (Toronto: Dundurn, 1991).

12 Data provided by respective political parties from their convention reports. George Perlin's surveys of the 1984 Liberal and 1983 Conservative conventions indicate that delegates 20 and under represented 6.6% and 19.2% of the delegates respectively; see Perlin, ed., *Party Democracy in Canada: The Politics of National Party Conventions* (Scarborough, Ont.: Prentice Hall, 1988).

13 Certainly the NDP leadership has been cautious in fostering youth wings of the party since

the Waffle episode. In the history of the CCF-NDP, it has not been uncommon for the youth section, when it existed, to take an ideologically more hard-line Marxist approach. See David Lewis, *The Good Fight: Political Memoirs* (Toronto: Macmillan, 1981).

[14] As John Courtney points out, a delegate-selection mechanism based on rewarding larger ridings with more convention delegates is hardly likely to alleviate this phenomenon; see Courtney, *The Selection of National Party Leaders in Canada* (Toronto: Macmillan, 1973).

[15] The small francophone and Québec samples are particularly revealing, since the 1987 convention was held in Montreal.

[16] Robert Michels, *Political Parties: A Sociological Study of the Oligarchic Tendencies of Modern Democracy* (New York: Free Press, 1962).

[17] Whitehorn, *Canadian Socialism.*

[18] The effect of much higher delegate convention fees ($175 in 1983, $300 in 1991) is unclear, but expense is certainly a likely contributing factor.

[19] Data from the 1984 Liberal and 1983 Conservative conventions are taken from Perlin's surveys. See Perlin, ed., *Party Democracy.*

[20] This is actually a conservative estimate, for undoubtedly the categories 'student', 'retired', and 'homemaker' would also include people from middle-class backgrounds; also, managers and executives account for 4.5% of delegates. See also Lele, Perlin, and Thorburn, 'The National Party Convention', for an elucidation on income, education, and occupational background of NDP delegates.

[21] See Keith Archer and Alan Whitehorn, 'Opinion Structure Among New Democratic Party Activists: A Comparison with Liberals and Conservatives', *Canadian Journal of Political Science* 22: 101-13; and Archer and Whitehorn, 'Opinion Structure Among Party Activists: A Comparison of New Democrats, Liberals and Conservatives', in Hugh G. Thorburn, ed., *Party Politics in Canada*, 6th ed. (Scarborough, Ont.: Prentice-Hall, 1991).

[22] Note, for example, the issues of bilingualism and abortion, which have divided all major Canadian parties. See also Donald E. Blake, 'Division and Cohesion: The Major Parties', in Perlin, ed., *Party Democracy*; Alan Whitehorn and Keith Archer, 'The NDP and Territoriality', paper presented at the annual meeting of the Canadian Political Science Association (1989). The NDP's fellow socialist party in Britain also exhibits such intra-party differences of opinion on policy issues; see Paul Whiteley, *The Labour Party in Crisis* (London: Methuen, 1983).

[23] Some care should be taken in the interpretation of these data. For a number of delegates several terms seemed equally apt, and certainly for many the terms 'socialist' and 'social democrat' are interchangeable; see Lewis, *The Good Fight*, 301.

[24] See Janine M. Brodie, 'From Waffles to Grits: A Decade in the Life of the New Democratic Party', in Hugh G. Thorburn, ed., *Party Politics in Canada*, 5th ed. (Scarborough, Ont.: Prentice-Hall, 1985); Robert Hackett, 'The Waffle Conflict in the NDP', in Thorburn, ed., *Party Politics*, 4th ed.; Robert Hackett, 'Pie in the Sky: A History of the Ontario Waffle', *Canadian Dimension*, special edition (Oct.-Nov. 1980).

[25] Louis St Laurent originally made this remark in 1949, but it has been reiterated by scholars such as Gary Teeple; see Gary Teeple, '"Liberals in a Hurry": Socialism and the CCF-NDP', in Teeple, ed., *Capitalism and the National Question in Canada* (Toronto: University of Toronto Press, 1972). D. Laycock suggests that the terms 'populism' and 'socialism' need not be incompatible; see Laycock, *Populist and Democratic Thought in the Canadian Prairies 1910 to 1945* (Toronto: University of Toronto Press, 1990). See also J. Richards, 'Social Democracy and the Unions: What's Left?', paper presented to the annual meeting of the Quebec Political Science Association (1983); J. Richards, 'Populism', in J. Marsh, ed., *The Canadian Encyclopedia* (Edmonton: Hurtig, 1988).

[26] See also Keith Archer, *Political Choices and Electoral Consequences: A Study of Organized*

Labour and the New Democratic Party (Montreal and Kingston: McGill-Queen's University Press, 1990).

27 Of course, union influence heightens in the midst of a leadership convention when union attendance rates increase, particularly if some of the candidates are seen as significantly more pro-union than others. Certainly David Lewis's candidacy in the 1971 convention saw a somewhat higher rate of union delegates. Lewis's long stewardship on behalf of the labour movement no doubt contributed to this phenomenon.

28 Indeed, Premiers Bob Rae and Roy Romanow have felt the effects of such attitudes among party activists.

29 For the first two CCF leaders, the procedure was actually a more complex hybrid: a two-step process involving first a vote within the caucus of MPs and than an election/ratification by convention of the leader as party president; see Lewis, *The Good Fight*, 499.

30 The six previous leaders served an average of 9.5 years. At 14 years' duration in 1989, Ed Broadbent was the party leader with the second longest tenure. M.J. Coldwell served the longest.

31 As of 1989 a leadership candidate was limited to a campaign expenditure of $150,000, was required to list the sources of his/her donations, and was allowed two free mailings to the convention delegates. In the past nominations were easier in that they required nomination signatures from fewer ridings or affiliated organizations. The result was that from time to time fringe candidates appeared with no chance of mounting a serious contest. At some point Douglas, Lewis, and Broadbent, as incumbents, all experienced such token contests. None of these votes was taken seriously.

32 For a discussion of this pattern, see Courtney, *Selection of National Party Leaders*.

33 Michels, *Political Parties*.

34 See Peter Woolstencroft, 'Social Choice Theory and Reconstruction of Elections: A Comment of Levesque's Analysis', *Canadian Journal of Political Science* 16: 785-9; R. Kenneth Carty, Lynda Erickson, Donald E. Blake, *Leaders and Parties in Canadian Politics: The Experience of the Provinces* (Toronto: Harcourt, Brace, Jovanovich, 1992); and Daniel Latouche, 'Universal Democracy and Effective Leadership: Lessons from the Experience of the Party Quebecois', in ibid.

35 When respondents to the 1989 survey were asked, 'Are you in favour of a change to a 'one member-one vote' system to choose party leaders?', 52.4% were in favour, 35.8% were opposed, and 11.9% were uncertain.

36 See Suzanne Hayward and Alan Whitehorn, 'Leadership Selection: Which Method?', paper presented to the Douglas-Coldwell Foundation (April 1991); Archer, 'Leadership Selection'.

37 Michels, *Political Parties*.

38 See Alan Whitehorn, 'The CCF-NDP: Fifty Years After', in Thorburn, ed., *Party Politics*, 5th ed.; Whitehorn, *Canadian Socialism*.

39 It should be noted that while in 1971 Broadbent was not among the final two leadership aspirants, at that time he could be labelled as centre-left, whereas in 1975 his position was seen as being more to the right of Rosemary Brown. For a discussion of the Brown campaign see her memoirs, *Being Brown: A Very Public Life* (Toronto: Random House, 1989). The 1989 leadership convention, discussed in more detail below, was seen by many observers as characterized less by ideology than by other matters.

40 Whitehorn, *Canadian Socialism*.

41 See also Audrey McLaughlin, *A Woman's Place: My Life and Politics* (Toronto: MacFarlane, Walter and Ross, 1992).

42 Roger Lagassé, a school teacher, was the only candidate not in caucus.

[43] For a more detailed application of the analysis in this section, see Archer, 'Leadership Selection'.

[44] Kenneth J. Arrow, *Social Choice and Individual Values* (New Haven: Yale University Press, 1961).

[45] Steven Brams, *Rational Politics: Decisions, Games and Strategy* (Boston: Academic Press, 1985), 58-60.

[46] Terrence J. Levesque, 'On the Outcome of the 1983 Conservative Leadership Convention: How They Shot Themselves in the Other Foot', *Canadian Journal of Political Science* 16 (1983): 779-84. For a reply, see Woolstencroft, 'Social Choice Theory'; and see Perlin, ed., *Party Democracy*.

[47] Note that these survey data overestimate McLaughlin's support among respondents and underestimate Barrett's. In general, Barrett's support in the survey is about 6 percentage points less than at the convention. McLaughlin's support is similarly overestimated by about 6 per cent, and the other candidates' support is accurately mapped. This is because of the relatively low response rate of union delegates, who were disproportionately supportive of Barrett, as well as the more generalized finding, from post-convention or post-election studies, that such studies overestimate the support of the winning candidate. However, the size of the error in estimation, and the fact that it applies only to McLaughlin and Barrett support, points to the reliability of the data on relative voter preferences. In particular, the relative-preference standings of Barrett and Langdon are unaffected by the error. For more detail see Archer, 'Leadership Selection'.

[48] Broadbent, the second most 'inexperienced' NDP leader, had been a member of Parliament for seven years when he won the leadership.

[49] Keith Archer and Allan Whitehorn, 'Speculation over NDP leadership', *Financial Post* 7 Feb. 1989: 12.

[50] Archer, 'Leadership Selection'.

[51] McLaughlin, *A Woman's Place*.

[52] Whitehorn and Archer, 'The Gender Gap'.

[53] Whitehorn, *Canadian Socialism*.

[54] A more detailed analysis incorporating the candidates' perceived characteristics, ideology, delegates' socio-demographic characteristics, and organizational factors can be found in Archer, 'Leadership Selection'.

[55] See Whitehorn, *Canadian Socialism*.

CHAPTER THREE

L E A D E R S   A N D   V O T E R S

The   Public   Images   of   Canadian
Political   Leaders

———

Lawrence   LeDuc

Party leaders occupy a prominent place in Canadians' perceptions of politics. In their day-to-day coverage of public affairs and political events, the news media treat the statements and activities of the party leaders as major news items; even issues and policy questions are frequently personalized and associated with individual leaders. During election campaigns, the media coverage of party leaders intensifies as reporters follow and report on the leaders' campaign tours. Each party pursues strategies explicitly designed to persuade the electorate that its leader has 'the right stuff' to confront the nation's most pressing social and economic problems. Election campaigns can easily turn into political 'horse-races' in which debate over substantive policies tends to lag behind the emphasis that the parties themselves place on cultivating positive images of their leaders, with the assistance of polling experts and advertising agencies. Attacks on the leaders of opposing parties have also become more common in recent years, as political strategists have come to realize that negative public perceptions of other leaders may be as valuable as favourable coverage of their own. And televised debates between the major party leaders seem to have become the critical events of recent election campaigns in Canada and elsewhere. While many Canadians decry this 'presidentialization' of parliamentary politics, it is a trend that is unlikely to be reversed any time soon.[1]

Canadian political parties have always afforded a prominent place to the role of the party leader. Rather than emphasizing social, regional, or linguistic cleavages, or laying out programs or clearly defined policy proposals, parties prefer to emphasize 'problems' that need to be addressed — not infrequently, variations of the same general ones identified by their competitors, such as 'the economy' or 'national unity'.[2] The images and personalities of the party leaders easily become intertwined with issues during the course of an election campaign, and 'leadership' itself is sometimes treated as an issue by one or more of the parties. Such a tendency to mix matters of policy with questions of leader competence is a natural part of modern political campaigning. But the Canadian political environment has been especially hospitable to this media-oriented emphasis on the attributes of the leader. This chapter will explore some of the linkages between party and leader images, and examine the impact that campaign strategies and high-profile media events such as televised debates can have on the public's perceptions of a party leader.

LEADERS AND PARTY IMAGES

A considerable body of data on Canadians' perceptions of parties and leaders has been collected over a sufficiently long period of time to permit comparisons of different leaders of the same party, the same leaders in different election campaigns, and the performance of individual leaders under different sets of political circumstances. Pierre Trudeau, for example, led the Liberal party in five election campaigns against different opponents, and was prime minister for fifteen years. In the 1984 and 1988 elections, the three parties were led by the same individuals, but the issues and circumstances of the two campaigns were markedly different. In both of these elections, however, televised debates between the leaders had a dramatic impact on the campaign. The large body of data collected in national surveys over the past 25 years provides an opportunity to measure in a variety of ways the effects of leaders on public perceptions of their parties, as well as the effects of external events on perceptions of the leaders themselves.

Two broad indicators of the role played by party leaders in Canadians' perceptions of politics were employed as standard items in the National Election Studies between 1974 and 1984.[3] One of these is an open-ended-style question concerning a respondent's 'likes' and 'dislikes' with respect to each of the three main parties.[4] Employed with repeated probes, this question indicates the number of times that respondents spontaneously mentioned party leaders compared to other political objects. As can be seen in Table 3.1, leaders have consistently occupied a prominent place in the images that Canadians hold of their political parties, generally ranking third behind issue or policy questions and items relating to 'style' or performance. The parties are most commonly viewed in terms of the dominant policies or issues of the day, and/or

TABLE 3.1 **THE STRUCTURE OF PARTY IMAGES IN CANADA, 1974-1984**[1] (percentages of respondents citing each category)

	1974	1979	1980	1984
Policy/issue	61	51	60	51
Style/performance	47	50	60	53
Leader/leadership	38	37	51	23
Parties/general	35	42	40	41
Area/group	28	27	31	34
Ideology	14	15	18	16
N =	(2,445)	(2,670)	(928)[2]	(3,380)

[1] Based on total national samples. Multiple response. 1974, 1979, 1980 and 1984 National Election Studies.
[2] Split half-sample.

in terms of their performance, particularly when in government. Parties are much less likely to be seen in ideological terms, and references to variables such as interest groups or regions are also distinctly less common than remarks of the two predominant kinds. For the most part, the images of parties that recur with the greatest frequency are those that tend to be most responsive to change over time. Images of parties that might be shaped by long-term social or political forces are much less in evidence.

Party leaders figure quite prominently in these perceptions of political parties. Through much of the 1970s, various references to Trudeau (both positive and negative) predominated in this category, and over half of all respondents spontaneously mentioned 'leaders' in the 1980 survey (Table 3.1). But in 1984, references to party leaders declined somewhat, in part because the two largest parties had new leaders who were less well known to voters. In addition, Brian Mulroney, John Turner, and Ed Broadbent, who led their parties in the 1984 and 1988 federal elections, did not tend to ignite strong passions in quite the same way that Trudeau could, and they were therefore somewhat less dominant in shaping the public images of their parties than he had been. This is not to suggest, however, that leaders have declined in importance. If anything, the pervasiveness of television and the use of televised leaders' debates in election campaigns have made them even more important. What is noteworthy is that images of political parties are shaped by current political trends, and can be subject to quite rapid change. Strong political leaders such as Trudeau and Diefenbaker were able to reshape their parties around their own images. One of the quickest and surest ways for any political party to give itself a new image is to choose a new leader. But new leaders can also drag their parties down. After 1984, the esteem

FIGURE 3.1   **Relative Ranking of Party, Leader, or Local Candidate as the 'Most Important Factor' in Voting Decision, 1974-1984**

(Shaded area indicates those respondents citing 'personal qualities' rather than 'stand on issues')

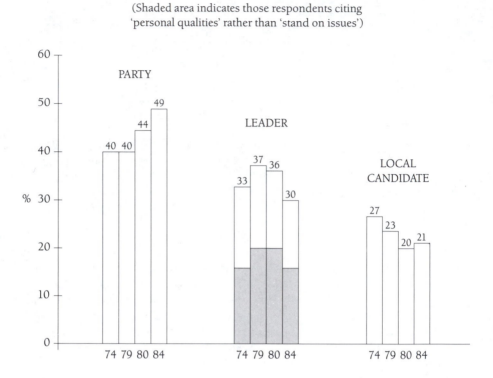

in which the public held all of the party leaders declined sharply (see Figure 3.2, p. 58 below), and these negative perceptions of their leaders reflected on the parties as well.

In each of four national surveys beginning with 1974, respondents were also asked to rate the party leader, the party as a whole, and the local candidate in order of importance as determinants of their personal voting decisions. For those naming 'leader' as the most important factor, a further probe was employed asking the respondent to indicate whether it was that person's 'personal qualities' or 'stand on issues' that mattered most.[5] As Figure 3.1 shows, leaders again occupied a prominent place in voters' perceptions of the choices presented to them in elections. The percentages who saw the elections as choices between party leaders are substantially higher than those mentioning local candidates, standing only slightly below 'parties as a whole' in the four studies. While parliamentary systems of voting by their very nature require that voters choose a 'package' of party, leader, and local candidate, it is evident that for most voters leaders have become a highly salient part of this package.

Although the importance of party leaders in parliamentary systems such as Canada's is widely recognized, there has been surprisingly little research on the ways in which the mass public forms its impressions of party leaders, and on the linkages between these perceptions and the images of political parties.[6] Part of the reason is that each leader seems a unique case, and the small number of cases, each with its own peculiar characteristics, inhibits generalization. However, the relative longevity of Canadian party leaders, together with the variations in political circumstances over several elections, allows several useful questions to be addressed. Do political parties tend to take on the images of their leaders? If so, then one might expect to see an abrupt shift in perceptions of the Liberal party following the transition from Pierre Trudeau to John Turner in 1984. Similarly, the change in leadership of the Conservatives from Joe Clark to Brian Mulroney in 1983 might have been expected to produce a similar transformation. On the other hand, well-established party images may tend to cling to the leader. Ed Broadbent's systematic attempt to position the NDP more firmly in the centre of the political spectrum seems to have been at least partly inhibited by the 'radical' image of the party that was well established in the minds of many voters.

There are also several questions to be addressed regarding the images of the leaders themselves. Is there a particular 'schematic' that individuals use in forming their impressions of party leaders? Are personality characteristics more important in this regard than issue positions? Can a leader's public image, once established, be reformed by an effective advertising campaign or reshaped by his/her performance in a debate? Trudeau's image, as well as his political fortunes, seemed to undergo several metamorphoses during his sixteen years as Liberal leader. Turner's strong performance in the televised debates of the 1988 election campaign, together with his embrace of the free-trade issue, helped at least temporarily to overcome the strongly negative components of his image that had lingered from four years earlier. Yet Joe Clark never seemed able to extricate himself from the image of bumbling incompetence acquired early in his tenure. By examining the stability and dimensions of the images of several of these leaders over a period of time, however, it should be possible to provide at least tentative answers to some of these questions.

THE DECLINE OF ALL LEADERS

In studies since 1968, respondents have been asked to indicate how much they liked or disliked particular political leaders using a summary statistic commonly called a 'feeling thermometer'. We thus have a comparable measure of the public's feeling about every major Canadian party leader of the past two decades. A summary of these indicators for seven of the party leaders over this period is presented in Figure 3.2. It is evident from these data that there has been a steady erosion of public support for party leaders, both as individuals and collectively. This is perhaps most obvious in the case of Pierre Trudeau, whose career as party leader spanned the longest period and included the entire decade of the 1970s. From his first election in 1968, positive feelings toward Trudeau declined sharply and steadily. But the sharp downward trajectory of public feeling about Trudeau illustrates a more general pattern. Every federal party leader of the past two decades has declined in public esteem from the benchmark established in his first election as leader, no matter how popular or

FIGURE   3.2   Thermometer Scale Ratings of Political Leaders, 1968-1992

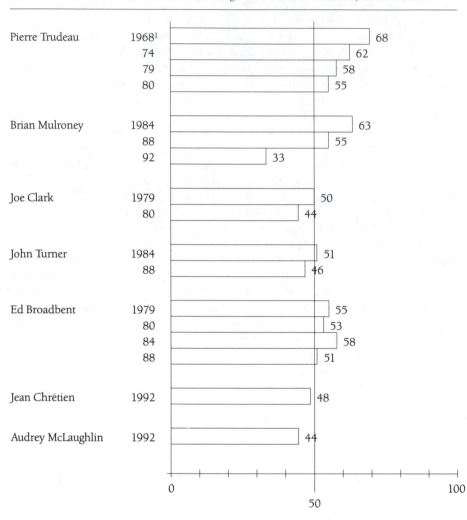

[1]1968 to 1988 National Election Studies. 1992 Carleton Referendum Study.

unpopular the leader was at that juncture. Taken as a group, the three party leaders of 1988 were all less popular than they had been four years earlier, and Brian Mulroney, the only one of these three who was still in public life, declined to historic lows in public esteem after 1988. Ed Broadbent presents only a modest exception to this pattern, as his standing with the public improved between 1980 and 1984 (Figure 3.2). But this upswing in Broadbent's popularity proved to be only temporary. In 1988 his rating resumed its decline, dropping to the lowest point recorded during his long political career. Time has not been kind to the leaders of our national political parties, even those who have enjoyed considerable electoral success.

The decline in the affection of the public for the nation's political leaders after 1984 is particularly instructive. At the time of the 1984 election Brian Mulroney, although still relatively unknown to much of the public, stood at what was to be the peak of his political popularity. At 63, his rating on the thermometer scale was second only to that recorded by Trudeau in 1968. Ed Broadbent was also at the highest point of his popularity, having defied the longer-term trend and actually improved his standing with the public from that of four years earlier. At a rating of 58 on the scale, he was the third most popular political leader of the past two decades, scoring higher than Trudeau in 1979 or 1980, or Mulroney in 1988. John Turner, although less well liked than Mulroney or Broadbent in 1984, was nevertheless rated just to the positive side of the scale, slightly more popular than Clark was in 1979 or Jean Chrétien subsequently.

Four years later, however, the feelings of the mass public about each of these leaders had undergone a steep decline. Mulroney, Turner, and Broadbent were all rated lower in 1988 than in 1984, a pattern that is somewhat surprising in the case of Turner, given his much stronger performance in the 1988 campaign. The most recent data available, collected at the time of the 1992 referendum campaign, show this decline in public estimation of party leaders to have accelerated further, with Mulroney's popularity at a record low and even the new leaders of the two main opposition parties, Chrétien and McLaughlin, rating on the negative side of the scale. Clearly, since 1988 the Canadian public has become more disillusioned with the party leaders than at any time in the recent past.

TRAITS AND CHARACTERISTICS

While the feeling thermometer provides a useful overview and comparison, it does not, of course, tell the whole story. Joe Clark won the 1979 election in spite of the fact that he was the least well regarded of the three party leaders at that time. Similarly, the NDP and Liberals both gained seats and votes in the 1988 election despite the slippage in popularity of their leaders. Some voters may not like a particular leader, but nevertheless may be quite prepared to support a party for issue or policy reasons, or because they believe that the leader has attributes that would be effective in office. In other words, the content of the images that the public holds of the party leaders can tell us as much or more about the perceived attributes of leaders as the thermometer scores. In a number of studies from 1968 onward, open-ended questions similar to the party-image questions discussed earlier were employed to discover particular characteristics that the public associated with various leaders. These more detailed data will be used to probe the images of the two most successful party leaders of recent times in Canada, Pierre Trudeau and Brian Mulroney.

More than any other party leader, at least since John Diefenbaker, Pierre Trudeau evoked strong public sentiments. Some loved him, some hated him, but few were indifferent. Certainly after 1988, Brian Mulroney provoked similarly strong feelings, more negative than positive, among the public. Trudeau's public image was complex, and underwent several significant changes during his long tenure as leader of the Liberal party and prime minister. Like Mulroney, he was not a well-known public figure when he assumed the leadership of his party, or even later when he became prime minister for the first time. But certain elements of both men's images have recurred again and again in national surveys. Voters were quick to recognize Trudeau's intelligence, his leadership abilities, and his personal magnetism. Indeed, respondents mentioned intelligence and leadership ability with increasing frequency as positive attributes even as politics took its toll on Trudeau's popularity. At the time of the 1980 election, even though the public's affection for Trudeau had declined considerably from its earlier high, 26 per cent of the national sample mentioned 'intelligence' as one of his positive qualities, and 18 per cent mentioned 'leadership' (Table 3.2). Even at the height of his popularity, however, certain aspects of Trudeau's personality were negatively perceived by much of the public. From the beginning there was a feeling that he lacked concern for ordinary Canadians, and that he was preoccupied with Québec and the Constitution at the expense of other pressing issues. The number of Canadians who saw Trudeau as arrogant and aloof rose steadily throughout his political career, with 22 per cent of respondents in the 1980 study describing him in this way, and additional numbers using terms such as 'conceited' and 'dictatorial' (Table 3.2). Toward the end of his career, these negatives weighed as heavily as the positives, in part accounting for the steady erosion of Trudeau's popularity. But despite responses such as these, Trudeau continued to be accorded at least a grudging respect, even among some who disliked either his personality or his policies.

Like Trudeau's, Brian Mulroney's rise to party leadership was sudden and unpredictable. Prior to becoming party leader in 1983, Mulroney had never held an elective public office. As a result, he was still a largely unknown quantity to much of the public when he faced the national electorate for the first time as Conservative leader in 1984. Tired of the Trudeau years and uninspired by John Turner, the voters were ready for change. Mulroney was able to put an end to the fractious conflicts among Conservatives after the 1983 leadership convention, and he led a united and determined party into the 1984 election campaign. This gave him an image of leadership ability and competence that Joe Clark had never achieved. Mulroney was effective in both French and English in the campaign debates and he projected an image of confidence and self-assurance that contrasted sharply with Turner's accident-prone campaign. The negatives in Mulroney's image were there from the beginning, but they did not become fully developed in the minds of voters until after he had become prime minister. Although many voters in 1984 saw him as 'honest' and 'sincere', a nearly equal number found him insincere or untrustworthy. As with Trudeau's perceived 'arrogance', the image that would most dog Mulroney throughout his political career was that of a man who could not be trusted. Having attacked Turner relentlessly over the issue of patronage, Mulroney dispensed it freely once in office. Proclaiming social programs a 'sacred trust', he later sought ways to bring about an end to universality of many benefits. Mulroney as prime minister forced through unpopular policies such

TABLE 3.2 FREQUENTLY MENTIONED TRAITS OF
PIERRE TRUDEAU AND BRIAN MULRONEY AS
POLITICAL LEADERS

Pierre Trudeau[1]
1974 (N = 1,203)

Positive	%	Negative	%
Intelligence	16	Arrogance	8
Speaking ability	10	Travels too much	5
Honesty	10	Doesn't attend to business	4
Leadership	9	Policies on inflation	3
Personality in general	9	Dodges issues	3
		General approach	3

1980 (N = 860)

Intelligence	26	Arrogance	22
Leadership	18	Too dictatorial	5
Speaking ability	8	Dishonesty	4
Experience	4	General attitude	4
Personality in general	5	Conceited	3

Brian Mulroney[2]
1984 (N = 3380)

Positive	%	Negative	%
Honesty, sincerity	11	Not sincere, untrustworthy	8
Speaking ability	8	Too many promises	5
Intelligent, capable	6	Too smooth, slick	4
Leadership ability	5	Arrogant	3
Confidence, self-assurance	5	Attitude in general	2

1988 (N = 1200)

Leadership ability, performance	7	Not sincere, can't be trusted, phony	19
Speaking ability	7	Pompous, arrogant	6
Honesty, sincerity	6	Too smooth, slick	4
Attitude, approach	5	Indecisive, vague	3
Works hard, tries	3	Not a leader	2

[1] 1974 and 1986 National Election Studies
[2] 1984 National Election Study and 1988 Carleton Panel Study

as the Free Trade Agreement and the GST, and presided over a long and deep economic recession. By 1992 his thermometer rating (Figure 3.2) was setting new records for personal unpopularity, in dramatic contrast to the positive ratings achieved earlier in his political career.

The traits that the public tends to associate with Canadian party leaders are consistent with a 'schematic' interpretation of the formation of leader images.[7] However, there appears to be no single model of 'leadership' against which leaders are measured. Personality characteristics tend to predominate among frequently mentioned attributes of Canadian party leaders. There are few mentions of issues or policy positions associated with leaders, and those that do occur tend not to persist over more than a single election. Only in the case of the NDP is there any significant transfer of party attributes to the leader, but even in that instance the personality characteristics associated with Ed Broadbent during his long tenure as party leader were more numerous. Leaders are perceived as being 'honest', 'sincere', 'capable', 'competent', 'trustworthy', 'intelligent', 'arrogant', 'slick', or 'indecisive'. They are not often evaluated as 'liberal', 'right-wing', or 'taxers and spenders'. There is also a great deal of consistency for the same leaders across two or more elections. The attributes associated with Trudeau, such as 'intelligence' and 'arrogance', became more firmly established over time, as did 'untrustworthiness' and 'insincerity' in the case of Mulroney. Once in place, such images do not change easily, because they are associated with the individual rather than with a particular set of circumstances.

Nevertheless, there are some traits evident in these data that, while falling within the general category of 'personality', do seem to be more driven by events. Some of these may be associated with a campaign style or theme, while others are products of what might be called 'performance', either in public office or as leader of the party. The 'concern for ordinary people' associated with Broadbent, for example, reflected the NDP campaign themes of 1984 and 1988 as much as it did the characteristics of the man himself. The fact that the two seemed to complement each other was in many ways a function of the party's strategy in those two campaigns. Similarly, the observations that Turner 'couldn't control his party' or that Clark was 'inexperienced' were at least partly related to performance. They were less pure personality traits than persistent images conveyed to the electorate by daily news programs. Like the personality traits noted above, these also do not change easily once established, in part because they tend to be continually reinforced over a long period of time. However, Johnston et al., in their study of the dynamics of the 1988 election campaign, did find that certain traits were affected by campaign strategies, media reporting, and other short-term factors.[8]

CAMPAIGNS AND DEBATES

How changeable are the images of party leaders, once they have taken shape in the voters' minds? Certainly new leaders who are relative political unknowns, such as Clark in 1979 or Mulroney in 1984, have the opportunity to use the techniques of modern campaigning to attempt to establish a favourable image with the public. But can other leaders, whose public images are more firmly established, employ those same techniques to retool those images or, more specifically, to counter those impressions that may be unfavourable? Could Brian Mulroney have been made to seem more trustworthy or John Turner more competent through a carefully crafted advertising campaign or electoral strategy? One test may be found in the effects that high-profile events such as televised leaders' debates have had on their images and on voting choice in elections. Because both the 1984 and 1988 Canadian federal elections featured such debates between the same three party leaders, and because the perceptions of their performances in those debates seemed in both instances to be at variance with the established images of the participants, it is possible to measure in at least a limited way the malleability of leader images through analysis of the effects of the debates in these two elections.[9]

The televised debates of the 1984 federal election campaign took place largely because they were consistent with the campaign strategies of each of three main parties in that contest. As the new leader of the opposition Conservatives and the least well known of the party leaders, Brian Mulroney was anxious to debate. He issued a public challenge to Turner, who had just succeeded Pierre Trudeau, at the very beginning of the campaign, even though the Conservatives probably did not need the debates in order to win. Mulroney was also anxious to debate in French, both because of his fluency in the language and because a French debate was essential if he was to make a major breakthrough in Québec. It was decided that two debates would take place, one in French and one in English, with the French debate occurring first. Turner was somewhat less enthusiastic about the debates than Mulroney, but he too quickly agreed. He was the incumbent prime minister in name only, and his party appeared vulnerable. But, less fluent in French than Mulroney and possessing a wooden speaking style, Turner started from a distinct disadvantage. The NDP also decided to participate in the debates, as it had on both previous occasions (1968 and 1979).

The debates (the first in French, the second in English the following night) took place early in the campaign, largely at the insistence of the Liberals, who saw debates held too close to election day (as they had been in 1979) as carrying greater risk. Mulroney, at ease in French and confident of his strategy, was highly effective in the French debate. Turner, naturally nervous and less at ease, although reasonably fluent in French, was less effective. The Québec newspapers quickly and uniformly named Mulroney the 'winner' of the encounter, many in banner headlines. Broadbent, the least fluent of the three leaders in French, nevertheless received some praise for his effort. Although Mulroney benefited from the French debate, the impact of the English debate the following evening was greater, if only because of the wider audience.[10] The English debate was also memorable for a dramatic incident in which Mulroney trapped Turner on the 'patronage' issue, referring to a string of unpopular political appointments made by Turner at Trudeau's behest immediately upon his assumption of the prime minister's office. Nervous and ill at ease, Turner responded weakly to Mulroney's stinging attack saying that he had had 'no option'. Facing Turner directly, Mulroney delivered the following riposte: 'You had an option, sir. You could have said: "I'm not going to do it. This is wrong for Canada. I'm not going to ask

Canadians to pay the price." You had an option, sir, to say no and you chose to say "yes" — yes to the old attitudes and the old stories of the Liberal party.'

It was dramatic television, and in many ways it illustrates the political potential of the televised debate forum. Mulroney used the 'no option' phrase extensively in the remainder of the campaign, continually taunting Turner with his ineffectual response. Most observers felt that Mulroney had won both debates. Broadbent also earned high marks for his performance, delivering thoughtful, articulate answers to questions and appearing every bit the equal of the major party leaders. Few felt that Turner had come through the two debates unscathed, and many viewed his performance in both debates as disastrous. When the Conservatives went on to win an election victory of landslide proportions, the debates were widely viewed as having contributed to the outcome.

Contrary to the circumstances in 1984, there was never any real doubt about whether a leaders' debate would take place in 1988. Such debates have begun to assume characteristics of institutionalization in Canadian elections, and it has become increasingly difficult for a party leader to refuse to participate. However, debates were also consistent with the strategies of all three parties in the 1988 campaign, so an agreement in principle between them and the networks was quickly achieved. As the governing party and front-runners in the early polls, the Conservatives pursued exactly the same strategy that the Liberals had in 1984: a French debate followed immediately by one in English, and an early date, allowing at least a month until election day to maximize the potential for recovery. Both the Liberals and the NDP were anxious for debates in 1988, as has generally been the case with opposition parties. All three leaders prepared extensively for the encounter, but the most detailed and elaborate preparations were undertaken by Turner and his advisers. The formats of the 1988 French and English debates were identical, differing only slightly in length and structure from those of 1984.

There can be little doubt that Turner's outstanding performance in the two debates turned the 1988 campaign around — at least temporarily. His ineffectiveness in the 1984 debates and low standing in the polls were in some respects advantageous, as he benefited from both low expectations and Tory over-confidence. In the six hours of televised debate, three in French on 24 October and three in English the following night, the momentum of the campaign abruptly shifted. The most dramatic segment of the debates, later used in Liberal campaign spots, occurred near the end of the second hour of the English debate, when Turner lectured Mulroney on the Free Trade Agreement. 'I happen to believe that you've sold us out. . . . With one stroke of a pen . . . you have thrown us into the North-South influence of the United States. . . . And, when the economic levers go, political independence is sure to follow.' Well-coached and confident, Turner appeared prime ministerial, while Mulroney, attempting to appear statesmanlike, came across as weak and ineffectual. Broadbent was simply relegated to the sidelines, particularly in the French debate where his lack of fluency was less kindly received than in 1984. Turner's success in the debates had an immediate and dramatic impact on the campaign. Public opinion polls quickly confirmed what many who saw the debates sensed almost immediately. Turner had

TABLE   3.3   **RATINGS   OF   LEADER   PERFORMANCE   IN
DEBATES   WATCHED,   1984   AND   1988
(mean   scores,   ten-point   performance   scale)**

	1988[1]	1984[2]
Turner	6.7	4.2
Mulroney	5.8	6.9
Broadbent	4.9	6.6

[1] Respondents who watched either of the debates and were able to give a rating of the leaders' performance in those debates which they saw; 1988 Carleton Panel Study (N = 744).

[2] Respondents who watched any of the three debates (including the 'women's debate'), and were able to give a rating of the leaders' performance in those debates which they saw; 1984 National Election Study (N = 2,144).

not only emerged as the 'winner' of the debate, he had vaulted his party into the lead. The Gallup poll taken in the week following the debates gave the Liberals 43 per cent, Conservatives 31 per cent, and NDP 22 per cent. An eleven-point gain in the Liberal percentage from the poll published a week earlier, it was the largest single shift ever recorded by the Gallup organization in Canada. Had the election taken place within a week of the debates as in 1979, the Liberals might have been able to ride this surge in support to victory. But the Conservatives' recovery began swiftly as the party's official campaign organization turned its fire directly on John Turner, emphasizing issues of 'trust' and 'competence' and borrowing selectively from the negative tactics seen in the US election campaign only a few weeks earlier. At the same time, outside groups, heavily financed by the business community, mounted an enormous advertising campaign to save the Free Trade Agreement. While the outcome remained in doubt until very near the end of the campaign, the Conservatives ultimately went on to win a solid majority of seats.[11]

National surveys available for 1984 and 1988 include several measures that capture respondents' perceptions of the relative performance of the leaders in the debates. Both the 1984 and 1988 National Election Studies also contain the thermometer measures of general leader affect, providing an indicator of a respondent's feelings about each of the three leaders that is conceptually independent of performance in the debates. Because of the wide disjuncture in the perceived performance of the three party leaders in the 1984 and 1988 debates, these measures demonstrate clearly the ability of viewers to recognize leader performance in a way that is independent of pre-existing evaluations or partisan affect. While debates may sometimes act to reinforce existing attitudes toward parties and leaders, they may also enable viewers to form impressions of the leaders that are distinct from such attitudes. Turner's strong performance in the 1988 debates was widely recognized by viewers in one 1988 sample, who collectively gave him a performance score substantially higher than that accorded either Mulroney or Broadbent (Table 3.3). This pattern existed for both French- and English-speaking respondents in 1988, although the spread between Turner and Mulroney was somewhat narrower among francophone respondents (data not shown).

Changes in the perceptions of the performances of the other two leaders are evident as well. Broadbent, who had been perceived as doing well in the 1984 debates, was rated much lower in 1988. Mulroney was also rated as having performed less well in the 1988 debates than in 1984, dropping more than a full point in mean rating for the entire sample on the performance scale. Even among francophone respondents, Mulroney declined from a mean rating of 7.5 in the 1984 study to a still respectable but much lower average score of 6.2 among French-speaking viewers of the 1988 debate.

These data should not necessarily be taken to imply, however, that respondents completely changed their opinions of the leaders following the debates, or that the debates determined the outcome of the election. It is entirely possible that, although recognizing Turner's strong performance in the televised debates, voters nevertheless continued to feel that he would make a poor prime minister, and were no more prepared to vote for his party after the debates than before. It is likewise plausible that neither Broadbent's strong performance in the 1984 debates, nor his much poorer one in 1988, had much effect on his overall image and/or on the NDP vote. Intuitively, it would seem that debates enabling a wide audience to form clear perceptions of the participants' performances should have made some difference. Yet we also know that in 1988 Mulroney went on to win the election in spite of the debates, just as Clark had in 1979. Likewise, Broadbent's apparently poor performance in the 1988 debates did not prevent the NDP from winning a record high of 43 seats. Clearly, if the effects of the debates are felt in the form of longer-lasting attitudes towards the leaders or their parties, or in votes cast on election day, it is in ways more subtle than these broad observations would suggest.

The thermometer scores provide a means of testing the effects of the debates on respondents' more general feelings about the leaders. Watchers and non-watchers of the various debates can be compared on these measures to determine whether or not those who watched one or more of the debates tended to feel more positively or more negatively about any of the leaders.

The fact that Turner's overall rating was substantially lower in 1988 than in 1984 despite his strong performance in the 1988 debates raises an important question. Although he was ranked higher than his competitors on the debate performance measures, Turner still received a low overall score on the thermometer from the same survey respondents. Clearly, debate performances alone do not account for the public's feelings about political leaders. Yet this does not mean that the debates had no effects. Comparison of watchers and non-watchers of the 1988 debates (Table 3.4) shows that Turner was regarded significantly more highly by those who saw the debates than by those who did not. But he was still rated lower than either Mulroney or Broadbent within each category of respondents. The 1988 debates did appear to cause Turner to be viewed more positively, but this in itself was not enough to prevent him from being poorly regarded as a party leader and potential prime minister, nor was it enough to win him the election.

TABLE 3.4 LEADER THERMOMETER SCORES BY EXPOSURE TO THE DEBATES, 1984 AND 1988 (mean thermometer scores)

	Watchers	Non-watchers	r[3]
		1984[1]	
Mulroney	*64	60	.05
Turner	*52	49	.04
Broadbent	*60	55	.10
		1988[2]	
Mulroney	56	54	.04
Turner	*49	45	.09
Broadbent	52	50	.04

* Between-group differences significant at .01
[1] 1984 National Election Study (N = 2,365).
[2] 1988 National Election Study, post-election wave (N = 2,794).
[3] Pearson correlation between watching/not watching the debates and thermometer scores.

There is something of a paradox, however, with regard to the effects of debates on the images of party leaders. In virtually every instance where a difference between watchers and non-watchers of a debate can be discerned, watchers tend to be more positive in their attitudes towards particular leaders than are non-watchers. This tendency is particularly evident in the case of the 1984 debates, where statistically significant differences between watchers and non-watchers are found for all three leaders. Even for Turner, whose performance in the 1984 debates was so dismally rated by journalists and survey respondents alike, the effect is both significant and positive. In the three cases for which data are available, no leader appears to have suffered in popularity as a consequence of a debate. There are a number of modest 'winners', but virtually no 'losers' among the cases examined here. This point is brought home more clearly by an examination of the correlations between debate exposure and the thermometer measures of affect toward leaders (Table 3.4). Although none of these is very strong, all are in a positive direction. In short, over the entire history of debates in Canadian election campaigns, a case cannot be found in which a party leader seems to have been harmed by his performance in a debate.[12] Debates, it would seem, tend to be mildly positive (or at least neutral) for everyone, even those whose performances leave something to be desired. This finding is similar to the patterns that have emerged in some American studies.[13] Images of virtually all of the participants benefit from the exposure associated with debates. The emphasis that is often placed on the single dramatic moment may be less important than a politician's ability to reach a mass audience in a positive setting. The effects of such exposure are probably most beneficial for smaller parties (the NDP), political unknowns (Mulroney in 1984), or those for whom expectations are low (Turner in 1988). There are parallels here to the way in which debates are generally thought to have affected the fortunes of American presidential candidates such as Kennedy in 1960, Carter in 1976, or Reagan in 1980.

LEADERS AND THE VOTE

The finding that debates tend to have positive effects on the images of party leaders does not in itself suggest any direct connection with election results. In previous research I have argued that although it is difficult to separate debates from other campaign effects, their direct influence on voting behaviour is minimal.[14] There is, however, some reason to suspect that 1988 may have been an exception. Having got off to a dreadful start, the Liberal campaign suddenly came alive after the debates. Journalist Graham Fraser quotes the experiences of candidates who noticed the change in mood almost immediately: said one Conservative, 'We knew within forty-eight hours. I could tell at the bus stops the next morning.'[15] Press coverage of the debates for the most part certified Turner as the 'winner', creating an effect that was instantly positive for the Liberal campaign. The change in mood brought about by the debates was quickly reflected in the public opinion polls. While there had been a fairly strong consensus among the various polls regarding the size of the Tory lead until the debates, virtually all polling organizations that were in the field within the following week or two picked up the Liberal surge. The size of the Liberal-Conservative spread varied somewhat among the various polling organizations, but there was little doubt about the overall direction of the trend. Johnston et al. also found a swing of about ten points in vote intention from Conservative to Liberal in the week immediately following the debates.[16]

Had the election taken place in that week, the Liberals might conceivably have won. But the debates' effect, such as it was, melted away quickly. The Gallup poll published on 14 November had the Conservatives back up to 35 per cent, and the final poll published by Gallup on 19 November estimated their support at 40 per cent. Other polls and surveys likewise documented the steady Conservative recovery. Having had the strategic foresight to insist that the debates take place a month before the election, the well-organized and well-financed Tory campaign was superbly positioned to regain the lost ground in the final three weeks.

We might, of course, simply attribute this turnaround to the effectiveness of the negative Tory campaign against Turner, or possibly to the widespread third-party advertising that saturated the final weeks of the campaign. Both of these were undoubtedly factors in the revival of Conservative fortunes. Although Turner had seemingly 'won' the debates, he remained an unpopular leader, with a number of weaknesses in his public image that were vulnerable to exploitation by an effective negative campaign. At the same time, however, the debates had the effect of focusing the final phase of the campaign around the free-trade issue, to the exclusion of nearly all other policy questions. On this issue, favourable opinion had to coalesce around the Conservatives, while opposition to it was divided between the Liberals and NDP. The debates thus triggered two quite separate phenomena in the final weeks of the 1988 campaign: one involving the image of a party leader (Turner), and the other the predominance of an issue (free trade).

It should perhaps not be surprising to discover that the effects of the 1988 debates on public opinion proved to be short-lived. Following the first of the debates between Reagan and Mondale during the 1984 US presidential election campaign, for example, the negative perception of Reagan's performance (and generally favourable reaction to Mondale's) registered in a number of polls.[17] But this effect also evaporated quickly, even before the second Reagan-Mondale debate, two weeks later. When a leader has succeeded in gaining an advantage over his opponents in a televised campaign debate, it is not easy to sustain that advantage through an additional three or four weeks of campaigning. Both the campaign itself and the attention of the public soon move on to other matters.

In part, this explains why the effects of debates on voting behaviour are not greater than they are. Most studies have found that, even where a debate seems to confer a clear advantage on a particular party or leader, the actual effects on individual voting behaviour or on the outcome of the election are slight. In the several Canadian cases for which data are available, statistically significant effects of exposure to debates on voting behaviour are relatively rare, and where they do occur, fairly weak. In the 1988 case, the debates appear to have helped the Liberals slightly at the expense of the Conservatives. Voters who saw one or more of the debates were also somewhat more likely to switch their votes from 1984 to 1988 than were non-watchers.[18] But the debates do not appear to have made any difference for the NDP, despite the negative ratings of Broadbent's performance in them. And the marginal differences in Conservative support are not statistically significant when treated as a simple dichotomy (Conservative/other) for the entire sample. In the 1984 and 1979 elections, both of which featured debates that were thought to be important to the campaign, the overall effects on voting behaviour were even more limited.[19]

This analysis of the effects of debates does not mean that leaders themselves are an unimportant factor in the voting behaviour of Canadians. Debates are single events in any election campaign, and their effects, however dramatic they may seem at the time, dissipate rapidly. The images of the party leaders, by contrast, are closely bound up with those of their parties, and are not as easily changed. For voters who pay scant attention to politics, leaders are perhaps the single most salient factor influencing their opinions. For others who maintain higher levels of interest in day-to-day political affairs, other considerations, particularly issues, may compete with leaders for attention.

Our studies of voting behaviour over the course of several elections have consistently found leaders to be an important, but not the most important, factor in understanding and explaining the outcomes of elections. Issue and leader effects on individual voting behaviour are often closely intertwined. Part of the explanation for the decline of public support for free trade lies in the fact that it was so closely

FIGURE 3.3 **Percentages of Variance Explained by Issues and Leaders, Flexible Partisans Only, by Levels of Political Interest, 1984 and 1988**

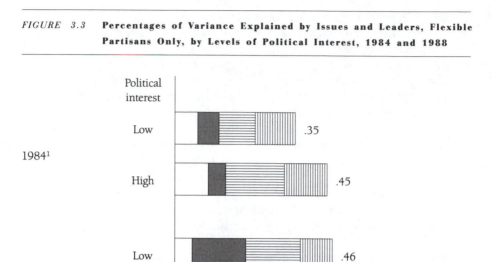

[1] National Election Study
[2] Carleton Panel Study

associated with an unpopular political leader. During the 1988 campaign, John Turner never missed an opportunity to tie the Free Trade Agreement to Brian Mulroney, always referring to it as 'the Mulroney trade deal'.[20] But it is also true that policies such as the FTA, the GST, and the Meech Lake Accord helped to drag down the popularity of the prime minister associated with them. It is not an easy matter to disentangle public attitudes toward issues and leaders, particularly over the course of an election campaign in which the interplay between them is so intense.

Nevertheless, it is possible to begin to isolate leader and issue effects. Figure 3.3 summarizes the results of such an analysis for the 1984 and 1988 elections, in which party, leader, and issue variables are entered in alternate orderings into a multiple regression analysis of voting for specific groups of respondents. This analysis is confined to those voters classified as 'flexible partisans': those whose partisanship is sufficiently weak or unstable as to make them more likely to switch from one party to another over the course of two elections.[21] These results show that leaders are a consistently important part of the electoral equation for these voters, both in their unique effects on individual voting behaviour and in conjunction with issues. They also show that the effects tend to be greater for those voters with relatively low levels of interest in politics. This result should not be underemphasized, as such voters constitute the largest single group within the Canadian electorate.[22] As recent elections in Canada have demonstrated, short-term forces are capable of moving large numbers of voters, producing quite sudden and unpredictable patterns of change. In the dealigned partisan environment that has characterized Canadian politics for at least a generation, such effects are likely to continue to be an important component of political change.[23]

CONCLUSION

The images projected by party leaders are clearly important in shaping the images of the parties they lead, even in parliamentary systems, such as Canada's, in which the party leader is not the sole focus of attention. Leaders have an important effect on voting behaviour, particularly for voters who are easily moved by short-term influences and who pay only modest attention to politics. Events such as televised debates are important elements in campaigns because of the large audiences they attract and the direct exposure they give to the party leaders. They are widely watched and commented upon, and they do affect, or at least help to shape, the public images of the leaders, particularly those who are not yet well known or whose images are relatively unformed. They stimulate interest in elections, and may have some positive effects on participation. But they do not really act to change in any fundamental way the perceptions of leaders that individuals already hold, and in some instances may serve merely to reinforce these. Where the public perceptions of debate performance are sharply out of line with established images or expectations, debates can produce measurable effects on public opinion. But these tend to be short-lived, and generally cannot be sustained through an entire campaign.

New party leaders in a parliamentary system have an opportunity to shape their public images through the media, through performance in Parliament, and through political advertising. But such opportunities tend to be limited until a leader gains the attention that comes with high public office. At this stage the process accelerates, and the image of the leader becomes more salient in the public's perception of the party that he/she leads. Margaret Thatcher was not well known to much of the British public prior to becoming prime minister in 1979, but her image came to dominate that of her party, as Pierre Trudeau's tended to do during the 1970s and 1980s in Canada.[24] A high public profile, coupled with long tenure in office, strengthens a leader's image to the point where it is unlikely to be permanently altered by a single event such as a debate, or by a concerted advertising campaign. Traits that are associated in the public mind with a particular leader are reinforced and solidified by time and events. Where such traits are negative, they may well be emphasized by opposing parties in carefully crafted negative campaigns. But images of leaders, like the images of the parties they lead, are shaped by performance over a period of time, and once established with the public are not abruptly changed. In a relatively fluid party system such as Canada's, therefore, it is easier for a party to change its image by choosing a new leader than it is for an established leader to procure a new image.

NOTES

[1] 'Presidentialization' is perhaps the wrong term to capture the increasing primacy of party leaders in parliamentary political systems. For some discussion of this phenomenon, see Joseph Wearing, 'President or Prime Minister?'; and Richard Neustadt, 'White House and Whitehall' both in Thomas Hockin, ed., *Apex of Power: the Prime Minister and Political Leadership in Canada* (Toronto: Prentice-Hall, 1971, 1977). See also Colin Campbell, 'Political Leadership in Canada: Pierre Elliott Trudeau and the Ottawa Model', in Richard Rose and Ezra Sulieman, eds, *Presidents and Prime Ministers* (Washington: American Enterprise Institute, 1980). For a more recent survey of the role of political leaders in a number of countries, see Anthony Mughan and Samuel Patterson, eds, *Political Leadership in Democratic Societies* (Chicago: Nelson-Hall, 1992).

[2] This is one of the principal themes developed in Harold D. Clarke, Jane Jenson, Lawrence LeDuc, and Jon H. Pammett, *Absent Mandate* (1984, 1991). See especially chapters 1 and 6 of *Absent Mandate: Interpreting Change in Canadian Elections* (Toronto: Gage, 1991).

[3] The 1974, 1979, and 1980 Canadian National Election Studies were conducted by Clarke, Jenson, LeDuc, and Pammett. Other analyses of these data may be found in *Absent Mandate: The Politics of Discontent in Canada* (Toronto, Gage, 1984), and in the same authors' *Political Choice in Canada* (Toronto: McGraw-Hill Ryerson, 1979, 1986). The 1984 National Election Study was conducted by Ronald Lambert, Steven Brown, James Curtis, Barry Kay and John Wilson. Reports of findings from this study are available in Kay et al., 'The Character of Electoral Change', in Joseph Wearing, ed., *The Ballot and Its Message* (Toronto: Copp Clark Pittman, 1991). A 1988 reinterview of respondents from the 1984 study was conducted by Lambert, Brown, Curtis, Kay, LeDuc, and Pammett. Additional analyses of these data may be found in *Absent Mandate* (1991). The 1988 National Election Study was conducted by Richard Johnston, André Blais, Henry E. Brady, and Jean Crête. Analyses of these data and a more wide-ranging discussion of the 1988 election campaign may be found in Johnston, Blais, Brady, and Crête, *Letting the People Decide* (Montreal: McGill-Queen's University Press, 1992). Neither the principal investigators of any of these studies, nor the Social Sciences and Humanities Research Council of Canada, which funded them, are responsible for the analyses or interpretations presented here.

[4] The open-ended questions employed in the 1974, 1979, 1980, and 1984 studies were: 'Is there anything in particular that you like about _____? . . . Anything else? . . . Is there anything in particular that you dislike about _____? . . . Anything else? . . .' This format was used for questions about both parties and leaders. For a more detailed description of the instrument used in these studies, see Clarke, Jenson, LeDuc, and Pammett, *Political Choice*, unabridged ed. (1979), 466-7, 421.

[5] The question was: 'In deciding how you would vote in the recent election, which would you say was the most important to you: the party leaders, the candidates here in this constituency, or the parties taken as a whole? . . . Which would you say was next most important? Which would you say was least important? _____ [If "LEADER"] When you say that "the leader" was the most important to you, are you thinking of his personal qualities or his stand on certain issues?' (*Political Choice*, p. 418).

[6] But see Steven Brown, Ronald Lambert, Barry Kay, and James Curtis, 'In the Eye of the Beholder: Leader Images in Canada', *Canadian Journal of Political Science* 21 (1988): 729-56.

[7] For a discussion of the 'schematic' concept of images of American presidential candidates, see Arthur H. Miller, Martin Wattenberg, and Oksana Malanchuk, 'Schematic Assessments of Presidential Candidates', *American Political Science Review* 80 (1986): 521-40.

[8] Johnston et al., *Letting the People Decide*, 168-96.

[9] For an analysis of the 1984 federal election campaign, see Allan Frizzell and Anthony Westell, eds, *The Canadian General Election of 1984* (Ottawa: Carleton University Press, 1985). For an account and analysis of the 1988 election, see Allan Frizzell, Jon Pammett, and Anthony Westell, eds, *The Canadian General Election of 1988* (Ottawa: Carleton University Press, 1989). For a discussion of the development of campaign debates in Canada and an analysis of the 1979 debates, see Lawrence LeDuc and Richard Price, 'Great Debates: The Televised Leadership Debates of 1979', *Canadian Journal of Political Science* 18 (1985): 135-53. On the 1984 and 1988 debates, see David J. Lanoue, 'Debates that Mattered: Voters' Reactions to the 1984 Canadian Leadership Debates, *Canadian Journal of Political Science* 24 (1991): 51-65; and Cathy Widdis Barr, 'Televised Campaign Debates: Their Impact on Voting Behaviour and Their Contribution to an Informed Electorate', in Frederich J. Fletcher, ed., *Media and Voters in Canadian Election Campaigns* (Toronto: Dundurn, 1991), vol. 18 of the Research Studies of the Royal Commission on Electoral Reform and Party Financing.

[10] About two-thirds of national samples of the electorate consistently report having seen one or more campaign debates. In the 1984 National Election Study 67% reported having seen one of the three debates (including the 'women's debate') that took place during that campaign. A 1988 study found 65% reporting that they had watched one of the two debates during that campaign. See *Absent Mandate* (1991), 102.

[11] See Richard Johnston, André Blais, Henry E. Brady, and Jean Crête, 'Free Trade and the Dynamics of the 1988 Canadian Election', in Wearing, *The Ballot*, 315-39. See also Johnston et al., *Letting the People Decide*, especially chapters 5 and 6.

[12] These findings are similar to those of the 1979 case as well. See LeDuc and Price, 'Great Debates', 144-8.

[13] In the 1980 Carter-Reagan debate, for example, one study found that perceptions of both Carter and Reagan were higher after the debate. See Richard Joslyn, *Mass Media and Elections* (Reading, Mass.: Addison-Wesley, 1984), 209-10; and John H. Kessel, *Presidential Campaign Politics* (Homewood, Ill.: Dorsey, 1984), 198-9. For a review of literature on American presidential debates, see S. Kraus and D. Davis, 'Political Debates', in D. Nimmo and K. Sanders, eds, *Handbook of Political Communication* (Beverly Hills: Sage, 1981), 273-96. See also A. Ranney, ed., *The Past and Future of Presidential Debates* (Washington: American Enterprise Institute, 1980); in G. Bishop, R. Meadow, and M. Jackson-Beeck, eds, *The Presidential Debates: Media, Electoral, and Policy Perspectives* (New York: Praeger, 1978); K. Jamieson and D. Birdsell, *Presidential Debates* (New York: Oxford University Press, 1988).

[14] LeDuc and Price, 'Great Debates', 148-53. See also *Absent Mandate* (1991), 101-4.

[15] Graham Fraser, *Playing for Keeps* (Toronto: McClelland and Stewart, 1989), 295-6.

[16] 'Free Trade and the Dynamics of the 1988 Campaign', in Wearing, ed., *The Ballot*, 316-18. See also Johnson et al., *Letting the People Decide*, 180-6.

[17] See the discussion of the 1984 Reagan-Mondale debates and their role in the US presidential campaign of that year in Paul Abramson, John Aldrich, and David Rhode, *Change and Continuity in the 1984 Elections* (Washington: CQ Press, 1986), 57-60.

[18] *Absent Mandate* (1991), 101-4.

[19] See Lawrence LeDuc and Richard Price, 'The Impact of Televised Campaign Debates on Public Opinion and Electoral Behaviour in Canada', Paper Presented to the Annual Meeting of the International Communications Association, Dublin, Ireland, 1990.

[20] Experiments with question wording in the 1988 National Election Study show that these associations did have an effect on respondents' support for the agreement. See Johnston et al., 'Free Trade and the Dynamics of the 1988 Canadian Election', in Wearing, ed., *The Ballot*, 319-21.

[21] 'Durable' partisans are those whose party attachment is strong, stable over time, and consistent between federal and provincial politics, while 'flexible' partisans are those who vary on one or more of these attributes. In studies of Canadian voting since 1974, it has been shown that flexible partisans are more susceptible to influences from various short-term forces and are more likely to switch their votes in any given election. See Clarke, Jenson, Le Duc, and Pammett, *Political Choice*, chapters 10, 11 and *Absent Mandate* (1991), chapters 3 and 6 for analyses of the behaviour of durable and flexible partisans in various elections.

[22] In the 1984 National Election Study, about two-thirds of all respondents were classified as flexible partisans, while about one-third were durable partisans. Of the flexible partisans, nearly half (28% of all respondents) reported low political interest, the largest single group in the sample. See *Absent Mandate* (1991), 46-9.

[23] See Lawrence LeDuc, 'Canada: The Politics of Stable Dealignment', in Russell Dalton, Scott Flanagan, and Paul Allen Beck, eds, *Electoral Change in Advanced Industrial Democracies* (Princeton: Princeton University Press, 1984), 402-24. See also *Absent Mandate* (1991), 49-54.

[24] For an analysis of the images of Thatcher and other British political leaders during the 1987 campaign, see William Miller, Harold Clarke, Martin Harrop, Lawrence LeDuc, and Paul Whiteley, *How Voters Change: the 1987 British Election Campaign in Perspective* (London: Oxford University Press, 1990). See also Anthony King, 'Margaret Thatcher: The Style of a Prime Minister' in Mughan and Patterson, eds, *Political Leadership*, 320-44.

CHAPTER FOUR

WOMEN   AND   POLITICAL   LEADERSHIP

A   Case   for   Affirmative   Action

—■—

Janine   Brodie

One of the 'babies' discarded with the 'bathwater' of the Charlottetown Accord was the promise that, in some provinces at least, gender parity would be one of the principles underlying reform of the Canadian Senate. The idea that Canada's representative democracy would be better served by formal guarantees for the election of both women and men was a radical one, which met with immediate resistance. This position had been advanced before by elements of the Canadian women's movement — most recently, by the National Action Committee on the Status of Women (NAC). Opponents, however, charged that formal guarantees of gender parity in the Senate subverted the fundamental democratic principle of formal equality. Others warned that gender parity would open the floodgates to countless groups (and their multiple permutations) for similar representational guarantees. Still others argued that gender-parity legislation would be detrimental to women because it would forever cast them as second-class political representatives — the ones who, unlike their male counterparts, were incapable of getting elected on their own merits. For many of these detractors, the idea of ensuring women's representation in the reformed Senate was far more ominous than many other elements of the Accord, including the entrenched quota for Québec's representation in the House of Commons, aboriginal representation, and provincial equality in the Senate. In other words, the concept of gender parity appeared more inconsistent with the fundamental principles of democratic representation than did either cultural or regional guarantees.

The issue of women's political representation has occupied the political agenda of Western democracies, with varying degrees of intensity, for most of the twentieth century. At the turn of the century, first-wave feminists in Canada fought for and won citizenship rights and formal political equality with men. Winning the right to vote and to become political leaders, however, failed to secure women any significant measure of political power. In the first fifty years after enfranchisement, women constituted less than one per cent of those elected in all federal and provincial elections. This dreary statistic led the Royal Commission on the Status of Women (RCSW) to report in 1970 that women had achieved only 'token recognition' of their right to be represented among the ranks of political leaders, and that the voice of government remained a 'man's voice'.[1]

In the years since the release of the RCSW report, Canada has witnessed a new round of feminist mobilization around the unfinished agenda of gender equality in political leadership. In fact, there has been an unprecedented increase in the number of women seeking and achieving positions of political leadership. In less than twenty years, the percentage of federal candidates, who were women increased from 6 per cent in 1972 to 19 per cent in 1988. During the same period women increased their representation in the House of Commons from 2 per cent to 13 per cent. Women's political representation in provincial legislatures and territorial assemblies reflects a similar upward trend. In 1990, women held approximately 15 per cent of sub-national legislative seats and four provincial party leaderships; indeed, in three provinces they constitute one-quarter of the assembly. The early 1990s also saw Canada's first woman prime minister, a woman leader of the federal New Democratic Party, and two women premiers, first in British Columbia and then in Prince Edward Island.[2]

It would be both premature and short-sighted, however, to suggest that these marginal gains signal the beginning of a inevitable or natural progression towards gender parity in political leadership in Canada. As the Charlottetown Accord débâcle demonstrated, public consensus is fragile and incomplete around the goal of increasing women's political representation and the means to achieve it. Moreover, some commentators point to growing evidence of backlash against feminist demands for political power and pressure for reversal of the marginal gains that women have achieved in politics.

Underlying the debate about women's political representation is considerable disagreement both about why increasing the number of women in political leadership is important and about how best to achieve this goal. Canadian political scientists, moreover, have offered little guidance on either question. Generally speaking, as Anne Phillips accurately points out, 'the literature on "women in politics" (more accurately, women not in politics) operated perilously close to the threshold of boredom. For those who knew that women were oppressed, the dreary statistics lacked any element of surprise.'[3] This chapter, then, will move from an enumeration of the obstacles confronting women in politics to a more proactive discussion of the goal of increasing women's representation in positions of political leadership. It will review political science's treatment of women's political representation, outline the reasons underlying the call to increase the ranks of women among political leaders, and assess the rationales for and the effectiveness of different strategies of affirmative action.

EXPLAINING MALE DOMINANCE IN POLITICAL LEADERSHIP

Until recently, political science did not question why, in a liberal democracy, the nominal majority — women — was virtually excluded from positions of political power. Male dominance in politics either was assumed to be natural, and thus not subject to academic investigation or political intervention, or was explained away by pointing to the alleged deficiencies that made women incapable of effectively competing with men for political office.

The idea that politics is an unnatural preoccupation for women was rigorously advanced by the early theorists of liberal democracy. As a political ideology, liberalism pronounced a new politics based on the values of individualism and formal political equality. From the outset, however, these values were not assumed to apply to women. Although early liberal theorists argued for fundamental equality among citizens, whether it stemmed from the state of nature or from the social contract, at the same time they denied that women could be citizens. Hobbes, for example, recommended that the family should be represented in the political sphere by the husband, while Locke argued that women voluntarily surrendered their political sovereignty when they entered into marriage contracts.[4] Liberal theorists deemed that women did not have the capacity to act as rational, independent and self-governing individuals and thus lacked the requisite attributes to participate in political affairs.[5]

The notion of political equality is always entangled with the issue of difference. In liberal theory, equality 'means the ignoring of differences for a particular purpose or particular context'; it represents a social agreement to consider obviously different people as equivalent for a stated purpose.[6] The expression 'one man, one vote' meant that, within the context of democratic elections, all men were equal. Formal political equality prohibited discrimination among men on the basis of class, caste, religion, race, or other differences. Paradoxically, however, the notion of equality has always been premised on discrimination rooted in difference. All men were equal in liberal democratic politics only to the extent that women were unequal.

While the early political theorists developed a variety of elaborate explanations for why women should be excluded from political leadership, later political scientists tended to take women's under-representation so much for granted that 'they did not even notice that they were leaving them out'.[7] The invisibility of women in political science was a partial reflection of its dominant paradigms. Empirical political science in particular focused on governmental institutions and the exercise of public power.

Because, almost exclusively, the exercisers of public power were men, women were, by paradigmatic definition, excluded from study.[8] Thus political science tended to reinforce the idea that women were unfit for political leadership precisely because it failed to acknowledge or question male dominance in politics.

When the discipline finally turned to the question of women's exclusion from the corridors of political power, it tended to rationalize the status quo by arguing that women's differences from men inhibited their entry into the ranks of the political élite. Among the numerous explanations offered were the notions that women were inherently less assertive than men; that they were primarily oriented to 'non-political' concerns such as the family; that few had the occupational and social skills required to compete in politics; and that women were socialized at an early age to identify politics as an inappropriate career choice in latter life. Most consistently, however, studies have found that situational factors, especially the role of mother, discouraged and delayed the political careers of potential women political leaders.[9]

For the most part, then, political science explained the under-representation of women in political power in terms of female deficiency and difference. Women did not 'measure up' to men in terms of disposition, preparation, or life experience, and for that reason did not get elected to political office. Underlying this approach is the assumption that women must be like men if they expect to become political representatives. In this view, therefore, the key to increasing the number of women in leadership is to transform women themselves through skills training, education, and resocialization.

There is an equally persuasive body of literature, however, that points to systemic and structural factors as the major obstacles to women's representation and hence the most appropriate areas for intervention and reform. The basis of this critique reaches back to the foundations of liberal democracy itself. Liberalism brought a revolutionary transformation of the social and political world that was based on the art of separation. Feudal society was reorganized into a series of different realms, each governed by its own institutions and power relations. Lines were drawn between the state and the church, the state and the economy and, most important for women, between the public and the private. The realm of the private, of personal and family life, was sacred ground, upon which the state could not tread.[10]

The public and private spheres were governed by different rules. The public sphere was defined by the rules of liberal democracy and the norms of universalism, equality, and reason, while the private sphere was a world of inequality, subjection, and emotion.[11] It was simply assumed that women's natural place was in the home and that they were subject to the rule of the man 'in his castle'.[12] In other words, the foundations of liberal democracy were profoundly gendered, and as a result, for most of its history, women were denied even the most basic individual and political rights. Although women eventually gained the formal right to participate in liberal democratic politics on the same basis as men, popular perceptions continue to reflect the patriarchal divisions of early liberal thought, according to which politics is a more appropriate 'masculine' than 'feminine' pursuit.

Research on systemic and structural barriers to women's election has tended to focus on more immediate and tangible factors such as the biases of political party organizations and electoral rules. In Canada, for example, Bashevkin has found that women's political careers were often stalled and circumvented because they usually were relegated to 'pink-collar' or secretarial roles within party organizations. Moreover, when women did rise to leadership positions within their party it tended to be during periods when the party was uncompetitive.[13] My own research indicates that when women did compete for political office, they were usually nominated in ridings where their chances for winning were low.[14] This trend has declined but has not disappeared. In the 1988 federal election, for example, only 13 per cent of women candidates were elected compared to 20 per cent of their male counterparts.[15] Both of these factors thus suggest that the number of women in political leadership roles would be increased by changing the practices of Canadian political parties—a strategy that was endorsed by the Royal Commission on Electoral Reform and Party Financing in 1992 (see below).

Still others point to electoral rules or the electoral system itself as the major impediment to increasing the numbers of women in political leadership roles. Numerous studies have argued that women are placed at a systemic disadvantage in systems where the financial costs of gaining party nomination, contesting election, and seeking party leadership are high, because as a group they have less access to personal financial resources and moneyed networks than men. Indeed, in a study of women candidates in the 1988 federal elections over three-quarters indicated that funding was an obstacle to their election, while 37 per cent found it the most significant obstacle they faced.[16] These findings suggest that more women would be elected if governments established rigorous spending limits on political candidates, to lower the threshold for women's entry into politics and partially level the financial playing field between women and men competing for office.

Finally, some point to Canada's first-past-the-post, single-member plurality electoral system as the major barrier to women's representation in legislative assemblies. This argument is based on the assumption that local party organizations generally do not seek out women candidates and afford them opportunities for election.[17] The cumulative result of local bias is that far fewer women than men are nominated, particularly in constituencies where they have a chance of winning. Proponents of this view argue that the adoption of a proportional electoral system would correct this bias because it would allow centralized control over party nominations. A proportional system enables political parties to devise candidate slates that more accurately reflect society.[18]

A report compiled for the Committee of Women's Rights of the European Parliament also suggests that electoral systems have an independent impact on the nomination and election of women to political office. It concluded that

- women benefit from systems where members are appointed to upper chambers;
- women are disadvantaged in chambers elected by indirect universal suffrage, because of the limited number of women in electoral colleges and the conservative spirit guiding this form of appointment;

- women, as candidates for nomination and election, are disadvantaged by the uninominal method because this method entails a choice of leaders already known to the electorate in the constituency; and
- women are advantaged in a proportional representation system because people vote for the party's program rather than any individual candidate, and the system entails large-scale constituencies with several seats to be filled, thereby offering more opportunities for women.[19]

In summary, then, political scientists have offered a number of explanations for the dramatic under-representation of women among the ranks of political leaders in Canada. These explanations range from the alleged deficiencies of individual women to systemic and structural factors, including the gendered division of labour and the electoral system. Each explanation, in turn, suggests a particular remedy, such as changing women themselves through skills training, changing the rules to account for women's competitive disadvantages, or changing the system in order to facilitate a conscious redress of the historical gender imbalance in political leadership. Each of these corrective measures has been applied with varying degrees of success in Canada and other Western democracies. Nevertheless, the idea that the election of women requires some form of affirmative action continues to be resisted. There is little consensus either about why increasing the representation of women in politics matters or about how to achieve more gender-balanced representation in political leadership. Proponents of affirmative action have perhaps too often assumed that the worthiness of increasing women's participation in politics is self-evident. The recent debate about gender parity in the Canadian Senate, however, demonstrates that for many it is not. Arguments for affirmative measures for women in politics must be well-grounded in order to succeed. In the next section I will argue that some rationales hold more sway than others.

WHY DOES ELECTING WOMEN MATTER?

Those who advocate increasing the representation of women in political leadership roles often meet with resistance from defenders of the status quo because the demand for affirmative action appears to contradict fundamental premises of representational democracy. For one thing, it appears to interfere with the electorate's right to choose. In addition, it is argued that guaranteeing gender balance in elected assemblies is inconsistent with Canadian parliamentary tradition, which rests on a Burkean model of representation. According to this model, guarantees for group representation are unnecessary because legislators are expected to act for the 'common' or community interest rather than identifiable or 'special' interests. In other words, the role of elected representatives, regardless of gender, is to legislate in the interests of all their constituents, including women. To do otherwise would result in endless factional infighting and legislative deadlock—neither of which serves the common interest. An associated argument is that women do not need to be represented because they do not have special or objective interests independent of men, the economy or the family.[20]

Advocates of affirmative action thus confront a powerful legacy of political conventions and mythologies that act to undermine their case. They are told that the gender composition of elected assemblies is irrelevant to the quality of political representation, and that there is nothing special about women that requires special representation.[21] Feminists historically have been divided in their response to these counter-claims. Generally speaking, however, the case for increasing the election of women can be made on three distinct, though not mutually exclusive, grounds. The first rests on the notion of basic justice; sexual segregation is unfair wherever it occurs, but it is perhaps most detrimental in democratic politics. The virtual exclusion of women from political power, it is argued, is an affront to the principles of democratic equality and representation because women constitute half of the citizens and only a handful of the lawmakers. The case for justice points to the dramatic under-representation of women in politics as indisputable evidence that something is wrong with a system that discriminates against women, and thus that considerations of democracy and equality alone demand change. This argument makes no assertions about representation of gender-specific interests or any special qualities that women might bring to the public sphere. It simply calls for measures that would advance democratic ideals, allowing women to realize the full range of their citizenship rights and participate equally with men in public affairs.[22]

The other two cases for women in political leadership stress women's difference from men and the need to incorporate these differences within democratic institutions.[23] The special interests/perspectives argument is that women carry different experiences and expertise into politics and that their increased representation would correct the distortions in representation and policy that result from excluding half of the population from political leadership. This approach stresses that representing gender difference in politics would make the system operate better because both sides of a gender-divided society would be represented and both sides of the story would be told. In other words, the special-interests argument suggests that the recognition of gender difference would improve the system of representation by making it more inclusive.

The third case, which might be called the 'essential woman' argument, pushes the idea of gender difference even further by suggesting that the inclusion of women in political leadership would make the system better because women *are* better. The central premise informing this position is that all women — whether by virtue of their biology, their mothering roles, or their shared oppression — exhibit specific values, orientations, and behaviours that make them better political representatives than their male counterparts. For example, all women are said to be more caring, more co-operative, and less motivated by personal ambition, than all men. The election of more women, therefore, holds the potential to transform the political system itself into a kinder, gentler, and more responsive forum for collective decision-making.[24]

All of these arguments have been raised, alone or in tandem, during Canadian feminists' century-long struggle for political equality. The early suffragists, for example, fought for women's citizenship rights on the basis of both justice and essentialist claims. Arguing that a democracy that denied women citizenship rights was undemocratic, at the same time they suggested that woman suffrage would help transform the political sphere by giving force to women's values, among them morality, sobriety, and family order.[25] Distinct, although equally essentialist, claims also underpinned the launching of the Feminist Party of Canada in 1979. In one of its early statements, for example, it suggested that women have taken historic responsibility for all that which renders communities more fully human. If politics is the process through which society safeguards the humanity of its members, then women belong in politics; and if politics is not such a process, then clearly women are needed to make it so.[26]

Not all feminist organizations, however, advance the claim that women are fundamentally and universally different from men. Key organizations that have lobbied for increasing the representation of women, such as the Committee of '94, the 52 per cent Solution, and, most recently, NAC, have used appeals to justice and special interests to support their demands for affirmative measures to promote the political representation of women.

Prospective women leaders also disagree about the significance of electing more women. In a study of 1988 federal women candidates,[27] the respondents were asked if it matters if more women are elected and why. The vast majority (95 per cent) agreed that electing women was important, but the reasons offered were almost evenly divided among the three rationales discussed above (Table 4.1). The largest group (38 per cent) offered justice-based reasons: for example: 'we need to have a balance'; 'women are 50 per cent of the population and should be 50 per cent of the House of Commons'; or 'all members of society should be represented'. By contrast, 30 per cent advanced the idea of women's special interests/perspectives, suggesting that 'women's point of view needs to be represented'; 'some issues need the participation of women'; or that particular issues such as abortion, women-headed families, childcare, and pay equity demanded women's participation in the policy-making process. Finally, 30 per cent expressed an 'essential woman' position, emphasizing the inherent superiority of women politicians. According to these respondents, increased representation of women is important because 'women are not as invested with power as men'; 'women have an instinct for economizing'; 'women are less competitive and more co-operative'; or 'women better feel the needs of people'.

The rationales underlying the call for the political representation of women are not simply a matter of academic curiosity. The success of efforts to challenge and reverse the historical legacy of male dominance in politics depends on the cogency of these appeals. In a sense, each of the three arguments outlined here calls women into political leadership for different reasons: to affirm a systemic commitment to democracy; to represent their special interests, or to transform politics with their unique qualities. It will be argued here that the two latter arguments, resting on women's difference from men, carry significant liabilities for women in politics and for those pursuing affirmative action to increase women's representation.

This is not to suggest that a better gender balance in political leadership would not have positive effects: policies would be more gender-sensitive, and some women would bring values into politics that would offer a beneficial challenge to traditional norms and behaviours. The promise of a feminist politics rests precisely on the

TABLE 4.1 **FEDERAL WOMEN CANDIDATES' RESPONSES ON REPRESENTATION**

1. Do you think electing more women matters?

	%	N
Yes	95.2	40
No	4.8	2
Total	100.0	42

2. Why does it matter?

	%	N
Balance/justice	38.4	15
Different experiences	30.8	12
Special qualities	30.8	12
Total	100.0	39

contention that both these goals are achievable, though not automatically. Rather, this argument posits that in the interests of equity and of strategic effectiveness, the justice argument holds the greatest potential for realizing a system of democratic representation that gives voice to women in all their diversity.

A strong case can be made for treating women as a distinct social category with distinct political interests. Newspapers and government reports are replete with evidence that women are segregated in the workforce and over-represented among the poor, among victims of male violence, and so on. These and many other issues that affect women disproportionately have been ignored and discounted in policy-making. Nevertheless, the special interests/perspectives argument too often uncritically embraces two assumptions that lose their force upon closer inspection. First, the claim that there are unique 'women's' interests indirectly reinforces a patriarchally ordered world view in which women's voices and actions are relegated to different (usually subordinate) places. In other words, it suggests that women should be allowed into the corridors of political power expressly to deal with 'their' issues, such as the family, reproduction, and child-care. Inclusion in leadership on this basis, however, releases men of responsibility in these fields of policy formation as a matter of community concern. At the same time, it assigns to them sole responsibility for the full spectrum of 'other' political issues that have a daily impact on the lives of women and men. Nominally 'non-women's' issues such as free trade have profound implications for women. Moreover, the notion that the policy field can be divided into women's issues and degendered 'common' interests virtually guarantees that, in cases of conflict, the 'common' issues will take priority.

Second, the 'special interests' rationale tends to convey the message that women share a common perspective on 'their' issues. This assumption has been widely contested among feminists because it tends to privilege the perspective of white, middle-class, heterosexual women. In other words, it conceals the very real diversity of political interests among women, and at the same time erodes the foundations of the special-interests argument. The terrain of politics for women cannot be confined to gender differences alone. The roots of racial, class, and heterosexist oppression run as deeply through women as through society itself. To deny that women have different and often conflicting stakes in politics serves to conceal these differences, and hence to deny the equality of all women to engage in politics to realize their policy goals. At the same time, to recognize these differences is to erode the very foundations of the special-interest argument, for if women do not share a common perspective, it is difficult to make claims for group representation.

Similar objections can be raised about the 'essential woman' argument. In particular, the assertion that all women approach political life in a similar 'co-operative' way reinforces the patriarchal construction of how women should act, and thus serves as a profound constraint on political women. Women leaders who appear to be ambitious, assertive, or just plain angry are judged to be unfeminine. It is simply not the case that all women bring the same qualities to politics, and the example of a Margaret Thatcher erodes the case that women should be elected because they are different (and better) political leaders than men.

Neither of the 'difference' rationales for increasing women's representation, then, is sustainable empirically or strategic politically. Both, in effect, tacitly accept the patriarchal 'othering' that constructs women as something different from the typical (read male) citizen and leader. While each argument emphasizes that it is precisely women's difference that recommends their inclusion in political leadership, the fact remains that neither of these tests — i.e., shared perspectives or behaviours — is applied to men as a requirement for entry into the ranks of political leadership. The assumption that women must somehow form a homogeneous bloc before they can be admitted into the political leadership denies them the same access to politics that is taken for granted by men. Women, like men, should be able to participate in political leadership to achieve policy goals and to resolve political conflicts regardless of whether these conflicts arise between women and men or among women themselves.[28] The central point here is that women should not be forced to demonstrate their difference from men as a rationale for their entry into political leadership. The only gender difference in politics that requires rationalization is the glaring one: women's virtual exclusion from the exercise of political power.[29]

We are thus left with the case for justice, which advances the claim that democracy itself is enhanced when women, in all their diversity, achieve equality with men in political leadership. Few would disagree with this goal; the question is how it can best be achieved. Classic liberal writings suggest that the foundations of gender equality in politics are guaranteed by the formal rules of democratic citizenship. Democracy is best served when the same rights and procedures apply to everyone, regardless of gender. Certainly this rationale was accepted by the early suffragists who fought for women's inclusion in the ranks of 'equal' democratic citizens. They assumed that the elimination of sex-based barriers to voting and running for political office would be sufficient for the realization of women's political equality. Despite the passage of decades, this goal has proved elusive. Increasingly, feminists have argued that formal citizenship rights not only are insufficient to ensure the election of women but, indeed, have acted to reinforce the historical legacy of male dominance in politics. Liberal democracy's construction of the non-gendered citizen denies the profoundly gendered origins of the system itself, and its 'very particular' definition of the public sphere has tended to make politics 'coterminous with the activities that have been historically associated with men'.[30] Liberalism, as Phillips argues, pretends that women 'can be equal in the public sphere when our differences are overwhelming in the private'. It offers women 'equality with one hand and takes it away with the other'.[31]

Liberalism treated women differently from the outset by defining the private sphere as lying outside the legitimate realm of politics, by confining women's 'appropriate' concerns to the home, and by denying that women had the qualifications to act in the public sphere. Thus they have achieved political equality in only a very formal and illusory way. The realization that guarantees of formal political equality, within the context of pervasive gender inequality, act to reinforce rather than diminish inequality has led many to conclude that the broader goals of justice and democratic representation demand a change in the rules. As will be argued in the next section, the case for affirmative action can be grounded on the concepts of systemic discrimination and either compensatory or distributive justice claims.

RATIONALES FOR AFFIRMATIVE ACTION

The call for affirmative-action measures to increase the representation of women in political leadership often meets with resistance both because the concept appears to contradict the liberal myth of equality of opportunity and because affirmative action effects a redistribution of political power. The issue of whether women should be treated differently from men in liberal democratic recruitment processes divides women themselves as well as women and men. Feminist legal scholars generally refer to this as the 'equality versus difference' debate. The 'equality' side argues that women's equality can be achieved only through strict adherence to gender neutrality in law. Treating women as a different or a special case, they argue, only invites gender stereotyping and gender-specific laws that could be injurious to women's equality in the long term. Those on the 'difference' side respond that women are different from men in terms of historical treatment and social position, and that women's equality therefore demands that laws make affirmative provision for gender differences.[32]

When this debate is transferred to the political realm, supporters of the equality and difference camps are equally divided. The former maintain that affirmative action designed to promote women's election subverts the fundamental principles of liberal democracy and threatens to stigmatize women politicians as people who can't compete on their own merits and are not legitimate representatives of their constituents. The difference side responds that women face historical and on-going obstacles that effectively reveal the supposed gender-neutrality of the rules of liberal democracy as illusory. Defining political equality as both the inclusion and the participation of all groups in representative forums, this position asserts that women's political equality will be achieved only through differential treatment, at least in the immediate future.[33]

It contends that affirmative-action measures are justified to end the hegemony of one group in politics, and that mandating the end of gender exclusivity in democratic institutions 'is not reverse discrimination but the beginning of equality'.[34] In other words, affirmative action represents an evolving commitment to the realization of a democratic society.

Opponents of affirmative action in politics often argue that these measures are unwarranted because available evidence does not demonstrate conclusively that the recruitment system overtly or intentionally discriminates against women. The real problem, they suggest, is that not enough qualified women offer themselves for political office. The courts, however, have long since moved away from the idea that affirmative-action measures require the demonstration of intentional discrimination. Rather, they have widely accepted that many forms of discrimination emanate from systemic factors, such as historical practices and deeply engrained cultural attitudes, that are often unacknowledged and unintentional. The term 'systemic discrimination' recognizes that pervasive cultural attitudes, behaviours, and institutional practices have more significant, though perhaps unintended, negative impacts on certain groups of individuals than obstacles constructed as a result of intentional discrimination.[35] When specific groups are shown to be dramatically under-represented in particular occupational categories, this fact in itself (rather than proof of intentional exclusionary practices) is taken as sufficient evidence of systemic discrimination and sufficient grounds for systemic remedies. In the United States, the courts have consistently mandated or upheld affirmative-action plans designed to reverse the impacts of systemic discrimination.[36]

Canada has had less experience than the United States with such policies, but in April 1985 Canadian courts gained the power, through the Charter of Rights and Freedoms, to uphold legislation designed to ameliorate the conditions of disadvantaged groups.[37] Section 15 (1) provides every individual with the equal protection and benefit of the law regardless of sex. Section 15 (2) allows for 'any law, program or activity that has as its object the amelioration of conditions of disadvantaged individuals or groups including those disadvantaged because of . . . sex.' The equality provisions of the Charter, therefore, recognize the individual's right to integrate into Canadian society notwithstanding differences and, at the same time, extend constitutional legitimacy to laws that acknowledge and accommodate differences rather than ignore and deny them.[38] The Charter, in other words, guarantees women the constitutional right to equal and different treatment under the law, so long as the different treatment takes as its aim the erosion of gender stratification in Canadian society.

Affirmative action for women has not as yet been challenged in Charter litigation. It is clear from the Supreme Court's decision in the Andrews case, however, that the Canadian courts, like their American counterparts, accept the concept of systemic discrimination and recognize the case for affirmative measures. In the judgement, Mr Justice McIntyre ruled that 'stereotyping' and 'historical disadvantage' constitute discrimination. Moreover, the presence of historical disadvantage can be determined 'in the context of the place of the group in the entire social, political and legal fabric of our society'. Finally, on the question of differential treatment, the Justice stated that 'there is no greater inequality than the equal treatment of unequals'.[39] While the Andrews case is complex, the ruling suggests that, under the Charter, any future affirmative-action legislation is likely to have a sympathetic reading from the courts, especially in the context of systemic discrimination and historic disadvantage.

The case for affirmative action for women in politics thus rests on evidence of systemic discrimination and is further advanced by appeals to either compensatory or distributive justice. Certainly there is abundant evidence of systemic discrimination against women in political leadership. Election results are a stark indicator that women have been systematically excluded from political office. From a compensatory perspective too, it can be argued that women continue to bear the weight of previous overt discrimination. Canadian electoral law now treats women and men as equals, but the adoption of gender-blind laws cannot erase the invisible and systemic inequalities that were created and sanctioned by law.[40] Policies of exclusion and subordination have left traces in the social fabric in the form of attitudes and denied opportunities. This historic legacy means that sex remains a relevant consideration in determining who will hold office, whether elected or appointed.

An equally strong case can be made for an affirmative-action program for women in electoral politics by appealing to a distributive conception of justice, emphasizing an evolving and expansive conception of equality and democracy. A distributive conception of justice begins with the premise that equality is not embodied in a static set of rules or institutions, but is a process involving 'constant and flexible examination, vigilant introspection and aggressive open-mindedness'.[41] It holds current evidence of systemic discrimination to be inconsistent with the broader and evolving social goals of democratic equality. Affirmative action, therefore, is justified as a collective declaration of the equality of all citizens and the integrity of the democratic process. In other words, an affirmative-action plan grounded on a distributive conception of justice is propelled by the moral force of democratic ideals and the recognition that 'sex segregation in political office' is unacceptable in a democratic polity committed to gender equality, because it 'perpetuates an image of women as less capable, less competent and less fully human than men'.[42]

The case for affirmative action for women in politics, therefore, can be firmly grounded in the liberal concepts of systemic discrimination and compensatory and distributive justice. Nevertheless, the question remains of how best to increase women's political representation. The next section will review the affirmative-action strategies that have been advocated and implemented in Canada and other Western democracies.

AFFIRMATIVE-ACTION STRATEGIES FOR WOMEN IN POLITICS

Constitutional Reform

Obviously the most effective way to ensure women's equal participation with men in political leadership is through constitutional reform. At present it appears that no country mandates gender parity in all aspects of public life, although the Norwegian Socialist Party has proposed just such a constitutional amendment. The Charlottetown Accord's proposal for gender parity in Canada's reformed Senate fell short of this ideal because under it gender parity would have been achieved through provincial law specifying selection/election procedures. Nevertheless, the idea that gender parity in public life should be constitutionally entrenched has been advanced before in Canada, and it has recently taken on some momentum in the United States.

Although they do not yet form a broad-based political movement, advocates of constitutional guarantees for gender parity in all forms of political leadership rest their case on appeals to compensatory and distributive justice. As we have seen, according to the compensatory rationale the state is justified in using the law to achieve gender parity in public life because historically the law has played a critical role in denying women access to public office. Examples include laws that deprived women of citizenship, constrained their property rights, and excluded them from a wide range of occupations.[43] Given this legacy of discrimination on the basis of sex, advocates argue that it is appropriate to employ the law to rectify the cumulative effects of law.

For other proponents of constitutional amendment, the compensatory argument is unnecessary. In their view, a distributive concept of justice, which takes ongoing discrimination rather than historic legacy as its departure point, is enough. They point to the virtual absence of women in American public life as a valid and sufficient indicator of systemic discrimination that, in a democratic polity, necessarily invites state intervention. A constitutional amendment grounded on a distributive conception of justice would provide a pro-active mechanism for reshaping gender relations in politics. According to a leading proponent of this position, gender parity in public office would not guarantee any specific substantive outcomes of the policy process. Instead, a constitutional amendment would commit the state to the principle of democratic equality between women and men, asserting that '[a]s half the population, half the citizenry, and half the taxpayers, women deserve half the positions that determine how public life will be regulated and how public resources will be allocated.'[44]

Gender-Balance Laws

For some, the idea of constitutionally mandating gender balance in public office constitutes a dangerous violation of the autonomy of political parties and the sovereignty of the electorate. Nonetheless, they concede that it is entirely within the prerogative of the state to ensure gender parity in non-elected positions of political authority. Gender-parity laws require the appointment of equal numbers of women and men to all public boards, commissions, committees, and councils. Five American states have adopted laws or resolutions supporting gender balance in state appointments. The first, enacted in Iowa in 1986, stated that 'all boards, commissions, committees, and councils shall reflect, as much as possible, a gender balance'. In the following two years, the scope of the Iowa gender-balance provision was extended to judicial nominations, and the voluntary provision was eliminated. Gender balance in state appointments is now required by law. North Dakota also has a gender-balance law, while Montana, Hawaii, Rhode Island, and the City of Los Angeles have adopted gender-balance resolutions, which though not mandatory recommend gender equity in state appointments 'to the extent possible'. As of 1991 seven other state governments — Alaska, California, Idaho, Minnesota, New Jersey, New York, and Wisconsin — were considering similar gender-balance laws.[45]

Although such laws mandating gender balance in appointed offices do not directly affect American electoral politics, it is argued that they have both symbolic and tangible implications for women's political equality. At the symbolic level, they represent a formal public commitment to women as a political constituency deserving of equal representation and voice in governmental bodies. At a more practical level, these laws may very well increase the pool of women recruits for elected office. Studies of American women office-holders show that they, much more than men, come to electoral politics through the door of appointed positions. It is reasoned, therefore, that in the medium and long term, gender-balance laws will generate growing numbers of women with the interests, skills, and connections necessary for elected office.[46]

Quota Systems

Many people have suggested that the election of women in Canada would be facilitated with the adoption of a proportional electoral (PR) system. They argue that PR systems afford the opportunity for parties to ensure the representation of women because the central party hierarchy draws up the list of candidates. Such systems therefore allow party élites more control over the composition of the national slate of candidates than do nomination systems that delegate candidate selection to local party organizations. Advocates of electoral reform point to the percentages of women elected under PR in countries such as Sweden, Norway, and Denmark to support their case. Nevertheless, the association between the type of electoral system and the success of women at the polls is much more complex than is generally acknowledged by the proponents of PR.

Closer examination of the European case indicates that the key variables underlying the apparent correlation between proportional representation and the election of women are the nature of the party system and the adoption of quota systems as an explicit and immediate corrective to the historic under-representation of women in public office. The examples of Norway and Sweden are cases in point. In Norway, attempts to increase the election of women began in the late 1960s and were aimed at encouraging women to vote for women candidates. In the early 1970s, women's groups, with the assistance of the Equal Status Council of Norway, launched a campaign to have women nominated to safe seats. The results of both these campaigns were modest. It was only after the Norwegian Labour Party adopted a statutory 40 per cent minimum rule in 1983 that the numbers of women elected began to increase and stabilize around the current level.[47] The percentage of women in the Norwegian lower house increased from 15.5 per cent in 1975 to 34.4 per cent in 1985.[48] This result was possible both because the socialists had a strong electoral presence throughout this period and because their actions forced other parties in the system to undertake similar initiatives.

The minimum rule that 'in all elections and nominations, there must be at least 40 per cent of both sexes' ensures that women are represented in key strategic positions within the Labour party as well as on party electoral slates. It also ensures that men are represented in the party 'housekeeping' roles that have traditionally been delegated to women. The 40 per cent rule has proved to be an effective and immediate way of integrating women into Norwegian politics. In fact, it now serves as a protective rule for men: when, in a recent Norwegian parliamentary election, more than 60 per cent of the Labour candidates who came forward were women, some had to be turned away to conform with the 40 per cent rule. Currently, the Labour party's parliamentary caucus is comprised of 31 women and 30 men.[49]

The Swedish case tells a similar story. The Social Democratic Party, which has dominated Sweden's legislature since the Second World War, followed the Norwegian example and adopted a voluntary 40 per cent rule. Again the results were immediate. In the decade between 1975 and 1985, the proportion of women in the Swedish lower house increased by 10 per cent, even though the SDP was out of power for almost half of this period, since its initiatives influenced the other four parties in the party system to respond in kind. In fact, all parliamentary parties now adhere to a 40 per cent rule. Moreover, since the 1970s it has been the agrarian Centre party rather than the SDP that has consistently returned the most women to the Riksdag.[50]

Throughout Europe, socialist parties have generally been the first to adopt quota systems and thus, depending on their electoral strength, to have a discernible impact on the gender composition of national legislatures. But there have been exceptions to this general rule — in particular, the Green party. Formed in West Germany in 1980 as a coalition of feminist, peace, and environmental activists, the Green party was the first to adopt a 50 per cent quota for both party positions and candidacy. Its party lists begin and end with a woman's name and this strategy has had an impact on the gender composition of the legislature. It has also been suggested that it was the success of the Greens in attracting West German women voters, rather than the example of the Socialist International, that initially led the West German SDP to adopt a 30 per cent quota.[51] Green parties have subsequently been launched in a number of other countries, including France (les Verts), Britain, and Canada. All subscribe to the 50 per cent rule.

All three of Canada's major federal parties have some experience with gender quota systems, but only the New Democratic Party has extended this affirmative measure to political candidacy. Both the Progressive Conservative and Liberal parties have mandatory quotas ensuring women's representation at leadership conventions. Although these quotas do no more than ensure party women of the right to vote for party leaders, they have had tangible results: over the last two decades, the percentages of women delegates to national leadership conventions have increased from approximately 15 per cent to 47 per cent.[52] The Liberal party, moreover, has recently taken steps guaranteeing women the co-chair of strategic national party committees, including the National Campaign Committee, which establishes guidelines for candidate selection.[53] By contrast, the federal NDP has guaranteed gender parity on all its governing bodies since 1983.[54]

None of Canada's political parties has established mandatory gender quotas for political candidacy, although both the Ontario and federal NDP have taken significant steps in this direction. In 1989, for example, the Ontario wing established voluntary guidelines recommending that 50 per cent of all constituencies and 75 per cent of priority ridings be allocated to designated target groups including women. Although the party fell short of this goal in the 1990 Ontario provincial election, the nomination of women to priority ridings brought many women (20 of 74 NDP members) to Queen's Park.[55] More recently, the federal party has endorsed similar, but still voluntary, affirmative-action measures for women candidates. In 1991 the Federal Council recommended that in the next federal election 50 per cent of all ridings and 60 per cent of priority ridings should be designated for women candidates. The party's Participation of Women Committee (POW), however, continues to lobby to establish these guidelines as mandatory quotas.[56]

Remedial Measures

By far the most common strategy for promoting the election of women in Canada has been the introduction of remedial measures designed to help individual women compete for public office. This strategy is based on a two-step approach of identifying the major obstacles to women's election and then tailoring programs to reduce or eliminate them. Some of these programs are directed at increasing the supply of women candidates through either skills training or the establishment of 'talent banks'. Leadership training seminars for women have been organized by groups inside and outside party organizations. More recently, the federal Progressive Conservative Party adopted and then deferred a plan to establish a talent bank of the names and résumés of women considered suitable for political candidacy.[57]

In general, however, remedial measures have been limited to offering women candidates incentives and token recognition of the financial obstacles that they face in politics. During the 1980s, for example, all three federal parties and many of their provincial wings established special funds for women candidates. The Progressive Conservatives' Ellen Fairclough Fund earmarks money to train women and assist in the financing of their electoral campaigns; the Liberals' Judy LaMarsh Fund has similar goals, while the NDP's Agnes MacPhail Fund distributes money to riding associations, rather than to individual women candidates, and the allocations vary according to need. Most evidence, however, suggests that these funds have little impact on the recruitment of women candidates. Such incentives are not available for women seeking nomination as candidates, and they are negligible compared to the total cost of conducting an election campaign. Women candidates in the 1988 federal election indicated that these funds did not even cover the costs of child care, day-to-day incidentals, or wardrobe expenses.[58]

The 1992 Report of the Royal Commission on Electoral Reform and Party Financing concentrated its recommendations for the election of women on such financial obstacles. But in many ways it is quite contradictory: although it accepts numerous rationales for affirmative-action measures, its recommendations fall significantly short of the practices of other Western democracies. For example, the Report clearly recognizes the case for affirmative action for women, arguing that 'sex . . . must not determine who can enter the political arena' and that 'a profile of MPs as a body over time constitutes a valid indicator of the openness, equity and fairness of our electoral process'.[59] It also accepts the concept of systemic discrimination and recognizes that 'there is a legitimate public interest in having equitable representation' in order to preserve 'the legitimacy of our democratic institutions' and to make public policy more sensitive to women's policy perspectives.[60] Yet it explicitly rejects the idea that the law should be used to implement gender parity or quotas in political leadership, focusing instead on 'the barriers that individuals face in seeking elected office, and the rules and practices of constituency organizations'.[61] In other words, it recognizes that women have a special case to make for affirmative action (the difference argument) but casts most of its recommendations in gender-neutral terms (the equality argument). Moreover, the one recommendation that is cast explicitly in gendered terms (see below) does little more than reinforce the uncertain status quo of incremental progress towards the goal of gender equity in political leadership.

Nevertheless, the Commission's recommendations for achieving a more equitable representational system, if implemented, would reduce some significant barriers for women in politics. Among other things, it recommended the adoption of spending limits and income-tax credits at the nomination stage; tightening of the rules governing voting at nomination meetings; child-care deductions during nomination and election campaigns; and the right to an employment leave of absence to seek nomination and election.[62] All of these reforms were designed to address systemic obstacles arising from electoral rules.

Although the Commission also recognized that systemic discrimination emanates from the attitudes and practices of political parties, it suggested that electoral law could only offer incentives for them to change their practices. In particular, it recommended that a registered party be eligible for additional reimbursements if it increased the proportion of women in its caucus. Parties would have to have a minimum of 20 per cent women MPs to qualify, and the incentive system would be eliminated once the overall percentage of women in the House of Commons reached 40 per cent. Importantly, however, this scheme would be implemented only if the overall percentage of women in the House of Commons was below 20 per cent following either of the next two elections.[63] Thus, in effect, the Commission appeared to endorse the view that evidence of incremental improvement in women's representation renders affirmative-action measures unnecessary. It trusts that the goal of gender parity in political leadership will be achieved by the magic hand of the political market in its own good time.

It is not surprising that the Royal Commission's recommendations were so clearly remedial and incremental. In many respects, Canadian feminists left the field open for others to define the legitimate parameters of electoral and democratic reform. The Commission did hear from a scattering of women's groups who pointed to the financial obstacles confronting women in politics, and its recommendations reflected these concerns. But a much louder chorus of vested interests told the Commission that public policy was an inappropriate mechanism for ensuring a more representative democracy in Canada. In particular, most representatives of Canada's political parties asserted that democracy was best served when parties maintained autonomy from the state. Few feminists, perhaps because of their long-standing suspicion of electoral and reformist politics, challenged this pervasive view. Little wonder, then, that the Royal Commission placed its recommendations for increasing the representation of women in a chapter entitled 'Political Parties as Primary Political Organizations'.

In summary, this review of affirmative-action strategies for women in politics suggests that the most effective way to ensure a gender-balanced political leadership is through gender-parity laws and quota systems. Remedial measures, while perhaps the easiest to achieve, promise only incremental and tentative results. In effect, there is an inverse relationship between the effectiveness of the affirmative strategy and the resistance it evokes, because the quest for gender equality in political leadership is a struggle over the distribution of political power. It is also a struggle that feminists are likely to lose if they continue to forfeit the terrain of liberal democratic politics to others, or if they accept prevailing definitions of the legitimate actors in democratic politics. In other words, it is unlikely that the goal of gender parity in political leadership in Canada will be achieved unless women are prepared to engage in a debate about what democratic equality means—a debate that must be grounded on principles of justice, emphasizing that the promise of democratic equality will not be met until women take their place in the democratic decision-making process.

CONCLUSION

No doubt the early suffragists would be shocked to realize that, some seventy years after women gained the right to vote, Canadian feminists are still struggling for political equality. If these years have taught Canadians anything, it is that women's quest for full citizenship in a democratic state is much more complex than was first thought.[64]

In the early days of the second wave of Canadian feminism, activists were deeply divided over whether they should attempt to reform existing institutions or fight for a revolutionary transformation of the social system. Over the past twenty years, this distinction has become blurred: feminists have won a series of seemingly reformist victories, but their cumulative effect has been transformative. Feminist victories, however, are always partial, contradictory, and reversible.[65] Indeed, in recent years women have seen a considerable erosion of some previously won gains. Governments have cut back on the funding of women's organizations and shelters, job-retraining programs, and crucial welfare services, and have delayed the implementation of pay equity and child-care programs. It is widely acknowledged that the 1990s have witnessed a backlash to feminism and feminist demands for women's equality. Ideas of social transformation have tended to falter in a climate of economic restraint, and many feminist organizations have retreated into a reactive posture.[66] Notably, this backlash is being enforced through the institutions of liberal democracy.

It is within this context of backlash and retreat that feminists have begun to re-examine the issue of women in liberal democratic politics and to recognize that the quest to increase the numbers of women in political leadership is a struggle for political power. This chapter has argued that feminists should take up this struggle on the grounds that Canadian democracy must evolve to include women as equal actors with an equal voice in the political process. Of course this was also the goal of the early suffragists; the difference today is that feminists no longer accept the notion that women do or must speak in a singular voice. Feminists can unite around the goal of achieving gender parity in political representation, but only so long as this goal opens political space for women in all their diversity. While the liberal democratic project is necessary if feminists are to realize their objectives, the feminist project of a politics that recognizes differences among women and conceives of equality as an evolving social goal is no less necessary for democracy.

NOTES

[1] Royal Commission on the Status of Women, *Report* (Ottawa: Information Canada, 1970), 339, 355; see also Janine Brodie, 'Women and the Electoral Process in Canada', in Kathy Megyery, ed., *Women in Canadian Politics: Toward Equity in Representation* (Toronto: Dundurn Press, 1991), vol. 6 of the Research Studies of the Royal Commission on Electoral Reform and Party Financing, 4-6.

[2] Brodie, 'Women', 5-6.

[3] Anne Phillips, *Engendering Democracy* (University Park: Pennsylvania State University Press, 1991), 61-2.

[4] L. Clark, 'Liberty, Equality, Fraternity — and Sorority', in Anne Bayefsky, ed., *Legal Theory Meets Legal Practice* (Edmonton: Academic, 1988), 267.

[5] Carole Pateman, 'Promise and Paradox: Women and Democratic Citizenship', Second York Lecture in Political Science, 1992.

[6] Joan Scott, 'Deconstructing Equality-Versus-Difference: Or, the Uses of Poststructuralist Theory for Feminism', in Marianne Hirsh and Evelyn Fox Keller, eds, *Conflicts in Feminism* (New York: Routledge, 1990), 142.

[7] Phillips, *Engendering Democracy*, 3.

[8] Joni Lovenduski, 'Toward the Emasculation of Political Science: The Impact of Feminism', in Dale Spender, ed., *Men's Studies Modified: The Impact of Feminism on the Academic Disciplines* (New York: Pergamon, 1981), 88.

[9] Brodie, 'Women', 34; Vicky Randall, *Women and Politics: An International Perspective*, 2nd ed. (London: Macmillan, 1987), 126.

[10] See Brodie, 'Women', 13; Michael Walzer, 'Liberalism and the Art of Separation', *Political Theory* (August 1984): 315-30.

[11] Birte Siim, 'Toward Feminist Rethinking of the Welfare State', in Kathleen Jones and Anna Jonasdottir, eds, *Political Interests of Gender* (Newbury Park, CA: Sage, 1988), 163.

[12] Carole Pateman, *The Sexual Contract* (Cambridge: Polity Press, 1985), 192.

[13] Sylvia Bashevkin, *Toeing the Lines: Women and Party Politics in English Canada* (Toronto: University of Toronto Press, 1985).

[14] Janine Brodie, *Women in Politics in Canada* (Toronto: McGraw-Hill Ryerson, 1985).

[15] See Brodie, 'Women', 7.

[16] Ibid., 44-5.

[17] For some empirical evidence supporting this view see Joni Lovenduski and Pippa Norris, 'Selecting Women Candidates: Obstacles to the Feminisation of the House of Commons', *European Journal of Political Research* 17 (1989): 534; Brodie, *Women in Politics*, Chapter 6.

[18] Randall, *Women and Politics*, 140-4.

[19] European Parliament, *Session Document*, 'Report drawn up on behalf of the Committee on Women's Rights on women in decision-making centres', Document A 2-169/88, 11.

[20] Brodie, 'Women', 47-8.

[21] Phillips, *Engendering Democracy*, 61.

[22] Ibid., 3, 62-4.

[23] Ibid., 63.

[24] Ibid., 3-5.

[25] Carol Bacchi, *Liberation Deferred? The Ideas of English Canadian Suffragists 1877-1918* (Toronto: University of Toronto Press, 1983), 3.

[26] As quoted in Nancy Adamson, Linda Briskin, and Margaret McPhail, *Feminist Organizing For Change: The Contemporary Women's Movement in Canada* (Toronto: Oxford University Press, 1988), 288.

[27] During the summer of 1990, 47 of the 300 women who contested the 1988 federal election were interviewed by telephone. For details see Brodie, 'Women', Appendix.

[28] Ibid., 48.

[29] Carol Mueller, *The Politics of the Gender Gap: The Social Construction of Political Interest* (Newbury Park, CA: Sage, 1988), 10.

[30] Phillips, *Engendering Democracy*, 6.

[31] Anne Phillips, 'Feminism, Equality, and Difference', in Linda McDowell and Rosemary Pringle, eds, *Defining Women: Social, Institutional, and Gender Differences* (London: Polity Press, 1992), 216.

[32] Diana Majury, 'Strategizing in Equality', in Martha Albertson Fineman and Nancy Sweet Thomadsen, eds, *At the Boundaries of Law: Feminism and Legal Theory* (New York: Routledge, 1991), 321.

[33] Iris Marion Young, *Justice and the Politics of Difference* (Princeton, NJ: Princeton University Press, 1990), 195.

[34] Canada, Royal Commission on Equity in Employment, *Report* (Ottawa: Supply and Services, 1984), 10.

[35] For a discussion of systemic discrimination see Royal Commission on Electoral Reform and Party Financing, *Report* (Ottawa: Supply and Services, 1992), vol. I, 97-8.

[36] Young, *Justice*, 194,

[37] The provision for the preferential hiring of veterans is still contained in the Public Service Employment Act, R.S.C. 1970, C.P.-32, as amended. See Canada, Royal Commission on Equity in Employment, *Report*, 197-200.

[38] Ibid., 13.

[39] *Andrews v. the Law Society of British Columbia* (1989), 56 D.L.R. (4th) 1, S.C.R. 143, 180, 152, 184. (This case concerned the eligibility of people who are not Canadian citizens to practise law in BC.) Although the Andrews decision did not directly relate to sexual equality, it was

the first to deal with the equality provisions of the Charter of Rights and Freedoms. In the decision the Supreme Court indicated that those provisions were intended to help the powerless and disadvantaged and thus could be used to justify special measures such as affirmative action.

[40] Mary E. Hawkesworth, *Beyond Oppression: Feminist Theory and Political Practice* (New York: Continuum Press, 1990), 177.

[41] Royal Commission on Equity in Employment, *Report*, 1.

[42] Hawkesworth, *Beyond Oppression*, 185.

[43] Ibid., 177.

[44] Ibid., 181-2.

[45] Fund for the Feminist Majority, 'Feminist Majority Campaign for Gender Balance Laws', Arlington, VA, 1991.

[46] Ibid.

[47] Fund for the Feminist Majority, 'The Feminization of Power: An International Comparison', Arlington, VA, 1988, 3-4.

[48] *Women's International Network News* 15, 4 (Autumn 1989): 64.

[49] Maria Rodriquez-Jonas, General Secretary of Socialist International, speech to British Labour Women Conference, April 1991, 2-3.

[50] Joyce Gelb, *Feminism and Politics: A Comparative Perspective* (Berkeley: University of California Press, 1989), 140, 151-2.

[51] Fund for the Feminist Majority, 'The Feminization of Power'.

[52] Sylvia Bashevkin, 'Women's Participation in Political Parties', in Megyery, ed., *Women in Canadian Politics*, 66.

[53] Lynda Erickson, 'Making the Ballot: Women and Party Selection in Canada', in Joni Lovenduski and Pippa Norris, eds, *Gender and Party Politics* (London: Sage, forthcoming).

[54] Brodie, 'Women', 31.

[55] Ibid., 38.

[56] Erickson, 'Making the Ballot'.

[57] Ibid.

[58] Brodie, 'Women', 47.

[59] Royal Commission on Electoral Reform and Party Financing, *Report*, vol. 1, 93.

[60] Ibid., 269.

[61] Ibid.

[62] Ibid., 270.

[63] Ibid., 273.

[64] Carole Pateman, 'The Patriarchal Welfare State', in McDowell and Pringle, *Defining Women*, 235.

[65] I thank my friend and colleague Shelley Gavigan for this point.

[66] Phillips, 'Feminism', 206.

BEING THERE

—■—

Governing in Canada

CHAPTER FIVE

PRIME MINISTERIAL
LEADERSHIP

Position, Power, and Politics

—▬—

Peter Aucoin

Within the Canadian system of government the prime minister is clearly the foremost political leader. The prime minister exercises the most crucial executive powers, heads the Cabinet that effectively controls the exercise of legislative powers, and selects the most important members of the judiciary. The prime minister has no equal within this structure of government. There are constitutional limits on the powers of the prime minister, as well as practical political limits on what a prime minister can do unilaterally. But, even within these bounds, a Canadian prime minister has powers that are not exceeded in any other democratic regime.

   This pre-eminent position of the prime minister, the powers of this office, and the politics of prime ministerial leadership derive from three interrelated dimensions of the Canadian system of governance. These are: (1) the constitutional conventions of 'responsible government'; (2) the organization and practices of 'party government'; and (3) the structure and operation of 'Cabinet government'. This chapter examines each of these in turn.

PRIME MINISTER AND RESPONSIBLE GOVERNMENT

The Canadian Constitution vests executive powers in the governor general acting on the advice of the prime minister in certain cases and on the advice of the Cabinet, of which the prime minister is head, in others.[1] The principal constitutional responsibility of the governor general is to ensure that there is a 'government' (prime minister and Cabinet) that has the confidence of the House of Commons—that is, a government supported by a majority of members in this assembly of directly elected representatives. It is in this sense that a government is 'responsible' to the House of Commons. If this support is removed, then either (1) the prime minister and Cabinet resign in order that a new government that can command this required support may be formed, or (2) the prime minister instructs the governor general to dissolve the House of Commons in order that a general election be held. In this latter case the prime minister and Cabinet do not resign but await the outcome of the election. Following the election the government either is able to command the support of the new House of Commons and thereby continue as government or, if it does not have the confidence of the majority, it resigns and a new government must be formed by a new prime minister.

Within this system of responsible government the role of the governor general is to accept the advice of the prime minister when the latter seeks a dissolution of the House of Commons or, when necessary, to appoint as prime minister that person who can form a government that will have the support of a majority of members in the House.[2] This second situation arises when a prime minister either resigns or dies in office. Whenever a prime minister resigns or dies, the 'government' no longer exists and a new one must be formed. The governor general does not actually form the government; he or she only appoints a prime minister to do so.

Appointing the prime minister does not assume the exercise of any personal discretion on the governor general's part. Rather, the choice of who is to form and head the government, following the resignation or death of a prime minister, depends on which party has the most members in the House of Commons. When a political party, following a general election, gains a majority of seats in the House of Commons, its leader will either continue to be or will become the prime minister. In the Canadian tradition, we call this a 'majority government'. In the event that no one party finds itself in this situation, either during the life of a Parliament or following a general election, the leader of the party that can command the support of a majority by obtaining the support of members from one or more other parties (or 'independent members') either continues as, or becomes, prime minister. In the Canadian tradition, we call this a 'minority government' because the 'governing party' has a minority of the seats in the Commons; the majority of seats are held by members from other parties or independents. In this instance, however, only members from the governing party actually serve in the government as ministers in the Cabinet. Finally, there could also be instances where a prime minister forms a government that includes members from more than one party. This was the basis of the so-called Union Government during the First World War, for instance, when the government included members from both the Conservative and Liberal parties serving as ministers in the Cabinet. Elsewhere such a government is normally referred to as a 'coalition government' because it consists of a coalition of two or more political parties. In the Canadian experience there has been only one such coalition; minority government has been the preferred alternative in situations where the governing party does not hold a majority of seats in the Commons.

Our major contending parties now have procedures in place to select a successor in the case of either the resignation or death of a leader. Even in the situation where a party leader does not hold a seat in the Commons (or Senate) no discretion is exercised by the governor general in determining who will be asked to form a new government. When John Turner was selected as Liberal leader in 1984, for example, he did not hold a seat in either the Commons or Senate, but was called upon by the governor general to be prime minister and to form a new government. The Liberals held a majority of seats in the Commons at the time and there was no question as to his claim to be prime minister. The fact that he did not hold a seat in Parliament, moreover, placed no restrictions on his constitutional authority as prime minister; he was fully head of the government, with all the powers attached to the office. He did call an election shortly after assuming the office, but this was primarily a function of the fact that the previous general election had been held in 1980. Had he assumed office shortly after the 1980 election, he would not have been required to call another general election for at least five years. In such a circumstance, however, convention would have required that he seek a seat in the Commons via a by-election; the norm here would be for a member of the House from the government party to resign to make way for a by-election. The convention in question requires, at the least, that a prime minister be a member of the House of Commons in order that, as the leader of the government, he or she may be subject to questioning by its members. Whether the prime minister has a seat in the House of Commons, however, does not affect the principle of responsible government: a government led by a prime minister without a seat in the House still requires the support of the Commons.

As outlined above, the constitutional principle of responsible government is effectively secured through our practice of 'party government'; the prime minister is the leader of the governing party in the House of Commons.[3] While voters elect a prime minister and government only indirectly—by voting in single-member constituencies for candidates who are members of a political party—Canadian electoral democracy assumes that the electorate can hold a government responsible via the practice of party government. A government can thus be 'defeated' at a general election if it fails to secure what the prime minister considers to be the confidence of the electorate. In such cases, the prime minister resigns and a new government is formed before the newly elected House of Commons is summoned. It is in this critical sense that political parties within our system of responsible government are 'primary political organizations'.[4]

Although this principle of responsible government requires that the government have majority support in the House of Commons, it does not mean that the government is indistinguishable from the Commons. The government, through either the prime minister alone or the prime minister and Cabinet together, exercises *executive powers*, as provided for in the Constitution Act, that are 'entirely separate' from the legislative powers that are also provided for in the Constitution.[5] The government, however, is also part of Parliament: Parliament consists of the Queen, the House of Commons, and the Senate.[6] The *legislative powers* of Parliament, accordingly, are *not* vested solely in the House of Commons and Senate; the Queen, and thereby the government (prime minister and Cabinet), is a component part of Parliament. Our system of constitutional government, in short, is composed of a government exercising separate executive powers, on the one hand, and a legislative branch of government wherein legislative powers are shared by an elected assembly (the House of Commons), an appointed assembly (the Senate) and the government (prime minister and Cabinet). In addition to the practice of party government that serves to assert the primacy of the government *within* Parliament, the Constitution itself also provides that all legislation relating to the raising or spending of public monies must be introduced exclusively by the government in the House of Commons. It is both inaccurate and misleading, therefore, to say, as many authorities do, that our system of responsible government is characterized chiefly by the 'fusion' of executive and legislative powers. This is only part of the constitutional structure of parliamentary government. Within 'parliamentary government' there is both a Parliament *and* a government; the latter is part of the former in the exercise of legislative powers, but is separate from it in the exercise of executive powers.

PRIME MINISTER AND PARTY GOVERNMENT

Although the practice of party government, as we know it today, took some time to develop, from the outset the prime minister, as head of government, was a party leader. Today the prime minister is expected to be that person who has secured the leadership of a governing party through election by the party membership. Since 1919, when the Liberal Party of Canada selected its leader by way of a leadership convention of party delegates, the norm for leadership selection has been selection by the party at large. Within this system, the parliamentary party, or party 'caucus', consisting of members of the party in the House of Commons and Senate, is now but one element of the party. The adoption of this practice by the leading parties in Canada has served to enhance the position and power of the Canadian prime ministership. It has done so precisely because it ensures that a Canadian prime minister's leadership position is not dependent upon the support of the prime minister's caucus colleagues.

Beginning with Canada's first prime minister, John A. Macdonald, the critical role of the party leader in party government was evident. Over time, nonetheless, the position of party leaders within their parties has been transformed in important ways. R.K. Carty describes the Canadian experience as exhibiting 'three quite distinctive party systems . . . [in] the country's political development'.[7]

In the first system (1867-1917), the prime minister as party leader required the support of the governing party caucus: 'for what the caucus had given it could also take away'.[8] The contending parties during this period were 'little more than coteries of political notables',[9] and, not unexpectedly, leaders emerged only from within these coteries. The second party system (1921-57) witnessed, among others things, the acceptance of the leadership convention as the route to party leadership. As Carty notes, this not only 'divided authority and responsibility within the parties' but, more important, meant that 'as Mackenzie King [Liberal leader from 1919 to 1948] is reported to have told his [caucus] colleagues, a leader not chosen by the caucus was not responsible to it'.[10] The third party system (1963-present) has seen the full flowering of the personalization of the prime minister's status as party leader. As Carty puts it: 'the parties have become more than ever an extension of the leader, a personalized machine to build and sustain a coalition of support for the leader's policies'.[11] To secure, and then to maintain, the leadership of a major party, one must have 'a highly personalized national network capable of penetrating and capturing the wider party'.[12]

Since 1867, Canadian prime ministers have been the leaders of only two parties: the Conservatives and the Liberals. Although these two parties have had different policy orientations and different bases of electoral support over time, deriving in part from their identification with the basic political cleavages of the Canadian polity,[13] their governance structures have evolved in ways that do not differ markedly. Indeed, their basic similarities over time are what enable Carty to identify three 'party systems'. The current party system, in what Carty calls the 'electronic age', has three distinguishing features that have enhanced the role of party leaders. First, the dominance of television as the principal medium of political communications has served to personalize party leadership. Second, the evolution of campaign technologies, particularly public opinion polling, media advertising, and 'direct mail', has strengthened the capacity of party leaders to centralize party electioneering. Third, the electoral law's provisions for election and party finance have given party leaders the financial resources to professionalize the central apparatus of the party under their personal direction.

In accordance with their personal power to direct the party apparatus as they see fit, to set party policy according to their preference, and to determine election strategy on the advice of their personal political advisers, the leaders of the Conservative (now Progressive Conservative) and Liberal parties assume that they must maintain their personal support within their respective parties, and that they will be held personally responsible for the parties' fortunes. This is not to say, however, that a party leader is totally secure in his or her position. The effectiveness of a leader is now subject to even greater media and public, and therefore party, scrutiny and evaluation. Since the advent of the third party system, three of the eight persons who have headed the Liberal and Conservative parties have been subject to formal challenges to their leadership, and two (Diefenbaker and Clark) failed to retain their positions, although neither was prime minister at the time. No prime minister in modern times has yet been displaced as leader while in office, but this does not mean that there have not been intra-party pressures on some to step down.

The position of a party leader while prime minister is buttressed both by the powers of the office itself and by the partisan dynamic that is commonly referred to as 'party discipline'. As prime minister, a leader has powers to foster party discipline within the ranks of the parliamentary caucus. Chief among these is the power to reward party members by way of appointments: for MPs, appointments as, *inter alia*, ministers, parliamentary secretaries, chairs of Commons committees, or members of special parliamentary or government missions to various international forums, and, for those contemplating retiring as MPs (and ministers), 'patronage' appointments to any number of government commissions and corporations or the courts. The prime minister can sanction members who stray, or threaten to stray, from the party by removing them from certain of these positions or by eliminating the prospect of future appointments. The ways in which this power is deployed will vary with individual prime ministers and, in some cases, political circumstances. The calculus of decision here depends upon both individual styles and the degree of leverage that such powers provide in particular cases. Nonetheless, the appointment power is generally a potent instrument of leadership.

It would be misleading, however, to suggest that prime ministers rely exclusively, or even primarily, on this instrument to secure party discipline. On the contrary, party discipline is above all a function of partisanship on the part of individual party members, and is reinforced by the group dynamics of political parties as partisan organizations with leaders and followers.[14] Party discipline arises as a consequence of our system of party government. Party members, including those elected to the House of Commons, are members of a partisan organization that seeks to secure and/or maintain political power through collective action. In order to achieve this objective, members subject themselves to party discipline. This means acceptance of the authority of the party leadership, however structured, and adherence to a party program, however defined. When discipline obtains, the net effect is a pattern of cohesive collective behaviour.

The dynamics of party government within the exercise of executive and legislative powers means that a prime minister can normally count on the members of his or her Cabinet to demonstrate, at least in public, what is referred to as 'Cabinet solidarity'. Ministers thus speak with one voice on matters of government policy and administration, however much they might disagree with one another in the private confines of Cabinet. In addition, and equally critical, the prime minister can normally count on the members of his or her parliamentary caucus, especially those in the House of Commons, to follow the lead of the government on public issues. It is this dimension of party discipline that is most widely seen as characterizing the government's role in the exercise of its legislative powers. MPs on the government side who are not in the Cabinet — and who are thus referred to as government 'backbenchers' — are expected to adhere willingly to government policy as it is debated in the House and its committees, and to support the government when the opposition attacks its management of public affairs. Although the organization and practice of our parliamentary parties allows for internal party debate and discussion within the private confines of party caucuses, the public behaviour of backbench government MPs, as is the case with the government's ministers, is expected to be in solidarity with the government.[15] Those who for one reason or another cannot conform publicly are expected to resign from the Cabinet and/or party caucus; in cases where they will not do so, and are an embarrassment to the government, they are asked to leave and/or pushed out.

Such discipline is crucial to the practice of responsible government within our system of parliamentary government. Party discipline, both in government and in opposition, clarifies publicly who is responsible for public policy and its administration and who should be held accountable for the same. It therefore plays an important role in our system of electoral democracy as well, in that such clarification enables voters in a general election to hold a government to account by voting for or against it: in the latter case, by voting for the candidates of an opposition party knowing who its leader is and what policies it promises to advance if successful at the polls.

At the same time it is clear that Canadians are increasingly dissatisfied with what they perceive to be the consequences of party discipline. Many view party discipline as detracting from, even subverting, the principle of representative government: their elected MPs follow the dictates of their party leaders instead of acting as the delegates or agents of their constituents. Although most Canadians see the advantage in this system in that it enables them, as voters, to determine which party will govern, they dislike the degree to which it results in the perceived subservience of their MPs to party policy, especially when such policy is considered not to advance their interests or represent their opinions.[16]

This negative view of party discipline is increasingly shared by many MPs themselves. However, a great many of these MPs are no more inclined to act merely as delegates or agents of their constituents. Rather, they would prefer, and may even demand, that they be able to exercise independent judgement on matters of public policy. For them, party discipline is a shackle to be loosened if not discarded altogether: they long to be considered independent 'legislators'. The British practice, in which discipline is seen as less confining, is a model for some; for others, the American model is even more appealing.[17]

The diminishing acceptance of party discipline by citizens and MPs alike constitutes a challenge to any leader of a political party, especially a prime minister. Although party discipline is critical to the leaders of all parliamentary parties, it is essential to a prime minister; under responsible government it is the support of the caucus of the governing party (and, in minority governments, the support of one or more other parties as well) that maintains the party in power. It is not surprising, for example, that Prime Minister Brian Mulroney devoted considerable effort to maintaining harmony within his Conservative caucus throughout his term in office. Not only did his party feel vulnerable to demands that MPs be more responsive to their constituents, but under his leadership it embarked on a number of major policy initiatives, after the general elections of both 1984 and 1988, that were not among its explicitly announced intentions and cannot be said to have been endorsed by the electorate.

The experiences of the Conservative party under Mulroney were not essentially different from those of other governments in the modern period. Recently, however, the demands for reform have intensified.[18] Although the upsurge in dissatisfaction may be transitory, it does highlight the extent to which prime ministerial leadership under party government depends upon a relationship between the prime minister and caucus that is built upon more than rewards and sanctions. As Léon Dion puts it:

> The successes of great political leaders . . . have been closely related to their ability to understand and express the sentiments of the followers. Simultaneously the leader will modify the goals of the group and transform, through manipulation or otherwise, the sentiments prevailing among the members, while the norms and structure of the group will tend to change so as to conform more and more to the leader's temper. In this second sense, the leader is by far the most influential member of the group.[19]

The partisanship that is inherent in party government does not stop with the caucus, however. Although a party can achieve electoral success with a prime minister who trails his or her party in public support, this is hardly a recipe for success and is invariably dependent on the fortuitous presence of an opposing party leader or leaders with even less popular support. As was noted above, no prime minister has been forced to resign as party leader, and thereby as prime minister, as a result of extra-parliamentary party pressures. Nevertheless, prime ministers have been pressured to alter their behaviour for the good of the party's electoral fortunes — the primary concern of party notables in the extra-parliamentary party.

PRIME MINISTER AND CABINET GOVERNMENT

Under our system of responsible party government, the government is clearly the prime minister's government: it lasts only as long as the prime minister remains in office. It is also the prime minister who forms the government. In the case of either a majority or a minority government, the prime minister is restricted to appointing ministers from the party that he or she leads. These ministers must be chosen primarily from the members of the governing party's caucus of elected MPs. Only in a few cases is it acceptable, according to constitutional convention, that Senators be made ministers. On occasion, persons who are neither MPs nor Senators may be appointed as ministers, but here convention dictates that they seek election to the House of Commons shortly after appointment, and if not elected that they resign as ministers. In addition, as Herman Bakvis points out in Chapter 7, there are numerous 'representational imperatives' that the prime minister must meet in the construction of a Cabinet. Given the regional and social diversity of Canadian society, these imperatives are especially strong in the Canadian case.[20]

The prime minister's decisions on appointments to the Cabinet and the assignment of particular portfolios to individual ministers are ultimately personal. But they are seldom taken without thorough consideration of the prime minister's personal relationships with, or the status and influence of, other leaders within the governing party. Although the prime minister can elevate the status and influence of members of the party by appointing them ministers, the Cabinet must represent, and be seen to represent, the collective leadership of the governing party. Under party government, the Cabinet is the apex of the governing party caucus.

Over time the Canadian Cabinet has grown significantly in size. Indeed, no other Cabinet in the British model of Cabinet/parliamentary government is as large as recent Canadian cabinets have been.[21] In Britain there are more ministers, but most do not sit in the Cabinet. There, as in Australia, each ministry has two tiers, and only senior ministers are members of the Cabinet; the other ministers assist the latter within the confines of their portfolios.

The Canadian Cabinet has been large in numbers primarily because of the representational imperative.[22] In the past, prime ministers have declined to introduce a two-tiered ministry system for fear of alienating those interests 'represented' by certain ministers; all such interests must be seen to be represented by ministers who are also members of the Cabinet. This is not to say that all ministers have equal rank or influence within the Cabinet: merely that there is no distinction between those who are appointed as ministers and those who belong to Cabinet.[23]

In a number of important respects — in fact, the most important ones — this structure of Cabinet is a legal fiction. It is so in two ways. First, nothing in our constitutional law or conventions demands that all ministers be equal in their authority or their influence over government policy. The fact that all ministers must accept the convention of Cabinet solidarity does not mean that they must be given an equal voice or vote in determining government policy; indeed, it does not even demand that they be involved in government decision-making. It simply means that when government decisions are taken, ministers either support them, at least in public, or resign. Cabinet solidarity in this sense is simply an extension of party discipline.

Second, there is nothing in our practice of Cabinet government that requires collective decision-making by the entire membership of the Cabinet to support the so-called principle of 'collective responsibility'. Certain decisions of Cabinet must be expressed as 'orders' of the governor general-in-council and a quorum of Cabinet ministers must decide in these instances. It is the prime minister, as head of government, who tenders advice to the governor general. The practical effect is that the prime minister may, and does, take decisions on behalf of the Cabinet, with or without discussion or consensus, and that Cabinet members must support such decisions, at least publicly. The fact that Cabinet business is, by law and by individual oath, secret greatly aids this convention of collective responsibility. The principle, in short, is merely another way of expressing the constitutional convention of responsible government: there is 'a government', consisting of the prime minister and Cabinet, and it must retain the confidence of the House of Commons; it is a government responsible, as a single entity, to the Commons. The Cabinet, as government, stands or falls together.

There is, of course, a powerful incentive for the prime minister to keep Cabinet ministers on side. Because Cabinet represents the leadership of the governing party, a prime minister must ensure that he or she does not lose the confidence of these leaders as 'followers'. Although these followers are perhaps even more susceptible than other MPs to the powers of appointment possessed by the prime minister, the latter must seek to ensure that the assignment of portfolios and the structures of Cabinet decision-making (both formal and informal) serve to secure his or her leadership position. This imperative constitutes the politics of prime ministerial leadership at its most significant level.

The structure of Cabinet decision-making has changed over time in response to various developments. At the outset, Cabinet was essentially a 'chamber of political compensation' wherein 'cabinet ministers, given the limited scope of their respective governments, pre-eminently articulate and aggregate matters of regional or local political concerns and are primarily in the business of dispensing patronage'.[24] The distributive nature of government activities, combined with the representational character of Cabinet, required a good deal of collective deliberation and decision-making. Although these decisions were governmental, the primary consideration was how to generate and/or maintain support for the governing party. Throughout this early period, patronage matters also preoccupied prime ministers, who as party leaders were well aware that patronage constituted their most potent instrument for developing their parties as cohesive national institutions.[25]

With the advent, in 1906, of the independent Civil (later Public) Service Commission to staff the public service on the basis of merit, the major source of partisan patronage disappeared. In turn, the introduction of the merit system for staffing the public service gradually resulted in the development of a professional public service. In combination with a continually expanding governmental role in various aspects of the Canadian socio-economic order, governmental decision-making increasingly shifted to individual ministers and their specialized departmental bureaucracies rather than the Cabinet as a collectivity. The prime minister, of course, was responsible for the assignment of ministerial portfolios as well as for the appointment of 'deputy ministers': that is, the senior administrative heads of each department, whose appointments were exempt from the jurisdiction of the independent commission responsible for staffing the public service below the level of deputy minister. In these ways, the prime minister was clearly the head of government within what Dupré describes as the 'departmentalized cabinet'.[26] Both departmental ministers and their deputy ministers served at the pleasure of the prime minister.

By the mid-1960s the continued expansion of the federal government in terms of its policies, programs, and public-service personnel, combined with the persistence, even elaboration, of the representative character of Cabinet, led to what Dupré has labelled the 'institutionalized cabinet'.[27] The institutionalization of Cabinet meant essentially three things. First, there was a new emphasis on collegial decision-making in order to overcome what were perceived as the dysfunctional consequences of the departmentalized Cabinet. Under a new system of Cabinet committees organized according to major sectors of government activities, such as social and economic policy, it was hoped that ministers would be less susceptible to capture by their departmental bureaucrats and their departmental clientèle. Collective ministerial decision-making, rather than individual ministerial decision-making, was also considered essential because the expanding role of the state had led to increasing interdependence between the activities of different government departments within broad sectors of government policy. Second, there were growing numbers of specialized functions for which government policy required a corporate perspective, one that encompassed the entire government. Corporate policies, by definition, reflect the fact that 'the government' is a single entity in, for instance, its fiscal plan, its expenditure budget, its internal administrative regulations, its intergovernmental and foreign relations, its political communications strategy, and its legislative agenda. Although responsibility for corporate policies had long been vested in others besides the prime minister—the minister of Finance for fiscal policy, and the Treasury Board (a Cabinet committee) for expenditure policy, for instance—the institutionalized Cabinet reflected a growing emphasis on extending corporate responsibilities both to other ministers and to the Cabinet collectively. Finally, the institutionalized Cabinet introduced a more formalized pecking order among ministers, enabling the prime minister to add new portfolios, particularly in the form of junior 'ministers of state' to assist senior department ministers.

The result of these changes has been the creation of a Cabinet that is essentially a system of portfolios wherein collective decision-making is confined to a hierarchy of committees; the full Cabinet no longer functions as an executive decision-making body. The formal structures of the institutionalized Cabinet have been subject to continual change since they were first introduced by Prime Minister Lester Pearson in the 1960s. Both the formal and informal dynamics of status and influence within the Cabinet system have been primarily influenced by the leadership paradigms of successive prime ministers.[28] Prime ministers not only appoint and assign portfolio responsibilities, but also organize their Cabinet's decision-making processes. The prime minister's authority over what is known, in bureaucratic terminology, as the 'machinery of government' encompasses everything from the most mundane procedural matters to the most significant decisions with respect to the exercise of political power. Prime ministers easily control the former. Their capacity to dominate the latter, on the other hand, depends on a number of factors.

A prime minister's powers within Cabinet government are influenced by at least three major factors. First, every prime minister must share power in the exercise of corporate responsibilities. Although prime ministers have varied in the extent to which they seek to take a leading role in various areas of corporate policy, none has been able to govern without delegating some power in areas of corporate responsibility to other ministers. As chief executives, prime ministers are forced by the exigencies of leadership, particularly demands on their time, to focus on a limited number of strategic issues at any one point in time. The increasingly specialized and demanding character of the issues involved in corporate policy decisions imposes severe restraints on the ability of any prime minister to engage in anything more than selective interventions in these decisions.

Second, political considerations and the interdependence of various policy areas have long demanded that Cabinet provide for a measure of collegial decision-making. Party government, as has been noted, demands that a prime minister lead a government that consists of the collective leadership of the governing party. Collegial decision-making, whatever its actual form, is the organizational expression of this inherently political dynamic. At the least, the government's most important ministers must normally be included in government decision-making in cases where partisan considerations loom large or portfolio responsibilities overlap, as happens frequently in such complex organization. The powers of the prime minister in this context are restricted primarily as a consequence, on the one hand, of the need to ensure party cohesiveness over matters that are partisan, and, on the other hand, of the need to allow ministers, and their departments, to resolve their interorganizational disputes through a process of mutual accommodation.

Third, while governments have always been complex organizations in one sense, they have become even more so with the development of the modern state. To some degree, accordingly, prime ministers and their Cabinets have had to allow executive authority to be exercised by individual ministers and their departments within the confines of their portfolio responsibilities. The institutionalization of the Cabinet has obviously reduced the ability of ministers and their departmental bureaucrats to function in the autonomous manner associated with the departmentalized Cabinet. At the same time, institutionalization of the Cabinet could not eliminate altogether the practical requirement that policy be developed and implemented by ministers heading operational departments. Despite the expansion of corporate portfolios, central co-ordinating agencies, and collegial decision-making processes, at the operating level — when public services are delivered and regulations enforced — the need for separate government departments remains.

In other words, the institutionalized Cabinet, with its elaborate structures for corporate and collegial decision-making, has not rendered obsolete the departmentalized structure of Cabinet decision-making. Rather, it illustrates that Cabinet government can encompass several different modes of government decision-making, depending on the issue at hand, the leadership style of the prime minister, the formal structure of ministerial portfolios and Cabinet committees, and the informal dynamics of political influence. For example, although in some instances the prime minister acts without reference to his or her Cabinet colleagues, these decisions are still government decisions. In other instances, individual ministers make decisions within the spheres of authority delegated to them by statute without reference to Cabinet, and yet these decisions are still considered government decisions. Finally, in some instances decisions are made collectively by Cabinet or Cabinet committees.

In order to appreciate the different modes of decision-making within Cabinet government, it is important to recognize that the Cabinet is an executive organization in which formal authority (or informal power) can be distributed in ways that are more or less centralized-decentralized and responsibility (or spheres of influence) can be assigned in ways that are more or less integrated-differentiated. Authority is at the centralized end of the centralization-decentralization continuum when vested in the prime minister, as chief executive, or in a minister, or committee, assigned a corporate responsibility; it is at the decentralized end of the same continuum when vested in the Cabinet as a whole, in one of its policy sector committees, or in individual ministers. Responsibility is at the integrated end of the integrated-differentiated continuum when assumed by the prime minister or assigned to the Cabinet or one of its policy-sector committees; it is at the differentiated end of the same continuum when assigned to a minister, or committee, with corporate

FIGURE   5.1   **Modes of Cabinet Government Decision-Making**

	Integrated	Differentiated
Centralized	Command	Corporate
Decentralized	Collegial	Conglomerate

authority, or to individual ministers. Viewed in this manner, Cabinet government permits four principal modes of decision-making, as illustrated in Figure 5.1.

The first mode, in which the prime minister acts in an essentially unilateral manner, I call the 'command' mode of government decision-making. Such decisions are ones either that prime ministers are expected to take on their own, given their constitutional powers, or that result from prime ministerial initiative. One of the most dramatic examples of the latter occurred in 1978 when Prime Minister Trudeau announced, 'without having consulted any of his senior ministers, including the finance minister', that $2 billion would be cut from federal expenditures.[29] As Mallory notes, the prime minister 'possesses the undoubted right to issue orders in any department without consulting the minister'.[30] Although the prime minister need not consult with ministerial colleagues, it is likely that he or she would first discuss any initiatives with advisers in the Prime Minister's Office (the political office that serves the prime minister as party leader) or the Privy Council Office (the public service office that serves the prime minister as head of government).

This mode of decision-making has always been open to prime ministers, at least with respect to those matters falling within the prime ministerial prerogative. Modern governments, however, have witnessed an increase in such decisions for at least three reasons: the increased independence of the prime minister as leader of the governing party; the increased personalization of the prime minister as party leader in our electoral democracy; and the expansion of governmental complexity and the need for a chief executive who can manage an increasingly complex political executive and state bureaucracy. It ought not to be surprising that prime ministers in Canada, as elsewhere, have been accused of 'presidentializing' their offices.[31] This accusation gained prominence while Trudeau was prime minister, and it has endured. In fact, of course, prime ministers have always possessed more unilateral executive powers than have presidents, as in the United States.

'Prime ministerial government' has also been regarded by some Canadian and British commentators as a deviation from the principle of collective responsibility.[32] Those who hold this view merge the constitutional principle of responsible government and the constitutional status of the prime minister as head of government. The two points should be kept separate, however. As heads of government, prime ministers will at times assert their primacy over Cabinet, either by overruling the majority view of ministers or by intervening in the portfolio responsibilities of individual ministers. No Canadian prime minister, though, has been able to govern primarily in this fashion. By contrast, most, if not all, have engaged in command decision-making. (Nevertheless, it should perhaps be noted that a small number of provincial premiers have made this mode of decision-making the defining characteristic of their governments.) If the Cabinet does not support these unilateral decisions it can revolt, but so long as it does support them they constitute government policy. Cabinet need not even be called upon to approve them.

The command mode of decision-making in the modern context is also characterized by a tendency for prime ministers seeking strategic policy advice to rely as much, if not more, on their personally appointed advisers as on their Cabinet colleagues. As party leaders and heads of government, recent prime ministers have strengthened their advisory agencies, especially those serving in the 'central agencies' of the Prime Minister's Office (PMO) and the Privy Council Office (PCO) respectively. In doing so, prime ministers have lessened their dependence on their Cabinet colleagues and provided themselves with independent sources of advice. It is now clearly the case that the most trusted advisers in these agencies—the people that Campbell and Szablowski call 'superbureaucrats'—have more access to influence with the prime minister than all but the most senior ministers.[33] In large measure this is a consequence of expanding Cabinet size, with many, perhaps most, members chosen primarily for the purpose of representing particular regions, segments of the society, or sectors of the economy. In the context of this kind of Cabinet, it is not surprising that when the prime minister shares strategic leadership it is with an informal 'inner circle' consisting of a few key ministers and PMO-PCO officials.[34]

The second mode is what I call the 'collegial' mode of decision-making. Decision-making of this kind is integrated because it acknowledges the need to co-ordinate the interdependence of different policy areas; it is decentralized in that the decision-making authority is assigned to the full Cabinet, a Cabinet committee representing the different ministers whose responsibilities must be co-ordinated, or, less formally, a group of ministers. The earliest cabinets, as 'chambers of political compensation', acknowledged the need to allow for mutual accommodation of local or regional interests in the distribution of patronage. In the departmentalized Cabinet, this co-ordination took place through the informal mutual adjustments of 'regional ministers'.[35] In the institutionalized Cabinet, such co-ordination was the rationale for the creation of Cabinet committees representing the major policy sectors of the government and involving all ministers in each sector.

To many observers, this mode of decision-making should constitute the norm within Cabinet government. It requires the collective participation of ministers in decisions for which they will be collectively responsible in the House of Commons. It also assumes a measure of collegiality and therefore equality among ministers. Once Cabinet became institutionalized, however, the fiction of all ministers' participating in Cabinet decision-making disappeared.

Under this arrangement, the Cabinet itself became, as we have seen, an organizational system of committees with a hierarchical structure; full Cabinet no longer met as a decision-making executive.[36] Once this system was established, moreover, it became known to ministers (and their officials) that certain influential ministers could obtain the decisions they wanted from quarters other than policy-sector committees: namely, by appealing to the prime minister, the inner circle of the prime minister, a corporate minister such as the deputy prime minister or minister of finance, or the inner executive committee of the Cabinet at the apex of the Cabinet committee system (variously called the Priorities and Planning Committee, the Inner Cabinet or the Operations Committee, the latter being a kind of inner Cabinet of the formal inner Cabinet). It is not surprising that the collegial nature of Cabinet committees has suffered almost the same fate as the full Cabinet. Committees continue to provide for collegial decision-making on matters that require co-ordination through mutual adjustment between ministers with interdependent responsibilities, but they are increasingly recognized as representing only one among several modes of Cabinet government decision-making.

The third mode of Cabinet decision-making I call the 'corporate' mode. It is in one sense an extension of the chief executive's primary responsibilities. Indeed, in the development of Cabinet government under the British constitution, the prime minister's principal corporate function, as *first minister*, was to ensure that Crown (i.e., public) expenditures were co-ordinated between the several ministers who served the Crown as constitutional head of both state and government; the British prime minister, it should be noted, still carries the title of First Lord of the Treasury.[37] If nothing else was co-ordinated across the government before the advent of what we call responsible government, wherein the prime minister rather than the Crown is head of government, there had to be a single budget, for there was only one public purse. Since the establishment of responsible government in the Canadian context, this corporate function has become particularly clear when prime ministers have assumed, or assigned to themselves, such portfolios as finance, external affairs, or federal-provincial relations. (This practice has been even more common among provincial premiers.)

The expansion and growing complexity of the role of the state has required an increasing differentiation of corporate responsibilities and hence the creation of new corporate portfolios and Cabinet committees. Beginning with the portfolios of the ministers of Finance (fiscal policy) and Justice (legal and constitutional policy) and the Cabinet committee called the Treasury Board (expenditure budget and financial administration), this system of corporate responsibilities has extended to, *inter alia*, foreign policy, trade policy, intergovernmental relations, regulatory policy, personnel policy, administrative regulations, political communications, and legislative strategy.

Over time, these corporate responsibilities have been assigned to different configurations of ministerial portfolios and Cabinet committees, but in all cases the aim has been to ensure that the government as a whole is horizontally co-ordinated. In practice this means that the operating responsibilities of ministers whose departments deliver public services or enforce regulations are subject to various forms of standardization from these different corporate centres. These corporate centres do not issue directives to the ministers of operating departments, instructing them what their programs or regulations should be; rather, they seek to co-ordinate their implementation in ways that promote government-wide adherence to corporate government policies. This constitutes a different kind of co-ordination from that practised in collegial decision-making, in which several ministers attempt to adjust their overlapping or interdependent responsibilities. Under corporate policy co-ordination, all departments are expected to adhere to the government's policy, whether it be foreign policy concerning a particular state, an employment-equity policy for government employees, an expenditure-restraint policy concerning travel by officials, or a communications policy relating to the release of certain kinds of government information.

The fact that prime ministers now share their corporate responsibilities with several different ministers and Cabinet committees is reflected in the pecking order in the Cabinet. In the prime minister's inner Cabinet/inner circle, corporate ministers are normally among the most important; along with key officials in the central agencies, in particular the clerk of the Privy Council/secretary to Cabinet (in effect, the prime minister's deputy minister), they are the ones who assist the prime minister in managing the government in an integrated manner. The importance of any particular portfolio or committee varies with political circumstance, but most, if all, such portfolios or committees remain near the centre of the Cabinet universe. The more critical the circumstance, the more influential such ministers become—the most recent example being Joe Clark's role as minister of Constitutional Affairs leading up to the Charlottetown Accord.

In the fourth, 'conglomerate', mode, decision-making is differentiated to the degree that government operations are managed by specialized departments for the government's various public services and regulatory programs, and decentralized to the degree that management responsibilities are delegated to the ministers and their officials in these operating departments. This mode of decision-making conforms to what Dupré calls the 'departmentalized' Cabinet. In this case, the prime minister and Cabinet defer to the individual ministers in their exercise of authority to make what in effect are government decisions. Although individual ministers must accept responsibility for their decisions, or those taken on their behalf by departmental officials, and account for them in the House of Commons, unless they are reversed by the prime minister or Cabinet they stand as government policy and must be defended by the government.

The complexities of managing the modern administrative state, coupled with growing realization of the limits of collegial and even corporate co-ordination, have resulted in a revitalization of this mode of decision-making within Cabinet government in recent years. In Canada and elsewhere, prime ministers and their advisers have recognized that they must delegate more authority to ministers and officials in operating departments if the tasks of government are to be accomplished.[38]

These four modes of decision-making within Cabinet government illustrate the pre-eminence of the position of prime minister. The prime minister is not simply the chair of a collective executive body, but the chief executive. In determining how and to whom formal authority will be delegated, the prime minister decides which of the four modes will be used for strategic decision-making. What constitutes a strategic government decision is also determined by the prime minister. No prime minister, however, can stay abreast of more than a few critical issues at any one time, and prime ministerial interest in particular strategic or critical issues will vary with the individual. These factors will determine the extent to which Cabinet decision-making will be differentiated and decentralized. At the same time, the political dynamics and managerial competence found within a Cabinet, and perhaps the governing party caucus, at any moment will inevitably serve to augment or constrain a prime minister's power. In large measure it is because of these factors that the formal structures of the Cabinet and its portfolios are so often at odds with the informal structures of power—and therefore so often changed—in the constant search for a formal system that might accomplish what is desired while accommodating the realities of ministerial and bureaucratic politics.

CONCLUSION

Prime ministerial leadership is obviously multi-faceted. A prime minister is a head of government under our constitutional structure of responsible government, a party leader under our system of party government, and a chief executive under our system of Cabinet government. The three roles overlap, of course, but in some important respects they are separate. Taken together, they make the prime minister's position in government pre-eminent and the powers of the office immense in relation both to other elected politicians and to the state bureaucracy. In conjunction with the internal practices of the two political parties from which our prime ministers have come, the competitiveness of our major parties under our particular electoral system, and the leadership expectations of the electorate and the mass media, the Canadian prime ministership is the most powerful head-of-government position in the democratic world. Given the contemporary dissatisfaction with political leadership generally, the populist democratic impulse that is now widespread in Canada and other Western democracies among citizens and politicians alike, and the decline and dispersal of political party allegiances among the voting public, one may well question whether it can survive as such for much longer.

NOTES

[1] The definitive study here is W.A. Matheson, *The Prime Minister and the Cabinet* (Toronto: Methuen, 1976).

[2] See Andrew Heard, *Canadian Constitutional Conventions* (Toronto: Oxford University Press, 1991)

[3] Peter Aucoin, 'Regionalism, Party and National Government', in Peter Aucoin, ed., *Party Government and Regional Representation in Canada* (Toronto: University of Toronto Press, 1985), 137-60.

[4] Canada, Royal Commission on Electoral Reform and Party Financing, *Reforming Electoral Democracy* (Ottawa: Minister of Supply and Services, 1991), vol. 1.

[5] Janet Ajzenstat, 'Comment: The Separation of Powers in 1867', *Canadian Journal of Political Science* XX, 1 (March 1987): 118.

[6] Canada, *Constitution Act, 1867*, Section 17.

[7] R.K. Carty, 'Three Canadian Party Systems', in Carty, ed., *Canadian Political Party Systems* (Peterborough, Ont.: Broadview Press, 1992), 563.

[8] Ibid., 563.

[9] Ibid., 564.

[10] Ibid., 574.

[11] Ibid., 577.

[12] Ibid., 580.

[13] Richard Johnston, André Blais, Henry Brady, and Jean Crête, *Letting the People Decide* (Montreal: McGill-Queen's University Press, 1992), 78-111.

[14] Léon Dion, 'The Concept of Political Leadership', *Canadian Journal of Political Science* 1, 1 (March 1968): 2-17.

[15] Paul Thomas, 'Parties and Regional Representation', in Herman Bakvis, ed., *Representation, Integration and Political Parties in Canada* (Toronto: Dundurn, 1991), 179-252.

[16] See Peter Dobell and Byron Berry, 'Anger at the System', *Parliamentary Government* 39 (January 1992).

[17] See C.E.S. Franks, *The Parliament of Canada* (Toronto: University of Toronto Press, 1987). The American model casts legislators as independent representatives who vote issue by issue. While party affiliation tends to divide the floor on a rough left-right spectrum, shifting coalitions and local concerns often supersede loyalty to party.

[18] See Report of Special Committee on Reform of the House of Commons (McGrath Committee), June 1985.

[19] Dion, 'The Concept of Political Leadership', 6.

[20] See Herman Bakvis, *Regional Ministers: Power and Influence in the Canadian Cabinet* (Toronto: University of Toronto Press, 1991).

[21] It should be noted that Prime Minister Campbell reduced her Cabinet to 24 ministers.

[22] Colin Campbell, 'Cabinet Committees in Canada: Pressures and Dysfunctions Stemming from the Representational Imperative', in Thomas T. Mackie and Brian W. Hogwood, eds, *Unlocking the Cabinet: Cabinet Structures in Comparative Perspective* (London: Sage, 1985), 61-85.

[23] See J.R. Mallory, 'Cabinets and Councils in Canada', *Public Law* 2 (Autumn 1957): 231-51. It is worth noting that Prime Minister Chrétien has adopted a two-tier system in his Cabinet.

[24] J. Stefan Dupré, 'The Workability of Executive Federalism in Canada', in Herman Bakvis and William Chandler, eds, *Federalism and the Role of the State* (Toronto: University of Toronto Press, 1987), 238.

[25] Gordon Stewart, *The Origins of Canadian Politics* (Vancouver: University of British Columbia Press, 1986).

[26] Dupré, 'Workability'.

[27] Ibid.

[28] Peter Aucoin, 'Organizational Change in the Machinery of the Canadian Government: From Rational Management to Brokerage Politics', *Canadian Journal of Political Science* XIX, 1 (March 1986) and G. Bruce Doern and Richard Phidd, *Canadian Public Policy: Ideas, Structure and Process*, 2nd ed. (Scarborough, Ont.: Nelson, 1992).

[29] Donald Savoie, *The Politics of Public Spending in Canada* (Toronto: University of Toronto Press, 1990), 153.

[30] J.R. Mallory, *The Structure of Canadian Government*, rev. ed. (Toronto: Gage, 1984), 93.

[31] See, for example, Denis Smith, 'President and Parliament: The Transformation of Parliamen-

tary Government in Canada', in Thomas Hockin, ed., *Apex of Power*, second ed. (Scarborough, Ont.: Prentice-Hall, 1977), 308-25.

[32] See George W. Jones, 'Presidentialization in a Parliamentary System?', in Colin Campbell, S.J. and Margaret Jane Wyszomirski, eds, *Executive Leadership in Anglo-American Systems* (Pittsburgh: University of Pittsburgh Press, 1991), 111-38.

[33] Colin Campbell and George Szablowski, *The Superbureaucrats: Structure and Behaviour in Central Agencies* (Toronto: Macmillan, 1979).

[34] Peter Aucoin, 'Cabinet Government in Canada: Corporate Management of a Confederal Executive', in Campbell and Wyszomirski, *Executive Leadership*, 139-60.

[35] Bakvis, *Regional Ministers*.

[36] See Herman Bakvis and David MacDonald, 'The Canadian Cabinet: Organization, Decision-Rules and Policy Impact', in Michael M. Atkinson, ed., *Governing Canada: Institutions and Public Policy* (Toronto: Harcourt Brace Jovanovich, 1993), 47-80.

[37] Matheson, *The Prime Minister*, 3.

[38] Peter Aucoin, 'Administrative Reform in Public Management: Paradigms, Principles, Paradoxes and Pendulums', *Governance* 3, 2 (April 1990): 115-37.

GOVERNING   MANITOBA

Reflections   of   a   Premier

—■—

Howard   R.   Pawley

MY PATH TO LEADERSHIP

My earliest political recollections were lively discussions around the family kitchen table. Later, I became active in student politics, as leader of the United College (now University of Winnipeg) CCF Club, and in 1958 I was elected chair of the Manitoba CCF following a successful challenge to the party's establishment. Eventually elected to the Manitoba Legislature in 1969 under the leadership of Ed Schreyer, I was appointed first minister of Municipal Affairs and Government Services, and then Attorney General. In those early years, few would have thought I had any leadership aspirations; I was considered too self-effacing, bookish, and reluctant to seek the media limelight. However, after two terms in Cabinet I was able to succeed Ed Schreyer as party leader.

Both of those Cabinet portfolios helped to promote my career. It was generally acknowledged that my handling of Municipal Affairs enhanced the NDP's popularity in some of the pivotal rural areas in the south of the province, where the party's political base is considerably weaker than in the north and urban centres. The Union of Manitoba Municipalities, a group of aging conservative-minded politicians, frequently applauded my relationship with them, and long after I had assumed the mantle of the Attorney-General, they successfully lobbied the premier for my continuance in the Municipal Affairs portfolio as well.

My baptism by fire had occurred early in the government's mandate, when as minister of Municipal Affairs I piloted a contentious bill concerning public auto insurance through a minority legislature. Despite massive protests, the bill was enacted and implemented in time to contribute substantially to our re-election in 1973, as well as to my future leadership aspirations. It was as Attorney-General, however, when I produced what was at the time considered to be virtually the most progressive family law in Canada, that I first contemplated the prospects for a leadership bid, whenever Ed Schreyer should step down.

Schreyer's sudden appointment to Rideau Hall in December 1978, the year following our election loss, shook the NDP caucus to its foundation. While his charisma had been crucial to our party's success, the election débâcle of 1977 resulted in our government's defeat and devastated the party's finances, membership, and organization. Most assumed we would be out of power for at least a decade, as Sterling Lyon's Conservatives had taken office with the highest popular vote ever received by a Manitoba party in the twentieth century; moreover, no Manitoba government had ever been defeated after only one term.

Some members would have preferred an interim leader who would not be a candidate for the vacant leadership position. However, that idea met strong caucus resistance, and the proposed candidate, the former Finance minister, Saul Cherniack, felt compelled to withdraw. Sydney Green, chief opponent of the idea, saw the effort as a manipulative attempt to focus on leadership image rather than on policy. Green had run twice for the leadership of the party, and while he was undoubtedly a master legislator, an eloquent orator, and one who never shirked his share of the ministerial load, he was perceived as too arrogant.

Other caucus members, though critical of the manoeuvring of the party's hierarchy, supported my candidacy. The caucus vote was close (Pawley 10, Green 8, Cherniack 3) but my win there unquestionably helped me to win on the first ballot at the convention nine months later.

The process of rebuilding the party commenced immediately after the caucus vote, despite two impediments. The first was the shadow of Ed Schreyer, from which I had to emerge with my own credentials or else we would be condemned to the opposition benches. The second was the degree of disarray in a party that was still reeling from electoral defeat and the departure of a highly popular leader. To win the next election, we needed an efficient organization, quality candidates, and a credible program.

An early reversal occurred when Green, after failing to win re-election to the national party's executive, left to form the Progressive Party. As several former members of the Schreyer Cabinet followed Green to the ranks of this new party and other MLAs announced their intention to retire, the legislative caucus was seriously weakened.[1]

In 1979, the resources available to the leader of the Manitoba Opposition were quite limited, consisting of only a secretary and assistant. But former Saskatchewan premier and NDP federal leader Tommy Douglas offered valuable advice on how to offset this deficiency: 'Form policy committees with Caucus members and prospective candidates, blitz the province and build the organization at the rank and file level, as you would tend a garden.' For the next three years I travelled extensively, staying not in hotels but with party members. Instead of flying I travelled by car to meetings that dragged on late into the night, waking early the next day to move on to the next town. This odyssey received useful media attention, but its principal aim was organizational. While good legislative performance and a well-devised communication plan are both important, to ensure success a leader must maintain close contact with the party's rank and file members. Such contact is probably even more imperative for the NDP than for other political parties, because the media attention it receives is generally less than positive.

All of this activity, which helped to triple the party's membership, eliminate its huge debt, and encourage hard-fought nomination battles, was not readily apparent to the overly confident Lyon government, which perceived the Opposition as weak and fragmented. The rebuilding process culminated on election day, 17 November 1981, when while travelling to the election centre and listening to the results on the car radio, an aide suddenly turned to me and addressed me as Mr Premier. The electorate had ignored Premier Lyon's charges that the NDP was the 'no damn progress Party' and that Manitobans feared more than any other the words, 'Premier Howard Pawley'. At the victory celebrations, one excited party supporter had amended a campaign sign with the original words 'Pawley for Premier' to read 'Pawley is Premier'. The governance of the province was now my responsibility.

That sobering thought dominated the next few days. Could we keep the promises we had made? Could the high expectations generated during the election campaign be met? Would I soon find myself needing to explain why they could not? More specifically, I had to decide the size and membership of both the Cabinet and the Premier's Office.

These appointments would provide an early signal of the new government's direction. My own role as leader would now include dealing with the inevitable tensions within the party while balancing its expectations with the public's customary caution and resistance to change. The following pages will indicate some of my responses to these questions during nearly seven years as premier and will examine various facets of the leader's role.

THE PREMIER AS PARTY LEADER

The source of any premier's power is his or her leadership of a political party. To achieve and to maintain electoral success, a leader must pay close attention to his or her party's needs, building a powerful organizational structure for electoral purposes while maintaining a common vision.

Leslie A. Pal's comments apply to a premier as well as a prime minister:

> The party is partisan while the government is in the broad public interest. The leader can only influence the party, whereas he may command the government. Party loyalty is to his person, government loyalty is to his position. The party is most alive during elections. The government is most alive between them. The leader is elected by the party but the government is elected by the people.[2]

Having moved through various levels of responsibility in the NDP, I required no persuasion about the critical role of the party in the political process. Unlike the older parties, the NDP encourages its rank-and-file members to play an active role in policy development.

In Manitoba, regular conventions are held and resolutions approved that reflect the party's policies and its vision, and these are not to be trifled with. At regular executive and council meetings, the leader is expected to respond to complaints that may be substantial — for example, why some particular legislation has not been expedited — or more personal, such as expressions of dissatisfaction with the behaviour of a particular minister. Although these discussions are not necessarily pleasant, they are indispensable for identifying problems, and will occasionally bring new ideas and potential solutions to the attention of the leader; they also provide an opportunity to explain the actions of the government and, most critically, to test the leader's perceptions against those of party activists.

To keep abreast of party activities, as leader I held monthly consultations with the party's secretary and president, and schedules and itineraries were devised to keep me in regular contact with the party's membership. At the same time, party membership must be kept abreast of government and party developments if they are to maintain the informed perspective and high morale required to provide effective electoral support for the party. Fostering that level of readiness is the ultimate responsibility of the leader, who must also ensure that the party's executive, staff, and advisers maintain the necessary organizational strength. Recruitment of new members and fund-raising activities are especially important.

Finally, the leader must always share with the party a vision that will instil confidence in the direction that he or she is taking. Sometimes discord may arise, but vital information must be shared, and debate encouraged when necessary. Tensions between the party and government frequently simmer, but as party leader one must never forget that the party is a voluntary organization, made up of individuals with their own minds, and that it is absolutely essential for electoral success.

THE PREMIER AND CAUCUS

To promote the objectives of the government, the premier must enjoy the confidence and the support of the caucus. And, since the premier, as an elected member of the Legislative Assembly, is a member of that caucus, he or she must function at caucus meetings as a facilitator rather than a director. To ensure that each one feels indispensable to the team—no mean feat with backbench members who are often heckled by the opposition for behaving as little more than the leader's 'trained seals'— all caucus members must be encouraged to participate in the decision-making processes of the government: for example, by serving on advisory committees to ministers.

One frequent complaint that a leader must deal with arises when a member discovers that the government has undertaken some important initiative pertaining to his or her constituency without due consultation. A member who has not been consulted will justifiably see such an omission as a lost opportunity to gain a little credit for influencing the accomplishment.

Sometimes tension emerges because of members' expectations for career advancement. On one occasion a member threatened to quit unless a Cabinet post was awarded; I had no feasible alternative but to resist the pressure, and the member left to sit as an independent. On another occasion, the contents of a member's written demand for a Cabinet post appeared mysteriously in the *Winnipeg Sun*. The request was denied, and the member later deserted the government on a confidence vote that culminated in the government's defeat in 1988.[3] Despite the possibility of such repercussions, no Cabinet appointment can be made under such circumstances unless the leader is prepared to set off a free-for-all among ambitious caucus members. To accede to such demands for promotion would risk a serious erosion of caucus morale, not to mention Cabinet competence, as less aggressive but more able members could be passed over.

The premier's tour schedule should include annual visits to all the constituencies held by his or her party. Keeping informed of constituency priorities can help to ward off the kind of unanticipated revelations that can emerge less than fortuitously during an election campaign. If possible, the leader should be accompanied on such occasions by the constituency's member, to ensure his or her visibility.

Contemporary politics insists upon a more representative array of candidates to create a caucus that reflects the demography of the general population. Thus the Manitoba NDP made serious efforts to recruit more women, aboriginal people, and visible minorities, not only for electoral purposes but also to improve the process of policy development by providing better representation of diverse groups.

THE PREMIER AND CABINET

Aspiring premiers should keep in mind this observation by George Cadbury:

> (An) important necessity . . . is the creation of Cabinet solidarity and the development of a Cabinet personality above individual Ministers who, while running their departments, will be asked as Cabinet Ministers to create an overall entity with a view above individual departmental needs.[4]

One of the most difficult and complex tasks confronting a premier, not only upon assuming office but subsequently, is the appointing or shuffling of Cabinet personnel. The consequences of a bad decision can take almost forever to undo. Cabinet appointees are frequently chosen from the ranks of successful opposition critics, but the people so appointed may be unsuited for parallel roles in a new government. Former Premier Schreyer discovered this with Joe Borowski, a populist hero in opposition, who by temperament was ill suited for government. More recently in Ontario, Peter Kormos, an effective critic of automobile insurance in opposition, did not survive long in the Rae Cabinet.

There is always the danger of appointing somebody to Cabinet who is too much the individualist and too little the team player. The extreme individualist may become preoccupied with promoting a pet cause. Among the problems that Premier Schreyer faced with Borowski was the latter's vigorous single-minded campaign, while a minister, against pornography and abortion.

A Cabinet should not only reflect various ideological points of view within the party, but maintain a balance among those with regional, ethnic and gender qualifications. Above all, it should demonstrate competence. At the same time consideration must be given to loyalty and seniority. A premier restricted to elected members is, of course, hindered by the fact that the group is usually not fully representative of the general population.

In 1981, three of the five women elected in Manitoba were appointed to Cabinet, a modest representation compared to some provincial cabinets in the 1990s, but nonetheless a major improvement over earlier years. In 1986, Elijah Harper became the first Treaty Indian ever appointed to Cabinet, joining an ethnic mix reflecting the province's population, including members with Ukrainian, Jewish, Mennonite, German, French-Canadian, Polish, and Anglo-Saxon roots.

The Cabinet should include people who complement the premier's own strengths and weaknesses. In my case that meant having colleagues to whom I could delegate project management duties while I concentrated on developing vision and ensuring co-ordination. Because of the egos involved and the jealousies that are bound to arise, a leader must assign such responsibilities in a very formal, straightforward, and consensual manner at the beginning of the government's term. The entire Cabinet must be aware of why particular delegations of authority are necessary and who is responsible for what activities.

Among the Premier's duties are the following: to control the Cabinet agenda; to shape Cabinet decisions; to supervise functioning of colleagues' departments; to co-ordinate and arbitrate the executive decision-making process; and to encourage cohesion and a sense of purpose among all Cabinet members.

Although the premier is often referred to as 'first among equals', such an interpretation doesn't suitably describe the office, since in the political sense none is the premier's equal. Nevertheless, it is wrong to assume that a first minister reigns in unquestioned supremacy. For example, although a premier may occasionally declare a consensus in favour of his or her position even when a majority of Cabinet colleagues disagree, such occasions must be rare if the leader's support is not to erode.

The first minister must strike a delicate balance between too little and too much delegation of responsibilities. Too little delegation may enhance the appearance of the premier's competence while creating a perception of Cabinet as weak and ineffective.

This was part of the reason for the defeat of the Schreyer administration in 1977, despite the premier's personal popularity.

On the other hand, substantial central direction is crucial, or the government may appear to lack focus. Even if ministers must sometimes pursue directions that seem at odds with those of their colleagues, they must always appear fully committed to the government's main thrust. Ministers must promote the government's general policies, not just their own specific goals.

It was my experience that a few ministers would often attempt to do end runs on procedures or rules by seeking approval for various policies from other ministers. Diligence must be exercised in refusing such attempts, or collective collegiality suffers. Log-rolling between ministers must be discouraged, especially during the preparation of the government's annual estimates of expenditures, when different ministers will often collude to protect each other's pet projects, sometimes to the detriment of overall objectives. A minister must remove the departmental hat on entering the Cabinet room so that the interests of the government as a whole take precedence. In every Cabinet, a few ministers tend to monopolize the discussions, frequently hindering possibly more useful contributions from more passive ministers. Consequently a first minister must encourage the input of all those around the Cabinet table.

Generally it is better during crucial Cabinet discussions for a premier to defer personal comment until various ministers have offered theirs, so that his or her comments do not prematurely shape the direction of the discussion. In addition, to enhance collegiality, various techniques must sometimes be used during Cabinet meetings to permit face-saving on the part of a minister who appears to be losing support. Sometimes an issue can be re-cast or put in a wider context so that the decision is not seen as a win-lose situation; in other cases the discussion may be deferred until a later time, in order to permit a consensus to form.

THE PREMIER AND THE PUBLIC

The premier speaks for the entire provincial community and is the human personification of the government. Cabinet ministers generally have limited profiles or public acceptance and are perceived as littler more than a supporting cast. The political focus is on the premier, who must be seen as active and aggressive on key issues and initiatives. The major issues must be carefully selected and few in number so as to not diminish their impact. Explaining these major themes to the public is the premier's responsibility. It will help to create a positive image for the premier if he or she can be seen as the source of good news, and any bad news can be attributed to the minister involved.

While a decentralized, group-consensus approach is generally necessary for effective administration, it is not effective in marketing a government. Especially when issues are contentious or difficult, the premier must demonstrate that he or she is in firm control. Thus in the mid-1980s I made all major economic announcements, although the minister responsible was usually present; examples included the initiation of economic or job-related projects such as the launching of the massive hydro-electric project in northern Manitoba. That the premier should be the only one to speak for the government is based upon strategic considerations. In Manitoba, we discovered the necessity of this principle after the disastrous effort to sell the controversial French-language constitutional amendments in the early 1980s, when, try as we might, we were unable to convince the public of the wisdom of our efforts. As a result, the proposals were withdrawn from the Legislature, and it became necessary to restrict official comments on this issue to those made by myself as premier.

Such a consistent and focused approach was fundamental to our success in achieving re-election in 1986, since the French-language debate had aroused the most emotional controversy I had ever witnessed. Our party dipped to record low levels of popular support at the height of this battle, but was re-elected in 1986 after devising and following a plan of action that focused on the economy for the remainder of our mandate.

Finally, identifying with ordinary people who enjoy public empathy does much for a leader's image. On one occasion, I intervened with the Manitoba Telephone System to assist an unemployed carpenter who had been charged business rates by the system. On another occasion, my personal intervention was required to prevent a government department from continuing the deplorable practice of allowing native children to be sent to other parts of Canada and the United States for adoption by non-aboriginal parents. Such interventions to rectify social injustices are personally satisfying as well as beneficial for a leader's image.

A premier must avoid casual remarks that could be taken out of context and blown up to inflict damage. Georgette Gagnon and Dan Rath, in *Not Without Cause*, tell of an anti-poverty protester confronting former Ontario Premier David Peterson during the 1990 election campaign. Premier Peterson responded: 'Someday you will grow up and find a responsible job.' Although the protestor was known as a professional troublemaker and had lost his credibility with the local media, this did not prevent the television reporters from seizing upon the exchange as one of the highlights of the campaign. As Gagnon and Rath write: '"Get a job" was riveting television. The clip became one of the most widely repeated of the campaign, showing up on the news summaries, weekly reports and campaign features until election day.'[5] A similar incident occurred in Manitoba when former Premier Sterling Lyon uttered from his Legislative seat an off-hand remark to the effect that his Conservatives were 'good breeders' during a stormy debate over his government's repeal of the Schreyer government's family law legislation. His perceived insensitivity not only aroused the anger of the feminist community but contributed to a negative image of his government in general.

Although selling the government to the public depends largely on the leader, it also requires the active participation of the entire team, including the Cabinet and caucus as well as rank-and-file party members, if the result is to be effective.

THE PREMIER'S OFFICE

Upon becoming Premier, I soon understood the importance of an effective office staff. In addition to the clerk of the Executive Council, principal secretary, and media secretary, the staff positions that must be competently filled generally include the following:

1. a speech writer capable of reflecting the premier's style and personality;
2. an executive assistant to brief the premier, serve as the liaison with other ministers and caucus, and provide staff support at outside engagements and on trips and deal with case files that can't be forwarded elsewhere for resolution;
3. a correspondence secretary with good writing ability and some administrative skills, who knows when a form letter can be used and when it can't, and understands that rapid turnaround is essential in responding to correspondence from the public;
4. a tour co-ordinator to organizes all the premier's outside engagements and ward off last-minute glitches;
5. a policy unit staffed by individuals conscious of the need for the government to have and remain true to a clearly articulated plan of action; and
6. an outreach co-ordinator to ensure contact with all segments of the population.

The pressure on this group of aides is enormous: their hours are long, and even their holidays may be interrupted. Since political staff enjoy no job security, they must be very rare and committed individuals who are prepared to run the same risks as their leader.

The strengths or weaknesses of the premier must be taken into consideration in the organization of the Premier's Office, which must be staffed by effective administrators —not mere hangers-on. If the leader pays little attention to detail, aides must pay a lot. If the leader lacks a policy orientation, the staff should have an intellectual base. If the leader has been aloof from party activists, then assistants with a detailed familiarity with the party are required.

The premier's schedule is intense. There is normally a morning briefing with the clerk of Council, principal secretary, and media secretary, at which planning is done. Meetings will also be required with party officials or Cabinet ministers. In addition, when the Assembly is in session there is the Question Period, in which the Premier must play a pivotal role; hence briefing is critical. There are meetings of Cabinet and key committees. There is correspondence—an excellent source of information—to be examined and answered. There are ribbon-cutting or sod-turning ceremonies to attend, and special delegations—municipal associations, labour organizations, business groups— to be received. On top of all this, there are ever-increasing demands for the premier's presence at intergovernmental conferences or trade missions outside Canada.

In conclusion, the manner in which the Office supports the premier will reflect on the latter and affect future prospects of success. If letters are constantly mislaid, appointments missed, or tour details not pinned down, the premier's public image will suffer.

THE PREMIER AND DEPUTY MINISTERS

Deputy ministers—the administrative heads of departments—are fundamental to the effective delivery of the government's policies and programs. The quality of the appointments to these senior administrators therefore have a crucial impact on the capacity of the premier and Cabinet to carry out their initiatives. In Manitoba, the choice of new deputy ministers normally takes place in an open competition, with the premier and relevant minister present during the interviews of those who make the short list. Dismissals of deputy ministers take place only with the premier's blessing.

After the defeat of the Schreyer administration in 1977, the new premier, Sterling Lyon, dismissed three deputy ministers several days before formally taking office. This badly handled incident stained the new government's image. Similarly, former British Columbia Premier Bill Vander Zalm, through his principal secretary, David Poole, tended to intervene in the operations of various government departments and their deputies, without appropriate consultation with the ministers involved. He once went so far as to shuffle all his deputy ministers without giving his ministers a chance to select the deputies they wanted.[6]

Deputy ministers with political and administrative skill will generally survive government transitions. Meetings between the premier and the deputies, at which deputies are informed of major government directions, are held once or twice a year. My first such meeting, shortly after assuming government, was essential to dissipate the usual apprehension characteristic of all transitions. The deputy ministers were reassured of their roles in the new administration, and in turn I gained greater confidence in their collective loyalty.

THE PREMIER AND CENTRAL AGENCIES

If necessary, a premier may restructure the government's central agencies and their decision-making processes so that they better reflect his or her personality and intentions. When former Premier Ed Schreyer, for example, established a Planning and Priorities Committee of Cabinet, with a supporting secretariat, he made it clear to the line departments, as well as the public, that an activist, policy-orientated government was in charge.

My administration, elected at a time in the early 1980s when the predominant necessity was to stimulate the economy, established a 'Jobs Fund' Committee of Cabinet included the key ministers responsible for the economic portfolios — Energy, Economic Development, and Finance — with myself as chair. Its function was to initiate job-related projects that needed to be launched expeditiously, without being delayed by the normal bureaucratic procedures. It helped significantly in getting Manitoba through the recession of the early 1980s.

Premiers Lyon and Filmon, by contrast, favoured powerful Treasury Board Committees of Cabinet, reflecting their emphasis on central control of the deficit.

THE PREMIER AND THE MEDIA

Successful political leaders have always mastered the skills associated with the principal mass media of the day. Alberta's Premier Bill Aberhart had unquestioned mastery of the radio broadcast, and Tommy Douglas's oratorical skills provided some of the best entertainment available in the post-World War Two era in Saskatchewan. Current leaders must be telegenic and expert at communicating complex ideas in fifteen-second sound bites.

Generally, if a leader has good contacts with the media, an opportunity exists to set the tone or mood for the government's style. The Premier's Office is often asked to provide clarification of various news stories. In addition, friendly relations or contacts established in opposition often continue during the early part of the mandate. To build on these strengths, we had a director of communications charged with overall responsibilities for public relations and a director of press relations with special responsibility for media relations. They were the ones who planned regular press conferences — a vast improvement over the impromptu scrums in the Legislative corridor that often generate ill-considered comments. While selective leaks may sometimes be undertaken through the Premier's Office, it was my experience that this practice caused alienation, and that the excluded media would take an anti-government stance on whatever issue was involved.

Recent trends in the media make it more difficult to convey information to the public. Little coverage, if any, is devoted to legislative debates. Fine oratorical flourishes pass unnoticed, and detailed analyses of estimates are ignored. Hard news is being replaced by 'soft copy'. For example, in a recent Manitoba Legislative session, little print coverage was given to the speeches of either Premier Filmon or Opposition Leader Gary Doer during the traditional debates on the Throne Speech and Budget Address. The same trend exists elsewhere in Canada. Regrettably, once the daily question period with its inevitable media scrum ends, the media show little interest in providing additional coverage.

These recent developments compel leaders to re-evaluate their means of communication. The results have been more direct mailings, open-line programs, direct advertising, and province-wide bus tours, at the expense of substantial debate.

THE PREMIER AND INTEREST GROUPS

The role of interest groups in policy-making has recently increased in importance, often eclipsing that of political parties. The ear of the premier — and sometimes the Opposition leader — is indispensable to interest groups. Frequently a premier must deal with large and powerful interest groups, who are strongly opposed to the government's policies.

While a premier must ensure sensitivity towards the array of interest groups, any suggestion that the office is their captive will bring a backlash from the public at large, diminishing a premier's credibility. This may be a particular danger for a New Democratic government if it appears to be too closely tied to the labour movement. On the other hand, the appearance of an overly snug relationship with the business community may threaten the NDP's traditional support.

I soon discovered that a premier cannot take any interest group, friend or enemy, for granted. I prepared a list of such groups describing where each might be expected to support or oppose policy. In addition, I sought to understand their leadership, their basic concerns, and, most important, whether they really represented those they claimed to lead and in the numbers of which they invariably boasted.

THE PREMIER AND THE LEGISLATURE

Contemporary premiers spend little time in the Legislative Assembly apart from the daily question periods and perhaps four or five major speeches during a session: the rest of the time they spend attending to more pressing demands. In the Assembly, the premier should appear as a statesman, standing above the often unruly and undisciplined fray and avoiding the offhand remarks that can do irreparable damage.

In confronting the opposition, the premier's attitude should be direct but courteous. Leaders must never forget that the public expects forceful, impassioned, but, above all else, statesmanlike behaviour.

THE PREMIER AND FEDERAL-PROVINCIAL AND INTERNATIONAL RELATIONS

A decade or so ago, the majority of provinces had separate ministries of intergovernmental relations. Now most premiers hold such responsibilities themselves and maintain an intergovernmental affairs secretariat in the Executive Council with its own staff. Thus it is imperative that the first minister stay abreast of all major developments in the federal-provincial field so that he or she can act as the key spokesperson for the province on all major issues. To maximize the impact of issues over which conflict occurs with the federal government, they should be relatively few in number and limited to areas in which the premier and provincial government enjoy credibility. To clash with the federal government in too many areas at one time can be counterproductive.

Sometimes a premier has little chance of success in reversing a federal government decision. One example occurred when I led a delegation of politicians, labour representatives and business leaders to Ottawa to protest and demand reconsideration of the awarding of the billion-dollar CF-18 maintenance contract to Canadair of Montreal rather than Bristol Aerospace of Winnipeg, whose bid was both lower and technically superior. I knew that the intervention would probably not change anything, but the entire provincial community demanded action, however futile. A clear objection had to be delivered to Prime Minister Mulroney, and although no constructive results were achieved, as premier I was seen as protecting the provincial interest when regional alienation had reached a boiling point. Such conflicts must always be structured so that the premier can stand up for the province without being seen as petty or divisive.[7]

Not all conflicts are so clear-cut. The endless federal-provincial wrangling on the constitutional front has jeopardized the political fortunes of many provincial premiers, as at times the provincial interest must be weighed against the national interest. The role of statesman is not always appreciated especially when endless debates appear to detract from more pressing issues. Seven of the ten premiers who were signatories to the Meech Lake Constitutional Accord either did not seek or failed to gain re-election.

Besides federal-provincial relations, premiers must sell their provinces on a global scale. Trade missions increase as premiers seek out new markets and increased trade for their provinces' products. In addition, in this period of heavy borrowing from offshore financial markets, a premier often plays a joint role with the minister of Finance in securing monies.

Finally, recent developments in relations between the United States and Canada have necessitated more joint conferences with US governors. While premier of Manitoba, I also initiated substantial contact with the governors of North and South Dakota, Minnesota, Iowa, and Nebraska, on issues such as hydro exports, the environment, and impediments to Manitoba's trade (for example, the export of hogs). In addition, of course, a steady stream of visits from ambassadors and consuls-general from foreign states demand a premier's attention.

CONCLUSION

In *The Prince*, Machiavelli refers to the leader as being subject to two forces: 'virtue', which is a combination of 'skill and courage', and 'fortune', which is an element of luck over which one may have no control. Although the general proposition is probably true, I would replace the word 'luck' with 'circumstances'. Among the circumstantial factors that may either constrain or provide opportunities for leadership are the existing economic climate; the demands on the social system and the tax system's capacity to finance them; the political base, including the interest groups and key decision-makers in the governing party and the extent of their influence upon the government; the pressure on the governing party from its own members as well as the opposition; and the government's power base within the Legislature, particularly its numerical position. Circumstances, then, in large part shape the manner in which the leader performs. With luck, the circumstances of the day will favour the leader's own inclinations. For instance, a visionary leader will be most appropriate during times of expansion or innovation, while a pragmatic leader will be better suited to lead in a period when programs must be cut back and expectations dampened. Thus a person who is an excellent leader in one environment may not do so well in another.

A leader must adjust his or her own style of leadership to suit the circumstances of the day. In some cases it may even be advisable to deliberately present a contrast to the leadership style of one's predecessor in office. (In my own case, if a consensual approach had not been my natural style, it would still have been a wise choice to counter the rather patrician, uncompromising style of Sterling Lyon.) One must then identify one's own strengths and weaknesses with regard to the challenges ahead and build a team accordingly. A premier cannot do it alone: he or she must be supported by a group of trusted individuals who are loyal not only to the leader personally but, more important, to the objectives of the party and to the government as a whole.

In conclusion, a premier must first lead the Cabinet as a team, then the government caucus, then the party, and, finally, the general public. To exercise leadership effectively, he or she must be able to inspire people to take action; to respond to circumstances; to shape compromise within a specific set of principles; to take a stand that reflects the best aspirations of a society, despite opposition; and to bring out the best in the team.

Finally, perhaps the most valuable attribute for a political leader, with respect both to the public and to his or her team, is the ability to exercise power through persuasion — and to do so without making it too obvious to people that they are being persuaded.

NOTES

[1] Green's case was not unique. Manitoba New Democrats have tended to be fractious, and when individuals have felt slighted, they have picked up and left, often noisily. Joe Borowski and Jean Allard quit the Schreyer government. Green, Ben Hanuschak, and Bud Boyce departed from the NDP when it was in Opposition. Henry Carroll, Russell Doern and Jim Walding quit the Pawley government, and Elijah Harper left the opposition NDP in 1993 to join the federal Liberal party.

[2] Leslie A. Pal and David Taras, *Prime Ministers and Premiers* (Scarborough, Ont.: Prentice-Hall, 1991), 93.

[3] On 8 March 1988, without notice, backbench NDP MLA Jim Walding voted with the Opposition on the annual budget.

[4] Manitoba, Provincial Archives, 'Notes on the Manitoba Situation' prepared by G.W. Cadbury, 1969; ref. p 941F 1969-76.

[5] Georgette Gagnon and Dan Rath, *Not Without Cause: A Cautionary Tale for Voters Everywhere* (Toronto: Harper Collins, 1991), 239-40.

[6] Gary Mason and Keith Baldrey, *Fantasyland — Inside the Reign of Bill Vander Zalm* (Toronto-Montreal: McGraw-Hill Ryerson, 1989).

[7] For background, see Robert M. Campbell and Leslie A. Pal, *The Real Worlds of Canadian Politics*, 1st ed. (Peterborough, Ont.: Broadview Press, 1989), 19-52, which explains the role of a premier in such circumstances.

CHAPTER SEVEN

CABINET MINISTERS

Leaders or Followers?

——

Herman Bakvis

Are federal Cabinet ministers leaders or followers? On the surface the answer seems obvious: they are both. On the one hand, they are expected to provide direction to the portfolios for which they are responsible, to participate in the collective leadership of the government's activities, and to help lead the party in Parliament and into electoral battle. On the other, they are expected to heed the prime minister's wishes with respect to government policy, the major tenets of party policy, and the collective decisions of Cabinet or Cabinet committees. This is the standard wisdom according to many textbooks on Cabinet government.[1]

Expectations are one thing, however; actual practice may be quite different. Many would argue that present-day Cabinet ministers in Canada lack both the public visibility (particularly in light of the prominence of the prime minister) and the capacity to manage complex issues that would enable them to provide much in the way of leadership to either their political party, their portfolios, or the country as a whole. By default, therefore, it might be suggested that in the present era ministers have become primarily followers rather than leaders.

It is the task of this chapter to assess the reality of the roles played by Cabinet ministers today as measured against expectations. Ministerial performance will be assessed under four headings: as departmental leaders, as members of Cabinet, as parliamentary and party leaders, and as public leaders. These four categories are based loosely on those used in Bruce Headey's classic study of British Cabinet ministers.[2] Before beginning discussion of the specific roles of ministers it may be useful to outline briefly the basic structure and constitutional standing of the Canadian Cabinet, as well as the constraints facing ministers in their efforts to exercise leadership in different settings.

THE CABINET: ORIGINS AND STRUCTURE

The federal Cabinet as we know it had its origins in the executive councils of the pre-Confederation period and British parliamentary government. The arrival of responsible government, first in Nova Scotia and then in the other British North American colonies, helped to establish two important constitutional conventions: first, that the governor general acts only on the advice of the 'Queen's Privy Council' and, second, that this council must secure and continue to enjoy the confidence of Parliament. In practical terms this means that the group of individuals sworn as members of Her Majesty's Privy Council to serve in a particular ministry must have the confidence of a majority of members in the House of Commons. Constitutional convention also requires that ministers be collectively and individually answerable to the House on matters for which they are responsible and, further, that they be drawn mainly from the elected lower House.[3]

The presence of organized political parties in Parliament, the election of members of Parliament on the basis of party labels, and strict party discipline within the House have made the term 'party government' interchangeable with 'Cabinet government'. A disciplined government party in the House means that, in contrast to the American congressional system, the Canadian system puts the political executive in firm control of the legislative agenda and the activities of the various government departments. Most students of Cabinet government have stressed that the Westminster model provides the ideal setting for the exercise of strong executive leadership: a relatively small body that reaches decisions in secret, that has full command over the levers of executive power vis-à-vis the bureaucracy, and that controls the legislative agenda.[4]

In the Canadian case, however, important qualifications need to be made. While the Cabinet deliberates in secret and makes effective use of party discipline to push through its agenda, it is certainly not a small body. Even at the reduced membership level of 35 at the end of the Mulroney period, the Canadian Cabinet was substantially larger than the 20-member British and 16-member Australian cabinets. No formal distinction is made between inner and outer cabinets, as in Britain; but clearly some ministers are much closer than others to the prime minister and enjoy greater authority. The real guide to power within the Canadian Cabinet is found in the structure and composition of Cabinet committees. Of the eleven committees in 1993, the 23-member Priorities and Planning Committee (P&P) came closest to constituting an inner Cabinet. The most powerful, however, was the Operations committee, a select group of the twelve most powerful ministers, which served as gatekeeper for P&P, and had considerable influence over its agenda. Significantly, in the Mulroney Cabinet the chair of this committee was *not* the prime minister.

Currently there are two types of Cabinet ministers: those formally in charge of one or more portfolios, and 'ministers of state to assist'. The last are the so-called 'junior ministers', who often have their own specific areas of responsibility (such as Seniors or Youth), but may also be responsible for some aspects of portfolios headed by regular ministers for whom they can speak in the House or elsewhere in their absence. There are also ministers of state for designated purposes, such as Urban Affairs and Science and Technology, but this category has not been used in recent years since the Mulroney government abolished the various ministries of state that were mainly legacies of the Trudeau era. And there have occasionally been 'associate' ministers, whose status is similar to that of 'ministers of state to assist'.

The formal power that ministers can exercise directly is primarily statutory in nature and relates almost entirely to their portfolio responsibilities. The more general prerogative authority exercised in the name of the Crown belongs to the prime minister and pertains to the power to appoint ministers, to assign portfolios, to organize Cabinet, and to appoint deputy ministers. There is also the collective authority of Cabinet as Governor-in-Council, which is given effect through the instrument of 'Orders-in-Council' (OICs). Even relatively minor matters of action relating to a single department may be decided by Cabinet, or at least in the name of Cabinet, rather than by a minister. This practice is much more prevalent in Canada than in the United Kingdom, and underscores the fact that the authority of ministers in Canada can extend into the domains of other ministers.[5] It also illustrates the fact that ministerial leadership in Canada is very much a collective enterprise.

MINISTERIAL LEADERSHIP

It should be stressed at the outset that the position of Cabinet minister is, by any standard, one of the more difficult posts imaginable. It demands that the occupant take on several different personae, often simultaneously, ranging from astute departmental manager to charismatic leader out on the hustings. The ideal minister would be strong on all counts; the constraint here is that all ministers are human. Some may have admirable personal qualities but relatively weak administrative skills and vice versa. To the extent, therefore, that ministerial leadership demands competence in a variety of functions, it would be unrealistic to expect high levels of effectiveness in any single area. Nevertheless, two essential criteria for ministerial leadership are the ability to set goals and the ability to mobilize individuals and institutions to achieve those goals.

Another factor that may be seen as a constraint is the role played by the prime minister. The prime minister is responsible not only for overall policy but also for the organizational paradigm under which Cabinet, its supporting agencies, and, to a large degree, even the line departments themselves conduct their business.[6] The prime minister's philosophy and style with respect to organizational matters may not always fit with the predilections of individual ministers, and thus one requirement of the latter is that they be able to adapt their leadership style to fit with the prevailing paradigm set by the prime minister.

Finally, as recent events—most notably the failure of the constitutional accord in the 1992 referendum—have illustrated, the Canadian public is profoundly distrustful of all politicians. There has always been a populist streak in Canadian political culture, but it has become more pronounced over the past decade, and has been particularly evident in a tendency to challenge the role and legitimacy of élites.[7] This can be attributed to two developments. First, the 1982 Canadian Charter of Rights and Freedoms has given rise to a phenomenon known as Charter politics, in which numerous special interest groups use the courts and the provisions of the Charter to promote their particular objectives. Second, younger generations have been far more accepting of what is called 'new politics', a development characterized by an emphasis on 'post-materialist' issues such the environment, women's and minority rights, and public participation, coupled with a willingness to use unconventional political channels.[8]

The impact of populism and, more specifically, Charter and post-materialist politics on ministerial leadership is twofold. First, the mere existence of numerous special interests aggressively seeking ministers' attention, and frequently operating outside normal channels, makes life difficult for ministers. Second, and more critical, the anti-élitist trend is in many ways profoundly at odds with the traditional constitutional basis of Cabinet government: that is, the responsibility of the executive not to the people but to Parliament. At a minimum, this trend makes it difficult for ministers to exercise leadership with respect to constituencies that have little regard for the normative basis of such leadership.

DEPARTMENTAL LEADERS

A minister in charge of a department can be seen as the equivalent of a chief executive officer (CEO) of a large corporation. He or she is responsible for giving direction to the department (that is, setting policy) and is ultimately accountable for its performance, its financial transactions, and all actions undertaken in the name of the department. There are some crucial differences, however, between ministers and CEOs of private-sector corporations.

First, many ministers—indeed, most ministers in a new government—have relatively little experience or training either in the substance of their portfolios or in the direction of a large organization. In fact, many new ministers may have relatively little parliamentary or even political experience of any kind—in sharp contrast to the situation in other countries, where experience plays a major role in ministerial recruitment. As Donald Savoie has noted: 'Overnight . . . it is possible for a teacher, a small town lawyer, or a small businessperson to be appointed to cabinet and be asked to direct the work of a large sprawling department with several thousand employees and a billion dollar budget. He or she will have little specific direction on what is expected and on the long-term direction of the department.'⁹ To the extent, therefore, that the department looks to the minister for leadership — to set policy, to act as a role model, to provide inspiration and to articulate the values of the organization — most ministers are ill-equipped to handle such expectations. They have little in the way of a policy agenda and limited skills in managing large organizations.

Second, ministers, though in theory accountable for all that happens in their departments during their tenure, do not have the formal powers commensurate with this responsibility — for example, to redesign the structure of the organization, to impart specific direction to appropriate divisions, or to choose their underlings. The actual running of the department is in the hands of the deputy minister, through whom all instructions and directions from the minister flow. The deputy decides how the wishes of the minister are to be translated into specific actions undertaken by the department. It should be stressed that the deputies are answerable not only to the prime minister, who appoints them, but also to the Clerk of the Privy Council, the Treasury Board Secretariat, and the Public Service Commission. A minister can ask the prime minister for a change of deputies, but such requests are only rarely granted. The important role assigned to the deputy and other senior officials in steering the department and advising the minister is intended in part to compensate for the limited experience of many ministers; but this practice can make the minister a follower or, worse yet, a hostage of vested departmental interests.

As well, recent efforts to reform the bureaucracy to make it more efficient and cost-effective, such as the Public Service 2000 plan, have given departmental managers more authority and freedom to make decisions concerning their units and agencies.¹⁰ In many ways this is a welcome development, but it does mean that the minister has even less opportunity, for good or ill, to intervene in the internal operations of the department.

The typical minister, therefore, in seeking to exercise control over the department, faces far more constraints in terms of experience, expertise, and formal powers than the average CEO of a corporation. As one former Liberal minister described the experience of being appointed to Cabinet:

> It's like I was suddenly landed on the top deck of an ocean liner and told that the ship was my responsibility. When I turned to the captain [i.e. deputy minister], I was told that he was appointed there by someone else and any decision to remove him would be made elsewhere. When I turned to others on the ship, I soon found out that they all report through the deputy minister, owe their allegiance to him and, more importantly, their future promotions. When I asked for a change in the ship's course, the ship just kept on going on the same course.¹¹

Clearly, the relationship between minister and deputy is crucial in determining how much influence any given minister will have on the course taken by the department. It is a relationship fraught with the potential for conflict. The minister is often leery of the influence that he or she feels the deputy possesses. The deputy in turn may feel that the minister is short on ideas and/or commitment to the long-term well-being of the department and its programs. The capacity of the minister to exert leadership over departmental activities may be further compromised by the limited experience of the deputy ministers themselves, at least with regard to specific portfolios. Deputies are increasingly being rotated from department to department, so that the average time spent by a deputy heading one department has declined from 4.5 years in 1966 to 1.4 years in 1986.[12] Given the increasing complexity of departmental operations, this means that deputies are often less helpful than they could or should be, and that ministers are even further removed from control over departmental operations.

Ministers do have direct control over their so-called 'exempt staff', personnel whom they hire directly, without reference to normal civil-service hiring procedures; this staff includes the 'chief of staff', a senior political adviser with a salary level comparable to that of an assistant deputy minister. One of the main responsibilities of exempt staff, and the chief of staff in particular, is to liaise with senior officials in the department. These staff are primarily concerned with the political dimensions of the department's activities and, like the minister, often lack specific expertise in the portfolio; most deputies, in turn, still cling to the notion that the operational aspects of the department are their prerogative.[13]

What is deemed political, however, can include a fairly extensive array of departmental activities, and in recent decades particularly ministers have used their exempt staff to penetrate into the internal operations of departments, by-passing both deputies and assistant deputies if necessary. Lloyd Axworthy, a member of the 1980-84 Liberal Cabinet, first as minister of Employment and Immigration and later as Transport minister, provides the most extreme example in this regard. At one point he had close to 100 staff working directly in his offices in Ottawa and Winnipeg, many of them exempt staff, others on consulting contracts, and still others civil servants seconded from their regular positions in the department. Decision-making power concerning a variety of programs was taken out of the hands of line-department officials and brought directly into the minister's office. Outside consultants were routinely hired to second-guess the advice tendered by officials on issues such as airline deregulation. As minister of Employment and Immigration, Axworthy systematically ignored his deputy and, when he felt it necessary, would communicate directly with junior officials several levels down in the organization.[14]

Axworthy's methods in seeking to influence the direction of his portfolios were regarded as fairly brutal, certainly by civil servants, and questions arose about his objectives. While he did have goals in mind that related to the mandate of his portfolios — achieving a more humane immigration policy, for example, and rendering the airline industry more responsive to consumer demands — these tended to be overshadowed by his primary preoccupation: channelling as many projects as possible to his home province of Manitoba. In successfully doing so Axworthy alienated a good number of the civil servants working under him.

Ultimately, for ministers to accomplish anything significant in their portfolios they need the active support of senior officials. These officials, in turn, in so far as they have their own vision of departmental objectives, need capable ministers to argue their case in Cabinet and in other arenas. Andrew Johnson notes that, particularly during the process of policy innovation or reform, a relationship of mutual dependence between ministers and senior officials tends to prevail.[15] The minister promotes and legitimizes the proposed policy in Cabinet and before the public, while the officials overcome obstacles within the department, draft the actual legislation, and subsequently implement it.

Johnson illustrates his point with reference to Bryce Mackasey, Liberal minister of Labour in the early 1970s, and the adoption of the Unemployment Insurance Act. Developed by senior officials in the department, the new scheme did not gain momentum until Mackasey decided to make it his personal cause, championing it both within Cabinet and within the department. What should be kept in mind, however, is that ministers who are policy-oriented or committed to the interests of their departments tend to be rare in the Canadian context. Most fall in the category of what Savoie refers to as 'process participants', ministers who generally eschew policy, political ideology, government organization, and even government programs. 'Projects are what matters, and the more the better. They will look to their departments to come up with specific projects for their own ridings or for regions for which they are responsible.'[16] This lack of a policy orientation on the part of ministers is corroborated by Sharon Sutherland, who, in a detailed examination of ministerial resignations from the Canadian Cabinet over a forty-year period, found that fewer than one-fifth of such resignations were policy-based; in Britain, by contrast, four-fifths of Cabinet resignations were.[17]

There are exceptions. Michael Wilson, as minister of Finance in the Mulroney Cabinet — one of the longest-serving ministers in that portfolio in post-war history — certainly had a distinctive economic agenda, relating to free trade, taxation policy, and expenditure reduction, that he was in good part able to implement. As well, he and his senior officials saw eye to eye on most issues, providing mutual support. Another exception was Marc Lalonde, minister of Energy, architect of the ill-fated National Energy Program (NEP), and the dominant force in staking out and implementing the Trudeau government's economic policy in the 1980-84 period. Both men had definite goals and were strong leaders, able to command the respect of the officials working under them and to infuse their own values into their policy areas.

On a different level one finds ministers who are less policy-oriented but do have a well-developed capacity for providing direction in a manner that fits with the government's overall itinerary, and who manage their portfolios well. To the extent that they have policy interests, these are frequently tied to their regional responsibilities. Recent examples of such ministers include Donald Mazankowski and John Crosbie. Both individuals handled a variety of portfolios in a highly competent manner, recognizing the essential functions of their departments and what needed to be done in order to serve politically important constituencies and keep the government out of trouble. Indeed, Mazankowski proved so adept at managing portfolios that the prime minister frequently turned to him as temporary custodian of other portfolios when the original ministers ran into trouble. Furthermore, as deputy prime minister Mazankowski became responsible for managing the government's overall agenda through the Operations committee of Cabinet. Both ministers used their portfolios to cater to regional constituencies — Mazankowski using Agriculture to help reinforce his western political base, Crosbie using first International Trade and then Fisheries to protect Newfoundland's interests — but did so without riding roughshod over their officials.

It should be stressed that the twin goals of looking after both one's department and one's region need not inevitably be incompatible or lead to conflict with departmental officials. Most officials realize that they need a minister to argue their case, in Cabinet and elsewhere, and that in the Canadian system a strong minister invariably enjoys a solid regional base. For this reason officials will try to assist their minister in doing good things for his or her province and riding. In turn it is expected that the minister will make all reasonable efforts to protect and support the department. A useful example here is irrepressible Marcel Masse. Much vilified, mainly in the English-language media, for his tendency to use his departments as pork-barrels and for his propensity to undercut the prime minister during crucial moments in the constitutional negotiations, he nonetheless served his portfolios well. As minister of National Defence he won the grudging admiration of officials after successfully steering the controversial $4.3 billion contract for the E-H 101 helicopter through Cabinet. The armed forces got a favourable decision, and Masse's home province of Québec received numerous contracts linked to the new project.

On a lower tier one finds a number of ministers who are competent in managing their portfolios and at the same time willing and able to take the lead from more senior ministers. Mulroney Cabinet ministers William McKnight and Doug Lewis fell into this category. In a sense the willingness of such ministers to recognize Cabinet hierarchy is a boon, in that any given government can contain only so many Michael Wilsons or Marc Lalondes: having thirty or more strong-willed individuals of this calibre in a single Cabinet would result in chaos. The other side of the coin, however, is that in Canada the majority of ministers — 'process participants' — tend to be lackadaisical with respect to the policy direction and management of their portfolios. Not only do they lack policy and management skills, but their attention is often focused elsewhere. Thus Benoît Bouchard, the Québec lieutenant in Mulroney's Cabinet from 1990 to 1993, and at one point minister of Industry, Science and Technology, was fully preoccupied with the constitutional issue on the one hand and finding money for projects in his home province on the other. As a consequence, according to one news report at the time, 'his department is positively floundering in frustration. The problem: an acute absence of political leadership. There is simply no evidence that Bouchard has any interest in using the resources at his disposal to develop the national policies needed to strengthen Canada's economic performance.'[18]

In summary, with a few exceptions Canadian Cabinet ministers tend to be weak both as initiators and developers of policy, at least with regard to the functional responsibilities of their portfolios, and as departmental managers. As will be seen below, these characteristics tend to be replicated in other arenas.

MINISTERIAL LEADERSHIP IN CABINET

Headey found that most British Cabinet ministers saw their primary role as that of promoting the well-being of their departments; in particular, they wanted to ensure that their departments' proposals received priority and that they would not be unduly meddled with by other departments. The case of Canadian ministers offers a distinct contrast. According to Savoie, ministers are often reluctant to push their departments' interests at Cabinet meetings, in part because they lack the interest to do so but also in part for fear of being seen by their colleagues as weaklings who have succumbed to the self-interested scheming of wily civil servants in their departments: 'Ministers suffering from departmentalitis are quickly spotted by their colleagues and they will find it more difficult to be heard in cabinet.'[19]

In the Canadian Cabinet it is also expected that ministers will meddle in the affairs of portfolios other than their own, not in order to promote their own departments but to see whether any given proposal affects the province or region from which the minister hails. Thus it is generally acknowledged that Newfoundlander John Crosbie was dictating the overall thrust as well as the details of fisheries policy on the east coast long before he actually became minister of Fisheries. When the Department of External Affairs negotiated a treaty with France over French access to northern cod stocks in 1987, Crosbie (at that time minister of Transport) made known his displeasure at not being adequately consulted, both within Cabinet and outside. Canada soon scuttled the treaty and the government offered a public apology in the House of Commons for failing to take into account Newfoundland's interests.[20] In the winter of 1993, Crosbie sat as an equal at the same table with Energy minister William McKnight, Industry minister Wilson, and Finance minister Mazankowski during negotiations with private-sector interests to reach an agreement to keep the Hibernia oil development off the shore of Newfoundland alive.

Clearly, leadership skills are often exercised within Cabinet to promote a minister's region rather than his or her department's interests. Much of the discussion that takes place in Cabinet committees and Cabinet as a whole revolves around distributional issues: which region will receive how much under a given program, or where some new installation will be located.[21] Given the nature of these issues, much of the discussion, negotiation, and conflict will take place outside the confines of Cabinet. Ministers will engage in intricate horse-trading and log-rolling with each other, swapping program items for mutual benefit. In this context ministers need to be skilled in persuading colleagues both in a collegial setting and on a one-to-one basis. They must also be adept at deploying their exempt staff, who should be constantly searching for possible projects of interest to the minister, or with potential for log-rolling with other ministers, and who must deal with both officials and exempt staff, working for other ministers. A key element in this framework of distributional politics is to line up support among the key ministers so that when the particular issue is discussed within the relevant Cabinet committee, the decision will be largely a foregone conclusion.

Not all issues are so easily resolved, however, particularly when substantial items are involved that are not readily divisible or that are seen in zero-sum terms. The result can be a drawing of battle lines, and ministers may well feel called upon to use all their rhetorical skills and evidentiary resources, such as public-opinion poll data, to make their case. During Cabinet debate over the EH-101 helicopter, Defence minister Marcel Masse broke new ground in seeking to persuade his fellow ministers of the merits of the multi-billion-dollar contract: his department hired a public-relations firm to lobby individual ministers and their staffs for their support. Issues that stir up considerable public sentiment, or that involve French-English relations, are invariably handled by a few key figures within Cabinet, and ultimately it is the prime minister who has the final say.

What role does collective leadership have in this apparent free-for-all for distributional bounty among Her Majesty's privy councillors? Mention was made earlier of Orders-in-Council (OIC), resort to which is much more frequent in Canada than in Britain. A decision announced as an OIC is one made in the name of the Cabinet as a whole rather than that of an individual minister. At first glance one might think that the issues involved would be mainly substantial ones cutting across a number of portfolios. In practice, however, most of the decisions covered by OICs tend to be fairly mundane, involving administrative convenience. At the same time, however, an OIC can disguise extensive log-rolling among ministers or the exercise of a veto which in some circumstances a regional minister may have. For example, minister X may have his or her department perform a certain action in response to a request from minister Y because the program in question involves minister Y's province; given that it is minister Y who is really behind the decision, it would be inappropriate to have minister X take full responsibility. Hence the OIC can be extremely useful as an instrument to cover the fact that many decisions, even minor ones, really do involve more than one minister.

One could argue that such use of the OIC is an exercise in subterfuge intended to disguise some distasteful practices among ministers. There is some truth in this; but it should also be kept in mind that Cabinet deals continually with highly sensitive issues related to regionalism, federal-provincial relations, and linguistic conflict. Even an apparently straightforward defence contract can become politically explosive if it appears to favour a particular province. In Canada such issues have a political salience that is lacking in Britain, for example. In this context, then, effective leadership may indeed require that responsibility, and blame, sometimes be extended beyond a single minister.

On a broader level, it is worth noting that Cabinet's collective preoccupations are not entirely restricted to the pork-barrel; it does have the capacity to address a number of more substantial issues on which the government hopes to make its reputation. In the case of the Mulroney Cabinet, these issues included national conciliation (i.e., the failed Meech Lake and Charlottetown accords), tax reform, monetary policy, and economic performance (i.e., the two free-trade agreements). This is not to say that the policies pursued in these areas were necessarily wise or effective. They did, however, represent distinct and successful efforts by Cabinet to assert its collective authority and to implement proposed solutions. If one aspect of leadership consists in presenting a united front in the face of opposition, then both the Trudeau and Mulroney cabinets fared quite well. In the case of the latter there was only one resignation based on an outright policy disagreement: that of Mulroney's first Québec lieutenant, Lucien Bouchard. Considering the diversity of opinion and personalities in his Cabinet and the controversial nature of the issues they faced, the degree of unity was remarkable, and reflected well both on his ministers and on Mulroney himself.

In light of the role that Cabinet is expected to play in giving collective direction to the bureaucracy on both major and minor matters, Cabinet as a collective body often needs advice and assistance in decision-making. By and large, this support has been provided by a number of central agencies, chief among them the Privy Council Office (PCO). Central agencies such as the Treasury Board Secretariat (TBS) and the Prime Minister's Office (PMO) are responsible for advising either specific Cabinet commit-tees or, in the case of the PMO, the prime minister, although agencies such as the Federal-Provincial Relations Office (FPRO) will assist the Cabinet as whole when issues such as Meech Lake and Charlottetown arise. The PCO co-ordinates all the information and agreements arising from the different departments and consciously attempts to help ministers in their efforts to assess them in a critical light.

Particularly during the Trudeau era, it was expected that the PCO and other agencies would act as countervailing sources of advice for ministers, to help them maintain some independence from the views of line-department officials. The presence of multiple and overlapping agencies does compromise this role, however. For example, officials from Finance, which also performs central-agency functions, may well com-pete with officials in the TBS or PCO in proffering advice to ministers. Lines of authority, and accountability, have also blurred. Thus the PMO has taken on responsi-bility for some things that formerly were in the domain of the PCO. The PCO in turn in recent years has become more politicized. For example, Dalton Camp, the *éminence grise* of the Conservative party, was appointed to the PCO rather than the PMO when he was recruited to help the Mulroney government find its way out of a political morass. The Deputy Prime Minister's Office, which expanded considerably under Donald Mazankowski in response to a perceived need for improved co-ordination, including liaison between Cabinet and the government caucus, encroached on some of the responsibilities of both the PCO and the PMO. The overall result of this fragmentation of authority has been a failure of co-ordination among the co-ordinating agencies themselves.[22]

Thus even though the Canadian Cabinet receives the most institutionalized sup-port of any in the Western nations, its ministers do not appear to be as well served as they might be by the considerable resources expended on central agencies. Ironically, it was the close personal co-operation between a number of key ministers that allowed the Mulroney Cabinet to overcome some of the problems of co-ordination at the agency level.

PARTY LEADERSHIP

Ministers must be able to sell their proposals not only to their fellow ministers but also to their political party. In addition, they are expected to steer their proposals through Parliament and to help lead the party at election time.

The Liberals and Conservatives, and to some degree even the NDP, can be character-ized as cadre parties. The extra-parliamentary wings of the parties, like their links with provincial parties, tend to be weak, coming alive only at election time. The focus for ministers, therefore, is generally the parliamentary party or government caucus.[23] The government caucus is further broken down into regional caucuses, which meet separately, and usually on a regular basis. The caucus expects to have the right of consultation if not direct input into the form and substance of government legislation. Woe betide the minister who lets slip at a press conference or in the House plans for even minor changes in legislation without letting the caucus know about them first. In a number of instances, policies accepted by Cabinet have been held up because of opposition in the caucus.

In this instance, therefore, ministers must cultivate a different set of skills, primarily the capacity to persuade or mollify a large and diverse group of frustrated backbench-ers, many whom are aspiring ministers. Ministers successful in this setting appear to have either a flair for rhetoric or the ability to make the caucus rank and file feel that they are genuinely part of the policy-making process. Thus, with respect to the latter, the astute minister will have his or her supporters within caucus raise the right questions or make the appropriate suggestions so that the minister can appear to pluck from the caucus these nuggets of brilliant advice, which will then be included in government policy. Given the imperative of linguistic duality, ministers, and the prime minister in particular, must be able to persuade both English- and French-speaking members of caucus of the importance of compromise in the interests of both the party and the country.

In the regional caucuses the orientation is more practical. The regional ministers — that is, the ten 'political ministers' representing each of the provinces — will be regularly queried on expenditures, the number of projects that will end up in their part of the country, and how these projects are to be allocated within the region. Each regional caucus will be aware of how other regions are faring, and in order to satisfy caucus members, ministers will need to deliver the region's proportionate 'fair share' of projects. It should be stressed that some regional ministers today have only a tenuous hold over their caucuses largely because prior to becoming ministers they had little standing in the party, either nationally or regionally. Traditionally, regional ministers were generally former premiers or substantial provincial figures who already enjoyed a strong political base in their region before entering federal politics. Currently, however, with the increasing separation of federal and provincial party politics, newly minted regional ministers may have little independent stature and authority. However, an important departmental portfolio will generate status.

Political ministers will also need to organize the regional caucuses and to maintain discipline so that their respective regional groupings of MPs can actually help them secure desirable projects. Historically, the Ontario caucus has always been consid-ered weak, and its political ministers invariably experience difficulty in maintaining order among the province's MPs and ministers. By contrast, the Québec caucus, in both Liberal and recent Conservative governments, has generally been a model of disciplined organization—a state of affairs that helps to explain why Québec ministers have been effective in getting what they want. Well-versed on future government needs and expenditures, Québec ministers and caucus members are better prepared than most others to present convincing arguments as to why certain projects are best located in their province.

Leadership in Parliament demands yet another set of skills. This is a critical arena, for it is here that ministers defend government policies, particularly those emanating from their own departments, and that government legislation is debated and eventually passed into law. In order to be effective, ministers must be well-grounded in the rules and customs of parliamentary debate. Of course, it also helps to be quick on one's feet and to have a facility for the well-turned phrase. Above all, however, experience tends to be the pivotal factor, and lack of it can easily get a minister into trouble. Sharon Sutherland points out that the opposition has an excellent nose for ministers who are inexperienced and unfamiliar with House procedures.[24] Such ministers become easy prey for the opposition's relentless pressure; many will stumble, discrediting themselves, the government, and their department. A number of ministerial careers have come to a premature end as a result of opposition attacks following inadequate performances in the House.

Conversely, a minister who is a skilled parliamentarian can save the very life of a government. Allan J. MacEachen, a long-time fixture in the Liberal governments of Lester Pearson and Pierre Trudeau, had his greatest impact as House Leader, especially during the 1972-74 period of minority government. Through adroit use of House rules and intricate negotiations with the opposition parties, he was able to keep the Liberal minority government alive, allowing it to rebuild public credibility in time for the next election—and win it by a majority. MacEachen's influence in Cabinet rose immeasurably after this singular accomplishment. By contrast, Walter Baker, House Leader in the Clark government of 1979-80, saw the destruction of both his career and his government after the budget débâcle that led to the Tory government's defeat. In brief, a high level of competence in Parliament is a prerequisite for successful ministerial leadership.

Ministers are also expected to help lead the party into electoral battle. Typically, a political Cabinet consisting of all the regional ministers and a few other high-level figures will be involved in election planning. In most cases, one of the co-chairs of this group will be the chief Québec minister, who will also have direct responsibility for the campaign in Québec. Election planning involves staking out the major themes for a national campaign; regional variations or issues will generally be regarded as sub-themes. Detailed planning, the development of specific proposals, and the conduct of the campaign itself will be left to a very limited number of party professionals.

Regional ministers were once regarded as indispensable at election time and were held responsible for delivering provincial blocs of seats for the government side. A classic example was J.H. (Jimmy) Gardiner, long-time Agriculture minister in the Mackenzie King government and former premier of Saskatchewan, who ran the Liberal machine in his province on behalf of the national party at election time, and who, when King lost his seat in an Ontario riding, found him a safe seat in Saskatchewan.

The advent of 'electronic politics' with the attendant focus on the party leader, however, has made the role of regional ministers in electioneering much less critical. Ministers obviously still play a role, and the more popular ministers will be in demand as speakers in the campaign efforts of individual candidates. But in the present era campaigns are centred primarily around television advertisements targeted at a national audience and featuring a national leader.

One role that regional ministers do play at election time — or at least attempt to play — is to channel as many visible projects as possible to winnable ridings in their region as well as to their own (even if the latter is not necessarily winnable). Whether expenditures on projects such as new wharfs, federal office buildings, or new enterprises supported under regional development programs actually improve the re-election of government incumbents remains an open question. Still, given the closeness of many electoral contests at the constituency level, even a few hundred votes swayed by the arrival of government largesse in the community may make the difference between winning and losing, and whatever election analysts might think, ministers and MPs certainly feel that these expenditures are necessary. In the 1988 election the main regional development agencies, such as the Western Diversification Office (WDO) and the Atlantic Canada Opportunity Agency (ACOA), were among the vehicles used for the delivery of election-related projects. In the case of ACOA, close to half of its five-year $1.05 billion budget was committed to projects in a ten-month period leading up to the election.[25]

The mad rush to spend for electioneering purposes has its down-side, however. With ACOA, the end came soon after the 1988 election, when a contrite Elmer MacKay, minister responsible for ACOA as well as political minister for Nova Scotia, announced that ACOA's budget was being 'reprofiled', an artful way of saying that the agency's five-year budget was being stretched to seven years and that the maximum amount of each grant was being radically reduced. More critically, while pork-barrel projects may help to save the electoral bacon of individual ministers or MPs, they can at the same time bring both the minister and the government as a whole into disrepute in the eyes of the broader public. For example, while Mazankowski's coup in the fall of 1992 in bringing a mail-in immigration processing centre (along with 200 new jobs) to his home town of Vegreville, Alberta, was hailed by his constituents, it was regarded with scepticism elsewhere, and positively reviled by those in the immigration community.[26] In other words, actions designed to serve immediate electoral needs can backfire when they undermine whatever support and legitimacy ministers and their government may enjoy in the broader public.

MINISTERS AS PUBLIC LEADERS

Maintaining a positive public profile can be problematic for many ministers. In particular, questions arise regarding ministers' stature, their ability to articulate the values and aspirations of citizens, and their capacity to command respect from the public.

This issue is important because one of the functions traditionally attributed to ministers, and to Cabinet as a whole, is regional and linguistic conciliation. According to élite accommodation theory, Cabinet ministers, at least in the past, have represented the interests of provinces and regions. Conversely, ministers have been able to persuade their constituents of the necessity of accepting compromises reached within Cabinet with ministers from the other regions. In this manner, so the argument goes, ministers have helped to perform the twin functions of regional representation and national integration.[27]

The current literature suggests that ministers no longer play a significant role in overcoming regional and linguistic divisions because they no longer have the stature and authority to do so. As Alan Cairns has noted, 'regional spokesmen of such power and authenticity are [now] only memories.'[28] The reason, according to most students of federalism, has been the rise of the federal-provincial arena, and especially the first ministers conference involving the prime minister and premiers, as the primary forum for decision-making on national issues as well as representation of regional interests. For the past three decades, federal ministers have simply been overshadowed by provincial premiers.[29]

There is no doubt that federal ministers are no longer as prominent or powerful as Jimmy Gardiner or C.D. Howe. Yet it would be misleading to say that they lack visibility or have been eclipsed by provincial premiers. On the basis of recent Gallup poll data, it is clear that senior ministers such as Joe Clark, Michael Wilson, and John Crosbie have enjoyed higher public recognition ratings than most provincial premiers. What is also clear, however, is that federal ministers are also somewhat more likely to make unfavourable impressions. As Table 7.1 shows, Joe Clark's share of 'favourable' impressions only marginally outweighed his 'unfavourable' ratings. John Crosbie fared poorly, and Michael Wilson was the least popular: 55 per cent of survey respondents had an 'unfavourable' impression of him versus only 22 per cent who were favourably impressed and 24 per cent who said 'don't know'. Among provincial premiers, only Bill Vander Zalm of British Columbia managed to garner more unfavourable than favourable responses.

One could argue that the premiers in question were simply more competent than the federal ministers; hence the more favourable impressions made by the former. But this is difficult to reconcile with the fact that even former premiers such as John Buchanan of Nova Scotia and Grant Devine of Saskatchewan, both regarded as having run inept governments during their last years in office, received, on balance, favourable ratings. A more plausible interpretation is that federal ministers face a much more formidable task in reconciling different interests and responsibilities, which makes it more difficult for them to make a favourable impression on the general public. Table 7.1 suggests that the ministers with the greater public visibility tended to be less popular. It should also be kept in mind that their different responsibilities included dealing with regional as well as sectoral constituencies: the demands generated by interest groups in these two competing constituencies are often implacable, and do not lend themselves to easy compromise.

As was noted above, the pork-barrelling activities of regional ministers in particular often serve to undermine their image as political leaders with a genuine interest in promoting the broader public interest. Regional ministers will frequently champion

TABLE 7.1 **PUBLIC IMPRESSIONS OF FEDERAL MINISTERS AND PROVINCIAL PREMIERS, 1990**

	Impression of federal Cabinet ministers		
	Favourable %	Unfavourable %	Don't know %
Joe Clark	41	38	21
John Crosbie	25	36	40
Don Mazankowski	21	16	63
Barbara McDougall	27	21	52
Michael Wilson	22	55	24

	Impression of provincial premiers		
	Favourable %	Unfavourable %	Don't know %
David Peterson	38	15	47
Robert Bourassa	34	34	32
Frank McKenna	25	9	66
Donald Getty	23	17	61
John Buchanan	19	10	71
Bill Vander Zalm	19	31	50
Clyde Wells	19	7	74
Grant Devine	18	11	71
Gary Filmon	17	9	74
Joe Ghiz	15	8	76

Question: 'In general, do you have a favourable or unfavourable impression of [name]?'

NOTE: Percentages may not add exactly to 100, because of rounding.
SOURCE: Based on Lorne Bozinoff and Peter MacIntosh, 'Tory Ministers Fail to Excite Canadian Public', Gallup, 8 Feb. 1990, and 'Provincial Premiers Largely Unknown to Canadian Public', Gallup, 11 Jan. 1990.

projects that are of benefit to their province as a whole, as distinct from their particular riding. Indeed, Crosbie, Mazankowski, and McKnight all argued for energy-related mega-projects in their provinces on the grounds that they would provide benefits extending well beyond provincial boundaries. It can be argued that in this they were merely following the lead set by the provincial governments.

In recent years the constitutional debates, while imposing some additional strains, allowed ministers to play the role of statespersons transcending regional and narrow sectoral differences. This role became particularly prominent following the failure of the Meech Lake Accord, when first ministers conferences were placed on hold. The Cabinet, specifically the Committee on Canadian Unity chaired by Joe Clark, hammered out a set of new constitutional proposals entitled *Shaping Canada's Future Together* that responded to issues raised by the provinces, aboriginal peoples, and Québec. These proposals later served as a basis for multilateral discussions with aboriginal people and the provinces, including Québec, a process that led ultimately to the Charlottetown Accord in August 1992. This experience suggests that under the right circumstances the Cabinet does have an important nation-building role to play. It is worth noting that in the period leading up to the referendum in October of 1992 several ministers, including Kim Campbell, John Crosbie, Benoît Bouchard, and, of course, Joe Clark made creditable efforts to sell the accord both to their regional publics and to the Canadian public.

Nevertheless, the defeat of the accord in the referendum would seem to indicate once again the limitations of ministerial leadership. In this instance the blame for the failure, if it can be construed as such, must be shared by all political élites, including the ten provincial premiers, the leaders of the aboriginal community, and, of course, the prime minister. Questions remain, however, about the overall effectiveness of ministers and what reforms might improve both the quality of individuals recruited to ministerial posts and their performance.

ASSESSMENT

In many ways the effectiveness of ministers as leaders has been found wanting. They appear not to have the capacity, or even any strong inclination, to provide policy direction for their departments or to act as managers. Ministers do have a capacity for collective leadership — ironically, because most are willing to defer to the lead of more senior ministers. But this quality tends to be diminished, in part because the collective authority of Cabinet is often misused. The OIC instrument, for example, is frequently used to disguise patronage or log-rolling among ministers, practices that elicit cynical responses from the electorate. Within Parliament, mastery of the rules of the game and the skills to deal with opposition attacks can be acquired only through experience. Unfortunately, these commodities are often in short supply, particularly in a new government, leading to performances that embarrass both the ministers involved and the Cabinet. Within the party at large, the fact that many ministers lack a robust base of support makes them more dependent on projects and expenditures associated with their portfolios, which they use to cultivate the respect of other MPs from their province or region. At election time, the importance of the national leader and the tendency to conduct campaigns primarily through the medium of television have made the role of all ministers, including regional ministers, much more limited than it was in the past. All this puts ministers in a rather weak position when it comes to cultivating their public images. When a minister does acquire a distinct public presence, more often than not it is a negative one.

As was noted above, at present Canadians judge all politicians harshly; thus the public's expectations of ministers may be unrealistic. Nonetheless, there are certain factors that have a direct bearing on ministerial performance, and that must be taken into account in any recommendations to improve ministers' capacity to exercise leadership. The first of these is the recruitment process. To the extent that we might wish to see more ministers with experience and expertise in the specific areas of their portfolios, or simply with expertise in managing large organizations, the blame can be attached to the political parties. Canada, unlike the UK, Australia, and a host of other nations, has a highly decentralized candidate-selection process. Essentially, the choice of candidates lies in the hands of the local constituency associations, and the national parties have very little control over how the associations conduct their business.[30] The attributes important to winning a nomination—above all, perhaps, good local connections—are not necessarily ones that make for strong ministerial leadership. Efforts by party leaders to hand-pick high-quality candidates and place them in winnable ridings are typically resisted by party activists at the local level. Overall, this system makes it difficult for parties to attract suitable candidates with broad regional or national stature, and reduces the pool of government MPs qualified for Cabinet.

A second factor is the competitive nature of the Canadian electoral system. Surprisingly, the turnover rate for MPs in Canada is far greater than elsewhere. The re-election rate for incumbents is much higher not only in the US but in the United Kingdom, a country that also uses the single-member plurality system. Furthermore, the margins of victory in individual ridings are much narrower in Canada. In other words, Canadian MPs, whether in opposition or in government, stand a much greater chance of being defeated than do their counterparts elsewhere.[31] This has a chilling effect on those contemplating the possibility of running for public office and is one of the reasons why so many ministers lack experience. It also provides incentives for pork-barrelling, since ministers who are vulnerable to defeat will do all they can to protect their positions. Unfortunately, such shoring up of electoral defences tends to be seen by the wider public as parochial, if not unseemly and crass.

The third factor relates to the representational imperative. Beginning with Sir John A. Macdonald, all prime ministers have paid diligent attention to the three 'Rs' of representation in constructing their cabinets: race, religion, and region. In recent decades religion has become less important and gender has been added to the list, but region still remains paramount. Since every province ought to be represented, even if it has elected only one government MP, the prime minister may be forced to include in Cabinet individuals who otherwise would not have been chosen. At the same time, individuals who would very likely make excellent ministers may have to be excluded. Not only tradition, but the very real regional differences that do exist, and the fact that Cabinet has served to some degree as an informal substitute for an elected Senate, make regional representation an important, perhaps indispensable, feature of Canadian Cabinet government. But a price is paid in terms of the quality of the ministers recruited and the additional burdens they carry in attempting to balance their regional with their portfolio responsibilities. The regional or 'political' ministers are primarily responsible for injecting the regional dimension into Cabinet discussion. The problem is that these ministers are often more concerned with their own ridings, or with pacifying government MPs from their own provinces, than they are with broader regional concerns. Given their frequent preoccupation with local matters, the term 'regional minister' is often a misnomer.

What are the remedies, if any? With respect to political recruitment, partial responsibility rests with political parties. Ways must be found to reduce the intensely localistic bias pervading candidate selection. This will require striking a new balance between the national party and local associations, a balance that would allow the national party a greater role in ensuring that the pool of potential candidates for nomination in any given riding is representative of the broader population. Some mechanism should also be found to permit the national party to reserve a number of ridings for individuals deemed to be outstanding or equipped with special expertise in various policy areas. This is no easy task, to be sure. The Liberal party recently changed its constitution to give the party leader the opportunity to reserve a limited number of ridings for special candidates. In attempting to exercise this new power, however, Jean Chrétien ran into strong resistance from unhappy grassroots Liberals. Nonetheless, all parties must take similar steps if they are to improve the calibre of those entering Cabinet.

Political parties should also strengthen their capacity for policy analysis and training. In virtually all Western democracies, including the United States and the United Kingdom, political parties and/or leading politicians have links with policy institutes, or at least have access to well-developed networks of expertise. In Canada such links are largely absent; this is certainly the case for the two largest parties. Party foundations, as such institutes are often called, serve several purposes. With respect to Cabinet recruitment and training, they would provide parties with connections to broader networks of people in universities and the private and non-profit sectors, people who would not normally be willing to become directly involved in electoral politics but who would agree to participate in policy debates and development. They would also help aspiring and actual MPs and ministers to acquire skills and knowledge in different policy areas. Finally, party foundations could assist newly elected governments with the transition to power by preparing the new ministers for the logistics of implementing their party's platform, including the recruitment of exempt staff.[32]

Canadian political parties and candidates still face a number of problems imposed by an electoral system that is highly competitive and that emphasizes short-term electoral gain. One possible remedy might lie in the adoption of partial proportional representation, perhaps along the lines of the German model, which combines individually held constituencies with the party-list system. This solution would alleviate problems in three areas. First, it would allow the national parties to place some of their key candidates on party lists rather than force them onto reluctant constituency associations. Second, in so far as there would likely be separate lists for each province (or for large electoral districts in the larger provinces), more individuals with a genuine province-wide basis of support would be elected. This might mean, in turn, that regional ministers would be *bona fide* representatives of a provincial electorate rather than of single constituencies. Third, the need for pork-barrelling would be much reduced, while the incentives to promote the broader welfare of both the province and the country as a whole would be increased.[33]

There is also room for improvement in the institution of Cabinet itself. For example, much could be done to rationalize the central agency apparatus supporting Cabinet. Decision-making within Cabinet could be further streamlined, and the size of Cabinet could be reduced, as was done by prime ministers Campbell and Chrétien in 1993, although for representational reasons it will need to remain somewhat larger than strict efficiency criteria might dictate. It must be stressed, however, that these are relatively minor considerations. The major factors affecting the behaviour of ministers and their capacity for exercising leadership lie outside Cabinet itself: namely, with the political parties and the electoral system.

The question remains whether current demands for transparency and broad public participation will allow those occupying public office to exercise leadership in any meaningful sense. In many ways the prevailing political climate requires that all our public leaders become followers; that they govern primarily by slavishly observing each and every dictate of public opinion. Nevertheless, even in this context most of us hope that our political leaders will succeed in making useful national policies out of the disparate and contradictory strands of group interests and public opinion without ignoring the needs of particular regions and social and economic sectors. This would appear to be the essence of political leadership in the late twentieth century. If federal Cabinet ministers are to improve their capacity to face this challenge, the reforms suggested above should be seen as necessary first steps.

NOTES

[1] For example, see William A. Matheson, *The Prime Minister and the Cabinet* (Toronto: Methuen, 1976); Michael Rush, *The Cabinet and Policy Formation* (London: Longman, 1984); Geoffrey Marshall, ed., *Ministerial Responsibility* (Oxford: Oxford University Press, 1989).

[2] *British Cabinet Ministers: The Roles of Politicians in Executive Office* (London: Allen and Unwin, 1974).

[3] Matheson, *The Prime Minister*.

[4] See introductory chapter in R.K. Weaver and B.A. Rockman, eds, *Do Institutions Matter?* (Washington: Brookings Institution, 1992).

[5] J.R. Mallory, 'Cabinets and Councils in Canada', *Public Law* (Autumn 1957): 236.

[6] Peter Aucoin, 'Organizational Change in the Machinery of Canadian Government: From Rational Management to Brokerage Politics', *Canadian Journal of Political Science* 19 (March 1986): 3-27.

[7] André Blais and Elizabeth Gidengil, *Making Representative Democracy Work: The Views of Canadians*, vol. 17 of the Research Studies of the Royal Commission on Electoral Reform and Party Financing (Toronto: Dundurn, 1991).

[8] Alan C. Cairns, 'Constitutional Minoritarianism in Canada', in R.L. Watts and D. Brown, eds, *Canada: The State of the Federation* (Kingston: Institute of Intergovernmental Relations, 1990); Neil Nevitte, 'New Politics, the Charter, and Political Participation', in H. Bakvis, ed.,

Representation, Integration and Political Parties in Canada, vol. 14 of the Research Studies of the Royal Commission on Electoral Reform and Party Financing (Toronto: Dundurn, 1991), 355-417.

[9] Donald J. Savoie, *The Politics of Public Spending in Canada* (Toronto: University of Toronto Press, 1990), 186.

[10] Government of Canada, *Public Service 2000: The Renewal of the Public Service of Canada* (Ottawa: Supply and Services, 1990)

[11] Quoted in Savoie, *Politics of Public Spending*, 187.

[12] Gordon F. Osbaldeston, *Keeping Deputy Ministers Accountable* (London, Ont.: National Centre for Management Research and Development, 1988).

[13] For a superb discussion of some of the problems of ministerial control and accountability *vis-à-vis* the bureaucracy see Sharon Sutherland, 'The Al-Mashat Affair: Administrative Accountability in Parliamentary Institutions', *Canadian Public Administration* 34 (Winter 1991): 573-603.

[14] For details on Axworthy as minister see Herman Bakvis, *Regional Ministers: Power and Influence in the Canadian Cabinet* (Toronto: University of Toronto Press, 1991), chapters 8 and 9.

[15] Andrew F. Johnson, 'A Minister as an Agent of Policy Change: The Case of Unemployment Insurance in the Seventies', *Canadian Public Administration* 24 (Winter 1981): 612-33.

[16] Savoie, *Politics of Public Spending*, 194.

[17] Sharon Sutherland, 'The Consequences of Electoral Volatility: Inexperienced Ministers, 1949-90', in H. Bakvis, ed., *Representation*, 303-54.

[18] G. Gherson, 'Benoit Bouchard Goes with the Flow', *Financial Times* (19 Nov. 1990): 7.

[19] Savoie, *Politics of Public Spending*, 195.

[20] Bakvis, *Regional Ministers*, 261-2.

[21] For the 'rules of the game' see H. Bakvis and David MacDonald, 'The Canadian Cabinet: Organization, Decision-Rules, and Policy Impact', in M. Atkinson, ed., *Governing Canada: Institutions and Public Policy* (Toronto: Harcourt, Brace, Jovanovich, 1993), 47-80.

[22] For a discussion of some of these problems see Peter Aucoin and Herman Bakvis, *The Centralization-Decentralization Conundrum* (Halifax: Institute for Research on Public Policy, 1988); S.L. Sutherland, 'The Public Service and Policy Development', in Atkinson, ed., *Governing Canada*, 81-113.

[23] For details on the role of party caucuses see Paul G. Thomas, 'Parties and Regional Representation', in Bakvis, ed., *Representation*, 179-252.

[24] 'Consequences of Electoral Volatility'.

[25] Bakvis, *Regional Ministers*, 255.

[26] See Estanislao Oziewicz, 'Mazankowski's Riding Gets Centre for Immigration', *Globe and Mail*, 25 Nov. 1992: A4.

[27] See Matheson, *The Prime Minister*; S.J.R. Noel, 'The Prime Minister's Role in a Consociational Democracy', in T. Hockin, ed., *Apex of Power: The Prime Minister and Political Leadership in Canada*, 2nd ed. (Scarborough, Ont.: Prentice-Hall, 1977), 154-8; see also K. D. McRae, ed., *Consociational Democracy* (Toronto: McClelland and Stewart, 1974), and Bakvis, *Regional Ministers*.

[28] Cairns, *From Interstate to Intrastate Federalism in Canada* (Kingston, Ont.: Institute of Inter-governmental Relations, 1979), 6.

[29] For example, D.V. Smiley, *The Federal Condition in Canada* (Toronto: McGraw-Hill Ryerson, 1987).

[30] The party leader, under the *Canada Elections Act*, is required to sign the nomination papers of the party's candidate in each riding. This gives the leader the formal power to withhold the nomination from an unsatisfactory candidate. However, this constitutes the proverbial sledge-hammer, which the national party is very reluctant to use, and hence it is an unsatisfactory mechanism for changing recruitment patterns.

[31] See Donald E. Blake, ed., 'Party Competition and Electoral Volatility: Canada in Comparative Perspective', in Bakvis, ed., *Representation*, 253-73.

[32] These were among the rationales given and recommendations made for the creation of party foundation by the Royal Commission on Electoral Reform and Party Financing, *Final Report*, vol. 1 (Ottawa: Supply and Services, 1991), 290-302.

[33] A study by Thomas Lancaster and David Patterson ('Comparative Pork Barrel Politics: Perceptions from the West German Bundestag', *Comparative Political Studies* 22 [Jan. 1990]: 458-77) found that legislators from single-member districts were much more likely than those elected under the list system to attach high importance to obtaining special projects for their districts, to make actual efforts to do so, and to claim success in acquiring them.

CHAPTER EIGHT

SCALING   THE   MATTERHORN

Parliamentary   Leadership
in   Canada

———■———

Ian   Stewart

The twentieth century has witnessed a steady decline in the power of most legislative assemblies. Rare indeed is the parliament that regularly has an independent impact on the affairs of the state, on the making of laws or the unmaking of governments. The underlying causes of this loss of legislative power are not difficult to identify. According to most observers, the major culprits have been the advent of mass political parties, the rise of the interventionist state, the growing complexity of public policy, the ponderous nature of the parliamentary process, and the appearance of corporatist forms of policy-making. In Canada there is some dispute as to precisely when the 'golden age' of our Parliament came to an end. For Gunther and Winn, the key year (1864) actually pre-dated Confederation,[1] while Hockin suggests that 1878 might be more accurate.[2] In either case, it has clearly been some time since the powers of the national Parliament began to wane.

This state of affairs is simultaneously ironic, paradoxical, and lamentable. It is ironic because, at least until 1982, the constitutional authority of the Canadian Parliament had remained largely unchanged since Confederation. Until the entrenchment of the Charter of Rights and Freedoms, the erosion of parliamentary power was mostly extra-constitutional in nature. This erosion is also paradoxical, since it paralleled (in fact, was linked to) the mushrooming of the Canadian federal state. While the Canadian federal state was exponentially increasing its influence over society, one of the three branches of that state appeared to be experiencing an absolute diminution of power. Finally, the relative impotence of our national Parliament is cause for lament. After all, in the Canadian federal state, only parliamentarians (and only some of those) are subject to direct election by the people. If Parliament does not play a vital role in the affairs of the state, the democratic legitimacy of our politics cannot help being called into question.

Given the foregoing, one could hardly be sanguine about the prospects for 'parliamentary leadership'. Indeed, the term may at first almost seem oxymoronic. If Parliament as an institution is sadly lacking in influence, there would appear to be no reason to anticipate that an individual operating within that institutional framework would be able to display leadership qualities. Yet such a conclusion would be too hasty. It is true that the opportunities for parliamentary leadership are significantly constrained; nevertheless, given a rather idiosyncratic set of circumstances, such leadership can come to the fore.

At this point it is essential to clarify our central concepts: 'parliament' and 'leadership'. With respect to the former, we will confine our attention to those members of Parliament (or of a provincial legislative assembly) who are not simultaneously part of the political executive. Given the intellectual division of labour that underlies this volume (see Chapter 7, on Cabinet leadership, by Herman Bakvis), such an approach is not difficult to justify. It should be noted, however, that it effectively eliminates certain types of parliamentary leadership from scrutiny. It should also be noted that the Senate has generally been a 'silent partner' in our bicameral system; as a result, the analytical focus of this chapter will be the House of Commons.

Conceptualizing 'leadership', unfortunately, is rather more complex. For such a seemingly ubiquitous phenomenon, the literature on political leadership is surprisingly insubstantial. As David Truman has noted, 'everyone knows something of leaders and leadership of various sorts, but no one knows very much.'[3] How, then, should the concepts be employed? Taras and Weyant submit that leadership can be defined as 'the process of influence between leaders and followers',[4] but that is too tautological to be helpful. In this chapter it will be argued that leadership exists if two conditions are met. First, leadership is fundamentally individualistic in nature. When a group acts as one, it cannot be said to be displaying leadership qualities (irrespective of the nature of these actions). Admittedly, the term 'collective leadership' has crept into the lexicon of political science in recent years, but in the absence of any qualifying adjective, 'leadership' is about the behaviour of individuals. Second, leadership must have significant consequences; it must make a substantial difference for the polity. This implies that in the absence of any act of leadership, important events would in some way have turned out differently, a prospect about which one may sometimes be able to speculate intelligently, but that can never be definitively proven. Notwithstanding these epistemological difficulties, the requirement that a leader's actions be of consequence will remain central to our understanding of the term. Leslie Pal makes a similar observation. 'In the modern state,' he suggests, 'the art of leadership consists of finding the modal points in existing networks of power and conflict and applying sufficient pressure *to alter flows in desired directions*.'⁵ In short, parliamentary leadership will be said to exist when an individual parliamentarian (who is not also a member of Cabinet) significantly alters the flow of events on matters of genuine importance to the polity.

Are there many instances of such leadership in the Canadian parliamentary context? For most observers, the answer is unequivocally negative. Consider, for example, Michael Atkinson's assessment that an MP has little influence in Ottawa. 'From the narrowest of details to the broadest of constitutional responsibilities,' he concludes, 'the government is in charge.'⁶ Many of those on the inside looking out share Atkinson's views. Of his experience as a Conservative backbencher, Garth Turner once observed: 'One person, no matter how well-intentioned, cannot accomplish very much. I've learned the importance of the team. Things get accomplished through the team, not the office of the MP.'⁷ Moreover, the prospects for parliamentary leadership seem to be growing progressively more gloomy. Long-time member of Parliament George McIlraith suggested in the early 1980s that 'there has been a sharp diminution in the influence of a private member in the last decade',⁸ while more recently Bill Blaikie asserted that the small amount of influence that individual parliamentarians used to enjoy has now declined to 'zilch'. According to Blaikie, constituents are starting to realize that 'it doesn't matter what you tell these guys [MPs], they have about as much influence as their next door neighbour.'⁹

Assuming that one does not reside beside Conrad Black, these assessments are obviously discouraging. Nor is the major cause of the problem especially mysterious. In essence, the Canadian Parliament is an institution in which the individual's identity is all but submerged beneath the collective will of the political party to which he or she belongs. Whatever their psychological predispositions, members of Parliament rarely behave like autonomous 'free spirits'. On the contrary, they are usually conformists, moving as one with their partisan cohorts. One observer has noted that an MP acts 'above all as a party member; the NDP, or Lib., or PC in brackets after the name is more important than the name. There is no person, just a party token.'¹⁰ Since leadership has been conceptualized as an attribute of individuals, the collective nature of legislative behaviour is obviously a major impediment to the emergence of parliamentary leadership.

One might not have expected such conformity from our MPs. After all, the pursuit of elected office is not for everyone: only individuals with an unusually well-developed sense of self-worth are likely to apply. Why, then, is a parliamentarian willing to subordinate his or her identity to that of the group? Part of the answer comes with the awareness that most MPs have internalized a fundamental loyalty to the party even before their arrival on Parliament Hill. They realize that they won their seats not principally on the basis of their own (undeniable) merits, but on the backs of their leader and party. One study of the 1988 national election, for example, discovered that only 27 per cent of the electorate cited the local candidate as the 'most important reason' for their vote (and even this figure, it should be noted, was unusually high by Canadian standards).[11] The pre-eminence of party comes, therefore, to be accepted as a necessary evil, one of the 'rules of the game'. For many MPs, the belief that they belong to a team with a coherent set of beliefs and values serves to reinforce their sense of loyalty. The degree to which Canadian political parties represent distinguishable ideologies has long been a subject of scholarly dispute. For some, the requirements of practising brokerage politics in a country rent with vertical social cleavages has robbed our political parties of their ideological identities. Nevertheless, at least one sample of MPs' orientations suggests that parliamentarians are, in fact, able to identify distinctive beliefs that they share with their caucus cohorts. For the Progressive Conservatives, these values are the family and free enterprise; for the Liberals, tolerance and diversity; for the New Democrats, progress and social justice.[12] Subordination to party can thus easily be legitimized as merely a means to further these shared long-term goals. In words that have clear relevance to the Canadian context, Edward Crowe has suggested that for most British parliamentarians, 'loyalty is routine and consensual; they explain their own actions as the products of agreement, positive affect toward their leaders, and feelings of obligation to the party.'[13]

Are internalized feelings of party loyalty all that stand in the way of the emergence of parliamentary leadership? The Special Committee on Reform of the House of Commons (commonly known as the McGrath Committee) did acknowledge that MPs must alter their own role perceptions if their independence is to be strengthened. Unfortunately, the McGrath Committee also stressed the need for attitudinal change among party élites, and the prospects of that are hardly encouraging. At present, party élites employ a judicious mixture of incentives and punishments to keep their backbenchers in line. With respect to the former, party leaders (especially those on the government side of the House) have a variety of perquisites to dole out to their faithful supporters. Cabinet positions can be promised, committee chairmanships can be bestowed, favourable publicity can be orchestrated, re-election assistance can be assured, lavish junkets can be arranged, and so on. Small wonder that many parliamentarians repress any misgivings they may have about their party's intended direction.

If these 'carrots' are insufficient to induce docility, then party élites may feel compelled to use (or at least threaten to use) the 'sticks' that are at their disposal. Dissidents may be denied the opportunity to participate in debates or Question Period, they may be removed from positions of authority, and they may be ostracized by their peers. Even the location and size of an MP's office is in the hands of his or her party. The party officer charged with keeping parliamentarians in line is the Party Whip. Although some observers claim that the Whips rarely have to coerce their charges,[14] the leather bullwhip on the Liberal Whip's desk and the 'ceremonial' whips on the wall of the Conservative Whip's office serve as symbolic reminders that dissidents will not easily be tolerated.[15] If all other means of persuasion fail, MPs who refuse to toe the party line can be banished from the party caucus. Two Conservative MPs from Alberta, David Kilgour and Alex Kindy, were expelled from the Tory caucus in 1990 over their refusal to support the government's controversial Goods and

Services Tax. Given the electoral fate that has customarily befallen independent candidates for elected office in Canada, such an expulsion can effectively terminate a political career. It is not surprising, therefore, that one observer graphically concludes: 'Whips and scorpions — that is what makes parliament tick today. Cattle were never so driven.'[16]

There is no reason to anticipate that party leaders will soon abandon these mechanisms of control. They may well engage in 'pious rhetorical support for the notion of strengthening the role of the private member',[17] but genuinely independent parliamentarians would render all but impossible an already difficult job. As the situation now stands, party leaders spend much of their time in a state of siege, dodging brickbats tossed by, among others, interest groups, provincial politicians, and the media. To these leaders the conformist behaviour of those who sit behind them in the House of Commons is their only reliable anchor in an increasingly unpredictable world. They will not willingly forego this anchor. Indeed, in order to sustain it, party élites have fostered the myth that any defeat of a government bill should be interpreted as a signal of non-confidence, with the fall of the government, the dissolution of the House, and the commencement of a general election campaign to follow swiftly. Successive administrations have managed to gull many of their supporters into playing what might aptly be dubbed 'the ultimate confidence game', despite advice to the contrary from Canadian constitutional experts[18] and experience to the contrary from other countries that employ the Westminster model of parliamentary government.[19] Fearful of precipitating a political cataclysm, many potential mavericks have quietly opted for conformity.

In summary, the prospects for parliamentary leadership in Canada would seem to be inversely related to the pre-eminence of party in the House of Commons. As long as MPs internalize loyalty to party, as long as their peers pressure them to conform, as long as their leaders reward dependence and punish independence, then the opportunities for parliamentary leadership will be few. Admittedly, some of these pressures seem to rest especially heavily on government MPs. Opposition leaders lack both some of the rewards and some of the punishments that are available to the government, and the consequences of dissident behaviour among opposition MPs would seem to be less apocalyptic. If opposition MPs are 'nobodies' as former prime minister Trudeau once remarked, then 'government supporters, given the force of party discipline, are rather less than that'.[20]

This state of affairs has significant democratic consequences. The chain of democratic accountability in our system extends from the voters to the members of Parliament, to the Cabinet ministers, and, finally, to the civil servants. If the first two links in that chain are weak, if parliamentarians submissively adopt the role of party delegates, then, at least from one perspective, the quality of Canadian democracy can be called into question. Certainly there is abundant evidence that the Canadian public is dissatisfied with the pre-eminence of party in the House of Commons. Public opinion surveys have repeatedly delivered the same messages, that politicians are not to be trusted, that MPs soon lose touch with the people who elected them, and that the government does not care what the people think.[21] On the specific question of whether parliamentarians should heed their party before their constituents, the answer is unambiguous. One poll discovered that 50 per cent of the respondents felt that MPs should vote as their constituents would vote; voting according to party demands was supported by only 8 per cent.[22] Nor should those numbers be surprising. As one member of Parliament has observed: 'Our constituents are demanding in part because our salaries come out of their taxes. They see us as their employees.'[23]

Although parliamentarians are certainly aware of public perceptions on this point, they do not necessarily share them. Most surveys discover that only a minority of MPs claim to be societal delegates,[24] and, of these the majority are oriented more to the nation than to their region or constituency.[25] Similar findings have been uncovered at the provincial level in Canada. One such survey revealed that only 16 per cent of MLAs considered themselves to be constituency delegates.[26] Even when the constraints of party discipline have been temporarily lifted — for example, during the 'free vote' on capital punishment in 1987 — many of our federal legislators have not perceived the reflection of constituents' views as their first priority. Although numerous polls revealed that a solid majority of Canadians supported the retention of the death penalty for certain offences, MPs voted 148 to 127 in favour of its abolition.[27] It has been observed of French citizens and deputies that 'mass preferences about deputy role emphasis show no congruence whatever with the élite distributions'.[28] That is, voters' expectations that elected officials should conform to public opinion, whatever their own views, is not an approach favoured by elected representatives themselves. This finding clearly has relevance in the Canadian context as well.

Of course, the interests of party and of constituency need not conflict. Political parties are organizations dedicated to maximizing their share of the popular vote; an open disregard for popular preferences is unlikely to facilitate that endeavour. Nevertheless, in a country as regionally divided as Canada, parties have to make strategic choices about the group or groups of Canadians to which they will pay particular heed. Given their disproportionate share of the national population, the voters of Ontario and Québec have historically been singled out for special attention from our major parties. For central Canadian MPs, therefore, the interests of party and of constituency may well be complementary: in other words, the party may be obliging these parliamentarians to respect the views of their constituents. For MPs elected from one of the eight hinterland provinces, however, the situation is altogether different; for them, the competing tugs of party and constituency may have an effect akin to that of a medieval rack. It is no coincidence that parties espousing parliamentary reform have consistently garnered their greatest support in western Canada, from the Progressives in the 1920s to Reform in the 1990s. Given their support for such plebiscitarian features as the initiative and, especially, the recall, it is apparent that these parties have not been intent on 'liberating' our MPs; instead, they have been concerned with substituting the yoke of constituency opinion for that of party discipline.

Can parliamentary leadership be rescued from these competing pressures, or must it be squeezed between the constituency rock and the party hard place? It is clear that the opportunities for an MP to exercise leadership are severely constrained. Even those, such as ex-Liberal MP Keith Penner, who claim that an individual parliamentarian can make 'an enormous difference' acknowledge not only that 'it doesn't happen immediately', but also that it is 'very hard for any MP to puff out his chest at the end of his parliamentary career and say, 'I accomplished these things'.[29] Individual accomplishments, however, are the essence of leadership. If they are to be found in our parliamentary system, there are plainly only a few possible locales. In the succeeding pages we will look for evidence of parliamentary leadership in party caucuses, legislative committees, private members' legislation, and voting against the party line.

PARTY CAUCUSES

Every Wednesday morning when the House is in session, a party's parliamentarians meet *in camera* to discuss matters of mutual concern. The rationale for convening behind closed doors is straightforward. Caucus meetings permit open discussion about the party's future direction; the frankness of such exchanges would undoubtedly be diminished were they to be held in public, especially given that 'the media will pay more attention to division than to harmony. Such, regrettably, is the nature of the beast.'[30] Moreover, MPs are under such pressure to conform to the party line in public that they require a private forum in which to air their frustrations. Several parliamentarians have stressed the importance of this cathartic function. Conservative Albert Cooper observes that MPs experience 'a lot of pressure and feelings are very tense. Very often, a Member can go into caucus and vent that steam.'[31] Similarly, according to Bud Cullen, 'caucus is one of the great escape vents for our feelings, particularly if we have some negative attitudes to bring across.'[32] MPs are already vilified by the public for their conformist behaviour in Parliament. Were it common knowledge that they spoke one way in caucus and voted quite differently in the House, charges of hypocrisy would echo about their ears.

Does the secrecy that surrounds the caucus meeting vitiate its potential as a forum in which parliamentary leadership can be exercised? Not necessarily. While we are accustomed to the public exercise of leadership, it is certainly not inconceivable that an individual MP's activities in caucus could have significant consequences for the polity. For that to occur, however, two conditions need to be met. First, public policy must be a central feature of caucus deliberations. Second, caucus must not operate in a hierarchical fashion. Certainly the first requirement has not always been fulfilled. A member of Diefenbaker's caucus once complained: 'We spent most of our time in caucus talking about secretarial service or parking space. We are never consulted about policy and hardly ever get to discuss it at all.'[33] More recently it has been suggested that the Liberal caucus under Prime Minister Trudeau was 'consulted infrequently on legislative priorities'.[34] Nevertheless, there is episodic evidence that caucus members do consider issues of public policy. During the Liberal regime of the early 1980s, for example, Atlantic MPs were able to use caucus to amend a bill on the prior employment period required to determine eligibility for Unemployment Insurance benefits, and their Québec counterparts were similarly able to block a proposal that would have limited the extent of provincial government ownership in transportation companies.[35] It is also true that, much to party leader John Turner's dismay, the merits of the Meech Lake Accord were actively debated during Liberal caucus meetings of the late 1980s.[36] Thus the possibility clearly exists for caucus to address issues of public policy.

Whether this consideration occurs in a hierarchical or egalitarian fashion, however, is another matter. Liberal MP Brian Tobin has no doubt that the latter characterization is more accurate:

> Caucus is like being in the corners in the third period of a hockey game. As a newly-elected Member of Parliament [in 1980, with a Liberal government under Trudeau], I was amazed at how free and outspoken Members were in caucus; nobody held back any punches. If somebody was mad at a Minister, a department or even the Prime Minister, that was the place to air concerns and Members did it with great candor. Caucus is not a place where we ceremoniously endorse government policy; it's the place where we get in elbows and knees.[37]

In this view, caucus meetings are places where the strictures of party discipline are removed, where the humble backbencher and the exalted frontbencher can joust on a level playing field. Others are less certain that caucus proceedings are not significantly stage-managed by party élites. One neophyte MP, amazed at what he took to be the democratic quality of caucus deliberations, was immediately chastened when a long-standing parliamentarian observed: 'They probably had this all settled before caucus, . . . we were just steered into approving.'[38] Herein lies the problem that bedevils many variants of élite analysis. Since the most successful élite will be the one that achieves its aims without visibly exerting its power, it is possible to interpret the absence of any direct evidence of leadership manipulation of caucus as confirmation of the skill and authority of that leadership. The Alberta Progressive Conservative caucus during the stewardship of Peter Lougheed provides a nice illustration of this phenomenon. For some contemporary observers, Lougheed's caucus meetings were strikingly democratic. The premier kept a low profile, backbenchers openly criticized Cabinet proposals, votes were invariably taken at the end of all discussions, and the majority sentiment prevailed. Caucus could even veto policies that had received prior Cabinet approval; it was, in short, a body that was 'active, effective, and even powerful'.[39] Following his retirement from politics, however, Lougheed indicated that appearances can be somewhat deceiving. Yes, the caucus vote was determinant on every major policy with the exception of the budget. The premier noted, however, that he did not proceed to caucus if the vote was going to be unpredictably close. In addition, Lougheed used his control of the speaking order to diminish the impact of his more articulate opponents. Finally, on those rare occasions when it seemed necessary, he would forcefully intervene on behalf of his preferred option.[40] If Premier Lougheed is to be believed on this matter, the egalitarian façade of Alberta Conservative caucus meetings served to cover a significantly hierarchical structure.

What, then, can be concluded about the prospects for parliamentary leadership in party caucuses? It would clearly be unwise to suggest that caucus is entirely a toothless tiger. It was caucus, after all, that toppled Pierre-Marc Johnson from his position as leader of the Parti Québécois, and it was caucus that sustained (for a while) the party stewardship of John Diefenbaker, when most of his Cabinet cohorts were demanding his resignation. If caucus, as a group, is occasionally able to flex its muscles on matters of policy and leadership, then the opportunity must exist for individual members of caucus to do the same. Exercise of parliamentary leadership in party caucuses may not be a common phenomenon, but it clearly can occur.

PARLIAMENTARY COMMITTEES

There are three types of ongoing committees in the Canadian parliamentary system.[41] First is the Committee of the Whole, the importance of which has diminished in recent years; Committee of the Whole is now largely reserved for the scrutiny of money bills. Second are legislative committees, which have the responsibility of studying specific legislative proposals. Finally, there are standing committees, which consider particular policy areas as well as the activities of relevant departments.

Before 1985 it was generally agreed that parliamentary committees played a rather marginal role in the political process. Attendance was spotty, party discipline was pervasive, and media attention was non-existent. One MP who lost his seat in the 1984 general election described committee work thus:

> It seems important at first and you feel you're doing something. And then the minister says to you at the end of the line, 'Well, I don't give a damn what you think about the bill, this is the way the bill is to be voted through and you just vote for it.'[42]

When the Conservatives swept to office in 1984, however, Prime Minister Mulroney had to concoct a method for keeping happy a group of party cohorts who were both unusually numerous (since the Tories had won three-quarters of the seats in the House of Commons) and demonstrably impatient (since the party had essentially been out of office for two decades). Mulroney's solution to this problem was to appoint the McGrath Committee. When the committee tabled its final report in 1985, the prime minister responded with characteristic understatement, describing the document as 'one of the most outstanding pieces of work that has ever been produced by parliamentarians'.[43] The centrepiece of the McGrath proposals, most of which were institutionalized, was an overhaul of the standing-committee system. Standing committees were made smaller and more cohesive, provided with greater material and staff resources, and given a mandate to initiate investigations without prior reference from the House.[44] Coupled with the exclusion of parliamentary secretaries from committee membership, these changes were thought to have the potential to increase greatly the autonomy and influence of members of Parliament.

A decade later, however, the jury is still out on the impact of the McGrath reforms. Admittedly, one 1987 survey of 92 MPs revealed that 12 per cent of respondents felt that the changes had given parliamentarians 'a lot more power', with a further 54 per cent suggesting that they had gained 'some power'.[45] Indeed, former Liberal MP Keith Penner has suggested that the post-McGrath committee system 'is a vast improvement over what it once was. . . . The system provides much more scope for the energetic, creative and intelligent MP.'[46] Particularly adept at capturing the attention of the government, the media, and the public has been the Standing Committee on Finance and Economic Affairs. Under the colourful leadership of Conservative backbencher Don Blenkarn, the SCFEA appeared to become a major player in matters of financial policy during the late 1980s. In fact, the committee was able to influence laws relating to bank service charges, financial self-dealing, corporate take-overs, and credit-card interest rates. In so doing, the SCFEA gave 'life to the role of a private member, increased the Finance department's accountability, humbled powerful lobby groups and raised issues of concern to the public that were ignored by the department and financial institutions'.[47] The committee aggressively challenged senior civil servants; in Blenkarn's words, it was 'rocking the bureaucracy'.[48] On the other hand, the SCFEA was forced to acknowledge the ultimate authority of Cabinet in matters of policy. While the government accepted (in some cases, reluctantly) a number of the committee's legislative recommendations, other proposals (notably in the area of tax reform) were ignored.

Moreover, other standing committees have not fared as well as the SCFEA in the post-McGrath era. Other chairs who have embarrassed the Mulroney administration (such as Fernand Jourdenais of the Standing Committee on Labour, Employment, and Immigration) have been peremptorily dropped, and other reports with which the government did not agree (such as those dealing with broadcast policy and access to information) have been ignored.[49] The media, furthermore, have paid little heed to the activities of most standing committees. One newspaper columnist has justified this inattention by noting that most committees are still characterized by 'bare quorums' and 'idiotic questions, at best'.[50] As the 1990s commenced, rumours swirled around Ottawa that many Conservative MPs were ducking their committee assignments and that the government was considering further reforms to the committee system.[51]

It would seem that the conclusion to this section must echo that of the preceding one. There are opportunities within the House of Commons' committee system to exercise parliamentary leadership. Don Blenkarn clearly fulfilled such a role in his capacity as chair of the Standing Committee on Finance and Economic Affairs; it is instructive that after Blenkarn was removed as committee chair, the SCFEA all but disappeared from public view. Yet even Blenkarn recognized that his influence was limited, that a 'renegade chairman who has a fundamental difference of opinion about government policy can be replaced without too much difficulty'.[52] In short, it requires a fortuitous combination of circumstances and some accessible cracks in the system for the exercise of parliamentary leadership in Commons' committees.

PRIVATE MEMBERS' BILLS

In attempting to strengthen the individual member of Parliament, the McGrath Committee also suggested new procedures for dealing with private members' bills (as opposed to those sponsored by the government). Certainly the traditional practices in this regard were in need of reform. Before 1986 there was essentially no chance that a private member's bill would find its way into the statute books; in fact, of the 3,170 introduced in the previous eighteen years, only 12 had received parliamentary approval,[53] and most of these were remarkably inconsequential. The National Flag of Canada Manufacturing Standards Act of 1984, for example, sponsored by MP Allan McKinnon, stipulated that 'a high quality of material, design and colour will be used in the manufacture of the Canadian Flag'.[54] The normal procedure was for a private member's bill to receive a single one-hour debate, after which it would fall to the bottom of the Order Paper where, given the limited time allotted to such matters, it would languish and ultimately die at the end of the parliamentary session. Small wonder that most MPs quickly became cynical about the process. Gordon Aiken, for one, asserted: 'Bluntly stated, private Members in Canada do not make new laws. Theoretically it is possible. They are encouraged to try. But everything is stacked against them.'[55] Echoed Doug Hogarth: 'What the private Member gets as a law-maker . . . is a fast ride on a square-wheeled chariot.'[56] By the early 1980s the situation had taken on farcical overtones. Realizing that their measures had no realistic chance of being adopted, many MPs began to submit only the titles rather than the completed drafts of their private members' bills; one study of the Official Commons Order Paper uncovered 165 of these 'phantom' bills.[57]

The McGrath Committee considered it desirable to 'widen the scope of Private Members' legislation and ensure that some Private Members' bills and motions come to a vote'.[58] Accordingly, several reforms were instituted. The new procedure has the deputy speaker randomly selecting twenty private members' bills from the hundreds submitted by individual MPs (in the second session of the 33rd Parliament, Liberal Charles Caccia alone submitted thirty-one motions or bills).[59] The Standing Committee on Privileges and Elections then designates up to six of the twenty as 'votable', which means that they will be allotted five one-hour debates and must ultimately come to a vote in the House. The remainder are disposed of in the traditional manner and new bills and motions are added as the original ones work their way through the parliamentary process.

It would appear that these reforms have been moderately successful. One study suggested that about half of those private members' bills or motions that have been designated as 'votable' have, in fact, received parliamentary approval.[60] Perhaps the most notable of these has been New Democrat Lynn McDonald's Non-Smokers' Health Act, guaranteeing that federal work places and transportation services would be smoke-free. Even though every member of the Cabinet who was in the House that day voted against the bill, it narrowly passed at third reading.[61] McDonald is convinced that her success has energized other MPs. 'It makes for a much livelier parliament,' she notes, 'when people think that it's possible to reach out even as an Opposition Member and, by organizing support from all parties, to change the laws of Canada.'[62]

One must be careful not to exaggerate the impact of the new procedures. Private members' bills still may not authorize the raising or expenditure of money, and the criteria employed by the standing committee in designating certain bills as 'votable' have been the subject of much controversy. Moreover, the Conservative government has not been fully animated by the spirit of reform; a parliamentary secretary has

generally been charged with ensuring that only those private members' bills designated as 'votable' by the Standing Committee on Privileges and Elections actually do
come to a vote in the House.[63] Nevertheless, if one acknowledges that leadership can
exist even if its consequences become apparent only over the long term, and, that
raising public awareness may serve as a necessary prelude to changing public attitudes, then parliamentary leadership could be found in the efforts of private members
even before the 1986 reforms. Jed Baldwin's long-standing crusade for greater freedom of government information is an obvious case in point. Baldwin did not draft the
access-to-information statute that ultimately found its way into law, but he could
legitimately claim indirect authorship. Since 1986, the prospects for a more direct
form of parliamentary leadership in private members' business have been greatly
enhanced. With enough good fortune (one's bill does, after all, have to be selected in
the deputy speaker's lottery), it is once again possible to exploit cracks in the system
and exhibit parliamentary leadership.

PARLIAMENTARY VOTING

Members who reject the party line provide the most compelling illustrations of
parliamentary leadership. 'Free votes', in which the constraints of party discipline are
temporarily removed, are about as common on Parliament Hill as bouts of prime
ministerial humility. According to one study, over a two-decade period only matters
relating to the Canadian flag and to capital punishment were decided by 'free votes'.[64]
And even in the latter case there has been evidence, at least in more recent debates,
that the 'party mechanisms within the House remain dominant' and that the party
House Leaders and Whips continue to be the 'backstage managers'.[65] The constitutional doctrine that Cabinet must be subservient to the will of Parliament has, in
practical terms, been stood on its head. Somewhat perversely, governments are now
said to be 'evading' their responsibilities if they permit parliamentarians to make
unconstrained choices.[66]

Such was not always the case. C.E.S. Franks notes, for example, that in the first five
years after Confederation there were 171 occasions when 'supporters' of the government voted against it.[67] More recently, though, the forces outlined earlier in the
chapter have cowed all but a few renegades. Former MP Pauline Jewett once observed:
'On several occasions, I had to vote against my conscience . . . and those times I felt I
had no character at all. But I could see no alternative.'[68] MPs who do break publicly
with their parties (such as those from the Yukon and Northwest Territories who voted
against the Meech Lake Accord) are sometimes able to return quietly to the party fold.
An irrevocable split, however, usually hurts the dissenter more than the party. Canadians may rail against the tyranny of party discipline, but they have exhibited a
marked reluctance to vote for 'independent' candidates. The case of Bill Yurko is by
no means atypical. Yurko split with the Conservatives over the patriation of the
Constitution and sat as an independent between 1982 and 1984. Although he had
received 54 per cent of the vote in the 1980 general election (at a time when the tide
was clearly running against the Tories), his support as an 'independent' candidate in

the 1984 national election plummeted to just over 8 per cent. A majority of Canadian voters are said to be 'flexible partisans'; that is, their party loyalties are weak, changeable, or inconsistent.[69] But this flexibility stops well short of support for candidates without any party affiliation.

Given the dangers of provoking a split with one's party, few parliamentarians can be expected to reject the party line on the floor of the legislature. Nevertheless, such breaches do occur, and they can provide some of the most dramatic displays of parliamentary leadership.

I. David MacDonald

During the October Crisis of 1970, the federal government claimed to have evidence of an 'apprehended insurrection' in Québec. Accordingly, it imposed the War Measures Act, and in so doing suspended a number of fundamental civil liberties. Three weeks later, the Trudeau administration attempted to replace the War Measures Act with a slightly less intrusive document, the Public Order (Temporary Measures) Act. On second reading, the House of Commons gave approval in principle to the new legislation by a vote of 152 to 1; the lone dissenter was David MacDonald, a Progressive Conservative MP from Prince Edward Island. The War Measures Act, in MacDonald's eyes, had 'already very detrimentally affected' Canada; the new bill would also be 'contrary to the interests of the country'.[70] According to one of MacDonald's caucus cohorts:

> The single act restored the faith of a lot of Canadians in the political system. One voice spoke for those who still thought the government was wrong. It requires some special kind of courage to stand alone against your party. But against the whole House is something else.[71]

MacDonald's actions legitimized dissent at a time when a creeping authoritarianism was infecting the body politic; shortly thereafter, a letter to the editor of the *Globe and Mail* observed with satisfaction that the 'frightened men who are the Government of Canada have not been able to still the non-conformist conscience of David MacDonald'.[72] Over the past two decades, the appropriate balance between the authority of the state and the rights of the individual have been a staple element of Canadian political discourse. For this, David MacDonald deserves at least a modest amount of credit.

II. Jim Walding

In March 1986, Manitoba voters narrowly re-elected Premier Howard Pawley's New Democratic administration; the NDP won 30 seats as opposed to the 27 garnered by the two opposition parties. Choosing a Speaker (who in the Manitoba legislature can vote only to break a tie) brought the government's margin down to two, however, and the subsequent resignation of Health minister Larry Desjardins reduced the majority to one. Compounding Pawley's problems was the presence of a visibly unhappy backbencher, Jim Walding, in the government caucus. Walding had previously served as Speaker of the Manitoba legislature and had clashed with other New Democratic MLAs over his willingness to countenance opposition filibusters. Although a fifteen-year veteran of the House, he barely survived a challenge from Pawley's former executive assistant for the 1986 nomination in his riding, and when he subsequently won re-election, Walding was not included in Pawley's Cabinet.

By early 1988, Walding's discontent with the government became a matter of public record. During the debate on the Speech from the Throne, Walding interjected: 'People are not sure of who's in charge of the store or, more frighteningly, is anyone in charge of the store.'[73] He was persuaded by some of his constituents not to support an opposition motion of non-confidence on the throne speech,[74] but shortly thereafter he brought down the government by voting against its budget. Walding's rationale for his vote was intriguing:

> It is time for the people of Manitoba to decide whether this government still has a mandate. The people of Manitoba can decide. I don't want that decision to be all on me. It's too much of a strain. I can't do it any longer.[75]

Such a justification, it should be clear, does not easily conform to popular preconceptions of the leader as a heroic figure. Walding apparently did not want the responsibility of determining the government's fate; in fact, he was having some difficulty coping with the idiosyncratic set of circumstances that had thrust him into the limelight. Nevertheless, by the criteria outlined earlier in the chapter, Walding's action was clearly an instance of parliamentary leadership. He had won his party's nomination by only a single vote; had his rival prevailed, it is very likely that the Pawley government would have survived at least through the 1988 sitting of the legislature. As it turned out, the NDP was routed in the 1988 provincial election and the Conservatives assumed office. In general terms, this meant that Manitoba experienced a shift away from the social-democratic policy thrust that had characterized the Pawley administration. More specifically, it erected a critical road-block to the passage of the Meech Lake Accord. While Pawley had been one of the original signatories (albeit a somewhat reluctant one) to the constitutional package, new premier Gary Filmon was decidedly unenthusiastic and delayed putting the Accord before the Manitoba legislature. In short, had Jim Walding not precipitated the fall of the Pawley government, it is entirely possible that the Meech Lake Accord would have been ratified in Manitoba and, subsequently, in New Brunswick (the other hold-out province) before anti-Meech crusader Clyde Wells was anything more than a distant blip on the Newfoundland electoral horizon.

III. Elijah Harper

The Constitution Act, 1982, stipulates that a proposed constitutional amendment expires if it is not ratified by the required number of legislatures within three years after it is first ratified by any legislature. For the Meech Lake Accord, which needed unanimous provincial consent, this meant that 23 June 1990 was the effective deadline. Two weeks before that date, the accord still had not been ratified in the provinces of Manitoba, New Brunswick, and Newfoundland (which had rescinded its earlier endorsement), but at a last-minute federal-provincial conference the premiers of these three provinces undertook to introduce the Accord promptly in their respective legislatures.

In Manitoba, however, this proved not to be a straightforward exercise. When Premier Filmon asked the legislature on 12 June for unanimous consent to waive the normal two-day period of notice, NDP backbencher Elijah Harper denied the request. Although some MLAs called his refusal 'legislative terrorism', Harper was adamant: 'It's about time that aboriginal people be recognized. We need to let Canadians know that we have been shoved aside. We're saying that aboriginal issues should be put on the priority list'.[76]

Harper again refused to waive the two-day notice requirement on 13 June, and on the following day, aided by the procedural advice of a former deputy clerk of the legislature, he raised a series of technical points of order. When the Speaker found that the government had erred in its previous notices of motion,[77] the government's timetable was pushed back to 18 June. Even then, Harper was able to use the rules of procedure to prevent the accord from being introduced in the Manitoba legislature until 20 June, a mere three days before the constitutional-amendment clock was to cease ticking. With dozens of MLAs wishing to speak on the matter, and with a legal obligation to hold public hearings on all proposed constitutional amendments, it was now abundantly clear that the 23 June deadline could not be met. A six-point federal offer to the aboriginal peoples was rejected out of hand and the accord was effectively killed when, on 22 June, Harper vetoed a government proposal to extend the normal sitting hours of the legislature.

Clearly, this was another instance of parliamentary leadership. A single MLA was able to take advantage of the legislature's standing orders to thwart the will of the government. Under normal circumstances, Harper's tactics would have been little more than a nuisance to the Filmon administration. But under the unusually severe time constraints of the moment (constraints for which the federal government must bear a large share of the responsibility), Harper's actions essentially eliminated any chance that the accord could be ratified. His behaviour was also consequential in other important ways. At the time, the *Globe and Mail* fulminated that his obstructionism would 'not produce a rush to address aboriginal grievances, however legitimate' and would engender 'a chill at the constitutional table for some time to come, a chill that will freeze out native concerns'.[78] Such, however, proved not to be the case. During the provincial election in the fall of 1990, the leaders of Manitoba's three major parties agreed to participate in a debate on aboriginal issues. 'This is really historic,' noted the head of the Assembly of Manitoba Chiefs. 'It's the first time ever, in any election, that political leaders have specifically set aside time to address the concerns of native people.'[79] In the constitutional talks of 1991-92, there was no doubt in any of the participants' minds that aboriginal concerns would have to be addressed, and the agreement that emerged from those discussions included an aboriginal right to self-government. Even though the Charlottetown package was rejected in the national referendum of 26 October 1992, it seems inconceivable that aboriginal issues will not be a central component of future constitutional negotiations. For galvanizing a shift in the Canadian political agenda, Elijah Harper deserves no small amount of credit.

CONCLUSION

That parliamentary leadership can exist in Canada is clear. One must keep in mind, however, that the examples cited in this chapter are exceptional. There have been many occasions when the body politic would have benefited considerably from some parliamentary leadership, but that commodity proved to be in distressingly short supply. A case in point would be the final years of Richard Hatfield's Conservative regime in New Brunswick. Although the premier had successfully led the Tories to four consecutive electoral victories, by the mid-1980s he had become something of an embarrassment to his party and his province. Among other things, Hatfield had been charged with (though not convicted of) possession of marijuana; had made unsubstantiated allegations that the RCMP was out to get him; had been accused of supplying drugs to university students; had made indiscriminate use of government aircraft; and had been charging to the Conservative party many of the personal expenses associated with his flamboyant life-style.[80] By May 1985, the chairman of the Tory caucus was publicly calling for Hatfield's resignation.[81] Nevertheless, one study of the recorded votes during New Brunswick's 50th Parliament (1983-87) discovered that every one of these was a 'party vote'.[82] To put the matter another way, a legislature of 58 members offers the possibility of 1,440,000,000,000,000,000 different groupings. Over a five-year period, not counting absences and abstentions, only one of those billions of possible permutations was to be found on the floor of the New Brunswick House of Assembly. One should not underestimate the impact of what has been dubbed 'the iron cage' of party government.

At which governmental level are legislators more likely to escape this iron cage? For some aspects of parliamentary leadership, the answer is clearly the national arena. Most provincial legislatures are significantly smaller than the House of Commons; as a result, many do not have a fully elaborated committee system and rely instead on Committee of the Whole. A stunted system of legislative committees closes off for many MLAs one of the more attractive avenues of parliamentary leadership. With respect to private members' bills a similar picture emerges. Although the situation is somewhat better in Ontario,[83] most legislatures dispense with private members' business in the same way that the House of Commons and before the McGrath-inspired reforms of 1986. In other words, private members' bills are briefly heard and rarely made law.[84]

With respect to the other aspects of parliamentary leadership, however, the opportunities would seem to be greater for provincial MLAs than for federal MPs. Other things being equal, a legislator's influence in party caucus should be inversely related to the size of that caucus. Whereas Progressive Conservative MPs over the past decade have had to jostle for influence with a group of colleagues who have numbered from 160 to over 200, in Prince Edward Island (to take an extreme example), Bennett Campbell's governing Liberals caucus, in 1979, had only 16 members. Similarly, the possibilities of casting a pivotal vote in the legislature should also be inversely related to the size of that legislature. Leaving aside minority administrations, there has never been a majority government in Ottawa that has had a margin of fewer than five over the combined forces of the opposition parties. By contrast, razor-thin majorities of the kind that Jim Walding was able to exploit are significantly more common in provincial legislatures. To take but one example, the Cameron government of Nova Scotia ruled the province from 1991 to 1993 with an effective working majority of a single vote. Even if provincial governments with slender majorities do not normally fall as a result of the defection of their own supporters (and the Walding instance was clearly exceptional in this regard), the need of such governments to keep their backbenchers happy must afford these individuals some opportunities for parliamentary leadership.

It would seem, then, that exercising parliamentary leadership is not unlike climbing mountains. At first blush, the imposing façade of party discipline may seem unassailable. It is not surprising that many legislators turn their attention to serving as ombudsmen and ombudswomen for their constituents. Yet even the smoothest of rock faces contains some fissures. Like skilled mountaineers, those who aspire to parliamentary leadership must take advantage of the few cracks that do exist in the system. Most people do not scale the Matterhorn; most legislators do not exhibit parliamentary leadership. With an idiosyncratic mixture of skill and good fortune, however, both goals can be achieved.

NOTES

[1] Magnus Gunther and Conrad Winn, 'Parliamentary Reform: A Background Note and Introduction,' in Gunther and Winn, eds, *House of Commons Reform* (Ottawa: Parliamentary Internship Program, 1991), 2.

[2] Thomas A. Hockin, 'Adversary Politics and Some Functions of the Canadian House of Commons', in Orest M. Kruhlak, Richard Schultz, and Sidney I. Pobihushchy, eds, *The Canadian Political Process*, 2nd ed. (Toronto: Holt, Rinehart and Winston, 1973), 363.

[3] Samuel C. Patterson, 'Party Leadership in the U.S. Senate', *Legislative Studies Quarterly* 14 (1989): 400.

[4] David Taras and Robert Weyant, 'Dreamers of the Day: A Guide to Roles, Character and Performance on the Political Stage,' in Leslie Pal and David Taras, eds, *Prime Ministers and Premiers* (Scarborough, Ont.: Prentice-Hall, 1988), 3.

[5] Leslie A. Pal, 'Hands at the Helm? Leadership and Public Policy', in ibid., 23; emphasis added.

[6] Michael Atkinson, 'Parliamentary Government in Canada', in Michael Whittington and Glen Williams, eds, *Canadian Politics in the 1990s* (Scarborough, Ont.: Nelson, 1990): 338.

[7] Graham Fraser, 'Four Years on Parliament Hill and How They Grew', *Globe and Mail*, 24 Nov. 1992: A2.

[8] 'Looking Back at Parliament: Interview with George McIlraith', *Canadian Parliamentary Review* 72 (Winter 1984-85): 25.

[9] 'Crisis of Confidence: A Roundtable Discussion', *Parliamentary Government* 9, 3 (1990): 6.

[10] George Bain, 'Raising the Profile of the Backbench MP', *Globe Magazine* November, 1985: 23.

[11] Jon H. Pammett, 'Elections', in Whittington and Williams, eds, *Canadian Politics*, 272.

[12] Robert Miller, 'The Meaning of Party', *Parliamentary Government* 6, 4 (1987): 6-7.

[13] Edward Crowe, 'The Web of Authority: Party Loyalty and Social Control in the British House of Commons', *Legislative Studies Quarterly* 11 (1986): 180.

[14] See Martin Westmacott, 'Whips and Party Cohesion', *Canadian Parliamentary Review* 6 (Autumn 1983): 14-19.

[15] Nancy Pawelek, 'Cracking the Whip?' *Parliamentary Government* 6, 4 (1987): 3.

[16] Morris Shumiatcher in 'The Great Debate: Parliament Versus Congress', *Canadian Parliamentary Review* 7 (Spring 1984): 5.

[17] J.R. Mallory, 'What is Parliamentary Reform About?' in Gunther and Winn, eds, *House of Commons Reform*, 198.

[18] Eugene Forsey and Graham Eglington, 'Twenty-Five Fairy Tales About Parliamentary Government', in Paul W. Fox and Graham White, eds, *Politics: Canada* 7th ed. (Toronto: McGraw-Hill Ryerson, 1991), 417-22.

[19] Philip Norton, 'Government Defeats in the House of Commons: The British Experience', *Canadian Parliamentary Review* 8 (Winter, 1985-86): 6-9.

[20] George Bain, *Globe and Mail*, 8 Nov. 1992: 6

[21] See, for example, Harold D. Clarke, Jane Jenson, Lawrence LeDuc, and Jon H. Pammett, eds, *Absent Mandate: The Politics of Discontent in Canada* (Toronto: Gage, 1984), 7-54 and 100-29.

[22] Jeff Sallot, 'Poll Suggests House is Irrelevant to Majority of Canadian Public', *Globe and Mail*, 19 Sept. 1983: 1. See also Robert M. Krause and R.H. Wagenberg, *Introductory Readings in Canadian Government* (Toronto: Copp Clark Pitman, 1991), 202.

[23] Lise Bourgault, 'A Private Member Speaks Her Mind', in Fox and White, eds, *Politics*, 429.

[24] See, for example, Robert J. Jackson and Michael M. Atkinson, *The Canadian Legislative System* (Toronto: Macmillan, 1974), 147.

[25] See Allan Kornberg, *Canadian Legislative Behavior* (New York: Holt, Rinehart and Winston, 1967), 108. See also David Hoffman and Norman Ward, *Bilingualism and Biculturalism in the Canadian House of Commons* (Ottawa: Queens Printer, 1970), 66-7.

[26] Allan Kornberg, William Mishler, and Harold D. Clarke, *Representative Democracy in the Canadian Provinces* (Scarborough, Ont.: Prentice-Hall, 1982), 181-2.

[27] See David Lord, 'Hard Choices', *Parliamentary Government* 7, 3 (1988): 3-7.

[28] Philip E. Converse and Roy Pierce, 'Representative Roles and Legislative Behaviour in France', *Legislative Studies Quarterly* 4 (1979): 549.

[29] Robert Miller, 'It's an MP's Life: Expectations and Realities', *Parliamentary Government* 8, 2 (1988): 6.

[30] Jeffrey Simpson, 'Keeping them in Line', *Globe and Mail*, 20 June, 1985: A6.

[31] Lynda Rivington, 'Sanctum/Sanctorum', *Parliamentary Government* 4, 1 (1983): 4.

[32] Ibid., 4.

[33] W.A. Matheson, *The Prime Minister and the Cabinet* (Agincourt, Ont.: Methuen, 1976), 182.

[34] Howard Gold, 'Revitalizing Caucus', *Parliamentary Government* 4, 1 (1983): 11.

[35] Paul G. Thomas, 'The Role of National Party Caucuses', in Peter Aucoin, ed., *Government and Regional Representation in Canada* (Toronto: University of Toronto Press, 1985), 97-8.

[36] Lord, 'Hard Choices', 4.

[37] Rivington, 'Sanctum/Sanctorum', 3.

[38] Gordon Aiken, *The Backbencher: Trials and Tribulations of a Member of Parliament* (Toronto: McClelland and Stewart, 1974), 115.

[39] Peter McCormick, 'Politics After the Landslide', *Parliamentary Government* 4, 1 (1983): 9. See also Frederick C. Engelmann, 'Alberta: From One Overwhelming Majority to Another', in Gary Levy and Graham White, eds, *Provincial and Territorial Legislatures in Canada* (Toronto: University of Toronto Press, 1989), 115.

[40] Robert Miller and Philip Rourke, 'Interview with Peter Lougheed', *Parliamentary Government* 9, 1 (1989): 4-5.

[41] For a detailed discussion of the committee structure of the national government, see Robert J. Jackson and Doreen Jackson, *Politics in Canada: Culture, Institutions, Behaviour, and Public Policy*, 2nd ed. (Toronto: Prentice-Hall, 1990): 344-53.

[42] Charlotte Montgomery, 'Bleak Picture Painted of Government Backbench', *Globe and Mail*, 25 Nov. 1985: A4.

[43] Hugh Windsor, 'Mulroney Challenged to Yield Some Cabinet Powers', *Globe and Mail*, 19 June 1985: A9.

[44] Magnus Gunther, 'Reform of the Committee System', in Gunther and Winn, eds, *House of Commons Reform*, 218-19.

[45] Ibid., 222.

[46] Keith Penner, 'Parliament and the Private Member', *Canadian Parliamentary Review* 14 (Summer 1991): 24. See also David Lord, 'The Role of the MP', *Parliamentary Government* 8, 2 (1988): 11-12.

[47] Robert J. O'Brien, 'The Finance Committee Carves Out a Role . . . And Bloodies Some Three Piece Suits in the Process', *Parliamentary Government* 8, 1 (1988): 3.

[48] John Holtby, 'The Standing Committee on Finance and Economic Affairs', *Parliamentary Government* 6, 3 (1986): 13.

[49] O'Brien, 'Finance Committee', 4.

[50] Christopher Harris, 'When It Comes to Committees, Are the Media Doing Their Job', *Parliamentary Government* 7, 1-2 (1987): 8.

[51] Susan Delacourt, 'Commons Panels Face Paralysis', *Globe and Mail*, 6 Nov. 1990: A1 and A5.

[52] O'Brien, 'Finance Committee', 5.

[53] David Blatt, 'Can MPs be Law Makers?', in Gunther and Winn, eds, *House of Commons Reform*, 52.

[54] Ibid., 54.

[55] Aiken, *Backbencher*, 50.

[56] Ibid., 53.

[57] Iain Wilson, 'Making a Difference: Private Members' Bills and Public Policy', *Parliamentary Government* 8, 1 (1988): 13.

[58] Nora S. Lever, 'New Rules for Private Members' Business', *Canadian Parliamentary Review* 9 (Autumn 1986): 7.

[59] Nora S. Lever, 'What's Happened Under the New Rules?' *Canadian Parliamentary Review* 11 (Autumn 1988): 15.

[60] Ibid., 16.

[61] Paul McCrossan, 'Parliament and the Private Member', *Canadian Parliamentary Review* 12 (Winter 1990-91): 9.

[62] Wilson, 'Making a Difference', 15.

[63] Blatt, 'Can MPs be Law Makers?', 65.

[64] Lucinda Flavelle and Philip Kaye, 'Party Discipline and Legislative Voting', *Canadian Parliamentary Review* 9 (Summer 1986): 8.

[65] John Holtby, 'The Great Capital Punishment Debate That Wasn't', *Parliamentary Government* 7, 3 (1988): 9.

[66] Hockin, 'Adversary Politics', 364.

[67] C.E.S. Franks, *The Parliament of Canada* (Toronto: University of Toronto Press, 1987), 21.

[68] Aiken, *Backbencher*, 118.

[69] Pammett, 'Elections', 272.

[70] John Burns, 'New Bill to Replace War Measures Act Approved in Principle With 1 Against', *Globe and Mail*, 6 Nov. 1970: 8.

[71] Aiken, 'Backbencher', 131.

[72] Letters to the editor, *Globe and Mail*, 13 Nov. 1970: A6. It should be noted that the author of this missive was not necessarily the stereotypical 'person on the street'. The letter was signed 'Donald V. Smiley'.

[73] Beverley Bosiak, 'By One Vote', *Canadian Parliamentary Review* 12 (Spring 1989): 15.

[74] 'Manitoba's New Democrats Escape Throne Speech Defeat', *Vancouver Sun*, 23 Feb. 1988: B7.

[75] Bosiak, 'By One Vote', 15. See also chapter 6 above.

[76] Geoffrey York, 'Native MLA Block Debate on Meech', *Globe and Mail*, 13 June 1990: A1.

[77] Geoffrey York, 'Manitoba MLA Throws Meech Into Jeopardy', *Globe and Mail*, 15 June 1990: A1.

[78] 'Native Groups should See Meech Lake as an Ally', *Globe and Mail*, 15 June 1990: A18.

[79] David Roberts, 'Manitoba Party Leaders to Debate Native Issues', *Globe and Mail*, 4 Sept. 1990: A3.

[80] See, for example, Chris Morris, 'Tory Caucus to Question Hatfield's Leadership', *Halifax Chronicle-Herald*, 29 July 1985: 5 and Julian Beltrame, 'The Rise and Falls of Richard Hatfield', *Vancouver Sun*, 14 Oct. 1987: B5.

[81] Alan Story, 'Top Tory Says Hatfield Should Resign', *Toronto Star*, 7 May 1985: A8.

[82] David L. E. Peterson, 'New Brunswick: A Bilingual Assembly for a Bilingual Province', in Levy and White, eds, *Provincial and Territorial Legislatures*, 160.

[83] Graham White, 'Ontario: A Legislature in Adolescence', in ibid., 37-38.

[84] One early study found no record in either Alberta or British Columbia of a private member's bill reaching the statute books. See Philip Laundy, 'Legislatures', in David J. Bellamy, Jon H. Pammett, and Donald C. Rowat, eds, *The Provincial Political Systems* (Agincourt, Ont.: Methuen, 1976), 292.

CHAPTER NINE

MAYORS AS POLITICAL LEADERS

Andrew Sancton

Robert Munsch is one of Canada's best-selling authors. His fanciful stories for children often depict bizarre variations on the problems of everyday life, always from a child's point of view. In one such story,[1] a boy named Jonathan living on Young Street is disconcerted to find that the living room of his apartment has become a subway stop. The book's illustrator, Michael Martchenko, makes it quite clear that Jonathan's errant Young Street subway is in Toronto. When Jonathan complains to a subway conductor, he is told, 'If you don't like it, go see City Hall.' At City Hall 'the lady at the front desk' tells him to see 'the subway boss', who in turn refers him to 'the Mayor'. The mayor, wearing his ceremonial chain of office, is depicted as an unsympathetic, white-haired, cigar-smoking male who trusts the city's computer for information rather than Jonathan. We soon learn from the 'little old man' who runs the computer that it is useless even though 'the mayor paid ten million dollars for it'.

It is noteworthy that a children's story about confrontation with governmental authority focuses on 'the mayor'. The mayor is the local person in charge—the chain of office makes that readily apparent. In this case, he is in charge of a subway system, an easily identifiable feature of everyday life in Jonathan's community. The mayor is not helpful; by the end of the story he is an object of ridicule. He spends money but has no idea what he is receiving in return or what his employees are actually doing. Fanciful as the story may be, there is nothing here that would be out of place in a cynical adult's account of what mayors of large Canadian cities really do.

But there are two important senses in which such an account would be structurally wrong. First, in relation to all that governments do in a community, the organization that the mayor heads — the municipality — is not really 'in charge' of very much; in fact, the mayor of Toronto has virtually no control over the city's subway system.[2] Second, mayors themselves have very little independent authority to direct city officials to do one thing rather than another; their room for manoeuvre is tightly circumscribed, and the chain of office bestows about as much political power as medals do to the governor general. A mayor alone certainly could not spend millions of dollars on a computer, useless or otherwise. If a mayor has any real power, it derives from political alliances and connections rather than from the official job description.

Mayors in Canada are directly elected by all eligible voters within the municipality. By contrast, in federal and provincial elections the names of the party leaders never appear on the ballot except in the individual constituencies in which they are candidates. In 1991 in Canada there were sixteen mayors whose municipalities' populations were greater than the most populous of all the federal or provincial electoral districts.[3] Each of these sixteen mayors (and the directly elected chairs of the municipal federations in Ottawa-Carleton and Hamilton-Wentworth in Ontario) can properly claim to represent directly more residents than any elected federal or provincial politician in the country.[4]

But the size of mayors' electoral constituencies has little bearing on the extent of their political power, even within their own municipalities. This is because securing one's own election as mayor does not necessarily mean that one has secured the political support of the majority of the rest of the council. For the prime minister and premiers, however, the nature of the parliamentary system ensures that they do have such support within their respective legislatures, although in cases of minority government it may be temporary.

As with prime ministers and premiers, a mayor's leadership role can be divided into three separate components: (1) leadership — both real and symbolic — of a community of people within a specified territory; (2) leadership within a large governmental organization; and (3) leadership of a party or faction dedicated to achieving certain declared political objectives. This chapter will examine each of these components in turn.

The analysis that follows will make it clear that mayoral leadership in Canada is quite different from political leadership in parliamentary systems. Unlike prime ministers and premiers, mayors do not share their symbolic role with an appointed representative of the Crown, mainly because the government of a municipality acts formally on behalf of its residents and property-owners, not the reigning monarch.[5] Because of the absence, at the municipal level, of Cabinet ministers and the doctrine of ministerial responsibility, the executive responsibilities of mayors are generally quite unclear. Sometimes they are even publicly challenged on particular issues by their own appointed officials—an impossible state of affairs in a parliamentary system. Finally, because mayors usually do not lead local political parties, they need to construct new coalitions of support for each policy position they wish to advance, a more complicated task than that facing prime ministers and premiers.

MAYORS AS COMMUNITY LEADERS

For a mayor to be a community leader, the office must have some degree of real political power. Such power could derive from the inherent importance of the municipality itself, or from the recognition by external forces that the mayor can influence the electors' behaviour in other political arenas. Each of these possibilities will now be examined.

What are the most important public-sector institutions in our larger cities that are subject, in some degree at least, to the control of local community representatives? For most people in most places the list would include public schools (and in some cases colleges and even universities), the local police force, hospitals, social-service agencies and residential facilities, the transit system, the fire department, and, of course the complete organizational apparatus at city hall, including land-use planners, engineers, tax collectors, garbage collectors, and outside maintenance workers. If the mayor is in fact the pre-eminent community leader, one would expect him or her to be 'in charge' of most, if not all, institutions of this kind. The reality in Canadian cities, however, is that direct municipal authority rarely extends to educational institutions, hospitals, social services, or even to transit and the police.[6] The mayor cannot possibly be 'in charge' of these institutions, because the municipality does not have functional jurisdiction.

Sometimes a given municipality does not have functional jurisdiction because it is part of a two-tier system of municipal government. In their purest form, such systems are found in the Municipality of Metropolitan Toronto (where, since 1988, voters have directly elected their representatives to both tiers) and in Ontario's eleven other regional municipalities. Mayors of 'area municipalities' within such systems must cope with the fact that a number of important traditional municipal functions (planning, roads, sewers, water supply) are partially or completely within the jurisdiction of the upper-tier government. Except in Ottawa-Carleton and Hamilton-Wentworth, the heads (or chairs) of upper-tier councils are not directly elected and hence are not nearly so visible to the public as mayors are. Nowhere in Canada are the heads of such councils called mayors, so they will not be considered further in this essay.[7]

It would be misleading to suggest that mayors have no influence over local public institutions that are not directly part of the municipal organizational structure. Typically, such institutions are run by provincially-established local special-purpose bodies or boards of directors. Often mayors are designated as municipal representatives; if not, they often have a crucial role in determining who the municipal representatives will be.

The fact that in most municipalities the mayor generally sits on more such bodies (or controls more appointments to them) than any other locally elected politician gives the mayor considerable influence. It also makes her political life exceptionally complicated. Not only must she line up support for her political objectives on her own council, but, in so far as other local bodies affect such objectives, she must convince their members as well, some of whom will have been appointed by provincial ministers precisely because they are not beholden in any way to local politicians.

Some local special-purpose bodies are themselves directly elected and are almost totally independent from any kind of municipal control. Boards of education in most provinces are the most obvious examples. Hospital and college boards are usually not directly elected, but they have their own direct access to provincial funds and to user fees. Mayors of Canadian cities therefore have virtually no influence whatsoever over schools, colleges, and hospitals. Since such public institutions are of vital importance in all large communities, no mayor can claim to be 'in charge' of the local public sector.

Perhaps mayors can have informal power in a community, power that derives more from their social and economic standing than from the legal status of the office they hold. Such an argument would have been a powerful one in some Canadian cities in the mid-nineteenth century. In those days, voting for municipal council was restricted to property-owners, and those elected then chose one of their colleagues — as is still the case today in Britain — to preside as mayor. Municipalities were then seen more as private business corporations than as popularly-controlled governments.[8] Between 1840 and 1873, nine of Montreal's twelve mayors were wealthy industrialists or merchants; two were lawyers, and one was a physician.[9] In many cases, early Canadian mayors were elected because they were already part of the community élite: becoming mayor added little to such an individual's status and power.

As the franchise expanded and as Canadians adopted new American ideas about mass democracy — including the direct election of the mayor — local élites retreated from municipal politics and more populist candidates won favour. Except in a few high-status municipal enclaves such as Rockcliffe Park in Ottawa or Westmount in Montreal, it is rare today to find established members of the community's social élite sitting on municipal councils, let alone becoming mayors. The differentiation between a community's social and economic élite and its municipal political élite is almost complete. Municipal voters do not now expect Canadian mayors to have held powerful positions in political parties or in the wider society prior to attaining municipal office.

This may be one of the factors that have enabled women to achieve leadership positions at the municipal level at a seemingly faster rate than at other levels of government.[10] Other factors favourable to the recruitment of previously full-time homemakers to municipal office are the importance of neighbourhood organizations, in which homemakers have traditionally been active, and the fact that municipal office does not require extended overnight periods away from one's family. In non-partisan city-wide elections, the presence of a serious woman candidate probably acts as an important cue attracting the attention of women voters who, after all, form the majority of the eligible electorate, if not the actual voters. In any event, in early 1993 six of the twelve cities with the largest populations in Canada had women mayors: Toronto, June Rowlands; Winnipeg, Susan Thompson; Edmonton, Jan Reimer; Scarborough, Joyce Trimmer; Mississauga, Hazel McCallion; and Ottawa, Jacquelin Holzman.[11] Women were also mayors of the three cities with the largest populations in Atlantic Canada: Shannie Duff in St John's, Moira Ducharme in Halifax, and Elsie Wayne in Saint John.

As mayors of large cities, however, women have hardly arrived at the pinnacle of political power. Even regarding matters apparently under their direct control, municipalities are still subject to considerable provincial supervision.[12] Sometimes the province's power stems from its control of essential financial resources, as in various conditional-grant programs. Often there are various administrative or quasi-judicial procedures that municipalities must negotiate prior to implementing their desired policies. In Ontario, the right of affected parties to appeal all local land-use planning decisions to the Ontario Municipal Board is an especially important factor in limiting municipal autonomy. On controversial planning matters, all the key players — including the mayor — realize that such issues will ultimately be fought out by lawyers and consultants in a quasi-judicial setting. Why, then, should a mayor squander scarce political resources in attempting to provide strong local leadership on issues that will be decided elsewhere, according to norms and procedures quite different from those at work within municipal councils?

If mayors are not really 'in charge', perhaps they are particularly well placed to lobby those who are, especially in the federal and provincial governments. Perhaps this is the real sense in which they are community leaders. Unfortunately for mayors, there is little evidence that this is the case. The most thorough study of federal-provincial-municipal relations in Canada[13] makes virtually no reference to the role of mayors. Nevertheless, in two case studies in Québec City Mayor Gilles Lamontagne, a well-known Liberal, is seen as a key player. Both cases involved all three levels of government at a time, in the early 1970s, when Liberals were in power in both Ottawa and Québec City. The close political relationship between the mayor and the federal minister from Québec City, Jean Marchand, was considered a key variable affecting the mayor's influence.[14]

Most of the time, however, the partisan political connections of local mayors appear to have little impact on the treatment of their municipalities. By contrast, in France such considerations have often been extremely important. Michael Keating, in a comprehensive comparative study of urban politics in the United States, Canada, Britain, and France, concludes that in Canada

> municipal leaders have limited opportunities to extract collective and individual advantages. At both federal and provincial levels, a British-style parliamentary system, with strong Cabinet government supported by disciplined legislative parties, serves to reduce the permeability of the centre by local interests. This separation is increased by the absence of involvement in local politics by the national and provincial parties. . . . Nor can Canadian municipalities play the federal and provincial governments off against each other, since the federal level has no direct links with local governments and provides virtually no resources for them.[15]

Mayors in Canada have high local political visibility. Their symbolic and ceremonial functions are very important. Some incumbents are so successful in building their image as the embodiment of all that is good in their community that they get re-elected time and time again. But this does not mean that they have any real political power to change public policy. Indeed, most such mayors find that municipal elec-toral success cannot easily be transferred to other levels of government. The number of modern-day big-city mayors who have gone on to become powerful figures at other levels is very small. As premiers (of British Columbia and Alberta) and former mayors (of Vancouver and Calgary), Michael Harcourt and Ralph Klein are notable excep-tions. Gilles Lamontagne and David Crombie,[16] former mayors of Québec City and Toronto respectively, became federal Cabinet ministers, but enjoyed less success than their earlier mayoral careers might have suggested.

MAYORS AS LEADERS OF MUNICIPAL ORGANIZATIONS

Having acknowledged that municipal power within a given community is relatively limited, we must now determine the power of the mayor in relation to the organiza-tion of which he or she is at least the nominal head. In this section the issue will be addressed without reference to the extent of the mayor's political support among elected members of council, a subject to be addressed in the next section. Here we want to explore only how a mayor can independently use the office to affect how the municipality functions.

In formal terms, Canadian mayors have slightly more authority than their British counterparts and considerably less than many American mayors, especially those operating in what is known as a 'strong mayor' system, in which mayors have the power to appoint officials of their choosing and can sometimes exercise a veto on council decisions. British mayors are not directly elected and in practice cannot exercise executive authority without the approval of the leader of the political party that controls the local council.[17] Their main functions are presiding over council meetings and formally representing the council at local ceremonies and public events. Most Canadian mayors do the same — and more.

Canadian mayors are expected to act as overseers of the municipal administrative apparatus, although their ability independently to direct municipal employees, espe-cially those whose positions are defined in provincial statutes, is actually quite limited.[18] They engage in a constant round of meetings, both inside and outside the municipality. Most of these involve attempts, in public and in private, to advance the economic health of the municipality, either by exploiting opportunities offered by federal- or provincial-government policies or by attracting new private-sector invest-ment. Mayors also spend a lot of time talking to members of their councils, searching in private for points of agreement and compromise prior to the public meetings.

Unlike many 'strong mayors' in the United States,[19] Canadian mayors have no authority to make their own appointments to top municipal offices. When, for example, a new mayor is elected in New York, all the senior bureaucratic positions become vacant and the mayor gets to shape his or her 'administration' in the same way that an incoming American president does.[20] A Canadian mayor is considered fortunate if he or she is given the luxury of using public funds to appoint a small staff of political and personal assistants. Mayoral appointment of such civic officials as the treasurer, city clerk, chief engineer, or planning director is out of the question. Such appointments are for the council as a whole, in which the mayor's voice is just one, albeit an important one, among many.

Except in the city of Toronto, all major Canadian municipalities appoint one official to be the administrative head of the municipal organization. The title of the position varies: chief administrative officer, director-general, city manager, chief commissioner, city administrator. So does its formal authority: some of these officials have almost complete administrative control over the heads of the major municipal departments, while others do little more than co-ordinate the paper flow to council meetings.[21] The key point, however, is that it is not the mayor's job to appoint, control, or direct the civic bureaucracy. Even where there is little or no central administrative control, the mayor is not usually expected to provide it. Instead, each department tends to go its own way, subject only to the council's allocation of funds through the annual budget and to the occasional intervention to sort out the most intractable of interdepartmental disputes.

In terms of the municipal organization, the most useful analogy to the role of the mayor is that of an unusually visible chair of the board of directors in a large corporation. The mayor acts as a crucial link between a highly independent, disparate, and unpredictable board of directors (the council) and a senior management that often has trouble determining what the board really wants. With easier access to senior officials than other council members enjoy, and the ability to interpret council's wishes when they have not been clearly stated, the mayor can exert considerable influence within the municipal bureaucratic apparatus. In all but the largest municipalities, the mayor's power is also enhanced because he or she is often the only council member working full-time on municipal business.[22]

Much is often made of the power a mayor gains by setting the municipal agenda and presiding over meetings of council. In smaller municipalities the mayor may indeed be able to control what goes on. But in larger cities the mayor, acting independently, can do little to determine what council discusses and how it does so. Councillors know their rights and political imperatives and are not likely to be intimidated by a mayor who suggests that a particular matter is best left untouched.

A mayor's influence on the political agenda does not derive from any extra authority in preparing the items for council discussion or in determining, as presiding officer, who speaks when. Much more important is the tendency for the media in a community to turn to the mayor for short summaries of municipal business or controversies. By telling the local television reporter on camera what just happened in the council chamber, or talking the next day to the newspaper when other council members are no longer around, the mayor can likely have more influence on the local political process than by attempting to manipulate proceedings in the role of council chair.

Indeed, when mayors really wish to exert leadership in council debates, they generally surrender the chair to a council colleague and speak from the council floor, like any other member. The mayors of Montréal, Québec City, and Winnipeg have permanently surrendered their positions as presiding officers at council meetings and behave in the council chamber more as prime ministers or premiers than speakers. In each of these three cities, understanding the role of the mayor requires understanding local political parties, the subject of the next section.

In some American cities, mayors can withhold their assent from council decisions, thereby nullifying them, at least until their action is overridden by a two-thirds vote at some future meeting of council. Once again, in the 'strong mayor' system the mayor's role in relation to council is similar to that of the president in relation to congress. By contrast, a Canadian mayor generally has only one vote, as does each of his or her council colleagues. If a motion receives an equal number of negative and positive votes, it is usually considered to be defeated.

In Québec, mayors often have what is called a 'suspensive' veto.[23] By refusing to assent to a council action, they can force their colleagues to consider it again at the next meeting, at which time the decision is made by a majority vote. Canada's most politically powerful mayors — most notably Jean Drapeau of Montréal — have generally come from Québec. But their power has had little to do with their right to exercise a suspensive veto. Rather, it has had everything to do with the existence of local political parties.

MAYORS AS LEADERS OF LOCAL POLITICAL PARTIES

Mayor Richard Daley was the leader of a local political party — the Democratic Party in Chicago. Democrats wishing to run for office in Chicago had to win his approval and support, whether they were running for federal, state, or local office.[24] The fact that he was mayor was almost incidental. It was his position at the head of the last of the great American 'urban political machines' that gave him his power. There have been no Canadian equivalents. Many Canadian mayors have been prominent members of federal or provincial political parties,[25] and a few have headed purely local parties. But none has controlled a party at the local level in the way that Daley and earlier American 'machine bosses' did. None can be considered to have been the local leader in a community for a party's operations at all three levels of government.[26]

The mayor who came closest to achieving such power was Montréal's Camillien Houde, who became leader of the Québec provincial Conservative party in 1929 after he had already been elected as mayor and as a member of the provincial legislature. By 1931, however, he had lost his provincial seat and been succeeded as Conservative leader by Maurice Duplessis.[27] During the period 1928-54, he was mayor of Montréal for all but eight years, four of which were spent in a federal detention centre for publicly opposing compulsory registration of young males for possible military service in the Second World War. As time went on, he built his reputation as a non-partisan 'Monsieur Montréal', a much more common role for the mayor of a large Canadian city, but one that few mastered as well as Houde.[28]

Unlike urban residents in most other Western democracies (including the United States), Canadians have rarely experienced municipal elections in which national (or even provincial) parties openly and explicitly sought municipal office. In 1969 in Toronto both the Liberals and the New Democratic Party ran slates of candidates, but neither were successful.[29] The NDP continues to sponsor candidates in a number of Canadian cities, but has never captured majority control in a council and formed an NDP municipal 'government', although Mayor Harcourt in Vancouver came close in the mid-1980s. From 1982 to 1986 he could usually rely on majority council support from a coalition of New Democrats, communists, and community activists.[30]

When we think of Canadian mayors as party leaders, we must usually think of them as leaders of purely local political parties, ones that are not formally connected to parties operating in federal and provincial politics. An influential scholar of American urban politics, however, has claimed that 'local politics is limited politics. Its issues are not great enough to generate its own partisan political life.'[31] For most Western democracies, the observation seems perfectly accurate. But Montréal and Québec City, and, to a lesser extent, Vancouver and Winnipeg, have indeed generated autonomous local political parties with mayors, or mayoral candidates, as their leaders.

Montréal deserves special attention in this context. It is Canada's largest municipality; it has a firmly established system of local political parties, and, as a result, Jean Doré and his predecessor, Jean Drapeau, have been unusually powerful. Since 1960, the mayor of Montréal has been backed in the municipal council by a majority of members belonging to the same local political party, the Civic Party for Drapeau and the Montreal Citizens' Movement for Doré. To govern the city on a day-to-day basis, each mayor has chosen members of an executive committee exclusively from among his own party's councillors. The committee meets behind closed doors and behaves very much like a cabinet in a parliamentary system. This places the mayor in as strong a leadership position as a prime minister or premier, except that to some extent he shares executive authority with the person he appoints as chair of the committee.[32]

It is the existence of the party, not the executive committee, that places Montréal's mayor in such a strong political position. The mayor's choices for the executive committee must be approved by the council as a whole. Without a party majority, the mayor could be forced to share executive-committee positions with political opponents and his position would be little different from that of most other Canadian mayors.

Until 1954, Montréal's council differed from that of other Canadian cities only in that it was much larger (100 members) and that it seemed more tolerant of open corruption. Starting in the early 1950s, a group of middle-class, nationalist, and devoutly Catholic francophones, known as the Civic Action League, tried to clean up the mess.[33] Their candidate for mayor, Jean Drapeau, won the 1954 election but the League did not control the council and it was incapable of holding together, particularly in the face of strong opposition from Premier Duplessis in Québec City, opposition that caused Drapeau's mayoral defeat in 1957.

Before the 1960 municipal election, Drapeau split from the League in order to lead a group of councillors and candidates specifically committed to establishing a strong parliamentary-style government. The object was to use a partisan council majority to advance a unified set of policies on which previous councils had never been able to agree. Drapeau's political background as a strong Québec nationalist initially helped to mobilize Montréal's francophones and antagonize its anglophones. After winning the mayoralty and a council majority without anglophone or business support in 1960, Drapeau and his Civic Party expanded their base throughout the city in the next election, in 1962, and did not face any significant council opposition until 1974. It was a period of remarkable achievement—building a subway system, presiding over Expo '67, bringing major league baseball to Canada for the first time.[34]

One of the main reasons Drapeau and his party were able to flourish was that Drapeau made it quite clear that he was not interested in pursing a political career at any other level: he would not threaten federal and provincial politicians as long as they left him free to pursue his own agenda within Montréal. But, starting in the late 1960s, local opposition began to emerge, mainly from groups believing that Drapeau's *politique de grandeur* was ignoring the needs of the city's neighbourhoods and their poorer residents. Since these groups themselves were split on 'the national question' (federalists supporting the New Democrats and sovereignists supporting the Parti Québécois), they agreed to unite for municipal purposes in a purely local political formation, the Montreal Citizens' Movement (MCM).[35] In 1974 its candidate for mayor won almost 40 per cent of the vote, and its candidates for council won eighteen of the fifty-five seats. A two-party system for Montréal local politics had emerged.

Partisan municipal politics was effectively institutionalized by the Parti Québécois provincial government elected in 1976. It amended municipal-election legislation for large cities to provide for public funding of municipal political parties, prohibition of corporate donations to municipal candidates' election campaigns, and the printing of party affiliations on municipal ballots. Such provisions helped the MCM through some difficult times in the late 1970s and early 1980s. Finally in the election of 1986, when Drapeau was no longer a candidate, Jean Doré and the MCM swept to power, gaining re-election in 1990. Doré was formerly a member of Premier René Lévesque's personal staff. While, unlike Drapeau, he is not an authoritarian figure, he leads the government in Montréal in almost exactly the same sense that any premier or prime minister does.

Montréal's experience with local political parties has been replicated in Québec City. From 1962 until 1989 a party known as the Progrés civique de Québec (PCQ) controlled the city's government. Perhaps, however, it was not so genuinely independent of other political parties, because one of its most successful mayors, Gilles Lamontagne, went on to a career as a federal Liberal Cabinet minister. In 1989 the PCQ was defeated by the Rassemblement populaire de Québec (RPQ), a kind of Québec equivalent to the MCM.[36] Curiously, the successful RPQ candidate for mayor, Jean-Paul L'Allier, was a former provincial Liberal Cabinet minister, while his PCQ opponent, Jean-François Bertrand, had been a minister for the Parti Québécois. Whatever links there once were between the two local parties and parties at other levels now seem tenuous at best. Like Montréal, Québec City has an autonomous system of local political parties, and as a result the mayor, as party leader, has real power within the municipal political system.

In its various restructurings of the city of Winnipeg, the government of Manitoba has done more than any other province to confront directly the issue of the political status of the mayor. In its 1970 White Paper proclaiming the need to consolidate the city of Winnipeg, ten suburban municipalities, and the Corporation of Greater Winnipeg into one 'Unicity', the NDP government stated:

> It is essential in our view that the Mayor . . . must be both consistently responsible to the members of Council and have the sustained confidence of the Council. Area-wide election of the Mayor, would, in our view, not merely dilute the supremacy of the popularly elected Council but leave ambiguous the question of who is really responsible, the Council or the Mayor. Hence the Mayor would be elected by the Council from among its membership.'[37]

However, in the face of strong representations from Winnipeg's flamboyant mayor, Steven Juba, in favour of maintaining city-wide direct election, the government relented.[38] Juba, who probably would not have been chosen mayor by the elected councillors, was elected by the people as Unicity's first mayor in 1972.

According to two of Unicity's chief architects, the government's decision to allow the direct election of the mayor 'undermined the leadership role that is essential to a structure using a parliamentary model'.[39] They had assumed that responsible party government would be a natural result of forcing council to choose a mayor. Their assumptions took account of Winnipeg's contemporary political realities. Juba was the most popular local politician, but he refused to align himself with any particular council faction, including the one committed to keeping party politics out of municipal government. Unicity's architects wanted voters to be able to choose clearly between the supposedly non-partisan group and the local NDP. Without Juba, they reasoned, one group or the other would clearly win control and could be held accountable.

We shall never know if the original scheme for choosing Winnipeg's mayor would have led to a system of municipal government in which a majority party on council could be held accountable for its actions. We do know, however, that such a system emerged in Montréal and Québec City without any changes to the system of electing the mayor. Ever since 1971 successive Manitoba governments have tinkered with the mayor's role, always insisting that they wanted to make the position and the whole system more accountable to the electors.[40] The latest change was made in 1991, when the Progressive Conservative government sponsored legislation reducing the membership of the council's executive policy committee to six: the mayor and five councillors appointed by the mayor. In legal terms at least, Winnipeg's mayor became the most powerful in the country. The declared objects of the changes were 'to make the political accountability of the city's elected representatives more visible [and] to enhance political leadership within City Council'.[41]

Winnipeg elected a new mayor, Susan Thompson, in October 1992, defeating the candidate sponsored by Winnipeg in the Nineties (WIN), a group with strong links to the NDP. WIN won five council seats and the anti-WIN group won six. Four 'independents' apparently hold the balance of power. In appointing her executive policy committee, Thompson chose three anti-WIN councillors, one from WIN, and one independent.[42] She is presumably leading a kind of non-partisan, pro-business executive policy committee, but since it meets in public and contains representatives from each of the council's three factions, it can hardly provide the kind of leadership expected from a majority government in a parliamentary system. It is difficult to see how Mayor Thompson will be able to lead Winnipeg in the sense that mayors Doré and L'Allier lead Montréal and Québec City.

CONCLUSION

By any conceivable measure, the political power base of mayors within most Canadian communities is low. According to Douglas Yates, who has analysed American mayors' leadership styles, mayors with weak power bases have two main alternatives in fulfilling their role.[43] They can be either 'crusaders' or 'brokers'. Crusaders attempt to innovate even in the absence of a strong political base. Yates's archetypal crusader was John Lindsay, mayor of New York City in the 1960s. Compared to Canadian mayors, however, Lindsay enjoyed considerable formal authority. Perhaps the best Canadian example was John Sewell, mayor of Toronto from 1978 to 1980. Even without the support of the majority on council, Sewell consistently advanced controversial reform positions and showed little patience with the day-to-day concerns of mayoral politics. The result was defeat, after only one two-year term in office.[44]

A much more common Canadian mayoral response to the absence of power is to act as a broker, working behind the scenes to mobilize support for incremental change. Sewell's successor (1980-91), Art Eggleton, clearly adopted this approach, and many of the more thoughtful, less flamboyant mayors across Canada fall into the same category. They understand the limitations of their office, but they also realize that they are uniquely placed to bring conflicting parties together. Most local political actors in most places — be they councillors, administrators, interest-group leaders, or citizen activists — are more likely to respond constructively to mayoral appeals for discussion or compromise than they would to similar appeals from people holding less prestigious local positions. A skilful mayor uses every ounce of moral authority that can be squeezed from the fact that in most large cities he or she is the only municipal politician elected by all voters.

According to Yates's typology, mayors who do have strong political power bases are either 'entrepreneurs' or 'bosses', the latter group being concerned only with maintaining power, usually through a complex system of patronage and rewards. 'Bosses' in this American sense have been rare among Canadian mayors and non-existent for at least the past seventy years. They simply have not had sufficient access to patronage and rewards. Mayor Drapeau has often been thought of as a boss, but he was really a perfect example of Yates 'entrepreneur', a mayor who uses his political and fiscal resources to provide large-scale public projects and other new services to build and consolidate political support.[45] Many recent Canadian mayors have consciously or unconsciously tried to emulate Drapeau — always pushing for one new public project or other, financed by some other level of government. They have never been as successful because no other Canadian mayor has had such loyal council support in such a large city during such sustained periods of economic growth.

The newer version of mayoral entrepreneurship involves the attraction of major private-sector investors. To some extent successful mayors have always acted as super salespeople. But now we have mayoral missions to foreign lands, complex twinning arrangements with allegedly complementary cities halfway around the word, and elaborate strategies to explain why mobile international capital should locate in the mayor's city rather than somewhere else. Mayors — or potential mayors — of big cities who seem out of place sipping cocktails with the heads of multinational corporations, or who are unwilling or unable to work co-operatively on foreign-investment issues with federal and provincial politicians from different political parties, are unlikely to remain long in office.

Some of the best-known of past Canadian mayors — Camillien Houde and Stephen Juba are among the most notable examples — built their political careers by personally symbolizing the hopes and aspirations of ordinary people in their respective cities. The fact that they did little else was not a political liability. As electorates grow more sophisticated, however, they want a mayor who will at least appear capable of playing a constructive role in making difficult policy decisions about the urban future. Mayors in Canada may not be as well placed as prime ministers and premiers to provide leadership within their respective governments. But it is in their offices that everyone can come together informally and work out a brokered deal that can later be formally presented to city council for further debate and ratification.

There is nothing wrong with being a broker. There is nothing unsavoury about encouraging people with conflicting interests to explore possible compromises in private. Indeed, without ongoing private efforts to work things out, our political life — and hence our society — would come to a standstill. Our parliamentary system of government at the federal and provincial levels expects party caucuses and cabinets to do their work in private. In large Canadian cities, except Montréal and Québec, there are no equivalent institutions, and it is the mayor's job to provide them. How skilfully he or she can do so — in the almost complete absence of any established set of procedures — will likely determine his or her success as a local political leader.

In the normal course of events, people do not win non-partisan elections merely because they are skilled brokers. They must present other attributes in their campaigns. Often voters are seeking someone with the apparent ability to convince outsiders that their community is a good one in which to invest private or public money. Sometimes they are looking simply for a new 'civic image', for someone who personally represents a different aspect of community life. Occasionally municipal voters may even believe that a particular candidate will be able to cut taxes, improve services, or even do both at the same time. The key point, however, is that a mayor elected in a non-partisan election cannot individually claim an electoral mandate to do anything. Each council member will insist on his or her individual interpretation of what the election meant, and the mayor is usually in no position to dispute it.

Explaining outcomes of mayoral elections is beyond the scope of this essay. However, it must be recognized that in non-partisan municipal elections with no public funding of campaigns (i.e., in most elections outside Québec), the raising of money is a crucially important task, especially in cases where the electorate is larger than that in most federal electoral districts. The extent to which mayors—and other members of council—are beholden to corporate donors concerned with property issues in their communities remains the most important issue in the study of the Canadian urban political process.[46]

Like the hapless mayor in Robert Munsch's story, Canadian mayors are generally expected to be responsible for what public authorities do within their communities. Countless schemes have been devised over the years to adjust reality to meet expectations: schemes to bolster municipal authority in relation to other local authorities, and to bolster mayoral authority in relation to the municipal organization in general and other members of council in particular. Most such schemes have never been approved or implemented. Canadians are comfortable with weak municipalities and weak mayors. But they also seem to expect their mayors to be leaders.

To provide leadership without possessing power and authority is among the most difficult of political challenges. Canadian mayors are expected to meet it almost every day. Some are more successful than others. If, as has been argued here, the most important form of mayoral leadership takes place behind closed doors, it is almost impossible for outsiders to distinguish effective leaders from ineffective ones. Municipal government is, in a trivial sense, the level of government closest to the people. It is also the most difficult to understand. In this more important sense it is the level of government most distant from the people. The confusing nature of the office of mayor is an important part of the problem.

NOTES

Helpful comments from Michael Keating and Ron Wagenberg on an earlier draft of this essay are gratefully acknowledged.

1 *Jonathan Cleaned Up—Then He Heard a Sound* (Toronto: Annick Press, 1981).

2 It is operated by the Toronto Transit Commission, an agency of the Municipality of Metropolitan Toronto of which the City of Toronto forms a part.

3 The federal electoral district of Mississauga West (209,706) was the most populous in the country. The municipalities with larger populations, in descending order, were Montréal (1,015,420), Calgary, Toronto, Winnipeg, Edmonton, North York, Scarborough, Vancouver, Mississauga, Hamilton, Laval, Ottawa, Etobicoke, London, Surrey, and Brampton. See Statistics Canada, *A National Overview*, 1991 Census of Canada, catalogue 93-301 (Ottawa, 1992).

4 The ten councillors in Vancouver and the four members of the Board of Control in London, Ontario, all of whom are elected at-large, could also make such a claim, but their political significance as individuals is obviously less than that of the mayor of their respective cities.

5 For a stimulating discussion of the significance of the fact that provincial governments act on behalf of the Crown, see David E. Smith, 'Empire, Crown, and Canadian Federalism', *Canadian Journal of Political Science* 14 (1991): 441-73.

6 Warren Magnusson, 'The Local State in Canada: Theoretical Perspectives', *Canadian Public Administration* 28 (1985): 575-99.

[7] Arguably, the two who are now directly elected are in political positions very similar to mayors'. One municipal political leader in Canada who has received academic attention is the first chairman of the Municipality of Metropolitan Toronto, Frederick Gardiner; see Harold Kaplan, *Urban Political Systems: A Functional Analysis of Metropolitan Toronto* (New York: Columbia University Press, 1967) and Timothy J. Colton, *Big Daddy: Frederick G. Gardiner and the Building of Metropolitan Toronto* (Toronto: University of Toronto Press, 1980). For autobiographical reactions to Gardiner from a contemporary mayor of Toronto, see Nathan Phillips, *Mayor of All the People* (Toronto: McClelland and Stewart, 1967).

[8] Warren Magnusson, 'Introduction,' in Warren Magnusson and Andrew Sancton, eds, *City Politics in Canada* (Toronto: University of Toronto Press, 1983), 6.

[9] Guy Bourassa, 'The Political Élite of Montreal: From Aristocracy to Democracy', in L.D. Feldman and M. D. Goldrick, eds, *Politics and Government of Urban Canada* (Toronto: Methuen, 1969).

[10] For a biography of Charlotte Whitton, the first woman mayor of a major Canadian city (Ottawa, 1951-56 and 1960-64), see R.L. Schnell and P.T. Rooke, *No Bleeding Heart: Charlotte Whitton, A Feminist on the Right* (Vancouver: University of British Columbia Press, 1987).

[11] For a listing of the other six cities and for the source of the population data, see note 3 above.

[12] Donald J.H. Higgins, *Local and Urban Politics in Canada* (Toronto: Gage, 1986), 74-101.

[13] Lionel O. Feldman and Katherine A. Graham, *Bargaining for Cities: Municipalities and Intergovernmental Relations, an Assessment* (Toronto: Butterworths, 1979).

[14] Ibid., 60-2.

[15] Michael Keating, *Comparative Urban Politics* (Brookfield, VT: Ashgate Publishing Co., 1991), 59.

[16] For accounts of Crombie's career, see Jon Caulfield, *The Tiny Perfect Mayor: David Crombie and Toronto's Reform Aldermen* (Toronto: James Lorimer, 1974) and Victor L. Russell, 'Remaking Toronto', in Allan Levine, ed., *Your Worship: The Lives of Eight of Canada's Most Unforgettable Mayors* (Toronto: James Lorimer, 1989), 99-124.

[17] Gerry Staker and Harold Wolman, 'Drawing Lessons from US Experience: An Elected Mayor for British Local Government', *Public Administration* 70 (1992): 241-68.

[18] For an account of the legal status of Canadian mayors, see Ian MacF. Rogers, *The Law of Canadian Municipal Corporations*, 2nd ed. (Toronto: Carswell, 1992) [Release No.3]), 280, 14-23.

[19] Barbara Ferman, *Governing the Ungovernable: Political Skill, Leadership, and the Modern Mayor* (Philadelphia: Temple University Press, 1985).

[20] Edward I. Koch, *Mayor: An Autobiography* (New York: St Martin, 1984), ch. 6.

[21] T.J. Plunkett, *City Management in Canada: The Role of the Chief Administrative Officer* (Toronto: Institute of Public Administration, 1992).

[22] Andrew Sancton and Paul Woolner, 'Full-Time Municipal Councillors: A Strategic Challenge for Canadian Urban Government', *Canadian Public Administration* 33 (1990): 482-505.

[23] Heads of council in Manitoba and British Columbia have a more limited form of suspensive veto. See Rogers, *Municipal Corporations*, 2nd ed., 280. 22.

[24] Mike Royko, *Boss: Richard J. Daley of Chicago*, (New York: Signet Books, 1971).

[25] For an account of the first Edmonton mayoral election campaign of Lawrence Decore, a well-known Liberal, see James Lightbody, 'The First Hurrah: Edmonton Elects a Mayor, 1983', *Urban History Review* 13 (1984), 35-42. Decore later became leader of the Alberta Liberal Party.

[26] Canadian municipal politics became detached from national politics under prime ministers Macdonald and Laurier. See Magnusson, 'Introduction' in Magnusson and Sancton, eds, *City Politics*, 9-10.

27 Paul-André Linteau, *Histoire de Montréal depuis la Confédération* (Montréal: Boréal, 1992) 407. See also Harold Kaplan, *Reform, Planning, and City Politics: Montreal, Winnipeg, Toronto* (Toronto: University of Toronto Press, 1982), 332-7.

28 For the origins of non-partisan urban politics, see Jack K. Masson and James D. Anderson, eds, *Emerging Party Politics in Urban Canada* (Toronto: McClelland and Stewart, 1972), Part 1. For brief biographies of other 'unforgettable' Canadian mayors, see Levine, ed., *Your Worship.*

29 Stephen Clarkson, *City Lib: Parties and Reform* (Toronto: Hakkert, 1972). See also Masson and Anderson, eds, *Emerging Party Politics,* Part 4.

30 Donald Gutstein, 'Vancouver Voters Swing Right', *City Magazine* 9-1 (1986-87), 30.

31 Paul E. Peterson, *City Limits* (Chicago: University of Chicago Press, 1981) 116-17.

32 Guy Bourassa and Jacques Léveillée, eds, *Le système politique de Montréal* (Montréal: les cahiers de l'AcPas, no. 43, 1986), ch. 2.

33 Kaplan, *Reform, Planning, and Politics,* 340-2 and 356-62.

34 For the best account of the career of any Canadian mayor, see Brian McKenna and Susan Purcell, *Drapeau* (Toronto: Clarke, Irwin, 1980).

35 Henry Milner, 'The Montreal Citizens' Movement Then and Now', *Quebec Studies* 6 (1988): 1-11; Warren Magnusson, 'Progressive Politics and Canadian Cities', in Desmond S. King and Jon Pierre, eds, *Challenges to Local Government,* (London: Sage, 1990), 173-94; and Jean-Hugues Roy and Brendan Weston, eds, *Montreal: A Citizen's Guide to Politics* (Montreal: Black Rose, 1990).

36 For a detailed account of the election, see Louise Quesnel and Serge Belley, *Partis politiques municipaux: Une étude de sociologie électorale* (Montréal: Editions Agence d'Arc, 1991).

37 Manitoba, Government of, *Proposals for Urban Reorganization in the Greater Winnipeg Area* [White Paper] (Winnipeg: Queen's Printer, 1970) reprinted as an appendix in Meyer Brownstone and T.J. Plunkett, *Metropolitan Winnipeg: Politics and Reform of Local Government* (Berkeley: University of California Press, 1983), 201.

38 Allan Levine, 'Stephen Juba: The Great City Salesman', in Levine, ed., *Your Worship,* 89-90. For details of Juba's pre-Unicity career, see Kaplan, *Reform, Planning and City Politics,* 495-8, 520-8, and 557-62.

39 Brownstone and Plunkett, *Metropolitan Winnipeg,* 100.

40 For background documentation, see Manitoba, Committee of Review, City of Winnipeg Act, *Report and Recommendations* (Winnipeg: Queen's Printer, 1976), 69-73; Manitoba, City of Winnipeg Act Review Committee, *Final Report 1986* (Winnipeg: Queen's Printer, 1986), 22-8; and Manitoba, Urban Affairs, *Strengthening Local Government in Winnipeg: Proposals to Change the City of Winnipeg Act* (Winnipeg: Queen's Printer, 1987), 9-13. All these documents were brought into being by the actions of NDP governments.

41 Manitoba, Legislature, Debates 35th Legislature, 2nd Session (1991), 3685.

42 *Winnipeg Free Press,* 4 Nov. 1992.

43 Douglas Yates, *The Ungovernable City: The Politics of Urban Problems and Policy Making* (Cambridge, MA: M.I.T. Press, 1977), ch. 6.

44 Warren Magnusson, 'Toronto' in Magnusson and Sancton, eds, *City Politics,* 123-6.

45 Yates, *The Ungovernable City,* 147.

46 James Lorimer has been the most effective proponent of this position. See his *A Citizen's Guide to City Politics* (Toronto: James Lewis and Samuel, 1972) and *The Developers* (Toronto: James Lewis and Samuel, 1978).

CHAPTER TEN

LEADERSHIP   IN   THE
PUBLIC   SERVICE

Renewing   an   Essential
Management   Skill

——■——

Joan   Price   Boase

Of the many qualities required for successful senior management in the public service, good leadership skills are perhaps the most important and the most elusive. In a large and complex organization such as the Canadian public service, where there is often the opportunity for employees to put discretionary effort into their jobs, 'productivity and motivation are inextricably linked'.[1] Motivation of subordinates is achieved by the successful exercise of management skills, particularly the nebulous skills of leadership.

In the decade of the 1980s, interest in public management development grew in many countries, and Canada was no exception. In 1988 the prime minister unveiled the Management Development Centre in Touraine, Québec, and in June 1989 the Organization for Economic Co-operation and Development (OECD) held its first-ever session on the issue of public management development.[2] Whatever the nature of a state's government — democratic, dictatorial, or communist — bureaucratic structures are essential, and many countries are looking to Western nations for new ideas in management development techniques. According to Donald Savoie, there is a growing perception that the study of public management has been too long ignored, in favour of policy development and policy issues. He also suggests that the primary reason for renewed interest in management skills can be traced, at least in part, to governments' need to pursue financial restraint.[3] Central to such restraint is the need to ensure that government programs and government operations are more effectively managed. It is necessary, therefore, to achieve a balance between policy development and management development.

The emphasis on policy development skills that emerged in the mid-twentieth century was a response to the move into the welfare state and the corresponding changes to the machinery of government; opportunities for policy analysts and policy advisers expanded rapidly. In the last decades of the century, however, governments have been forced to downsize and retrench, and to give less importance to policy development. Instead, they have found it necessary to place 'greater emphasis on such managerial concerns as increasing productivity and improving the delivery of services to the public'.[4] Effective management has become a priority for the public service, and although management and leadership are not the same thing, good managers require strong leadership skills. If managers are to be more than rational problem-solvers, they must learn to use their positions of power 'to influence the thoughts and activities of other people'[5] in positive ways.

This chapter has been organized around the above themes. The first section will review the development of leadership theory; the second will outline the complex relationships among senior civil servants that require the exercise of strong interpersonal and communicative skills; and the final section will examine these issues in relation to the ongoing Public Service 2000 initiative for renewal of the Canadian public service, and the serious challenges that it poses for all levels of the public service. It is important to emphasize at the outset that the conduct of politics and the implementation of policy decisions will be achieved differently within the institutions of different states. Canadian government officials, unlike their American counterparts, operate within a British parliamentary system that is founded on the doctrine of ministerial responsibility. Fundamental to this concept is the assumption of neutrality and anonymity on the part of the public service.[6]

THEORIES OF LEADERSHIP

Any discussion of leadership in bureaucratic structures must begin with the classic work of Max Weber,[7] who first developed the concept of legitimate authority. Weber identified three sources of legitimate authority: charismatic, traditional, and legal/ rational. The *charismatic* leader is one who, by virtue of intrinsic, visionary, even spiritual personal qualities, instils a loyalty in associates and subordinates that inspires them to respond positively to the leader's vision; taken to its extreme, charismatic authority can lead to religious fundamentalism. Weber's second category, *traditional* authority, is based upon the leader's hereditary position in society rather than any intrinsic qualities; for Weber, traditional authority was to be resisted, since it was based on the holding of privilege and right because of parentage or ancestry, and

led to class distinctions in society; a less threatening conception of traditional authority is that vested in parents over children.

Finally, *legal/rational* authority is exemplified by those people who thrive in formal,
bureaucratic structures. In their personal characteristics, according to Weber, they are
impersonal and impartial, detached, disciplined, monocratic, rigidly hierarchical,
and emotionless; they favour rules and regulations, and behave in a rational manner.
In his view, the more inflexible and dehumanized a bureaucracy becomes, the more
effective it will be. Weber believed that bureaucracy is permanent, and when well-
entrenched, indestructible. Its strength lies in its impersonal characteristics and the
vesting of authority in positions rather than persons. Clearly, for Weber, the rational/
legal structure of authority is what large organizations should strive for, and although
he presciently predicted the alienation that would result, for him this was preferable
to the unpredictability of charismatic leadership.

Subsequent writers have built on Weber's work and have developed their own
typologies of leadership. Amitai Etzioni, for example, groups leaders into types based
on their organizational position or personal power.[8] He lists *officials*, whose authority
rests on their hierarchical position (Weber's legal type), *informal leaders* who are able
to command because of their intrinsic qualities (charismatic), and *formal leaders*, who
combine the power features of the first two. Other writers have distinguished between
leaders and administrators in institutions, seeing leaders as taking a broad, unifying
and visionary role while administrators perform the technical, day-to-day bureaucratic work that keeps the organization running. A helpful distinction between the
roles of leaders and managers has been provided by John Kotter, who suggests that
leadership 'ultimately is about "coping with change", while management is about
"coping with complexity."'[9] These distinctions are not always evident, however, as
will become clear later in this chapter, in the discussion of Public Service 2000 and
the need for the entire public service to cope with change within complexity.

The many approaches to the study of leadership attest to the difficulty of defining
this significant yet nebulous concept. In attempts to identify which individuals are
more inclined to be good leaders, theories have focused on the traits and skills of
leaders and the different styles of leader. A contingency theory of leadership that
recognizes the many changing variables important to effective leadership has also
been developed.

Early writers on leadership focused on leadership traits, including inherited characteristics that leaders supposedly shared. For example, it was believed that leaders
tended to be taller, heavier, older, and possessed of greater athletic and speaking
abilities than non-leaders.[10] The results of research based on these assumptions proved
to be inconsistent, however, and subsequent studies focused on specific leadership
skills. A typology was developed in 1955 by Robert Katz that enunciated the skills
needed for leadership.[11] Katz grouped these skills under three headings. First were
technical skills, including specialized knowledge and proficiency in the specific discipline. In the case of the public service, this would require that senior managers have
specialized knowledge of their policy areas, as well as the technical skills related to
management. Second, Katz suggested that leaders need important *human skills*: that is,

the ability to motivate individuals and obtain co-operation for group projects and co-ordinated team effort. Finally, Katz believed that leaders need *conceptual skills*, or the ability to develop a broad view of their organization and its relations with its environment. These skills would include intelligence, originality, good judgement, adaptability, initiative, self-confidence, and a strong sense of responsibility. Some mixture of all these skills is needed at all managerial levels, but their importance changes at different levels. Closer to the delivery of services, technical skills become more important, while greater conceptual skills are needed by the more senior managers. Managers at all levels must possess human-relations skills, for no section of an organization will function effectively in the absence of productive interpersonal relationships.

Leadership style has also been broken down into three categories.[12] In the *authoritarian* style the leader dictates all aspects of policy and work activity, and remains detached from the group (although not necessarily unfriendly); decision-making is totally dominated by the leader. *Democratic* leaders have a more participative style, and are open to discussion and group participation in decision-making; they solicit feedback from the workers, are generally more involved themselves in a hands-on way, and let members of the group decide many of the details of their working relationships. Finally, a *laissez-faire* leader gives the individual and the group complete freedom in the determination of work procedures and makes no attempt to become involved, but remains available to answer questions. This type of leadership style does not have many supporters, for it allows relationships to deteriorate, is unstructured and confusing for the workers, and easily leads to chaos.

Nevertheless, studies have not unequivocally established that any one style of leadership is more effective in all situations; hence a contingency theory of leadership has been developed,[13] which suggests that the best leadership style depends on the characteristics both of the individual leader and of the group's members, as well as the specific situation or environment. Good leaders must be prepared to alter their leadership styles to suit changing circumstances. That is, an alert and flexible leader will deliberately choose a style of leadership on an authoritarian-democratic continuum in consideration of prevailing conditions and based on past experience. In some situations an authoritarian approach will produce the desired results, while in others a democratic approach will be more effective. A good leader must recognize the need to shift approaches and define the degree of independence or direction required by subordinates.

Good leadership, then, is both elusive and essential for effective government. Among the senior managers in government there are many opportunities to exercise leadership skills, and an increasing need to motivate people in a positive way. As the emphasis in the Canadian public service shifts from a demand for policy advisers to a greater demand for effective managers, the functions of leaders will change, as will the exercise and study of leadership skills. Sandford Borins argues that universities with programs in public administration will have to respond to the new demands by emphasizing management rather than policy skills. He suggests that 'public management is primarily concerned with explaining and interpreting the *processes* (for example, personnel and financial management) by which the public sector is managed'.[14] John Manion agrees that management training and development in the federal public service must be improved, as the machinery of government becomes more complex and decentralized.[15] With an increased emphasis on management practices to address new challenges, human resource management and leadership will become critically important components. As one deputy minister pointed out in a speech in 1988: 'Management experts tell you to plan, organize, staff, direct, budget and control with insight and finesse and if you do, you will get positive management results. But without motivating your staff, you simply have technical management'.[16]

Tim Plumptre addresses the need to possess more than just competence or even expertise in the procedural criteria for management, in his well-named book *Beyond the Bottom Line*. Evaluation of the effectiveness of managers, he argues, requires considerably more than just examining their procedural rectitude and the empirical evidence of their managerial approach as outlined in manuals, flow charts, and tables of organization.[17] While these may often be tangible evidence of familiarity with leading-edge management techniques, they indicate nothing more than the accepted means to achieve desired ends, with no guarantee of results. Plumptre believes that in both Canada and Britain, too much emphasis has been placed on means and processes in an attempt to improve management. 'It is relatively simple', he says,

> to tell departments, 'You shall have a commitment control system', and then go out and inspect to see if such a system has been installed. To say to departments, 'You shall have a well-motivated work force' is an injunction that is much less precise and much less susceptible to measurement. Yet the issue is surely of equal, if not greater importance.[18]

The emerging view of leadership as the ability to motivate others suggests that good leaders are really facilitators who are able to arouse the leadership that lies dormant in every individual.[19] It is the belief that each employee possesses self-leadership skills that has led to such innovations as participative management, employee involvement, and self-managing work teams. It also is at the heart of the move to 'empower' front-line public servants and give them a sense of 'ownership' of their jobs (a subject that will be discussed below).

We know, then, that leadership is important, but it is often easier to identify where it has failed than to explain how it has succeeded. Futhermore, it has a reciprocal aspect that is not often analysed; a leader who is successful in one situation, and with one group of employees, may fail in a similar situation but with a different group of subordinates. It is also difficult to discern good leaders during hiring sessions. Public servants are chosen by the merit system, which mechanically identifies the person who has the needed expertise, the right education, experience and technical skills; that is, the one who is most suited to the position. It is much more difficult to determine the strength of individuals' commitment to the values and vision of the organization, or their power to persuade and motivate others to embrace those values. A résumé may identify the 'best' person in a technical sense but give little guidance on the crucial issue of interpersonal skills; too often, organizations must live with the disastrous results.

CHALLENGES FOR SENIOR MANAGERS

Changes in the public-sector environment, particularly the focus on restraint and retrenchment during the 1980s and the concomitant emphasis on efficiency and effectiveness, have served to underline the many challenges that modern governments face. Whatever policy decisions are taken, their successful implementation depends on the ability of senior public servants to inspire others, to motivate members of their departments so that their support for and commitment to the policy direction is assured. Successful senior public servants are rarely just good administrators, although they are at the apex of the administrative hierarchy. They are, rather, visionaries, decision-makers, communicators, innovators, and developers of the management team.[20] The latter function requires an ability to stimulate team effort, using interactive techniques, to enable people to perform at their maximum capacity and give them a sense of 'ownership' of their jobs.[21] This is closely linked to individual job satisfaction, which in turn enhances the implementation effort, and ultimately the success of the organization.

In sum, it must be stressed that no one leadership style is appropriate in all situations. Senior managers in the public service must be prepared to be flexible, for they function in a complex and unstable organizational environment. Governments in Canada have often put their faith in restructuring the administrative machinery, in the expectation that extensive structural and institutional change will lead to improved performance and responsiveness. In one three-year period (1985-88), for example, there were more alterations to the organization and processes of government than in any similar period in history, many of which have broad implications for the public service. Among these changes are the following:

- radical changes in parliamentary procedures and in the relations between public servants and Parliament,
- a new and powerful role for the deputy prime minister;
- a new role for ministerial aides/chiefs of staff;
- significant changes in the Cabinet decision-making process
- a sharp reduction in the number and power of central agencies, and the beginning of massive decentralization/deregulation.

In the context of often massive organizational and institutional restructuring and the uncertainty and insecurity that it engenders among employees, senior managers must respond, adjust, and continue to influence the actions of their traumatized subordinates in a positive way. It is an intimidating challenge.[22]

RELATIONSHIPS IN THE CANADIAN PUBLIC SERVICE

Central Agencies

Government administrative structures are hierarchical, although they level off somewhat at the top as relationships become more collegial in nature. In Canadian government there is often not a clear line between collegiality and hierarchy, especially in the relationships among the 'central agencies'—that is, the staff departments—and the administrative heads of the various line departments.[23] The relationships do not always adhere to Weber's ideal of strict hierarchical structure, with a single responsible person—never a committee—at the apex. There is one person who is, however, indisputably the head of the public service, and that is the clerk of the Privy Council and secretary to Cabinet, who is in effect the prime minister's deputy minister.

The clerk/secretary heads the Privy Council Office (PCO), which is the prime minister's department and the agency that services most of the committees of Cabinet. Within this office there are sections, or secretariats, that parallel the standing committees of Cabinet such as Priorities and Planning or Legislation and House Planning, and these secretariats perform the crucial functions of strategic planning and policy analysis.[24] The PCO's massive co-ordination and communication functions, its officials' easy access to both the prime minister and the Cabinet committees, and its responsibility for substantive policy development clearly identify it as the predominant government staff department. It is from within the PCO that plans for government reorganization often emanate, and the leadership of its officials is crucial not only to the day-to-day functioning of the machinery of government, but also to the smooth implementation of the recommendations of the many commissions that have examined government operations.[25]

PCO staff are the important liaisons between Cabinet decisions and departmental officials. This role gives them considerable influence over departmental staff in the interpretation and communication of memoranda to Cabinet, as well as the decisions and direction articulated by Cabinet committees.[26] Richard French discusses the highly sensitive nature of the responsibilities of PCO officials in this liaison role. The PCO official is expected to brief the chair of the relevant Cabinet committee or even the prime minister on a memorandum to Cabinet from departmental officials. In so doing, the 'PCO official is counterposing his overview of developments in the policy sector and his experience with cabinet and its committees against the substantive expertise of department officials'.[27] If the PCO officials possess good leadership qualities, they will be circumspect in their interpretation so that the result will not be frustration of the department staff, who often have more specific technical expertise. PCO officials will also seek advice from other central agencies, particularly the Treasury Board Secretariat (TBS) whose officers may have greater knowledge of departmental programs and personalities.

The purpose of this interactive role is to present advice to Cabinet that is as broad and objective as possible, without discouraging or alienating departmental officers. A cautious approach is important as well when the information flow travels in the opposite direction, and the PCO official is required to communicate the Cabinet Records of Decision to departmental staff. In all these consultations and discussions there are many opportunities for influence and pressure, and for playing 'numerous bargaining and advocacy roles within the bureaucratic politics behind each initiative'.[28] These roles include advising department officials on the best way to proceed, monitoring development of the new policy in the department, deciding when the proposal is ready for Cabinet, ironing out any conflicts among officials that might occur, and ensuring that decisions are properly implemented.[29] PCO officials must pursue their advisory role with tact and sensitivity if they are to be perceived as supportive rather than arbitrary and intrusive.

Within the PCO, the role of the clerk/secretary is a pivotal one, calling for highly developed motivational and leadership skills and, in particular, the conceptual skills required for a broad perspective on the entire machinery of government. Gordon Osbaldeston, a former clerk, says that the clerk has 'important responsibilities in providing a role model for deputy ministers and public servants, establishing standards of behaviour for the public service, and ensuring that minister-deputy minister teams are working satisfactorily'.[30] Another sensitive role for the clerk/secretary that is important to deputy ministers particularly is the role of chair of the Committee of Senior Officials (COSO). This small committee, composed of perhaps four other deputy-minister level officials, advises the clerk on performance appraisals for deputy ministers, and also makes recommendations regarding assignments and salaries; its review of the performance of the very senior managers in the public service is the basis on which the prime minister decides their performance rating. This role is clearly one that must be pursued with prudence and careful objectivity.

It is necessary for the clerk/secretary to maintain excellent relations with the senior staff in all the departments of government, including the other central agencies. One relationship that is critical to the smooth functioning of government is that between the clerk and the prime minister's principal secretary, who is the head of the Prime Minister's Office (PMO). This office is staffed by partisan political appointees, the prime minister's personal staff. The purpose of this office, in the words of a former principal secretary, Thomas Axworthy, is 'to join policy and politics, structures and process in a coherent plan that can change with events (but not too often) and that takes into account constraints and available resources'.[31] This office is critical to the pursuit of a strategic approach to politics, which includes decisions regarding objectives and assessment of possible approaches, likely obstacles, and necessary resources. Implementation of chosen strategies can be extremely challenging, even 'excruciatingly difficult', requiring timing, organization, conviction and effective communication. 'Organizational politics', says Axworthy, 'is coalition building, pure and simple. Who can you bring onside and with what degree of intensity?' He also suggests that there is a need for the 'intuitive arts . . . knowing when to proceed and when to delay, sensing when to be bold and when to be prudent, calculating the forces pro and con'.[32] These intuitive arts must extend also to the relationship between the principal secretary and the clerk of the Privy Council, for their 'close partnership . . . is crucial to the workings of a strategic prime ministership'.[33] Yet Axworthy also underlines the need to adhere to our tradition of separating the neutral public service from the partisanship of the PMO, as represented by the clerk and the principal secretary respectively. Their discrete functions must not be blurred, for a prime minister requires the perspectives of both.

Another central agency that plays a major co-ordinative role in the federal public service is the Treasury Board Secretariat (TBS), which services the Treasury Board of

Cabinet. The TBS is the management arm of Cabinet, responsible for giving advice on resource allocation, both financial (in the sense of expenditure budgeting) and human, since the Treasury Board is the employer of the public service. In both these roles, particularly the latter one, TBS officials must call upon their leadership/management skills to achieve top-down co-ordination and a unified civil service. They have a very demanding role:

> It is they who must set regulations and policies which reach far into the domain of departmental management, it is they who must police these regulations and policies, it is they who must say 'No!' to the usually well-meant ambitions of departments and agencies. For departmental personnel, the Treasury Board and its staff are the most omnipresent bogeymen in the never ending bureaucratic maneuvering between co-ordinator and co-ordinatee.[34]

The officials in the TBS examine and assess the short submissions that come from department officials, and they have broad influence on the reception of these submissions by the Treasury Board Committee of Cabinet.[35] It is their responsibility to make recommendations on the acceptance, rejection or modification of these departmental proposals. Like the PCO officials, they must fulfil this interpretive and advisory role with circumspection and sensitivity, in recognition of the importance often attached to the submissions of departmental staff. They are not always successful. For example, the Lambert Commission of 1979 identified the serious, even debilitating, tensions that have arisen between the TBS and departmental officials. The Lambert Commission saw this as a power struggle, and one senior departmental manager said that with their many interventions in departmental decision-making, the TBS officials have been 'sapping the line manager of authority and [have] been imposing [their] judgment on departmental operations without any continuing responsibility for the consequences'.[36] Empire-building, top-down directives, and authoritative interference in departmental affairs are clearly not effective management techniques, and while it might be unrealistic to expect to totally extirpate these undesirable and destructive management traits, the ongoing efforts to renew the public service are reminders of their tenacity, and their extensive manifestation.

The Federal Provincial Relations Office (FPRO) also serves an important co-ordinative function for the machinery of government. This function brings FPRO specialists into frequent contact with officials within the departments, several of which have their own federal-provincial specialists. While it is a truism to state that the reality of politics in Canada is an immense interdependence between the two levels of government, it is more difficult to determine the implications of this interdependence for the functional side of policy development and implementation. The establishment of the FPRO as an entity separate from the PCO in the mid-1970s was evidence of the growing importance of federal-provincial relations, especially in view of the election of the Parti Québécois in 1976, the increasing interest in constitutional reform, and the proliferation of federal-provincial conferences.

This office is responsible for overseeing the operation of federal-provincial programs and maintains a liaison with officials involved in these programs. The head of this office, the secretary to the Cabinet for federal provincial relations, reports directly to the prime minister and enjoys a status just slightly below that of the clerk of the Privy Council. FPRO officials play a key role in the preparation of federal-provincial conferences, and they focus more on their co-ordinative role than on substantive policy issues. However, they also establish a network of contacts with officials in provincial departments, quite independent of those established by officials in the special federal-provincial divisions of the federal departments.[37] This gives the FPRO 'many opportunities to become involved in the activities of operating departments, i.e., in any area in which a department operates an intergovernmental program. This engenders some of the same love- hate relationship between departments and FPRO as [occurs] in connection with PCO.'[38]

The primary purpose of the department of Finance is to advise the minister of Finance and the Cabinet on matters of economic policy. This function means that officials from this department do not have the same intrusive, day-to-day role in departmental affairs that those from the TBS and PCO have. Nevertheless, the Department of Finance has a pervasive influence on the entire public service. Its role in the preparation of the budget and the determination of spending priorities has broad implications for the policy plans of individual departments. Although the influence of the Finance department fluctuates, and during the 1980s there were moves to decentralize its powers, 'power rather abruptly returns to the centre when the economic environment is difficult'.[39] Fiscal restraint and retrenchment increase the influence of officials in the Finance department, and their ability to intervene at the level where expenditures are decided compels officials in the line departments to be prudent in their policy proposals and to develop persuasive arguments to substantiate their positions.

Among the duties of the central agencies that bring their staffs into frequent and close relationships with departmental staff is their role in interdepartmental consultation. Since officials in the central agencies are able to influence Cabinet action regarding departmental priorities, it is imperative that discussions take place for the purposes of co-ordination and information exchange. Many of these meetings (for example, the Co-ordinating Committee of Deputy Ministers, and the monthly deputy ministers' luncheon) are called by the secretary to the Cabinet and many are initiated, often on an *ad hoc*, policy-specific basis, by departmental officials. Some committees that meet regularly are at the assistant deputy minister level, and there are many interdepartmental committees at less senior levels as well. Clearly, at all of these consultative, functional meetings, where the department's purpose is to put forward its priorities, and the agency's purpose is to evaluate, assess and make recommendations on these priorities, interpersonal skills are as critical as technical skills to the eventual outcome.

Intradepartmental Relationships

Within the department, the deputy minister is the effective head: the equivalent of the chief administrative officer, while the minister is in a way the chief executive officer. (See Herman Bakvis's discussion of this relationship in Chapter 7 above.) For deputy ministers, the relationship with their ministers is a crucial one, and helps to determine their relations with the central agencies of government as well as with their subordinates in the department. This relationship must be handled with great care, since the minister is the indisputable political head of the department, but is frequently a neophyte with regard to its substantive policy issues. The deputy minister has both the policy expertise and the administrative ability to run the department, yet must proffer advice and knowledge discreetly, offering departmental support and briefings that will enable the minister to pursue the department's priorities with confidence in Cabinet. A good relationship with a strong and confident minister can provide reciprocal benefits for the deputy minister and other departmental officials. 'For the deputy minister', says Sharon Sutherland,

> having a political boss is a lifeline to decisiveness. When the party in power is not willing to think of the civil service as a partner in government, the senior department officials become prey to the circling sharks in the central agencies and regulating bodies whose job it is to ensure that their organization's governing values are given primacy. On the other hand, it is within the minister's discretion to give senior officials permission to pursue policy substance before bureaucratic form.[40]

A relationship that is predicated on an awareness of and respect for these reciprocal benefits can encourage policy development that is practical and effective and that efficiently exploits the discrete capabilities of the minister and the public servants.

Another important relationship that can be problematical or productive is the one that develops between the deputy minister and the ministerial staff, particularly the ministerial chief of staff.[41] The ministerial staff is the minister's personal, partisan political support staff. As political appointees, members are 'exempt' staff; that is , they are outside the neutral public service, and are not controlled by the Public Service Commission or hired on the merit system. They often have no more program expertise than the minister does, but their purpose is to counterbalance advice from the department. They are expected to bring a partisan political perspective to policy proposals, and to keep the minister informed of the implications of policy moves for the fortunes of the party and for the minister's personal political future. Ministerial staffs have essentially the same functions as members of the PMO (although they are much smaller in number) and they also look after the minister's agenda. Tim Plumptre, while conceding that ministers do need support staff, succinctly describes the problems encountered:

> . . . many staff members do not in fact have the background to give the minister the kind of mature political advice that is required; the nature of the job (short term, ill defined, resented by the public service) is such that it is unlikely to attract the type of people wanted in such a position; ministerial aides tend to be ambitious individuals who, lacking supervision, develop private agendas unrelated to the minister's interests, thereby causing the minister more harm than good; assistants interfere in the work of the department in ways that serve partisan political purposes, unrelated to the general public interest.[42]

This description suggests that the deputy minister, and the senior staff in the department, may require considerable interpersonal skills to manage the conflicts that may arise with the ministerial staff.

Ted Hodgetts, in an article titled 'The Deputy's Dilemma', describes the complexity of the many relationships that must be managed by the deputy minister. He says that deputies' heads need to be on a 'well-oiled swivel' to address the many individuals and groups to whom they owe responsibility.[43] These would include the prime minister, their own minister, Cabinet committees, central agencies, Parliament, the Public Service Commission, the various other federal 'watchdogs' (such as the Official Languages Commissioner or the Human Rights Commissioner) as well as their own department colleagues. Osbaldeston says that deputy ministers

> 'manage by radar'; they must adapt to an uncertain, changing environment, and balance their inter and intra departmental responsibilities; the quality of their judgement is therefore the key indicator of their ability to manage.[44]

In Canada the hierarchical nature of public administration, combined with parliamentary structures and the doctrine of ministerial responsibility, presents a 'significant bias in the direction of the centralization of formal authority'[45] and a concomitant downplaying of the role of middle managers. Recent changes in the environment of the public service, however, have led to a new perception of the importance of the role of middle managers:

> Restraint and downsizing, technological changes, demographic developments, new accountability regimes, regional decentralization and administrative deregulation, politicization, contracting out, and increased expectations and assertiveness on the part of subordinates and citizens, have all radically changed the environment of middle managers.[46]

For these reasons it may be appropriate to examine the management traits and leadership skills of the critical mass of middle managers.

Richard Paton uses three terms to describe management levels in the public service: supervisors, middle managers and senior executives.[47] Supervisors are responsible for directing small groups of technical or professional staff, or small groups that provide service directly to the public. Senior executives are the top two or three levels — the deputy ministers, assistant deputy ministers, and perhaps the directors general — who have overall management responsibility for the department and its relations with other government structures. Middle managers provide the crucial link between supervisors and senior executives and are responsible for the overall management of programs, districts, and regions.

Middle managers are responsible for setting priorities specific to the department; establishing departmental/external support, which would include co-operation with both internal and external groups; managing resources (both human and monetary) within public-sector constraints; and managing operations, such as the appropriate delivery of the service or program.[48] These responsibilities are not unlike those of the senior executives in government, although they are usually on a somewhat smaller scale. Nevertheless, middle managers must also learn to adapt to an uncertain and changing environment, develop a broad perspective on the department's mandate, maintain a sensitivity to the political milieu within which they operate, proceed with initiative, enthusiasm and vision, and call upon superior interpersonal skills to motivate and inspire their subordinates. These are essential qualities that escalate in importance when an exercise such as Public Service 2000 is launched.

PUBLIC SERVICE 2000 — LEADERSHIP IN ACTION?

Prime Minister Brian Mulroney, in December 1989, announced Public Service 2000 (PS2000), an ambitious initiative to renew the public service of Canada. His statement said that the intention of the initiative was to 'foster and encourage a public service that:

- is professional, highly qualified, non-partisan and imbued with a mission of service to the public;
- recognizes its employees as assets to be valued and developed;
- places as much authority as possible in the hands of front line employees and managers; and
- provides scope for different organizational forms to meet differing needs, but in the context of a single Public Service.'[49]

He also stated that it was the government's intention to reduce the complicated and burdensome management regime; relax central administrative controls; clarify and simplify the roles of central agencies; and develop innovative ways to encourage efficiency and improve program delivery.

Clearly this undertaking was intended to prepare the public service to 'rise to the challenges of a world that is increasingly interdependent and fiercely competitive'[50] and to provide it with the structures, skills, and personnel to respond to the increasing complexities of the 1990s and beyond. Is it just another manifestation of the hyperbole that accompanies the approach of a millennium, or does it have real meaning for the managers and leaders of the public service, as well as the thousands of public servants whom they are expected to manage and lead? To answer this question it is necessary to examine the thrust behind the reform initiative, how it was pursued, and some perceptions of the process.

Background to the Reform Initiative

By the time of the prime minister's announcement, there was growing evidence that the 1980s had been a difficult period for Canada's public service. The pursuit of restraint and reduction by successive governments meant that by 1990, the public service was the same size that it had been in 1973.[51] A study published in 1981 showed that ambitious and talented public servants had 'nowhere to go' — the routes to senior management were being closed off, and 'plateauing' was a new phenomenon in government service.[52] Relations between the Trudeau government and its employees were severely shaken in 1982 when the Public Sector Compensation Restraint Act was passed, limiting employee compensation and suspending for two years the rights to bargain collectively and to strike. Furthermore, when the Mulroney government took office in 1984, it was deeply suspicious of the public service, and was determined to seek policy advice from political rather than administrative sources.[53]

By the mid-1980s, 'the talk in the corridors of power in Ottawa . . . was of cutbacks and reductions, of difficult relations between the elected Government and the public service, and of interference by officials of the Prime Minister's Office in departmental administration'.[54] A survey of senior public servants conducted in 1986 (with a follow-up in 1988) 'revealed a public service in trouble: demoralized, losing confidence in its public service leaders and themselves, unsure of their roles and their futures, overburdened with work, chafing under perceived unfair criticism, lacking the tools and skills to face new challenges'.[55] Phrases such as 'a growing malaise', 'low morale', 'a separate management culture' [between upper and middle levels], and 'negative responses' were used to describe the attitudes of many public servants. Tellingly, there was a clear gap between the satisfaction expressed in the surveys by the very senior levels (including central agents) and the middle and lower level managers; the authors described this phenomenon as 'vertical solitude'.

These discouraging indications of low morale, discontent, and the need for improved productivity, quality and effectiveness appeared to amount to a condemnation of the leadership skills of senior management, although the situation was not always perceived that way. However, if strong leadership involves instilling vision, dedication, enthusiasm and motivation among subordinates, recognizing, understanding and solving problems, and communicating shared purpose and values, then there was clearly a leadership lapse in the public service.

In response to this challenge the COSO (Committee of Senior Officials) developed a plan to improve the working environment by giving managers more authority and reducing administrative restraints; to improve human resources planning, leadership, and communications; and to review the roles of the central agencies. Ironically, implementation of the plan 'was largely the responsibility of central agencies which had little motivation for change and which lacked a focal point for leadership in the human resources field (as the Auditor General criticized in his 1989 report)'.[56] The follow-up survey in 1988 did not show the expected improvement in morale and confidence, and in the Department of Communications public servants at all levels expressed frustration and malaise. The problems were clearly more deep-rooted than had at first been suspected. It was recommended that a major review of the public service in Canada be undertaken, with a focus on the level of the individual, the machinery of government, and the government infrastructure. Accordingly, in December 1990 the Mulroney government produced a white paper entitled *Public Service 2000; The Renewal of the Public Service of Canada*. PS 2000 was launched.

The process was initiated by Paul Tellier, the clerk of the Privy Council. Unlike previous reforms, it was to be led from within, in the belief that 'massive cultural change was required, and hence broad support ("ownership") within the public service, especially the management cadre, was essential'.[57] Ten task forces were established to examine specific areas (such as staffing, workforce adaptiveness, staff

relations, the management category, service to the public), and hundreds of recommendations were produced. On 18 June 1991 the government introduced Bill C-26,
the Public Service Reform Bill, an omnibus bill that incorporated changes to several of
the existing acts governing the public service. Describing this bill as 'intended to give
statutory effect to the goals and values of PS 2000' Tellier said that it had been
'developed through a long process of consultation with employees and with public
service unions,'[58] and that its passage would have a 'significant and positive impact
on the way in which the Public Service will operate in the years to come.'[59] By
February 1993, many of the recommendations had been acted upon or were under
consideration. In general, the task forces called for a balance between decentralization
and accountability, with an updating of public-service values and a major emphasis
on people, both clients and employees. Significantly, none of the reports dealt with
the 'very heavy and duplicative roles played by central agencies'.[60]

Carrying Out the Plan

In his first annual report to the prime minister, on 30 June 1992, Tellier was optimistic:

> I am pleased with the progress we have made. It reflects above all the imagination and
> dedicated effort of many thousands of individual public servants. If there is any credit
> due for what has been achieved, it belongs to them.[61]

In particular he singled out the role of deputy ministers in achieving reform, which he
said had been one of his priorities, and suggested that a reform exercise must be top-
down as well as bottom-up. He emphasized that there had been a focus on the
management skills of the deputy ministers and the need to hold them 'more clearly
accountable for how well they manage people and organizations [and] we are sending
a strong signal to the entire Public Service that reform is a continuing priority.'[62] He
went on to enumerate several of the 'milestones' that had already been passed, and
identified other areas in need of special attention. Among the latter was the need to
combat scepticism among the employees 'in the middle' who 'recognize the need for
change but are perhaps uncertain or apprehensive about how to bring it about' and
who wonder whether the reforms are genuine and beneficial.[63] The quality of leadership in the public service will clearly be crucial if such scepticism and apprehension
are to be overcome and an organizational climate that will permit the successful
pursuit of consensual goals is to be achieved.

The fanfare with which Public Service 2000 was announced and pursued precipitated much discussion. The key word used to describe the planned changes was
'empowerment'; the intention was to decentralize decision-making, encourage participatory management, and place more discretionary power in the hands of upper- and
middle-level managers. The term evoked memories of the Glassco Commission
(1962), which was often identified by the phrase 'let the managers manage'. A.W.
Johnson commented that 'if Glassco could be styled the "let the managers manage"
report, and Lambert the "make the managers manage" report, Public Service 2000
might be styled the "make the managers good managers" report.'[64] Frequent

invocation of a 'vision of service' and the need to develop a 'client-oriented' service was reminiscent of Weber's belief in the inevitable bureaucratization and alienation associated with large organizations. The need for repeated reminders that the purpose of public service is to serve the public was disheartening; it appeared that the public service of Canada was a manifestation of goal displacement theory: that is, that the obvious goals of the public service had been displaced by others of its own making.

There was much emphasis in the PS 2000 documents on the need to change public-service culture. The Human Resources Development Council,[65] for example, published a report in July 1992 under the title *Strategies for People: An Integrated Approach to Changing Public Service Culture*. It focused on the vision of 'client- centred service' that would 'put PEOPLE — clients, stakeholders and staff — at the centre of our efforts to achieve a revitalized Public Service'.[66] Clearly aware of the magnitude of the challenge, the Council enunciated four strategic statements to guide its activities and promote more responsive client service through the development of

- A responsive work environment that attracts and retains Canadians who have talent, commitment, and imagination required to provide client-centred service and make a contribution to the national well-being and who reflect the diversity of Canadian society.
- A continuous learning culture that places a high value on learning and career development for all employees and that encourages managers and employees to learn from each other through every day experiences and formal training.
- Leadership and management practices and behaviours that empower — or enable — employees to make full use of their skills, creative energies and formal training.
- A participatory approach to management that is rooted in jointly developed priorities, clear standards and personal accountabilities, and an appraisal and reward system focused on achieving service results and good human resources management.[67]

The profound change in public-sector culture that was implied in the task-force reports led to some scepticism about the outcome, although the authors of the reports evinced cautious optimism.

Bruce Rawson, who served on the Service to the Public Task Force, has called the report 'trail blazing', since it not only provided research and recommendations but also included a detailed analysis of the route to better service in government:

> In articulating a definition of good service and how to achieve it, we were tackling the same challenges which government departments and agencies would confront as they set out to transform their own service. All our work rested on the fundamental premise that the federal government is, through and through, a service organization . . . it exists to serve the people'.[68]

Rawson also describes the need to focus on the creation of a service-oriented environment or 'culture', and clearly perceives this to be a challenging prospect. Although he says that public servants across Canada already have a strong service ethic, he suggests that '[a]t every level and in every occupation, the employee's value to the team would be measured in terms of service. As traits such as innovation and initiative acquired a new and higher value, so the collective corporate personality would change. A preoccupation with results rather than process would become *not an exception but the mandated norm*.'[69] He clearly understands that to develop a service culture within the public service will require a major transformation, and he foresees that some managers may resist the needed adjustments as they are called upon to play a decisive role in implementing a new system.

In a paper examining the potential for a 'career public service 2000', Kenneth Kernaghan expresses several concerns about the attainability of success with the PS 2000 initiative.[70] He believes that there has been an inadequate appreciation of the magnitude of the challenge implicit in changing the culture of an organization as large as the Canadian public service. The new culture envisioned, he says, 'will be results-oriented and client-oriented, based on management principles falling into the four categories of service, innovation, people and accountability'.[71] However, success would demand a significant culture change to a client-oriented public service, and 'it has not been customary for the public service to regard Canadians as customers.'[72] This change in culture will require a firm commitment at both the political and the senior management levels, and success will depend on the efforts of the individual managers involved in implementation. Kernaghan questions whether governments have the political will to pursue such massive, fundamental organizational change, particularly since it will require several years for effective implementation.

An indication of the severity of the resistance that could be encountered is provided by Robert McIntosh, who offers the unionized employee's perspective.[73] As the head of the Professional Institute of the Public Service, McIntosh laments the lack of involvement of employees in the process of renewal. Paul Tellier's statement about broad consultation notwithstanding, he says the process has been 'unabashedly management driven', and that the 'refusal to permit the involvement of employees diminishes the prospects for the successful introduction of the sweeping reforms sought by all interested parties'.[74] This is a serious grievance, and since the vast majority of federal public servants are unionized, extensive reform is unlikely to occur unless they are open to it. If McIntosh is representative of the unionized public service, then the concept of 'ownership' of the reform process by front-line employees has not taken hold. He makes the grave accusation that the exercise has been created 'by management for management' and without the participation, encouragement, and commitment of the great bulk of the public service.[75] Apparently there is still a wide gap between the rhetoric of good leadership (the ability to motivate and promote a vision and a commitment to shared values) and the practice of leadership in the public service.

CONCLUSION

'The only way in which anyone can lead us is to restore to us the belief in our own guidance.'[76] At the beginning of this chapter it was suggested that in a large organization such as the Canadian public service, employees have many opportunities to choose the amount of effort they wish to invest in their jobs; if they are to be productive and responsible, the incentive must come from within. In the absence of leadership that can facilitate the development of incentive, however, a responsible and productive public service will not be forthcoming. Senior managers, especially in times of retrenchment,[77] must transcend the perception of hierarchical, top-down direction and motivate their employees to be self-leaders. 'Effective leaders should be judged more on their ability to tap the leadership potential within each person . . . at the heart of any empowerment effort should be an emphasis on employee self-leadership.'[78]

Along with increased autonomy for the individual public servant, however, comes a need for 'prudence and probity, [and] clear accountability'.[79] The Auditor General's Office has correctly suggested that the 'flip side' of empowerment and management freedom and flexibility is the need for improved accountability mechanisms.[80] It reminds us that 'the history of the federal public service shows a swing of the pendulum from centralization, rules and control, to decentralization, deregulation and autonomy', and that the Auditor General's role is to ensure that a proper balance is maintained. The Office also suggests that previous efforts at reform have neglected accountability — in effect, that this has been the 'missing link'.[81] However, it can also be argued that effective leadership that successfully taps the inherent self-leadership capabilities in each employee will give that employee a sense of ownership of the job, and that the resultant self-motivation should lessen the need for elaborate external accountability controls.

Canadians, and public servants, should not be too discouraged by the apparent need for frequent major reforms to the public service. It is, after all, a large, complex, and hierarchical bureaucratic structure, and as such will always be predisposed to the pitfalls so accurately described by Weber. In contrast to the mechanical, emotionless rationalism of Weber's ideal bureaucratic construct, however, the modern public service is composed of individuals, each with his or her own career aspirations, character strengths and flaws, and personal agenda. At the same time, they will always be susceptible to encouragement to maximize their potential and develop their potential and develop their inherent capabilities in response to effective, encouraging, honest, and visionary leadership.

NOTES

[1] Timothy W. Plumptre, *Beyond the Bottom Line: Management in Government*, (Montreal: Institute for Research in Public Policy, 1988), 377.

[2] Donald J. Savoie, 'Developing Leaders for the Public Sector: Discussion Summary', *Canadian Public Administration* 33, 3: 287-305, 271.

[3] Ibid., 272.

[4] Sandford F. Borins, 'The Role of the Universities in Public Administration Education', *Canadian Public Administration* 33, 3: 348-65, 352. Barbara Wake Carroll, however, has found that senior managers in the federal government often have not been long enough in

their positions to fully develop their policy-specific skills. One of the objectives of Public Service 2000 is to have deputies remain longer in their departments.

[5] Abraham Zaleznik, 'Managers and Leaders: Are They Different?', *Harvard Business Review* 70 (March/April 1992): 126.

[6] Sharon L. Sutherland poses serious questions about the implications of the Al-Mashat affair for ministerial responsibility and administrative accountability in 'The Al-Mashat Affair: Administrative Responsibility in Parliamentary Institutions', *Canadian Public Administration* 34, 4: 573-603. Nevertheless, the government's White Paper entitled *Public Service 2000: The Renewal of the Public Service of Canada* (Ottawa: Minister of Supply and Services, 1990) reiterated the importance of ministerial responsibility (7-8).

[7] For an expansion of these points, see *From Max Weber*, H.H. Gerth and C. Wright Mills, eds, (New York: Oxford University Press, 1946); Seymour Wilson, *Canadian Public Policy and Administration: Theory And Environment* (Toronto, McGraw-Hill Ryerson, 1981), chapter 2.

[8] Amitai Etzioni, *Modern Organizations* (Englewood Cliffs, NJ: Prentice-Hall, 1964); also see discussion in Nicholas Henry, *Public Administration and Public Affairs* (Englewood Cliffs, NJ: Prentice-Hall, 1975), 128-32.

[9] John P. Kotter, 'What Leaders Really Do', *Harvard Business Review* 68 (May/June 1990): 104; quoted in Henry, *Public Administration*, 131.

[10] Kenneth Kernaghan and David Siegel, *Public Administration in Canada* (Toronto: Methuen, 1987), 83.

[11] Discussed in Kernaghan and Siegel, *Public Administration*, 84, and by Robert D. Pursley and Neil Snortland, 'Leadership', in Kenneth Kernaghan, ed., *Public Administration in Canada: Selected Readings*, 5th ed. (Toronto: Methuen, 1985), 28.

[12] Ibid., Kernaghan and Siegel, 86-7; Pursley and Snortland, 29-31.

[13] Ibid., Kernaghan and Siegel, 87; Pursley and Snortland, 33-4.

[14] Borins, 'The Role of the Universities', 352.

[15] John Manion, 'New Challenges in Public Administration', *Canadian Public Administration* 31, 2: 234-46.

[16] Quoted in Gordon Osbaldeston, *Keeping Deputy Ministers Accountable* (Toronto: McGraw-Hill Ryerson, 1989), 121.

[17] Plumptre, *Beyond*, chapter 2.

[18] Ibid., 40.

[19] Charles C. Manz, 'Self Leadership . . . The Heart of Empowerment', *Journal for Quality and Participation* 15, 4 (1992): 80.

[20] Osbaldeston, *Keeping*, 119-20.

[21] Manion, 'New Challenges', 238.

[22] See Albert A. Vicere, 'The Strategic Leadership Imperative for Executive Development', *Human Resource Planning* 15, 1 (1992), for a discussion of the need for leaders to 'stay the course in an organization while continually "rocking the boat"', 15.

[23] For an excellent discussion of Canada's central agencies, see Colin Campbell and George J. Szablowski, *The Superbureaucrats: Structure and Behaviour in Central Agencies* (Toronto: Macmillan, 1979).

[24] See ibid., chapter 2.

[25] For example, Royal Commission on Government Organization (the Glassco Commission), 1962; Royal Commission on Financial Management and Accountability (the Lambert Commission), 1979; Special Committee on Personnel Management and the Merit Principle (the D'Avignon Committee), 1979.

[26] Richard French, *How Ottawa Decides: Planning and Industrial Policy-Making 1968-1980* (Toronto: James Lorimer, 1980), 6-7.

[27] Ibid., 6.

[28] Colin Campbell, 'Central Agencies in Canada', in Kernaghan, ed., *Public Administration*, 118.

[29] Ibid.

[30] *Keeping Deputy Ministers*, 55.

[31] Thomas Axworthy, 'Of Secretaries to Princes', *Canadian Public Administration* 31, 2: 251.

[32] Ibid., 252.

[33] Ibid., 260.

[34] French, *How Ottawa Decides*, 11.

[35] See ibid, p. 10. There are thousands of these submissions to cabinet each year. They are short, only about two pages each, and they indicate a department's program priorities.

[36] Hubert L. Laframboise, 'Counter-Managers: The Abandonment of Unity of Command', *Optimum* 8, 4 (1977): 21-2, quoted in French, *How Ottawa Decides*, 11.

[37] Audrey Doerr, *The Machinery of Government in Canada* (Toronto: Methuen, 1981), 179.

[38] Kernaghan and Siegel, *Public Administration*, 149.

[39] Sharon L. Sutherland, 'The Public Service and Policy Development', in Michael M. Atkinson, ed., *Governing Canada: Institutions and Public Policy* (Toronto: Harcourt Brace Jovanovich, 1993), 92. The difficult economic environment of the early 1990s has had profound effects on the whole public service.

[40] 'The Public Service', 95.

[41] When the Mulroney government took office in 1984, it was deeply suspicious of the senior departmental staff. To counterbalance administrative advice, the position of executive assistant to each minister was upgraded to ministerial chief of staff, comparable to an assistant deputy minister.

[42] *Beyond the Bottom Line*, 138.

[43] *Policy Options* 4, 3: 14-16.

[44] *Keeping Deputy Ministers*, 155.

[45] Peter Aucoin, 'Middle Managers — The Crucial Link: Summary of Discussions', *Canadian Public Administration* 32, 2: 187.

[46] Ibid., 189.

[47] 'Middle Managers: Upscale Supervisors or Emerging Executives?', *Canadian Public Administration* 32, 2: 245.

[48] Ibid., 249.

[49] Government of Canada, *Public Service 2000: The Renewal of the Public Service of Canada* (Ottawa: Minister of Supply and Services, 1990), 3.

[50] Paul M. Tellier, 'Public Service 2000: The Renewal of the Public Service', *Canadian Public Administration* 33, 2: 132.

[51] John Manion, 'Prospects for Career Public Service', presentation at Dalhousie University, Conference on 'Career Public Service — Principles, Practices and Prospects', Halifax, 5-7 Oct. 1990, 2.

[52] Nichole S. Morgan, *Nowhere to Go* (Montreal: Institute for Research on Public Policy, 1981).

[53] Plumptre, *Beyond*, 333.

[54] Ibid., 327.

[55] David Zussman and Jak Jabes, *The Vertical Solitude: Managing in the Public Sector* (Montreal: Institute for Research in Public Policy, 1989). Discussed in Manion, 'Prospects', 5.

[56] Manion, 'Prospects', 6.

[57] Ibid., 8.

[58] Paul Tellier, *Public Service 2000, First Annual Report to the Prime Minister* (Ottawa: Supply and Services Canada, 1992), 12-13.

[59] Ibid., 13.

[60] Manion, 'Prospects', 10.

[61] *First Annual Report*, covering letter, 30 June 1992.

[62] Ibid., 12.

[63] Ibid., 15.

[64] 'Reflections on Administrative Reform in the Government of Canada, 1962-1991' (Office of the Auditor General, 1992), 20.

[65] This is a new central agency, created in conjunction with PS 2000.

[66] *Strategies for People*, Treasury Board Secretariat (July 1992), i.

[67] Ibid., 28.

[68] 'Public Service 2000 Service to the Public Task Force, Findings and Implications', *Canadian Public Administration* 34, 3 (1991), 491.

[69] Ibid., 493; emphasis added. This statement might be a source of amazement to many, but it certainly conforms to Weber's classic description of bureaucracy.

[70] 'Career Public Service 2000: Road to Renewal or Impractical Vision?', *Canadian Public Administration* 34, 4: 551-72.

[71] Ibid., 555.

[72] Ibid., 556.

[73] 'Public Service 2000: The Employee Perspective', *Canadian Public Administration* 34, 3: 503-11.

[74] Ibid., 504.

[75] Ibid., 511.

[76] Author Henry Miller, quoted in Megan Smolenyak and Amit Majumdar, 'What is Leadership?', *Journal for Quality and Participation* 15, 4 (July/Aug. 1992): 28.

[77] Robert D. Behn, 'Leadership for Cut-Back Management: The Use of Corporate Strategy', *Public Administration Review*, Nov./Dec. 1980: 613-20. Behn makes some interesting arguments about the extra challenges facing management in times of retrenchment. Managers must become more active and intrusive, because 'cutback management requires [firm] leadership' (618).

[78] Manz, 'Self-Leadership', 80.

[79] 'PS 2000 . . . Developing a Common Understanding' (Office of the Auditor General, August 1991), 14.

[80] Ibid., 5.

[81] Ibid., 14.

CHAPTER ELEVEN

JUDGES AS LEADERS

—■—

Ian Greene

One might question whether a chapter on judges is really needed in a book about political leadership. It might end up being embarrassingly short: one paragraph about why our laws do not allow judges to be political leaders because this dual role would compromise judicial impartiality and independence, in fact as well as appearance. (It should be remembered that this was not always so in Canada. Prior to Confederation, colonial judges frequently held positions in the appointed executive council. The separation between the judicial and 'political' branches of government came about as the rule of law gained in prominence, and as a larger population base made the separation of the judiciary from the other branches of government economically feasible.)

Regardless of political theory, however, Canadians do perceive judges as playing a leadership role, especially since the advent of the Charter of Rights in 1982. After all, it was the Supreme Court of Canada that struck down the Lord's Day Act in 1985, the abortion law in 1988, and the law that prohibited spreading false news in 1992.[1] Moreover, even before 1982, judges sometimes behaved as leaders. It was the

London-based Judicial Committee of the Privy Council (Canada's top court until 1949) that from the 1880s until the Second World War interpreted the British North America Act in such a way as to expand provincial powers.[2] Nor should we forget the Supreme Court's Constitutional Reference of 1981 — the decision that set the stage for the 1982 constitutional reforms that included the entrenchment of the Charter of Rights.[3]

Judges, then, are indeed political leaders. But the leadership skills they require must necessarily be somewhat different from those of leaders in the overtly 'political' branches of government—the executive and the legislature. The leadership skills needed by judges are more like the talents possessed by a Margaret Atwood, a Bruce Cockburn, a Wayne Gretzky or a Peter Russell than a Kim Campbell, a Jean Chrétien, or an Audrey McLaughlin. Judges lead through the persuasiveness of their writing, unusual displays of creativity within the rules of the judge's art, their industry, their intellect, and their skill in working in small groups, rather than through charisma, their grasp on complex policy issues, their ability to direct a large bureaucracy, or their public image.

This chapter will analyse the leadership role of judges from three perspectives:

- judges as leaders within the legal-judicial community,
- judges as administrative leaders; and
- public expectations about judicial leadership, and the judicial response to these.

First, though, it is necessary to clarify what 'successful leadership' means with reference to the judiciary. Clearly, judges are successful leaders if their decisions advance the law and contribute to greater social harmony, and if their administrative decisions result in greater efficiency and procedural fairness. As Canada's democracy matures, however, it may be that more is required. Patrick Monahan has argued that the judiciary's interpretation of the Charter of Rights ought to further democratic ideals by promoting higher levels of public involvement in public policy-making.[4] Building on this approach, I will define a good judicial leader as one who is successful not only in achieving the goals mentioned above, but also, where appropriate, in fostering the goals of participatory democracy. Examples of such successes might include writing decisions that promote democratic ideals,[5] helping to make the court system more responsive to public demands for more considerate treatment of witnesses and litigants, and promoting an atmosphere in the courts in which all judges and lawyers can be encouraged to excel.

It could be argued that the rule of law requires judges to be impartial even with regard to the fundamental values of our political system: democracy and its prerequisites of equality and freedom. Such an expectation, however, would be not only impossible to achieve, but self-defeating. One purpose of the court system, as a branch of government, is to defend these basic constitutional principles. These principles underlie the Charter of Rights and Freedoms, which as part of our Constitution the judiciary is sworn to uphold. But these values are sometimes difficult to put into practice. Democracy can be broadly participatory or merely representative; equality and freedom can be interpreted narrowly, so as to protect entrenched privilege, or broadly, so as to encourage development of the higher human potentials. There are no easy solutions to these dilemmas, but the insight, depth of analysis, and compassion that judges bring to bear when considering them are indications of their leadership qualities.

THE LEADERSHIP ROLE OF JUDGES
WITHIN THE LEGAL COMMUNITY

Research indicates that between 50 and 60 per cent of Canadian judges accept judicial appointments for reasons related to the chance of being recognized as leaders in the legal-judicial community.[6] For 10 to 20 per cent of judges, accepting a judgeship represents the pinnacle of their legal careers. Another 35 to 40 per cent look forward to the challenge of being a judge, which usually includes expecting to make a contribution to the development of the law. For members of both these groups, a leadership role could consist in writing solid and sometimes innovative decisions that provide guidance both to other judges and to lawyers. One of the best examples of such a leader is former Ontario Court of Appeal judge Arthur Martin, who is mentioned by appeal court judges across Canada as one whose opinions set a standard for Canadian criminal law.[7] Another is Chief Justice Bora Laskin (1973-84), whose opinions judges at all levels generally felt obliged either to adopt or at least to debate.

With regard to how judges command the respect of other judges and lawyers through their written decisions, three factors need to be examined: legal and intellectual insight, writing ability, and personal reputation. Judges tend to admire other judges who are intelligent without being arrogant, and have a thorough knowledge of the law without being too rigid in their interpretations.[8] But intelligence and background knowledge are wasted unless a judge can write clearly. A good judicial writing style implies a concise, straightforward approach. (The National Judicial Institute, a continuing education centre for Canadian judges which was established in 1987 in Ottawa, offers judgement-writing courses that are already highly regarded by the judiciary.)

A new judge who writes intelligently and clearly will arouse the curiosity of other judges, who will want to know something about the newcomer's personal reputation in order to assess how much store ought to be placed in his or her opinions. The qualities that other judges admire most among their colleagues, according to a study of judges in Alberta, are industry, courtesy, empathy, and patience.[9]

One measure of success in the legal-judicial community is a judge's reputation in the law journals. All the law schools in Canada publish journals, and these are filled with articles criticizing or applauding recent important decisions. Over time, journal articles tend to praise some leading judges more than others, and this contributes to a judge's reputation. For example, in the first years after Madame Justice Bertha Wilson was appointed to the Supreme Court of Canada in 1982, journal articles were sometimes critical of her decisions, which they found to be too unorthodox. By the time she retired in 1991, however, she was regarded as one of the most innovative and intellectually solid judges on the court—someone whose opinions set new standards in certain areas of law.[10]

In situations where the law is somewhat unclear, judges may have the opportunity to be innovative or 'activist' — to actually bring about a change in the application of the law that may occasionally be as far-reaching as any legislation. On the other hand, they may choose to be 'restrained', that is, to find a way of avoiding adding anything new to the law, and leaving it to the legislature to enact fundamental changes. Is a good judicial leader activist or restrained? There is no clear consensus among judges themselves. Research indicates that, in Alberta, about 40 per cent of the judges are solidly 'restrained', 10 per cent are enthusiastic 'activists', and half think that it is acceptable to dabble with activism on occasion.[11] The issue is further complicated by the fact that activism can be either progressive or regressive, and can serve either to promote participatory democracy or to restrain it.[12]

In sum, to be regarded as a leader in the legal-judicial community, a judge needs to demonstrate hard work, courtesy and patience, a keen intellect, and a clear writing style. Obviously, the higher the court the judge sits on, the greater the chance of being recognized as a leader in this sense.

To be a successful leader from the perspective of democratic ideals, a judge would need, in addition to all of the above skills and attributes, a sense of where it is appropriate to promote participatory democracy through judicial decision-making. For example, in the opinion explaining why the Lord's Day Act was contrary to the Charter of Rights, Chief Justice Brian Dickson went beyond what was strictly necessary in a legal sense to stress the importance of democratic values:

> A truly free society is one which can accommodate a wide variety of beliefs, diversity of tastes and pursuits, customs and codes of conduct. A free society is one which aims at equality with respect to the enjoyment of fundamental freedoms. . . . Freedom must surely be founded in respect for the inherent dignity and the inviolable rights of the human person.[13]

At the same time, it should not be forgotten that, in their Charter decisions, Supreme Court judges have probably missed opportunities to further democratic values at least as often as they have deliberately chosen to use them.[14]

THE LEADERSHIP ROLES OF JUDGES
WITH ADMINISTRATIVE RESPONSIBILITIES

In order to analyse the nature of leadership among the administrative judges, it is necessary first to understand exactly what administrative responsibilities these judges have.

Administrative Responsibilities

Most of the judges in Canada with administrative responsibilities are the chief judges and chief justices. (The term 'justice' refers to judges in the provincial 'superior' trial courts, the provincial courts of appeal, the Federal Court, and the Supreme Court of Canada. All of these are appointed by the federal government, and they constitute about half of Canada's nearly 2,000 judges. The rest of the judges, appointed by the provincial governments, preside in 'inferior' courts, most of which are known as 'provincial' courts.[15]) The chief justices and judges in the larger courts are assisted by associate chief judges or justices, as well as by the 'senior' judges in local court centres. But these administrative judges do not have a free hand to direct as they please; they are constrained by the constitutional principle of judicial independence, buttressed by the mind-set that respects professional autonomy (see below).

In the provincial trial courts, the chief judges determine in which districts the regular judges sit (although there is usually an understanding about the judges' home districts at the time of appointment), and make temporary re-assignments to the busier courthouses. In multi-judge courthouses, a system is required for assigning cases to judges, and this system is designed by the provincial chief judge, the associate chief judge, and the local senior judges (often the longest-serving of the local judges).

In the superior trial courts, the chief justices are responsible for developing a system of assigning cases to judges in multi-judge court centres. In addition, most superior courts are travelling courts; superior court business in the smaller court centres is handled through visits from a superior court judge several times a year. The travelling schedules of the superior court judges are set by the chief justice.

Judges on appeal courts hear cases in panels. In the provincial appeal courts, most cases are heard by panels of three judges, although the most important cases are considered by five-judge panels. In the Supreme Court of Canada, the norm is the seven-judge panel, while the most important cases are heard by the full complement of nine judges. Five-judge panels are utilized for civil law appeals from Québec (so that the three Québec judges will be in the majority), for some less-important cases, or when caseload pressures make seven- judge panels impractical.

The chief justices decide on the size of the panels, the panel members (usually changed on a monthly or bi-weekly basis) and the system for assigning cases to panels. In panels that include the chief justice, the latter presides over the 'conferences', or discussions after the hearings. As well, the chief either assigns a judge to write the court's decision when the decision is 'reserved', or announces the oral decision in court after the conference. When the chief is not on the panel, the senior judge on the panel is usually the 'presiding judge', although sometimes this responsibility is carried out by a 'lead judge' (appointed by the chief justice) who is not necessarily the senior judge.

Independence and Autonomy

Judicial independence is a constitutional convention, parts of which are incorporated into the Constitution Act, 1867 (Sections 96, 99, and 100) and the Charter of Rights and Freedoms (Section 11[d]).[16] This principle, according to which judges must decide cases without interference, evolved to promote the rule of law demanding that the law be interpreted and applied as impartially as possible. In the Anglo-Canadian legal system, judicial independence carries the implication that even chief and senior judges cannot attempt to interfere with the decision-making processes of more junior judges. Thus judges with administrative responsibilities tend to tread lightly to avoid being perceived as violating judicial independence.

Judicial independence aside, because of their professional experience judges are unlikely to be amenable to the kind of supervision and management to which those who work in a typical bureaucracy are accustomed. Lawyers learn to appreciate their autonomy during their years in private practice, and they are not inclined to surrender this professional freedom when they become judges.[17] An administrative judge is in a position somewhat analogous to that of a university department chair: both have the unenviable task of co-ordinating a group of prima donnas who are among the best-educated over-achievers in the country, who stress their professional autonomy, and who can back up their demands for autonomy with principle (judicial independence in the case of judges, academic freedom in the case of professors). There is general agreement among judges about what constitutes a reasonable workload, but specific assignments are made by administrative judges more through negotiation than by decree.

Administrative Challenges

There are two general systems for the assignment of cases to judges in multi-judge trial courts. (Such trials are always presided over by judges sitting alone; in fewer than 5 per cent of cases in superior trial courts is the judge assisted by a jury). One approach is to divide up cases according to type and then assign the same kinds of cases to the same courtroom. For example, in a criminal court with four courtrooms and four judges, incoming cases might be divided into traffic offences, minor non-traffic cases, cases involving assault, and cases involving property. The judges would rotate courtrooms every month, although the rotation schedule is rarely made public.

One problem with this system is that a litigant may prefer a different judge from the one assigned. When this happens, the litigant's lawyer may invent a reason to request that the case be adjourned for a month or longer in the hope either that the preferred judge will be assigned to the courtroom the next time around ('judge-shopping') or that a particular judge can be avoided ('judge-avoidance').

In busy courthouses, judge-shopping and judge-avoidance can contribute to an unacceptable backlog of cases,[18] and therefore the senior judge or the chief judge may insist that every case be decided by the judge first assigned to it. Such scheduling systems are more complex, however, and are more likely to be successful if the senior judge has some expertise in administration, if the court administrator is skilled, and if there is a good working relationship between the senior judge and the court administrator.[19] Even when these conditions are present, however, many judges, having acted as counsel themselves, view judge-shopping or judge-avoidance as legitimate or inevitable, and so may not take action to prevent these practices.[20]

In any case, two reasons for unnecessary delays in trial courts that are even more common are the inefficient use of judicial resources and unnecessary delays caused by counsel.[21] The former occurs when cases are disposed of unexpectedly quickly in one courtroom, while in another the cases are taking longer than expected, so that some will have to be adjourned. It makes sense for the judge finished early to take cases over for the busy judge, but this is easier said than done. In criminal cases, such arrangements would depend on the last-minute re-assignment of some cases to a different Crown attorney for prosecution; as well, care must be taken to ensure that a police witness does not end up having to appear in two courtrooms at the same time. Most important, delay caused by counsel can only be tackled in a court where the chief justice believes that the pace of case-flow should be controlled by the court, not by counsel.

It should be clear from these examples that the success, as leaders, of trial court judges with administrative responsibilities depends on both administrative skills and personality. Since all judges are recycled lawyers, and very few lawyers have any formal training in administration, most of the administrative skills of successful administrative judges are learned 'on the job'. The judges who develop these skills are those who are willing to recognize their skill deficit and who have the energy to remedy it.

With regard to the required personality traits, successful administrative judges in trial courts require diplomacy above all. Because of judicial independence and professional autonomy, administrative judges do not have the legal or moral authority to give orders to the regular judges. Rather, they must persuade, suggest, and encourage. However, this soft-touch approach does seem to work tolerably well much of the time, and can sometimes be made to work very well. One reason is that most judges have developed a professional attitude through their years of experience as lawyers. On average, judges have about twenty years of experience practising law before judicial appointment, and the majority have been partners in law firms. In addition, most have held executive positions in law societies, bar associations, service clubs, or fraternal organizations.[22] They tend to operate most efficiently when left alone to do their jobs. When the administrative system works unusually well, it is often because the administrative judge has a combination of administrative skills and personality traits that encourages co-operation on the part of the regular judges.

The personality of administrative judges becomes an even more critical factor in appeal courts, where cases are always heard by panels. For these panels to work effectively, the presiding judge needs to combine 'task leadership' and 'social leadership' skills.[23] An effective task leader has the ability to focus on the main issues in a case, summarize alternative views clearly and concisely, and assign the 'most appropriate' judge to write the opinion. To choose the most appropriate judge, an effective task leader should take into account the existing workload of each judge, the judges' individual areas of expertise, and the 'politics' of the panel; the latter consideration arises because the panel may include a mixture of judges with 'liberal' and 'conservative' reputations. Sometimes the best judge for writing the panel's opinion is not necessarily the one who has the most knowledge of the case's subject-matter, but the one with the greatest chance of commanding the respect of both the liberal and conservative judges on the panel.[24]

An effective social leader has the ability to encourage the judges on the panel to get along with each other and to enjoy working together. As David Danelski wrote of US Chief Justice Hughes (1930-41), a successful task and social leader, never in his eleven years as Chief Justice did he lose his temper . . . , pass a personal remark or even raise his voice. Never [was he witnessed as] interrupting or engaging in controversy with an associate. . . . [He] had a keen sense of humor which aided in keeping differences in conference from becoming discord. Moreover, when discussion showed signs of deteriorating into wrangling, Hughes would cut it off. On the whole, he was well liked.[25]

Hughes's style contrasted sharply with that of Chief Justice Stone (1941-46), who seemed to fail on both counts. As a task leader, Stone frequently did not appear to grasp the essential issues in a case; as a social leader, he did little to control the debate in conference, and sometimes made insulting comments to the other judges. The result included 'serious conflict, ruffled tempers, severe tension, and antagonism' on the US Supreme Court during Stone's tenure as Chief Justice.[26] The productivity of the court declined, and dissenting or concurring opinions became more common.

Chief Justice Bora Laskin is probably the Canadian equivalent to Hughes: someone who demonstrated strong task and social leadership skills. A retired judge who sat on the Supreme Court with Laskin observed that he

had a very sharp and concentrated mind. He was an intellectual leader; he knew where he was going. He had a decisive mind. It was usually obvious to him what the outcome [of a case] should be, and he didn't want [the court] to waste time debating unimportant issues. When it got to be his turn [in conference], he would usually say,' Well, it's clear that this is the outcome, and for this reason.' He didn't do this in a heavy-handed way, but in a kindly way. It was a joy to work with him.[27]

The Canadian answer to Stone may be Chief Justice Sir Henry Strong (1892-1902), who was 'widely considered to be bad-tempered, chronically ill, and intellectually lazy'.[28] Under his (lack of) leadership, the Court's performance and productivity set record lows.[29]

Some judges sitting on panels may try to influence the thinking of their colleagues in order to bring the majority around to their conclusions.[30] There are indications that Canadian appeal court judges do not exercise this sort of leadership very often.[31] When they do, however, a variety of strategies may be employed, including writing a 'red herring' draft opinion, and then offering to withdraw it if the other judges compromise; having a friendly chat at a social occasion with a judge open to being persuaded; or offering to yield to another judge's perspective in another case if the latter will yield in this instance.[32] Although, on occasion, chief justices have been known to 'stack' panels with judges they know will support their point of view,[33] it is generally agreed by Canadian appeal court judges that this rarely happens today.[34]

To recap, judges exercising administrative responsibilities need a combination of administrative skills (usually learned 'on the job') and personal diplomacy that will allow them to persuade without threat or sanction. Those sitting on appeal courts will require, as well, a combination of task and social leadership skills appropriate to a small group of highly-trained and independently-minded professionals.

Keeping in mind the principles of participatory democracy, successful administrative judges will try to promote administrative practices that take into account the needs of litigants and witnesses, and not just those of lawyers and judges. After all, the purpose of courts is to provide an efficient and effective public dispute-resolution service for the public at large. Nevertheless, as Peter Russell points out, 'For too many lawyers and judges, judging is still not regarded as the provision of a basic social service but the exercise of a private professional craft.'[35] Among those who are putting the interests of the public ahead of their personal convenience are a newly- appointed district court judge in northern Ontario who told me he was so concerned with the suffering that unnecessary delays in the court caused some litigants (particularly children) that he planned a procedure for hearing some cases on evenings and Saturdays, and a Toronto judge who has developed a system for attempting to ascertain whether the sentences he imposed had the desired impact.

PUBLIC EXPECTATIONS OF JUDICIAL LEADERSHIP AND THE JUDICIAL RESPONSE

Public Expectations

Public opinion polls show that Canadian judges are among the most highly-respected officials in our society. They command far more respect than politicians.[36] No doubt part of the reason is that, at least over the past few decades, they have honed a reputation for competence, impartiality and fairness.

One implication of the public image of judges is that many people expect them to play the role of 'official public philosophers.'[37] Judges are expected not only to decide cases 'correctly', but to present the appropriate philosophical justification for their decisions when the law is unclear. Judges are sometimes revered as role models, especially in smaller communities.[38]

These expectations place judges in a difficult situation. It is in the nature of the legal process that in many criminal cases, and most civil cases, litigants are convinced they are right; otherwise they might have settled out of court. One side is bound to lose, and the losing side will perceive that the 'official public philosopher' is not quite so omniscient as first believed. For example, after Joseph Borowski failed to persuade the Supreme Court to declare that foetuses have a right to life, he announced to the press his disillusionment with judicial wisdom:

> I'm glad I did not come to Ottawa for the decision. . . . I probably would have gone into the court and punched the judges in the nose. It looks to me like it [hearing the case] was a gimmick, a charade, a trick they played on us. . . . I think it would be a waste of my time to ever go back before those gutless . . . judges who wasted 10 years of our time.[39]

The Charter of Rights has given Canadian judges more opportunities than ever before to play the role of official public philosophers. The Charter is a vague document, which by its nature cannot possibly be perfectly clear about the meaning and application of the rights and freedoms listed in it. It is up to the judiciary to declare the precise meaning of the Charter on a case-by-case basis, and many Canadians expect judges to use this power to be leaders in social and political change.

Yet the impact of this judicial 'philosophizing' on the thinking of ordinary citizens is uncertain. Very few Canadians read judicial decisions, and although the gist of some of the more media-worthy opinions eventually filters down through lawyers, academics, and journalists, the leadership role that judges do play is rarely evident to the public. Once in two or three decades, a judicial decision may have a major impact on public opinion — for example, the US Supreme Court decision in 1954 that pronounced racial segregation to be contrary to the US Bill of Rights,[40] the 1930 decision of the Judicial Committee that women are 'persons' and may therefore sit in the Canadian Senate,[41] or the 1981 constitutional reference in which the Supreme Court of Canada declared that a convention did indeed exist that a substantial majority of provinces must agree to any constitutional amendment affecting provincial powers.[42] The vast majority of the time, however, we ordinary Canadians pay very little attention to our 'official philosophers'.

Thus there is a dissonance between the high expectations that Canadians have of their judges, and the ability of the judges to make their fulfilment of those expectations visible to the public.

The Judicial Response

Judges are human beings that some members of the public expect to have almost super- human qualities. It would be difficult for anyone put into the shoes of a judge to avoid developing a swelled ego. In response to a question about whether the judicial role affects judges' personalities, two-fifths of a sample of Ontario judges whom I interviewed in 1980, as well as three-fifths of a sample of lawyers and Crown attorneys, thought that judges tended to develop 'swelled egos'. Another fifth of the same groups, however, thought that the judicial role resulted in judges' further developing their most positive personality traits.[43]

How do judges cope with a situation where there are public expectations for them to play a leadership role in society, but because of institutional constraints, the opportunity to play a community-wide leadership role (in contrast to a leadership role within the courts or the legal-judicial community) is extremely limited?

Some judges 'escape' to a higher public profile by accepting temporary positions on commissions of inquiry. Here are a few recent examples. Ontario's Supreme Court Chief Justice William Parker was appointed by Prime Minister Brian Mulroney to inquire into the Sinclair Stevens affair in 1986. Mr Justice Charles Dubin (now Chief Justice of Ontario) was appointed to inquire into the use of performance-enhancing drugs in Canadian sports after sprinter Ben Johnson was disqualified for drug use in the Seoul Olympics of 1988. Supreme Court Justice Willard Estey was commissioned in 1987 to inquire into the collapse of the Canadian Commercial Bank and the Northlands Bank. Clearly, the Canadian public expects that judges can be trusted to make an impartial assessment of such situations, and will not be swayed by partisan political considerations. The judges' reputation for impartiality, which is at the centre of the public's leadership expectations concerning judges, might however be compromised when the judge-commissioner eventually has to take sides regarding these controversial issues.

Given the inherent danger presented to judges in accepting such appointments, it is somewhat ironic that some judges seem so willing to accept these challenges. There are two major reasons why judges will accept these positions. First, some consider it their duty as perceived leaders in Canadian society. Second, some judges simply get bored with the judicial routine, and view work on a royal commission or inquiry as a relief from the usual tedium.[44]

Sometimes, however, a judge may exceed the boundaries of judicial propriety in making a sincere attempt to play a national leadership role. An example is Mr Justice Thomas Berger, a former superior court judge in British Columbia, who in November 1981, while speaking at a university convocation, criticized the constitutional accord that had been reached earlier that month by all of Canada's first ministers except Québec's. The Canadian Judicial Council, a group of superior court chief justices that, among other things, acts as a disciplinary body, received a formal complaint and investigated. In the end, the Council issued a reprimand to Berger, and noted that judges cannot make public statements about current political issues without compromising judicial independence.[45]

Nevertheless, even though judges cannot speak in public about current political issues, it is a common perception that some judges attempt to lead public opinion by making far-reaching, trend-setting decisions such as those that struck down the Lord's Day Act, the old abortion law, and the legislation prohibiting the spread of false news. Not only do these kinds of decisions have a major impact on public policy, but they arouse nation-wide debates. Moreover, it is no secret that judges themselves are divided on such issues. Some past and present Supreme Court judges, such as Bora Laskin, Brian Dickson, Bertha Wilson, and Antonio Lamer, are perceived as small-'l' liberals, while others, such as William McIntyre, Gerald LaForest, and John Major, are viewed as small-'c' conservatives. Depending on how many judges the government in power can appoint, either the 'conservatives' or the 'liberals' will be in the majority, and the public perception is that the judges with the greatest influence act as leaders in reforming the law in the directions they prefer. Occasionally, leading judges will give speeches or interviews commenting on their approaches to judicial interpretation, and the resulting news coverage reinforces the public perception that Supreme Court judges have a great deal of latitude in shaping the law according to their views on how the country should develop.[46]

Such perceptions, although they contain a grain of truth, distort the reality of judicial leadership. In the great majority of cases at all levels below the Supreme Court of Canada, the legal issues are straightforward and there is little opportunity for judges to influence the development of the law. The Supreme Court is different because it controls its own caseload. Nearly all the cases that go to the Supreme Court must be granted 'leave', or permission to go forward, by the Court itself. The Court tries to focus its energy on 'hard' cases—those containing legal issues that have not yet been settled. But even in these 'hard' cases, research indicates that judges tend to see themselves as leaders only with respect to the legal-judicial community, not the Canadian public. They realize that when the law is unclear, different judges have different approaches to resolving the ambiguity, but they also realize that judges usually tackle these issues by applying what they consider to be the most appropriate legal and intellectual standards, rather than taking into account the kinds of political considerations that would be of utmost concern to elected politicians.[47]

For example, the Constitutional Reference of 1981 gave Supreme Court of Canada judges the opportunity to act as national leaders by contributing to the resolution of the constitutional impasse. I asked a retired Supreme Court of Canada judge who participated in that decision whether the judges tried consciously to find a politically acceptable solution. He replied: 'No. We were given a job to do and we did the best we could with it.' Another retired judge told me that making this decision 'was like a great friendly discussion in which we tried to find what's useful [rather than what is politically acceptable] for the country'.[48] There was no indication that the judges saw themselves as 'political' leaders; their primary purpose was to interpret the law in what appeared to them to be the most logical and sensible way, from the perspective of legal rather than political norms.

There is no doubt that judges enjoy the prestige accorded to them by the public. However, good judicial leadership requires that judges have the strength of character to resist opportunities for public leadership, and concentrate any leadership hopes they may have on the legal-judicial and administrative aspects of leadership. The closest they can legitimately come to playing a public leadership role is in accepting a temporary appointment on a commission of inquiry or royal commission.

CONCLUSION

Lawyers who want to be community leaders and tackle current political issues in the public limelight would be well advised to seek leadership roles in the political branches of government rather than in the judiciary. Most judges with leadership aspirations seem content with seeking to be leaders in the legal-judicial community or leaders among administrative judges.

The leadership roles, and therefore the skills required, of a 'leading' judge are somewhat different from those of other leaders in our political system. Judges must be more intellectual and more impartial; as well, since in most instances they lack the power to give administrative orders, judges need to lead through diplomacy.

But there are also some similarities. The leadership qualities that judges require to be effective leaders in the legal-judicial profession — industry, courtesy, empathy, patience — are also required of the most successful leaders in the legislative and executive branches of government, as well as the public service. Just as successful administrative judges must have the interpersonal skills to encourage a group of prima donnas to work together, prime ministers and provincial premiers need similar skills to manage their cabinets effectively. Furthermore, for both judicial and political leaders to be regarded as successful in the current era, they need a realistic understanding of and deep commitment to the principles of participatory democracy.

Ironically, then, while successful judicial leaders need many of the same skills and attributes as political leaders, they also require the ability to resist the temptation to exercise 'political' leadership in the usual sense.

NOTES

1 *Regina v. Big M Drug Mart et al.* [1985] 1 S.C.R. 295; *Regina v. Morgentaler*, [1988] 1 S.C.R. 30; *Regina v. Zundel*, [1992] 2 S.C.R., 731.

2 Peter Hogg, *Constitutional Law of Canada*, 3rd ed. (Toronto: Carswell, 1992).

3 Peter Russell, 'The Supreme Court Decision: Bold Statecraft Based on Questionable Juris- prudence', in P.H. Russell et al., *The Court and the Constitution* (Kingston, Ont.: Queen's University, 1982).

4 Patrick Monahan, *Politics and the Constitution: The Charter, Federalism and the Supreme Court of Canada* (Toronto: Carswell, 1987).

5 Such opportunities are particularly evident in cases involving voting rights and the right to run for office (Section 3 of the Charter); see Ian Greene, *The Charter of Rights* (Toronto: Lorimer, 1989), 110 ff. However, because the basic principles of democracy are closely linked with the fundamental freedoms outlined in Section 2 of the Charter, the legal rights in Sections 7 to 14, and the equality rights in Section 15, there are many other opportunities for judges to promote democratic values.

6 Peter McCormick and Ian Greene, *Judges and Judging: Inside the Canadian Judicial System* (Toronto: Lorimer, 1990), 83-100.

7 This information was obtained from the Canadian Appeal Courts Project, which is funded by the Social Sciences and Humanities Research Council. This project involves interviews with most Canadian appeal court judges by Carl Baar, Ian Greene, Peter McCormick, Martin Thomas and George Szablowski.

8 McCormick and Greene, *Judges and Judging*, 102 ff.

9 Ibid., 102-17.

10 James MacPherson, 'Canadian Constitutional Law and Madame Justice Bertha Wilson— Patriot, Visionary and Heretic', 1993 *Dalhousie Law Review* vol. 16 (forthcoming).

11 McCormick and Greene, *Judges and Judging*, 231.

12 Rainer Knopff and F.L. Morton, *Charter Politics* (Toronto: Nelson, 1992).

13 *Regina v. Big M Drug Mart Ltd.* et al. [1985] 1 S.C.R. 295.

14 For example, see the commentary on the Alberta Labour Reference, the decision in which the majority on the Supreme Court concluded that the Charter does not protect the right to strike, in Leo Panitch and Donald Swartz, *The Assault on Trade Union Freedoms* (Toronto: Garamond, 1988).

15 For a description of the Canadian court system, see Peter H. Russell, *The Judiciary in Canada: The Third Branch of Government* (Toronto: McGraw-Hill Ryerson, 1987), 101ff., and McCor- mick and Greene, *Judges and Judging*, 3-34.

16 See Andrew Heard, *Canadian Constitutional Conventions: The Marriage of Law and Politics* (Toronto: Oxford University Press, 1991), ch. 6, and Ian Greene, 'The Doctrine of Judicial Independence Developed by the Supreme Court of Canada', *Osgoode Hall Law Journal* 26 (1988), 177.

17 Ian Greene, 'The Politics of Judicial Administration: The Ontario Case', unpublished Ph.D. dissertation (University of Toronto, 1983), 149 ff.

18 Ian Greene, 'The Politics of Court Administration: The Ontario Case', *Windsor Yearbook of Access to Justice* 2 (1982), p. 124.

19 Perry Millar and Carl Baar, *Judicial Administration in Canada*, (Montréal: McGill-Queen's University Press, 1982).

20 Greene, 'Politics of Court Administration'.

21 McCormick and Greene, *Judges and Judging*, 30-4.

22 Ibid., 64-70.

23 These are terms developed by David J. Danelski in 1960 in 'The Influence of the Chief Justice in the Decisional Process', reproduced in Walter F. Murphy and C. Herman Pritchett, eds, *Courts, Judges, and Politics: An Introduction to the Judicial Process*, 3rd ed. (New York: Random House, 1979), 695. See also Walter F. Murphy, 'The Supreme Court as a Small Group', in S. Sidney Ulmer, ed., *Courts, Law, and Judicial Processes* (New York: Free Press, 1981), 363.

24 Walter F. Murphy, 'Courts as Small Groups', *Harvard Law Review* 79 (1966), 1565.

25 Danelski, 'Influence', 697.

26 Ibid., 698.

27 Ibid., 203.

28 Ibid., 191.

29 See James Snell and Frederick Vaughan, *The Supreme Court of Canada: History of the Institution* (Toronto: University of Toronto Press, 1985).

30 S. Sidney Ulmer, 'Leadership and Group Structure', in Ulmer, ed., *Courts*, 368.

31 Canadian Appeal Courts Project.

32 See Murphy, 'Courts as Small Groups'.

33 Interview with a retired Supreme Court of Canada judge, discussing cases from the 1950s.

34 Canadian Appeal Courts Project.

35 Peter Russell, 'Judicial Power in Canada's Political Culture', in M.L. Friedland, ed., *Courts and Trials: A Multi-Disciplinary Approach* (Toronto: University of Toronto Press, 1975), 75.

36 See, for example, Paul M. Sniderman, Joseph F. Fletcher, Peter H. Russell, and Phillip E. Tetlock, 'Liberty, Authority and Community: Civil Liberties and the Canadian Political Culture', paper delivered at the annual meetings of the Canadian Political Science Association and the Canadian Law and Society Association, University of Windsor, 9 June 1988.

37 Russell, *Judiciary*, ch. 1 and 2.

38 For examples, see McCormick and Greene, *Judges and Judging*, 100-1.

39 *Globe and Mail*, 10 March 1989. See also F.L. Morton, *Morgentaler v. Borowski: Abortion, the Charter, and the Courts* (Toronto: McClelland and Stewart, 1992).

40 *Brown v. Board of Education* 1954, 347 U.S. 483.

41 *Edwards v. A.-G. Canada* [1930] A.C. 124.

42 *A.-G. Manitoba et al. v. A.-G. Canada et al.* [1981] 2 S.C.R. 753.

43 McCormick and Greene, *Judges and Judging*, 102.

44 Personal interviews with superior court judges.

45 See Peter Russell, *The Canadian Judiciary*, 85 ff.

46 For example, see 'Inject Female Values into Judiciary, Supreme Court Judge Urges', *Globe and Mail*, 10 Feb. 1990: A 4, regarding Madame Justice Bertha Wilson, or 'Making the Law Make Sense', *Globe and Mail*, 10 April 1993: A 1, referring to Madame Justice Claire L'Heureux-Dubé.

47 In the Canadian Appeal Courts study, appeal court judges were asked whom they perceive as their 'audience' when writing opinions: the litigants in particular cases, other judges, lawyers, or the community at large. Preliminary results indicate that most appeal court judges write primarily for the legal-judicial community.

48 McCormick and Greene, *Judges and Judging*, 240.

CHAPTER TWELVE

CONSENSUAL POLITICS

Political Leadership in the Aboriginal Community

———■———

Kathy Brock

Aboriginal political leadership in Canada is undergoing a dynamic and vital process of change. The emergence of aboriginal self-government as a constitutional and community issue has caused analysts and practitioners alike to ask how traditional methods of governance may be combined with contemporary practices of governance and adapted to contemporary social and economic realities. Within local communities, the question surfaces in the tension between elected band governments and traditional governments. Beyond the community level, the dilemma becomes more acute as aboriginal communities construct nationally representative organizations and regional governments that must work with other Canadian political organizations and governments. As the aboriginal and Canadian traditions clash, new and innovative structures and styles of leadership are emerging.

Perhaps one of the most demanding areas of innovation concerns the adaptation of the traditional aboriginal principle of decision-making by consensus to accommodate the adversarial decision-making process that is characteristic of the Canadian political system. A survey of the government in the Northwest Territories, which blends aboriginal and parliamentary traditions, and the Assembly of First Nations, which represents aboriginal interests in negotiations with the federal and provincial governments, reveals that consensual traditions are being combined with Canadian political practices, although some problems of leadership remain unresolved.

This chapter is divided into three sections. The first briefly describes what is meant by consensus politics; the second examines how the principles of consensus politics affect the operation of the Legislative Assembly of the Northwest Territories; and the third examines the application of the principles of leadership by consensus in a nationally representative organization (the Assembly of First Nations). Both of the latter sections identify areas of unresolved tensions. The chapter concludes that the attempt to develop politically representative, relevant, and effective institutions to serve aboriginal interests and to serve as intermediaries between aboriginal peoples and the federal and provincial governments is an evolutionary process requiring creativity and imagination on the part of the aboriginal political leaders. This process may reveal some lessons on political leadership from which the rest of Canada could benefit in the current period of voter disillusionment, when political leadership is being fundamentally questioned and criticized.

POLITICS BY CONSENSUS

'A pair of good Ears will drain dry a Thousand Tongues.'

Poor Richard's Almanack, 1753

To discuss aboriginal traditions and practices of government is a complex and difficult task. Governing institutions derive from and reflect the broader culture. As Menno Boldt observes:

> Indian culture is not easily delineated because the Indian continental race . . . is made up of hundreds of distinct societies representing many languages and a variety of customs. However, in the total tribal mosaic it is possible to discern certain cultural features common to most Indian societies, that may be regarded as representative of those Indian peoples located within Canada's borders.[1]

Thus, although aboriginal cultures and political systems may appear similar when contrasted with their European counterparts, when compared among themselves their diversity is remarkable. Nevertheless, some principles and practices are common, though not universal, among traditional aboriginal political systems, and decision-making by consensus is one.

The practice of making decisions by consensus is based upon three essential principles widely shared in aboriginal philosophy. First, consensus is embedded in the principle of equality upon which most aboriginal societies were based. Boldt and Long underline the contrast between aboriginal and European concepts of equality:

> In European thought the Enlightenment concept of egalitarianism emerged as a reaction and response to excesses resulting from the hierarchical doctrine of sovereignty. Egalitarianism was imposed on, and interacted with, the hierarchical concept of sovereign

authority to produce more humane political structures. In traditional Indian society, however, the idea of egalitarianism did not emerge as a reaction to excesses of hierarchical authority. Equality was derived from the Creator's founding prescription. The creation myth held that, from the *beginning*, all members of the tribes shared and participated *equally* in all privileges.[2]

Egalitarianism was embraced because all creatures were imbued with the spirit of the Creator. This meant that the views of each member of the communities had to be treated equally.

The power of this statement becomes even more apparent when it is coupled with a second principle in aboriginal societies: respect for the individual. Aboriginal people participated in their societies as individuals who were part of a collective whole. Boldt quotes Alvin J. Josephy:

> Belief in the freedom and dignity of the individual was deeply ingrained in many Indian societies. In some tribes it was observed to such an extent that at any time — even when his people were fighting for their lives — a man could go his own way and do whatever seemed right to him. Among many tribes, also, councils decided on courses of action by unanimous, rather than majority, agreement; the feelings and opinions of each person were considered too important to override.[3]

Respect for the individual gives rise to the associated ethic of non-interference. According to Dr Clare Brant, a Mohawk: 'We are very loath to confront people. We are very loath to give advice to anyone if the person is not specifically asking for advice. To interfere or even comment on their behaviour is considered rude.'[4] The opinions and behaviour of each individual were treated as valid.[5] Thus no one opinion could be imposed upon another individual. Instead, for one person's opinion to be accepted and followed, that person had to convince the other members of the tribe of its worthiness.

Finally, aboriginal communities tended to strive for harmonious relations. Communities emphasized sharing, along with collective and voluntary action. These principles were reflected in the justice systems that endorsed gift-giving and reconciliation, rather than punishment or retribution, as means of rectifying wrongs. In political circles, the importance of harmony was reflected in the relationship between a chief and his people. In the League of the Six Nations, according to Chief Tom Porter,

> When a Chief is chosen, he is told: 'Your skin has to be seven layers thick, because people will be ungrateful and they will throw sharp words at your heart when you are tired. You must not let the sharp words penetrate your heart. . . .
> A chief cannot get angry with his people. He cannot call anyone down. He must speak with kind words at all times.[6]

Leadership by persuasion and example seems to have been the prevalent mode in North American aboriginal culture. Through these means harmony could be maintained and divisions avoided.

These philosophical principles were reinforced by the harsh exigencies of everyday life. 'Among those Dene who followed the large herds of caribou' co-ordinated collective action was essential to 'ensure the survival of the entire group.'[7] Political decisions had to reflect the interests of the group as a whole. Another pragmatic consideration encouraging decision-making by consensus has been pointed out by Grand Chief Michael Mitchell of the Mohawk Council of Akwesasne: 'No agreement is lasting until it is unanimous.'[8] Although the process of arriving at a unanimous decision may be arduous, the result is more stable than one obtained through a process where factions are created or issues are left unresolved. In communities that were vulnerable to attack from their neighbours, cohesion and a shared sense of purpose were essential.

Decision-making by consensus is a difficult and time-consuming process. One of the clearest descriptions of that process and the rationale behind it is provided by Oren Lyons, subchief of the Iroquois:

> The first lesson to be learned when dealing with Indian government is one of patience and one of thoroughness, because there are no shortcuts. As soon as you begin to short-cut, you begin to detract from the complete thought and the process for its achievement. This process works through discussion until consensus is reached, not by voting. The problem we have with voting is that you may have more than half the people not agreeing with the decisions of government. Those who don't agree with the decisions are just going to lie back and wait their chance to get even. Under these circumstances, actions are often taken from a desire to get even rather than on the merits of the action itself. That is why it is important to have a decision-making process whereby you avoid disagreement, and the process Indians advocate is consensus. Consensus involves long discussions, and, if agreement cannot be reached, the issue must be set aside until agreement is possible.[9]

Whereas voting fosters an adversarial style of politics, consensus decision-making encourages co-operation. Deliberators become stake-holders in the result of their deliberations, and thus will be more inclined to promote and abide by the decision than to distance themselves from it or even defy it, as they would if a decision had been forced to a premature conclusion by a vote and they did not support the majority view. Consensus ensures that deliberators are convinced of the merits of a proposal, and it instils in the broader community a sense of confidence that the leaders have thoroughly and thoughtfully considered the issue with the best interests of the community in mind. Moreover, consensus does not promote factionalism or retaliation on future issues. The primary grounds for evaluating and accepting a proposal are the merits of the proposal itself, rather than the character, status, or identity and affiliations of the initiator.

Under the consensus process, an issue would be raised at a meeting of the council, and often a possible solution would be proposed. Speakers would then take turns addressing the issue. While a speaker was talking, the audience would listen attentively. Speakers had unlimited time to make their case and were usually given a few moments afterwards to reflect upon their remarks and make any additions before the next person spoke. Benjamin Franklin reflected on the merits of this system, in comparison with the British one, upon attending the councils of the Six Nations: 'To interrupt another, even in common Conversation, is reckon'd highly indecent. How different this is to the conduct of a polite British House of Commons, where scarce a day passes without some Confusion. . . .'[10] He concluded that in the Six Nations system, the 'Persuasion of Men distinguished by Reputation of Wisdom is the only means by which others are govern'd or rather led'.[11] Acceptance of a decision rested upon open debate and clear justification of its necessity. Often incorporating amendments suggested by various speakers, the end result would represent the opinion not of any one individual, but of the broader community. Decision-making by consensus, then, emphasizes agreement, reason, and wisdom, reflecting in the principles of equality, respect for the individual, and harmony embedded in aboriginal philosophy.

Consensus decision-making operates best in small communities where shared values, beliefs, and philosophies will facilitate agreement.[12] Since every individual may participate in the decisions being taken, all share an equal responsibility for them. An individual who refuses to comply may be reminded of the decisions, criticized, shunned, or, in the extreme case of disobedience, banned from the community. In such situations social norms may exert sufficient pressure for responsible community action while still allowing individuals to govern their own conduct.

Decision-making by consensus and the principles it embodies were not universal, but they were sufficiently widespread to be considered an important dimension of aboriginal culture. Thus it is not surprising that during the current renaissance of aboriginal cultures in North America, the principle of consensus decision-making is being revived and invoked at the supra-community level of governance as a means of linking the present with the past and uniting diverse communities in a common struggle to survive. However, this principle is difficult to uphold in the context of contemporary society, as the following discussions of the Legislative Assembly of the Northwest Territories and the Assembly of First Nations reveal.

A UNIQUE ASSEMBLY

The Legislative Assembly of the Northwest Territories is unique in Canada in that it embodies the conflict between traditional aboriginal and Canadian political practices. Although it is modelled on the Westminster style of government, its procedures and principles have been adapted to accommodate aboriginal culture. It provides a good example of the tensions and difficulties as well as the opportunities that arise in the effort to combine consensus and adversarial styles of government.

As presently constituted, the Legislative Assembly of the NWT is relatively young.[13] Originally established in 1875 under the Northwest Territories Act, the Northwest Territories Council was a branch of the federal government designed to allow it to govern the region directly. After 1905, when Alberta and Saskatchewan were created out of the Territories, the official head of the territorial government was a Commissioner appointed by the federal government. By 1951, the Northwest Territories Council had increased to eight members, five appointed by the federal government and three elected by non-aboriginal residents of the Mackenzie Valley. In 1954 the Council expanded to include an additional member elected by residents in the western Territories, and in 1960 the franchise was extended to aboriginal peoples.

Council sessions consisted of two weeks in Ottawa during the winter and one week during the summer at a location in the Territories.

Between 1955 and the present, the Council evolved into a more representative, responsible, and autonomous legislature. Various acts between 1955 and 1967 significantly increased the administrative powers of the territorial government, and devolution of powers from the federal government continues to the present. In 1967 the seat of government was moved from Ottawa to Yellowknife, and in 1970 the balance of power shifted when Council was increased to ten members, six of them elected. By 1975, with the advent of the first fully elected Council, the shift was complete. The Council named two members to the executive and could elect its own Speaker. Although the Commissioner remained head of government and was still appointed by the federal government, the role of the ministers of the Council increased while that of the Commissioner declined. The growing independence of the Council was reflected in 1976 when it was renamed the Legislative Assembly. In 1979, the first aboriginal majority was elected to the Assembly. The expanded responsibilities and autonomy of the Government of the Northwest Territories (GNWT) were evident in 1984, when the Legislative Assembly was expanded to include 24 members representing all regions of the Territories, and the Executive Council comprised eight members. Shortly after, in 1986, the Commissioner withdrew entirely from the daily administration of government and became more the equivalent of a provincial lieutenant governor. The Assembly now meets regularly and is responsible for the governing of the Territories.

In 1993 the Legislative Assembly comprised 24 members representing a population of approximately 55,000.[14] Members are elected through a single-member plurality electoral system. The majority in the Assembly is aboriginal, with nine Inuit, six non-native, five Dene, and four Métis members. The Executive Council (Cabinet) comprises three Inuit, two Dene, two non-native, and one Métis. The Government Leader is Nellie Cournoyea, an Inuvialuit. The Assembly's aboriginal majority distinguishes it from the other legislatures in Canada and is evident in various symbolic adaptations to aboriginal customs.[15]

The operation of the Legislative Assembly closely resembles that of the provincial legislatures. Following the Westminster model of government,[16] the government leader is the equivalent of a premier; the Executive Council functions like a Cabinet, its members are ministers of the Crown, each of whom is responsible for one or more government departments; the Council is responsible to the Assembly; and it may be dismissed upon a vote of non-confidence. Nevertheless, in some key areas the Assembly's practices depart from those of the provincial legislatures, reflecting the influence of aboriginal traditions, most notably the principle of concensus decision-making.

This is not to say that the territorial legislature is a pure example of consensus government. Dacks, for example, claims that to describe the Assembly as consensual 'is to overstate the case' since the basis for consensus government—namely, shared beliefs and identity—is necessarily lacking. Given that the primary difference usually ascribed to the Assembly is 'the absence of formal party organization and party discipline', he concludes that it is more accurately described as 'non-partisan'.[17] O'Keefe points out that 'there are obvious complexities in modern society that make traditional consensus decision-making virtually impossible for the day-to-day administration of government policies, programs, and services.'[18] And although White does not see this debate as central to an understanding of the territorial government, he does observe that non-native members are more likely than aboriginal members to view the links to consensual government as significant. Aboriginal members 'find little in common' between the operations of the House and 'true consensual decision-making'; instead, 'They view the legislature as too majoritarian and believe that power is far too centralized in cabinet.'[19] It would be misleading, therefore, to treat the operations of the Legislative Assembly as a model of consensus politics. Nevertheless, examination of the influence of the consensus tradition on the workings of the Westminster model reveals that the two traditions have been adapted to accommodate one another.

For example, the process of debate in the Legislative Assembly bears an uncanny resemblance to Benjamin Franklin's account of the Council of the Six Nations. As White observes:

> Although intemperate language and passionate debates do occur, compared to the raucous, rough-and-tumble standards of behaviour of other Canadian legislatures, proceedings in the NWT Assembly are strikingly civil. MLAs listen politely and attentively to one another; heckling occurs infrequently and is decidedly mild; speeches, questions and answers are typically prefaced and concluded with 'thank yous'; when points of order are raised, even on contentious issues, the MLAs sit quietly as the Speaker ponders a decision and accept rulings with good grace.[20]

Although the rules of the House stipulate time limits for speeches, 'these rules can be waived with the unanimous consent of the Assembly and, in practice, that consent is almost always given.'[21] Respect for the individual and for oratory tempers debate and guides members' conduct in the House.

Consensus principles also affect the operations of the House at more fundamental levels. Reflecting on the Assembly's differences from southern legislatures, W.H. Remnant commented: 'In the south, the fate of an issue rests on which party raised it; in the north, the fate of an issue rests on its merits. You cannot accurately forecast the outcome of most votes.'[22] For a council initiative to pass in the House, the other members must be convinced of its merits, and ministers tend to be very solicitous of their concerns.[23] While Dacks is correct to attribute this approach to the absence of party discipline,[24] it also reflects the traditional practice of leadership through persuasion, based on respect for the views of all members.

The influence of the consensus tradition is evident in other aspects of the Assembly's operations as well. O'Keefe notes that 'there is an underlying assumption that the consensus tradition puts everyone on the same side; there is an expectation of openness and equal participation.[25] Instead of dividing members into government and opposition and operating in hierarchical fashion, the territorial legislature functions as a single caucus in which all 24 members work as equals to discuss and resolve common problems. Conscious efforts are made 'to emulate the traditional consensual decision-making model by avoiding votes except for elections and on clearly defined either/or questions on which agreement cannot be reached' and 'to accommodate all members' views'.[26] Similarly, the Executive Council differs from southern cabinets in that membership is more fluid, solidarity is weaker, and ministers will step down more readily if they side with ordinary members on an issue.[27] In addition, ministers generally ensure that information is supplied to members and that bills are tabled early enough to allow members to consult their constituents and give direction to the Council.[28] In effect, then, the Council follows the bottom-up or delegated leadership model of the consensus tradition, rather than top-down, representative leadership model of the parliamentary tradition. In return, members rarely exercise the privilege of introducing private members' bills, and although organized into a loose coalition to hold the government to account, they emphasize harmony over strenuous opposition.[29]

Perhaps one of most remarkable respects in which the Westminster model has been tempered by aboriginal traditions is in the selection and dismissal of the Speaker, Government Leader, and Cabinet.[30] Under Assembly rules, the Speaker is selected prior to the Leader and Council by members of the House, with the longest-serving member presiding. This practice signifies the independence of the Legislature and the impartiality of the Speaker. The Government Leader is then elected by a majority vote of the members of the House, with the Speaker-elect presiding. Candidates are nominated by other members and then are required to give a twenty-minute speech followed by questions. The vote is by secret ballot. In practice, however, the result will be known to members of the Assembly before the ballots are cast, since members confer among themselves when choosing the House Leader in an effort to determine not which person is most popular, but which is the best suited for the position. Council is elected by a similar procedure, following informal discussions focusing on which members are the most capable.[31] Thus the merit principle characteristic of the consensus style of political leadership is clearly evident in the selection of leaders. On the other hand, if a minister is perceived to have failed to perform the job properly, or to be disrespectful of other members, then members may draft dismissal notices and require the minister, Leader, or entire Council to step down.[32] The selection and dismissal of leaders ensures that they remain individually responsible for their conduct to the Assembly and to the public. They cannot impose their own will, but must be responsive to the general will.

The Legislative Assembly of the Northwest Territories is not a fully functional example of consensus government. However, its points of departure from other legislatures clearly indicate that the tradition of consensus government has tempered the workings of the Westminster model. The principles of equality, respect for the individual, and maintenance of harmony all operate to ensure a more open and participatory style of leadership and government.

How long this style of leadership can continue to function is open to question. Many members of the aboriginal community question the legitimacy of the Assembly as presently constituted, and its compatibility with the consensus tradition.[33] Others feel alienated from its process of decision-making and would prefer government to be closer to the community, in accordance with traditional practices.[34]

Future developments in the Northwest Territories could also threaten the principles and practices of consensus government in the Assembly. For example, the emergence of an élite class, or the possible encouragement, by multinational corporations, of class differences and interests could further erode the social basis for consensus politics.[35] Similarly, the natural maturation of the political system could give rise to the development of parties, while contentious issues such as land claims could create sharp divisions within the population. Either case would foster a move towards a more adversarial form of government in the Assembly.[36] Indeed, such a move has been encouraged by a government report on the operations of the GNWT that recommends changes in the interests of more efficient government. These recommendations include strengthening Cabinet and the central machinery of government; simplifying and streamlining the government agenda to focus on important items of business and to reduce duplication and debate; and providing more autonomy and Cabinet support to the bureaucracy.[37] Finally, a shift in population towards a non-aboriginal majority could influence the operation of the Assembly towards southern principles.

Thus the influence of consensus politics at the level of the territorial government may be waning. Nevertheless, at present the Legislative Assembly offers a model of how aboriginal traditions of government may be used to moderate Canadian practices in the direction of a more open, inclusive, and participatory form of leadership.

USING CONSENSUS TO BIND

The practice of consensus politics is not limited to the north. In the south, the Assembly of First Nations (AFN) is a nationally representative institution that reflects aboriginal traditions and acts as a liaison between the First Nations and the federal and provincial governments. As in the case of the GNWT, the traditions of consensus and adversarial government do not always blend easily, but the AFN has thus far managed to balance the pressures from the two divergent traditions with some degree of success.

Although attempts to organize aboriginal peoples on a national level to improve their conditions began early in the century, they did not begin to bear substantial results until the 1940s and 1950s.[38] The grandparent organization of the present AFN, the National Indian Council (NIC), was formed in 1954 and became the official representative of both status and non-status Indians in 1960-61.[39] However, in 1968, largely as a result of difficulties arising from the attempt to unite the two divergent populations in one organization, the NIC voted to disband. The National Indian Brotherhood (NIB) was formed to represent status Indians, while the Canadian Metis Society, which later became the Native Council of Canada, was created to represent non-status Indians.[40]

The NIB operated throughout the 1970s, lobbying and working with the federal government for changes in the conditions of the First Nations, and galvanizing aboriginal peoples into political action. But by the end of the decade it was evident that the NIB required restructuring if it was to survive as a national organization and represent aboriginal interests effectively in the constitutional negotiations and the battle for self-government.[41] In 1980 an Interim Council of Chiefs, attended by most of the 573 band chiefs in Canada, was established to develop a new structure for the NIB. In 1982 this was accomplished, and 'the Chiefs formed a Commission on Structure with a mandate to complete the transition from an organization with a statuting foundation to an organization with the First Nations as its foundation'.[42] After meetings in 1983 and 1984, the AFN assumed its present structure, adopting its Charter at Vancouver on 31 July 1985. Amendments were made to the Charter in 1990.[43]

The AFN represents status Indians in Canada, namely those Indians registered under the Indian Act. The Department of Indian Affairs and Northern Development estimates that there are '521,000 Status Indians, of which 316,000 reside on-reserve and 205,000 off-reserve'.[44] By 2001, projections of population growth estimate the status population at 623,000.[45] Currently, approximately 633 bands are registered with the Department of Indian and Northern Affairs. Under the AFN Charter, all First Nations possess the right to be members (Art. 4).

The five-part structure of the AFN ensures that it is directly accountable to the Chiefs. The First Nations-in-Assembly consists of all Chiefs of First Nations who have exercised their right to be members. Accountable, through the Chiefs, to the communities, it 'is a forum for First Nations to conduct nation-to-nation discussions, consultations and deliberations and to collaborate on any matter within the jurisdiction of First Nations' (Art. 7. 1). This Assembly serves as the empowering body of the AFN and provides guidance and direction to the AFN and Executive Committee. It meets in regular annual sessions in June and July and in special sessions when required (Art. 6-10). Next in the structure of the AFN is the Confederacy of First Nations, which is directly accountable to the First Nations-in-Assembly. It represents aboriginal peoples on the basis of regions corresponding to the territories and provinces, and allots an additional representative for every 10,000 First Nations citizens in a region. The Confederacy of First Nations meets quarterly and functions as the governing authority between assemblies, ensuring that the wishes of the First Nations-in-Assembly are acted upon and that the Secretariat and Executive Committee do not exceed the limits of their authority (Art. 11-16).

The three remaining bodies provide checks on and supports for each other in executing the directions of the Assembly and Confederacy. The Executive Committee comprises the National Chief, Regional Chiefs drawn from the territories and provinces, and the Chair of the Council of Elders, who sits in an advisory capacity. The Executive Committee is accountable to and guided by the Assembly and Confederacy. In addition to its administrative functions, the executive is expected to represent the interests of the AFN in accordance with its delegated and mandated authority, and to advise the Confederacy and Assembly of 'any matters which, in their opinion, may jeopardize the security, survival, rights, aspirations and jurisdiction of First Nations' (Art. 18. 5; cf. Art. 17-19). Although the National Chief is the primary spokesperson for the AFN, he is only one member in the collective leadership constituted by the Executive. Thus the National Chief has a political role but no inherent political authority (Art. 20-22). The AFN Secretariat (also called the National Indian Brotherhood) comprises the Executive Committee and the administrative, technical, and support staff required to implement decisions of the Assembly and Confederacy (Art. 25-26). Finally, the Council of Elders consists of an unspecified number of elders who are representative of the First Nations. It is a political and advisory body intended to provide independent advice and direction to the AFN organs on any matters, including issues that endanger First Nations' relations (Art. 23-4).

The structure and Charter of the AFN are designed to promote leadership by consensus. First, the AFN is a highly structured organization with clearly defined lines of accountability. Authority flows from the communities through the Assembly to the Confederacy to the Executive and Secretariat. Checks and balances are provided through the interaction of these four bodies and the advisory role of the Elders. Although the structure provides for individual input and participation in decision-making, particularly at the level of the Assembly, the body functions as a collectivity, and the ability of any one individual to take independent action is constrained. In the case of the Executive and National Chief, independent action is disallowed under the provisions of the Charter (Art. 18. 1 and 20.1). The accepted style of political leadership is collective.

Second, the language of the Charter reflects this commitment to collective action. The preamble speaks of the sovereign independence of the First Nations, the equality and dignity of each individual, and the collective commitment to tolerance and respect for diversity, among other things, as giving rise to the resolution to combine their efforts 'to accomplish common aims'. Thus the ideals of the First Nations include recognition of the common struggle 'based upon the Indian values of trust, confidence and toleration', respect for the sovereignty of each Nation, acknowledgement of the capacity for collective action, and commitment to equality of treatment of the First Nations (Art. 1). The principles that follow from these ideals emphasize that the 'authority, responsibilities and jurisdiction of the Assembly of First Nations shall be derivative in nature and scope' (Art. 2. 2). The powers of the AFN are clearly circumscribed by the First Nations. Thus any authority of the AFN is delegated: it does not direct the First Nations, they direct it. This ensures that the AFN, unlike its predecessor the NIB, must have the consent of the member Nations before it acts.

The provisions delineating the operation of the Assembly and its constituent organs make the preference for consensual leadership clear. For example, Article 2.6 stipulates that

> Any decision or direction on a subject matter of a fundamental nature that may affect the jurisdiction, rights and survival of First Nations, may be undertaken as a national or international matter provided the First Nations-in-Assembly have reached a consensus to grant delegated power, mandate or responsibility to the Assembly of First Nations.

Similarly, Article 8. 1 encourages decision-making by consensus or general agreement in the First Nations-in-Assembly. The basis for these provisions was provided by the

Working Committee on the AFN Structure when it maintained that 'Consensus is a prerequisite for a national front or approach on matters, concerns, problems, issues goals or aspirations before any actions or initiatives can be undertaken at the national level as a national matter.'[46] Only consensus would be consistent with the underlying principles of coexistence, diversity, and solidarity.

Recognizing the need to temper this principle in the interests of organizational efficiency, both sections of the Charter provide for a vote to occur 'when all efforts at achieving consensus have been exhausted'. However, a 60 per cent majority is required for a measure to pass. Substantial consent is an acceptable last resort. Similarly, the National Chief is elected by a 60 per cent majority of registered representatives of First Nations at an Assembly convened for that purpose and may be removed by a 60 per cent majority at a special meeting as well. However, in accordance with tradition, it would be the norm for the elders first, and then the other Chiefs in Assembly, to remind an errant Chief of the duties, responsibilities and limits of the office before forcing such a vote. In this way, traditional practices have been adapted to modern constraints and realities.

In practice, these procedures work effectively. At the June 1991 annual meeting of the Assembly of First Nations, held in Winnipeg, 29 resolutions were passed from the floor of the First Nations-in-Assembly over a four-day period which encompassed the election of Ovide Mercredi as National Chief. The session was completely open to members of First Nations and registered observers. Although a restricted area was reserved for delegates to the Assembly, all business was conducted in public. Motions were submitted the day prior to being tabled. When a motion arose, the initiator would have ten minutes to speak and the Chiefs would have five minutes. What was striking was the willingness of the Chair and the initiators to accept amendments to the motions. Whereas in an adversarial system the initiator tends to defend the motion, under this system motions became rolling drafts. Where a difference arose between two speakers, a third speaker would suggest a compromise. In the case of clear differences, votes were held. An atmosphere of constructive good will characterized the passage of most motions. Very likely the efficiency of the meeting could be attributed in large part to the extensive background materials on key motions that were circulated prior to the meeting.[47]

Finally, the amending formula for the Charter reflects the commitment of the First Nations to collective political leadership. Article 27 provides that the Charter 'may be amended by consensus or general agreement of the Chiefs or their duly accredited representatives of the First Nations-in-Assembly.' The Charter was adopted by the same procedure. A logical result of the turbulent past of the national organization, this formula ensures that the AFN remains representative of all First Nations equally — unlike the NIB, which was accused of excluding certain First Nations while privileging others.[48] As Grand Chief Michael Mitchell observed, lasting agreements are unanimous agreements.

Both the AFN's commitment to political leadership through consensus and the difficulties it entails were evident in the months leading up to the 1992 constitutional referendum. In preparation for the negotiations that produced the Charlottetown Accord, the AFN established a First Nations Parallel Constitutional Process. Then, in response to the initiatives by the federal and provincial governments to consult their citizens, the AFN undertook inclusive consultations,[49] on the basis of which the Chiefs delegated responsibility to the Executive to negotiate an agreement. However, difficulties arose after the Accord had been signed.[50] First, questions arose as to whether Ovide Mercredi and his team of negotiators had exceeded their delegated authority in agreeing to certain clauses without first consulting the Chiefs. Second, and more important, the AFN failed to arrive at a consensus with respect to its position on the Accord. At a special meeting in Vancouver a few weeks before the referendum, the Chiefs did not vote on the Accord. Apparently a number of Chiefs believed that more time was required to assess its merits, and that a premature vote would have proven too divisive and harmful to the AFN. Shortly after, the AFN Executive contacted the YES Committee and received funding to campaign on the Accord. Although the AFN did not officially join the YES Committee, Mercredi did speak on behalf of the Accord.[51] However, many of the Chiefs and aboriginal opinion leaders, including Elijah Harper, the Assembly of Manitoba Chiefs, and most of the Alberta Treaty Chiefs, chose to boycott the referendum.[52] Although the Treaty Chiefs, among others, criticized the Accord and the actions of the AFN leadership, the majority or consensus view seemed to be that more time was required to reflect on the Accord. This decision was consistent with the traditional practice of delaying contentious decisions and allowing for lengthy deliberation on important matters. However, the AFN was brought to the brink of a crisis.

The Charlottetown experience revealed the difficulties that an organization such as the AFN faces in attempting to deal with complicated issues within a relatively limited time. The deadline of the referendum limited the Chiefs' ability to consult with their communities and prepare their positions on regional and provincial levels. Moreover, as national spokesperson, Ovide Mercredi was constrained by the delegated nature of his authority, which put him at a disadvantage in negotiations with leaders of the federal, provincial, and territorial governments. Finally, where there are sharp differences in opinion or interests between groups, as in the case of Treaty and non-Treaty First Nations, consensus decision-making becomes even more difficult, especially when time is limited.

In summary, the AFN employs a qualified form of consensus decision-making with mixed results. Given the diversity and range of interests included in the AFN, it is not surprising that consensus is not always possible. However, it is through the rules of consensus and accountability that the AFN has gained the co-operation of the majority of First Nations and the opportunity to define a coherent direction for aboriginal peoples at the national level, providing aboriginal peoples with a stronger and more united voice in negotiations with the federal and provincial governments. Its experience suggests that political leadership based on principles of consensus decision-making faces significant but not insurmountable challenges in a system where the adversarial model is dominant.

CONCLUSION

The circumstances that gave rise to consensus decision-making in traditional societies no longer exist; hence this style of leadership can function only in a modified form today. However, the operations of the Legislative Assembly of the Northwest Territories and the Assembly of First Nations reveal that the consensus tradition continues to influence aboriginal governance at the supra-community level. In the case of the Northwest Territories, elements of consensus decision-making temper the workings of the Westminster model of parliamentary government. The result is a legislative assembly that emphasizes deliberation over opposition and co-operation over confrontation. Similarly, the tradition of consensus government ensures that the AFN operates according to strict lines of authority and responsibility, and that, like the GNWT, it attempts to balance equality and respect for the individual with the community interest. But the results are not always ideal or immediate. Aboriginal leaders will face significant challenges in the future if the principles of consensus government are not to be further eroded.

NOTES

[1] Menno Boldt, 'Indian Leaders in Canada: Attitudes Toward Equality, Identity and Political Status', unpublished Ph.D. thesis (Yale University, 1973), 59.

[2] Menno Boldt and J. Anthony Long, 'Tribal Traditions and European-Western Political Ideologies: The Dilemma of Canada's Native Indians', *Canadian Journal of Political Science* 17, 3 (Sept. 1984): 542. Boldt and Long refer to such classic studies of Indian cultures as J.B. Mackenzie, *The Six Nations Indians in Canada* (Toronto: Hunter Rose, 1896); M.W. Smith, *Indians of the Urban Northwest* (New York: Columbia University Press, 1949); A.M. Josephy, Jr, *The Indian Heritage of America* (New York: Bantam Books, 1968); and Philip Drucker, *Indians of the Northwest Coast* (Garden City, NJ: Natural History Press, 1963). To this list I would add the important, albeit controversial, surveys of Indian and Inuit cultures by Diamond Jenness, *Indians of Canada* (Toronto: University of Toronto Press, 1977); Harold Driver, *Indians of North America*, 2nd ed. (Chicago: University of Chicago Press, 1969); and Frederick Hodge, *Handbook of Indians of Canada* (Ottawa: King's Printer, 1913; reprinted Toronto: Coles Publishing, 1971).

[3] As quoted in Boldt, 'Indian Leaders', 62.

[4] As quoted in Rupert Ross, *Dancing with a Ghost: Exploring Indian Reality* (Markham, Ont: Octopus Publishing, 1992), 13.

[5] For an expression of this principle in Dene culture, see George Barnaby, George Kurszewski, and Gerry Cheezie, 'The Political System and the Dene', in Mel Watkins, *Dene Nation: The Colony Within* (Toronto: University of Toronto Press, 1977), 120.

[6] Tom Porter, 'Traditions of the Constitution of the Six Nations', in Leroy Little Bear, Menno Boldt, J. Anthony Long, eds, *Pathways to Self-Determination: Canadian Indians and the Canadian State* (Toronto: University of Toronto Press, 1984), 20.

[7] Lesley Malloch, *Dene Government Past and Future* (Yellowknife: Western Constitutional Forum, 1984), 14.

[8] Michael Mitchell, 'An Unbroken Assertion of Sovereignty', in Boyce Richardson, ed., *Drumbeat: Anger and Renewal in Indian Country* (Toronto: Summerhill Press, 1989), 135.

[9] Oren Lyons, 'Spirituality, Equality, and Natural Law', in Little Bear, Boldt, and Long, *Pathways*, 5.

[10] As quoted in Bruce Johansen, *Forgotten Founders: How the American Indian Helped Shape Democracy* (Harvard and Boston: Harvard Common Press, 1982), 87.

[11] Ibid., 88.

[12] Gurstan Dacks, 'Politics on the Last Frontier: Consociationalism in the Northwest Territories', *Canadian Journal of Political Science* 19, 2 (June 1986): 348.

[13] This chronology is compiled from the Commission for Constitutional Development, *How Can We Live Together? Towards a Common Future for the Western Northwest Territories* (Yellowknife: CCD, October 1991), 24-6; W.H. Remnant, 'Speaking Notes on the Northwest Territories', (Winnipeg: February 1993); Mark O. Dickerson, *Whose North?* (Vancouver: UBC Press, 1992), 94-6; Kevin O'Keefe, 'Northwest Territories: Accommodating the Future', in Gary Levy and Graham White, eds, *Provincial and Territorial Legislatures in Canada* (Toronto: University of Toronto Press, 1989), 214-17.

[14] The population is divided as follows: non-natives 42.1%; Inuit 35.5%; and Dene Metis 22.4%. See Dickerson, *Whose North?*, 23.

[15] Many of the decorations in the Chamber are reminiscent of aboriginal traditions and lifestyles. For example, while the British House of Lords has a wool bench in the centre of the Chamber to symbolize the basis of its wealth, the Territorial Legislature has a polar bear hide on a table in the centre of its Chamber to represent its livelihood. Similarly, while the dress codes in the southern Chambers require men to wear a tie and jacket, the Territorial dress code includes such traditional dress as buckskin jackets, fur vests, and sealskin boots. These differences in dress were noted in an interview with Mr W.H. Remnant, Clerk of the Manitoba Legislative Assembly and former Clerk of the NWT Legislative Assembly (1966-82), Winnipeg, Manitoba, April 1993; and in Graham White, 'Westminster in the Arctic: The Adaptation of British Parliamentarianism in the Northwest Territories', *Canadian Journal of Political Science* 24, 3 (Sept. 1991), 505.

[16] For a discussion of the Westminster model of government see Michael M. Atkinson, 'Parliamentary Government in Canada', in M.S. Whittington and G. Williams, eds, *Canadian Politics in the 1990s*, 3rd ed., (Scarborough, Ont.: Nelson, 1990), 336-58; C.E.S. Franks, *The Parliament of Canada* (Toronto: University of Toronto Press, 1987); Robert J. Jackson and Michael M. Atkinson, *The Canadian Legislative System: Politicians and Policy-Making*, 2nd rev. ed. (Toronto: Gage, 1980).

[17] Dacks, 'Politics', 350-1; cf. Dacks, 'Devolution and Political Development in the Canadian North', in Dacks, ed., *Devolution and Constitutional Development in the Canadian North* (Ottawa: Carleton University Press, 1990), 340-1.

[18] O'Keefe, 'Northwest Territories', 209.

[19] White, 'Westminster', 510.

[20] Ibid., 506; cf. Dacks, 'Politics', 353.

[21] Dacks, 'Politics', 351.

[22] Remnant, interview, Winnipeg, April 1993.

[23] White, 'Westminster', 510-1.

[24] Dacks, 'Politics', 351-3.

[25] O'Keefe, 'Northwest Territories', 209-10.

[26] White, 'Westminster', 511; cf. M.S. Whittington, 'Canada's North in the 1990's', in Whittington and Williams, eds, *Canadian Politics*, 32.

[27] Sandy Gillies, former team leader of Project to Review the Operations and Structure of Northern Government, interview, Winnipeg, January 1993.

[28] O'Keefe, 'Northwest Territories', 209-11; Dacks, 'Politics', 351-2.

[29] White notes that this may be attributable more to the size of the legislature and the opportunity for retaliation than to the tradition of consensus government. However, the same type of thinking underlies this behaviour as in traditional societies.

[30] This account of procedure is based on the notes on election procedures prepared for and provided to the Territorial Leadership Committee, 12 November 1991.

[31] Gillies, interview, Winnipeg, January 1993.

[32] Remnant, interview, Winnipeg, April 1993; Gillies, interview, Winnipeg, January 1993; Dacks, 'Politics', 351.

[33] White, 'Westminster', 521-2.

[34] Malloch, *Dene Government*, 31.

[35] Doug Daniels, 'Dreams and Realities of Dene Government', *Canadian Journal of Native Studies* 7, 1 (1987): 105-6, 108-9.

[36] Dacks, 'Politics', 354; White, 'Westminster', 518-19.

[37] Northwest Territories, Project to Review the Operations and Structure of Northern Government, *Strength at Two Levels* (Yellowknife: November 1991), 100, 57-8, 100, 110, 111, 172. However, the report recommends enhancing aboriginal culture by strengthening government at the community level.

[38] See, for example, Harold Cardinal, 'Hat in Hand: The Long Fight to Organise', in J.R. Miller, ed., *Sweet Promises* (Toronto: University of Toronto Press, 1991), 393-401; J. Rick Ponting and Roger Gibbins, *Out of Irrelevance* (Toronto: Butterworths, 1980), 196-7.

[39] James Frideres, *Native People in Canada*, 2nd ed. (Scarborough, Ont.: Prentice-Hall, 1983), 239.

[40] Ponting and Gibbins, *Out of Irrelevance*, 197-8; Sally Weaver, 'Towards a Comparison of National Political Organisations', lecture series for the Institute of Social Sciences, University of Tromso (Tromso, Norway, 19-26 October 1983), 25.

[41] For details see Weaver, 'Towards a Comparison', 25-36; Ponting and Gibbins, *Out of Irrelevance*, 198-216; Frideres, *Native People*, 241-2.

[42] AFN, Working Committee on Assembly of First Nations Structure, *Final Report to Assembly of First Nations* (Ottawa, 18-21 February 1985), 3; cf. Weaver, 'Towards a Comparison', 31.

[43] Charter of the Assembly of First Nations, 31 July, 1985, as amended December 1990.

[44] Department of Indian and Northern Affairs, *Growth in Federal Expenditures on Aboriginal Peoples* (Ottawa: DIAND, February 1993), 29, 31.

[45] Ibid.

[46] AFN, Working Committee on AFN Structure, *Final Report*, 13.

[47] See AFN, Draft Agenda, 12th Annual Assembly of First Nations, Winnipeg Convention Centre, 8-12 June 1991; AFN, Rules of Assembly, as amended to prohibit cellular phones in the Assembly, June 1991; 'AFN General Assembly and Elections', *AFN Bulletin* 8; 2 (April/June 1991): 7. For example, at this meeting Draft Resolution No. D-ll, which created the First Nations Circle on the Constitution, was amended through this discussion process and passed by consensus on 10 June. These comments are based on my observations of the meeting.

[48] AFN, Working Committee on AFN Structure, *Final Report*, 6-7, 11, 14-5.

[49] See for example, AFN, First Nations Circle on the Constitution, *First Nations and the Constitution: Discussion Paper* 21 Nov. 1991, 3; AFN, *First Nations Parallel Constitutional Process*, August 1991.

[50] For an account of some of the difficulties encountered by the AFN, see Susan Delacourt, 'Loss of Faith', *Globe and Mail*, 24 Oct. 1992: Dl. See also her book, *United We Fall: The Crisis of Democracy in Canada* (Toronto: Viking, 1993). For a brief account of the concerns of the

Treaty Chiefs, see Sharon Venne, 'Treaty Indigenous Peoples and the Charlottetown Accord: The Message in the Breeze', *Constitutional Forum* 4, 2 (Winter 1993): 43-6.

[51] Les Campbell, NDP representative of the YES committee, interviews, February and April 1993.

[52] In October, the Assembly of Manitoba Chiefs passed a two-part resolution urging that aboriginal peoples boycott the referendum, or, if they chose to exercise their franchise, then to vote against the Accord. A spokesperson for the Assembly of Manitoba Chiefs stressed that the Chiefs believed that the referendum was premature. They required more time to study the Agreement and develop a position that would reflect the opinions of their citizens. It was a decision not to participate rather than a rejection of the Agreement (AMC, interview, April 1993).

LEAVING THERE

—■—

Exiting Political Office

CHAPTER THIRTEEN

SHOULD I STAY
OR SHOULD I GO? *

Career Decisions of Members
of Parliament

—▬—

David C. Docherty

In the United States, the overwhelming re-election rate of politicians, often topping 90 per cent federally, has resulted in a move towards limiting the terms of state and federal representatives. In the 1992 US election, term-limit measures — putting a ceiling on the number of years a politician can hold one particular office — passed in all fourteen states that included such initiatives on the ballot.[1]

The 1993 Canadian general election caused two hundred and five members of Parliament, over 69 per cent of the total House of Commons, to leave elected life. Although many Canadians hold politicians in such low esteem[2] that they might welcome term limits, some Canadian political scientists have argued in favour of keeping members in the House longer.[3] Just as their counterparts to the south argue that term limits will not by themselves increase turnover rates,[4] Canadian academics are not convinced that the House of Commons would benefit if it had fewer career politicians. If anything, Canada may have too much turnover: perhaps more careerists would improve the House of Commons.

This chapter will not argue the merits of professionalism versus amateurism. Instead, after briefly examining and accepting the arguments that amateurism in the Canadian House of Commons is present and potentially problematic, and that turnover levels are high, this chapter will focus on the final stages of parliamentarians' careers. As every Parliament draws to a close and a general election becomes increasingly likely, all members must decide whether to continue or leave their political careers. Those who choose the latter are considered voluntary vacators, or retirees. The election splits the remaining group, those who have chosen to stay, into winning and defeated incumbents. High rates of turnover in Canada are caused by this combination of voluntary vacators and defeated incumbents.

This chapter will explore three main questions. Does the career of a member while in the House of Commons influence the manner in which he or she leaves it? Which members are likely to retire, and which to leave only at the urging of the voters? Finally, which MPs are more susceptible to electoral defeat, and which are relatively shielded from the wrath of an often unappreciative electorate?

To date, little attention has been paid in Canada to the relationship between the type of career enjoyed in the House and the manner in which an MP leaves it. Concentrating on the members of the 33rd Parliament, 1984-88,[5] this chapter will show that there are more than two stages—getting there and staying there—to most politicians' careers, and that MPs confront career choices at each of these stages. A relationship does exist between an MP's parliamentary career and the way in which she or he leaves the House of Commons. A parliamentary veteran who holds or has held a leadership position is electorally all but invulnerable. Simply put, veteran MPs in positions of leadership are electorally safe, while newcomers on the back bench enjoy little job security.[6]

THE PROBLEM OF AMATEURISM AND TURNOVER

High levels of turnover in a legislative assembly can be problematic for a number of reasons. First, as Franks argues, 'competent, experienced personnel are the backbone of any organization.'[7] If turnover is so high that an organization has few experienced members, long-term plans will too often be interrupted before completion. Maintaining the continuity of an organization under such conditions is also difficult, since many of the members leave just as they become familiar with the formal rules and informal norms of their work environment. This problem is exacerbated if turnover depletes one segment of a legislature while leaving others relatively unscathed. For example, observers of the Canadian House have long noted a clear division between parliamentary leaders and private members. Party leaders, Cabinet ministers and key frontbench opposition members (such as House leaders and Whips) tend to be parliamentary veterans, while their peers on the back benches are less experienced. Norman Ward, John Porter, and C.E.S. Franks have all identified this gap in legislative experience between parliamentary leaders and the back benches.[8] Part of their concern is that veterans dominate leadership positions and rookies are held to minor positions, and as a result the Cabinet dominates both the government and the House of Commons.

This gap between the executive and other members of Parliament is particularly problematic in view of the House of Commons' duty to serve as a watchdog over the government and opposition parties' responsibility to offer viable governing alternatives.[9] The larger the gap in experience between leaders and non-leaders, the less capable the House of Commons is of performing these essential functions.

But turnover is only part of the problem; the other part is amateurism. When used in connection with politics, the term 'amateur' can have many different meanings.[10] Observers of the Canadian House of Commons, however, have been content to call amateurs people who fall into one of two categories: people who come to Parliament with little previous elected experience, and/or those whose stay in the House is marked by its brevity (usually no more than one term). By contrast, parliamentary veterans who may or may not have spent some time in the electoral minor leagues are considered to be political careerists.

Individuals who enter the House after spending some time in provincial assemblies may not require the same lengthy learning period as their colleagues whose previous experience is either non-existent or limited to the municipal level. They will be familiar with legislative rules and norms, and sometimes come to Ottawa with established reputations as politicians. Generally, they often go directly onto the front bench or into Cabinet.

However, whereas in the United States movement from state legislatures to the nation's capital is common,[11] such a career ladder is unusual among Canadian politicians. V.S. Harder argues that the most astounding feature of previous elected experience among MPs is 'the overwhelming lack of any'.[12] Doreen Barrie and Roger Gibbins point out that from Confederation to 1984, only 14 per cent of all parliamentarians had served in a provincial legislative assembly.[13] Indeed, gaining experience at the provincial level before entering the federal arena is actually becoming less common. Before the First World War, it was not unusual for up to one quarter of all members in any Parliament to have served some time in a provincial assembly, but of the 282 individuals elected in 1984, only twenty, or 7 per cent, had served some apprenticeship in a sub-national assembly. Thus the effect of provincial training is limited, and it differs by region.[14] As a result, the lack of such a career ladder in Canada contributes only minimally to amateurism in the House of Commons.

In terms of the primary measure of amateurism, years of experience in the House of Commons, few argue that Parliament is a club too full of veterans. In his seminal 1950 study on the House of Commons, Norman Ward found that anywhere from 35 per cent to over half of each new Parliament was made up of newcomers to Ottawa, and that an additional 20 to 35 per cent had less than five years' experience. Little has changed in four decades.[15] The 1993 election produced a House in which 68 per cent of members were newcomers, and just 12 per cent have more than five years' experience.[16]

Immediately after the September 1984 election the average length of service for MPs was 4.3 years. In spite of the large turnover that the 1984 election brought, the House of Commons as a whole did contain a large contingent of members with at least one full term of federal legislative experience. In the 33rd Parliament there was no doubt that the lion's share of legislative experience among Conservatives rested in the den of

TABLE   13.1   LEGISLATIVE   EXPERIENCE   IN   THE   33rd
PARLIAMENT,   SEPTEMBER   1984

	Average years' experience	Total years' experience	Number
Conservative party	3.55	749	211
Conservative leaders[1]	9.5	410	43
Conservative back bench	2.0	339	168
Opposition members	6.5	463	71

[1] Cabinet members, party whips, and caucus chairs.

Cabinet. Table 13.1 outlines the average and total years' experience for the 33rd Parliament as of September 1984.

Although outnumbered by their backbench colleagues 168 to 43, the Conservative leaders had on average almost three times the experience of the caucus as a whole. The total in person-years of legislative experience among the Conservative leadership is actually higher than that among its very large backbench counterpart. When choosing his first Cabinet, Prime Minister Mulroney clearly favoured experience over new blood.

Table 13.1 also demonstrates that the level of experience of opposition members in September 1984 was only slightly less than that of the Conservatives occupying positions of leadership. Despite the Liberal party's electoral decimation, particularly in Québec, the Liberals were able to compete on an experience basis with the new Cabinet, as were the New Democrats. If experience is a factor in the ability of some members to dominate others, the Conservative leadership enjoyed an advantage over its caucus (particularly the back bench) but not the opposition. The gap between Cabinet and opposition was not large, and opposition parties had the experience at least to set forth viable policy alternatives and keep the government accountable.

In contrast to amateurism, the turnover issue concerns not who is in the legislature but rather who is leaving, and why. Social scientists have argued that the predominant cause of turnover can tell us something about the institutions of representative democracy. If, for example, young members who have just recently entered the legislature choose to leave it, then the assembly may be seen as having a difficult time holding onto its future leaders. If, on the other hand, the major cause of turnover is electoral defeat, the problem may reside in an electoral system that makes it difficult for individual legislators to construct a personal vote.

In the United States, an electoral system with no campaign-spending limits and high levels of interest-group financial support favours incumbents. The re-election rate for both representatives and senators is so high that for most lawmakers the only way to leave is through retirement. In fact, however, voluntary retirement is increasing among 'younger and more electorally secure' legislators, and this suggests an increasing dissatisfaction with life in the US Congress.[17] This lack of desire to pursue a long political career is seen as an indication that it is the congressional life-style, and unwillingness to suffer the public's low perception of lawmakers, rather than a tough electoral system that is to blame for short political careers.

In Canada observers of Parliament have pointed to both the lack of 'safe seats' and the unattractiveness of the job as the two main reasons for high levels of turnover. William Irvine argues that most elections are won and lost by parties, and that individual candidates can do little to offset national swings.[18] There is little personal vote for Canadian members of Parliament. C.E.S. Franks states that job dissatisfaction is the second major cause of turnover, close behind the lack of safe seats. He argues that many MPs, upon arriving in Ottawa, discover 'that they do not like the job', and that long hours, a lack of privacy, and substantial financial sacrifices all take their toll.[19]

In an examination of the seven elections between 1968 and 1988, Atkinson and Docherty demonstrate that over half (56 per cent) of all turnover is caused by MPs' losing their re-election bids.[20] The remaining 44 per cent of turnover is the result of voluntary retirement. The combination of electoral defeat and voluntary retirement means that at least one-third of each new Parliament will tend to be rookies. And some elections bring even more drastic results. After the 1984 election, for example, nearly half the new members were rookies—and almost two-thirds of the changes were the result of incumbency defeat. In 1988, 64 incumbents were defeated and 46 retired.

More interestingly, Atkinson and Docherty's study of 225 former members of Parliament found that individuals who were defeated in elections had served an average of 6.3 years; this compares with an average of 11.4 years of service for MPs who left by choice.[21] They also found that a larger proportion of Cabinet or former Cabinet members were to be found among the ranks of the voluntary vacators and the more experienced MPs. Few people who had experience in positions of leadership were among the defeated members of Parliament.

There can be little doubt that electoral defeat is the primary cause of turnover in Canadian politics. Voluntary retirement is an important, but secondary, cause of turnover. Nonetheless, with at least one-third of the House generally comprised of rookies, concern about turnover seems well founded.

Studies of turnover in Canada have to date studied three different groups of MPs: leaders and non-leaders, amateurs and careerists, and voluntary retirees and defeated members. While there has been some examination of the relationships within each of these groups, little has been done to explore the relationships between them. The rest of this chapter is an initial attempt to examine these latter relationships.

CAREERS IN PARLIAMENT
Getting to the Exit Stage

The analysis thus far suggests that a distinct line can be drawn between amateur and veteran parliamentarians. Members enter the House as amateurs, and at some point in their political careers cross an imaginary experience line and become parliamentary veterans or careerists. Yet a closer look at what John Hibbing describes, in the US case, as the 'contours of elected life'[22] shows that the House of Commons does not easily break into groups of rookies and seniors.

Most parliamentary observers and politicians agree that an apprenticeship period exists for all new MPs. Individuals rarely enter the House of Commons completely at ease with the formal rules and the informal norms of parliamentary life. Those few individuals who apparently need no apprenticeship period and are 'natural leaders from the time they enter' Parliament are the exception. For most members there is a learning period in which they learn to how to become 'effective in the House' and gain 'credibility from [their more experienced] peers'.[23]

Just how long this apprenticeship period lasts is not clear. Like John Porter,[24] both Lovink and Franks suggest that the learning period for a member of Parliament is four years, or one full term. As a result, they suggest, up to half the members at any time are in this learning period and, as Lovink states, 'unable to work at their potential capacity'.[25] More recently, however, Sharon Sutherland has argued that two years is sufficient time for members, or at least potential Cabinet ministers, to familiarize themselves with the nuances of parliamentary life.[26]

Members seem to concur with Sutherland's assessment of the apprenticeship period. Those members of 34th Parliament (1988-93) who responded to a survey regarding their attitudes toward Parliament self-assessed their apprenticeship period at an average of one and a half years.[27] This self-assessment differed by party. Members of the Liberal caucus believed their apprenticeship lasted just over one year; NDP members believed that the learning time was, on average, a year and a third; and members of the Conservative caucus, on average, believed that the apprenticeship period lasted a full two years. Among all parties, however, many members mentioned four years or 'one term' as their apprenticeship stage. Certainly the length of time varies by individual, and while this period may not consume an MP's entire first term, it rarely exceeds it.

Graduating from MP spring training, of course, does not automatically turn a rookie MP into a wily veteran, and members who have survived one re-election bid are not by definition political careerists. A further benchmark in many politicians' careers is what some former MPs have dubbed 'the threshold': the point at which they must decide if they wish to turn their backs on their previous careers or whether their time in Parliament is just an 'interlude or short-term break in a career outside of politics'.[28] The longer one stays in politics, it is argued, the less likely one is to return to a previous career. Like the end of the apprenticeship period, the timing of reaching the threshold is unique to individual members, and often depends on the type of career pursued before entering politics. As one former MP explained:

> The fact that I am a lawyer meant that I could afford to stay in politics longer than some, without breaking all ties to my previous profession. I knew I wasn't assured of returning to my old firm, but I did know I could return to the law. But businesses, who always argue they need more business [people] in government, are very bad at taking back former members. Unless you were at the top of your company or it was a family owned

business, many members are afraid that if they stay too long [in Ottawa] they will have nowhere to go to when they leave.

Thus members of Parliament pass through as many as three stages in their political careers. All enter as apprentices; some become knowledgeable and potentially effective members; and, after crossing a threshold, a few become career politicians who treat their work in the same way that most professionally trained individuals treat theirs.

The time spent in each of these career stages is unique to each member and depends on a variety of factors, including political party, attention paid to House of Commons duties, promotion within the House, and ability to return to previous occupations. And at any time along the way, retirement from the House, either voluntarily or via electoral defeat, may claim a member before she or he has passed through these stages. All members enter as amateurs or apprentices. Not all return after their first term in the House, and fewer still survive to cross the threshold into careerism.

CAREER TYPES
Leaders, Non-Leaders and Career Stage

While the career stage is a simple time continuum, the progression in rank of an MP, in terms of positions held in the House or party, is not so uniform. Some MPs do climb a leadership ladder, moving from the back bench to the position of parliamentary secretary to Cabinet. Others may enter Cabinet relatively early in their political careers but, through either a shuffle or a change of government, be relieved of their Cabinet duties and spend the remainder of their careers as private members. Others may spend most of their careers in positions of authority in the House. Still others never get to Cabinet or, in the case of opposition members, one of the few leadership positions available to the non-governing parties.

For the purposes of this paper, the term 'leaders' will be used to designate any member who, *at some point in his or her federal career,* served either in the Cabinet or as a party leader, House leader, whip or caucus chair. Since the discussion here will focus on the 33rd Parliament, these 'leaders' will include MPs who held federal leadership positions prior to the 1984 Conservative victory: namely, former Liberal Cabinet ministers, and Conservative ministers under Joe Clark. The term 'private member' will refer to MPs who have not held any of the above positions but includes committee chairs, parliamentary secretaries, deputy House leaders, deputy whips and other less senior positions.

Table 13.2 compares leaders and private members of the 33rd Parliament in terms of a three-stage breakdown of political careers. Excluded from the table are MPs who had left the House of Commons before the spring of 1988. The first stage, amateur, includes all those individuals who by spring 1988 had served no more than one full term; that is, they were first elected to the House of Commons in or after the 1984 general election. The second stage, seasoned politicians, includes members who had

TABLE 13.2 **LEGISLATIVE EXPERIENCE (SPRING 1988)**
Amateurs, Seasoned Politicians,
and Careerists

Status	Amateurs	Seasoned politicians	Careerists
Leader	20	21	31
	7.2%	7.6%	11.2%
Private member	117	61	26
	42.6%	22.0%	9.4%

served at least one full term but who were first elected after 1974. The final group, political careerists, consists of members who by spring 1988 had served for at least fourteen years.

The relationship between career stage and leadership is evident. The further one moves along in a federal career, the greater the likelihood that one will spend some time in a leadership position. Very few amateurs are found within the ranks of leaders. Among 'seasoned politicians' there are almost three times as many private members as leaders. However, once members pass their so-called threshold and become 'political careerists' they are more likely to be leaders (or former leaders) than private members.

It is important to note the absence of directional arrows. Some members are appointed to leadership posts early in their careers and then go on to enjoy lengthy political careers. Others must first gain the vaunted veteran status before getting their turn at a leadership position. For some there are rewards for surviving the rigours of electoral battles. Others may survive electoral contests in part because of their status as present or former leaders.

It is reasonable to expect that the inclusion of NDP members, who have never tasted federal government power and are therefore limited to only a few leadership positions, may exaggerate the number of private members compared to leaders. Removing members of the NDP from Table 13.2 does alter the ratio of leaders to private members, but only slightly. The only real change occurs among the 'seasoned politicians', where the number of private members falls from 61 to 44 and the number of leaders drops from 21 to 19. This changes the ratio in this category from almost three private members for every leader to just over two to one. In both other categories, removing NDP MPs does not alter the ratio between private members and leaders.

All of this suggests a fairly simple relationship between career stage and position within the House of Commons. MPs in positions of leadership tend to be parliamentary veterans, and a number of them are, at least by the definitions employed here,

TABLE 13.3 **THE 1984 ELECTION RESULTS BY MEMBER'S STATUS**

Group	Margin of victory in riding (%)	Share of vote in riding (%)
Leader amateur	18.1	51.8
Leader seasoned	27.4	56.4
Leader careerist	30.5	56.3
Private member amateur	17.3	50.4
Private member seasoned	21.3	51.6
Private member careerist	23.7	53.2
Total average	21.1	52.1

career politicians. Is there a similar relationship between experience and the ability of MPs, both leaders and private members, to achieve re-election?

In fact, those with more federal experience do appear to be electorally more secure than their rookie counterparts. Table 13.3 shows the average margin of victory for MPs and the average share of the vote for members in the 1984 election for each of the six categories outlined above.

The margin of victory is the difference between the individual's total percentage of the vote and the vote percentage of the person who finished second. Amateurs, both non-leaders and leaders, were elected with the smallest margins of victory in 1984, with 17 and 18 per cent respectively. Going into the 1988 election, therefore, first-term members had the smallest cushion of all incumbents. By contrast, 'leader careerists' had the largest margin of victory in 1984, at just over 30 per cent. It is interesting to note that 'private member careerists' had a smaller margin of victory than 'seasoned leaders', although the difference is less than 4 per cent.

In terms of the total percentage of the vote won by a member in his or her constituency in the 1984 election, 'private member amateurs' held the lowest share, at just over 50 per cent. The largest total constituency votes were achieved by 'seasoned' and 'careerist' leaders in the House of Commons, with just over 56 per cent in both cases. It is interesting to note that 'private member careerists', with more elections under their belts than either 'leader amateurs' or 'seasoned private members', also managed to obtain a larger overall portion of the vote, and a larger margin of victory, than these two other groups.

Both indicators therefore suggest that the less experience one has, the more vulnerable one may be to electoral defeat. With electoral experience comes electoral security. But how does this type of electoral cushion affect MPs' chances in their next electoral battle, should they choose to stay?

TABLE 13.4   EXPERIENCE, STATUS, AND THE
              1988 ELECTION[1]

Group	Won N %		Lost N %		Retired N %	
Leader amateur	15	(75)	3	(15)	2	(10)
Leader seasoned	15	(71.4)	1	(4.8)	5	(23.8)
Leader careerist	20	(64.5)	2	(6.5)	9	(29)
Private member amateur	66	(56.4)	40	(34.2)	11	(9.3)
Private member seasoned	35	(57.4)	14	(22.9)	12	(19.6)
Private member careerist	15	(57.7)	4	(15.4)	7	(26.9)
Total	166	(60.1)	64	(23.2)	46	(16.7)

[1] Some percentages do not add to 100 because of rounding.

WINNERS, LOSERS, AND LEAVERS

It was suggested earlier that a relationship exists between the structure of a legislative assembly and the type of turnover that it experiences. For instance, a legislature that is dominated by a few leaders and provides little opportunity for new members to break into this select group should have a high number of voluntary vacancies among young private members, and few veteran members outside positions of authority. Conversely, an organization in which promotion is based solely on seniority and merit should show a more orderly pattern of transition from junior private members to senior leaders.[29] Here defeat should be the overwhelming cause of turnover, particularly among junior members.

In typically Canadian fashion, the House of Commons is a compromise between these two extreme types. Table 13.4 shows the records of each member in the 1988 general election, as well as those who chose not to fight in that contest, according to the six categories of leadership status and career stage.

The success rate of politicians as a group varies from just over 56 per cent to 75 per cent. Not surprisingly, 'private member amateurs' enjoyed the lowest re-election rate. The re-election rate for more experienced private members, however, was not overly encouraging either. Both 'private member seasoned' and 'private member careerist' MPs had a 57 per cent re-election rate. Members of the 'leader' group had much better luck at the polls. 'Leader amateurs' had a 75 per cent re-election rate, while among the 'leader seasoned' and 'leader careerist' MPs 71 and 64 per cent respectively were successful in their re-election bids. The re-election rates of all seasoned and career MPs held up across region: in other words, veteran MPs can be found in all regions of the country.

The differences in re-election rates between leaders and private members are even more striking when those members who choose to leave are temporarily excluded. In total, fewer than 11 per cent of MPs in the leader categories who ran in 1988 were defeated. This compares with a one-third defeat rate among private members in 1988. The most politically vulnerable group of MPs, perhaps not surprisingly, were amateurs who had yet to taste the fruits of leadership. Almost 35 per cent—40 out of 117—lost their first re-election bids. And while the private-member veterans did better than their seasoned and amateur counterparts, one-fifth of this group were also defeated at the polls. Only two of 22, or 9 per cent, of 'leader careerists' who ran in 1988 were rejected. These figures suggest that the members most vulnerable electorally as a result of unpopular policies or legislation are usually not the ones who shaped the latter—that is, the individuals in the front benches—but rather the rookie back-benchers who agreed to them.

The key variable in the decision to leave seems to be not status but the length of time one has spent in the House. The less experience a member has, whether on the back or front benches, the less likely it is that he or she will choose to go. Among both 'leader amateurs' and 'private member amateurs' the voluntary retirement rate was approximately 10 per cent. This contrasts with drop-out rates of 27 per cent among 'private member careerists' and 29 per cent among 'leader careerists'. And among 'seasoned politicians', both leaders and private members, the drop-out rate varies between 19 and 24 per cent. Somewhere between one-fifth and one-quarter of all members, then, reach their threshold of careerism and decide not to cross it. The rest make the leap and put their career fate in the hands of the voters.

Thus it appears that an MP's status and career stage are in some way linked to the manner in which he or she will leave political office. Careerists, both private members and leaders, are more likely to leave by choice than by force. Amateurs, on the other hand, are much more susceptible to the whims of the electorate. While the low numbers of 'leader amateurs' make any generalization difficult, it is clear that among 'private member amateurs' the most common departure route is the least enjoyable: namely, choosing to stay and being voted out. Leadership status in the House seems to have the most effect in terms of method of exit among seasoned politicians. 'Seasoned leaders' are fairly safe electorally should they choose to cross the career threshold, while exits amongst 'seasoned private members' are almost evenly split between voluntary retirement and electoral defeat.

What other differences exist between winning, defeated, and retiring members? In the spring of 1988, 230 members of Parliament decided that the benefits of elected life outweighed the negative aspects and chose once more to offer their services to the country. Of these, 64 were handed their pink slips and 166 were 'rehired'. An additional 46 members chose not to face the electorate again, some of whom did not even wait until the election was called before vacating their seats. Most, however, continued to represent their constituencies until the public chose their replacements. The factors and issues that helped to determine the outcome of the 1988 election are thoroughly detailed elsewhere and need not be examined here.[30] However, given the concern with high levels of turnover and its role in reducing the overall levels of

TABLE 13.5 THE FATE OF THE 33rd PARLIAMENT

	Re-elected (N = 166)	Defeated (N = 64)	Retired (N = 46)
Years served	8.4[1][2]	6.1[1]	11.6[2]
Age at exit	49.6[2]	51.5	58.2[2]
Margin of victory, 1984 (%)	22.7[1]	15.5[1]	23.3
Member's percentage of vote, 1984 (%)	53.1[1]	49.0[1]	53.1
Regional party vote, 1984 (%)	45.3	43.5	47.4
Transposition of votes, 1987 (%)[3]	53.2[1]	47.3[1]	52.3
Party support in Dec. 1987 (%)[4]	33.4	30.6	33.5

NOTE: With the exception of party support in December 1987, in each case a difference of means significant at $p < .001$ exists between those defeated and those retired.

[1] Indicates difference of means significant at $p < .001$ between re-elected and defeated members.

[2] Indicates difference of means significant at $p < .001$ between those re-elected and those retired.

[3] For explanation see text.

[4] Source: Angus Reid poll.

experience in the House of Commons, it is important to examine other factors that distinguish electoral survivors from electoral victims.

Table 13.5 compares the career experience and electoral history of members who in 1988 were re-elected, were defeated, or did not run for re-election.[31] As the table indicates, members who decided not to fight the 1988 election were older, legislatively more experienced, and electorally more secure than either of the other groups. Among the voluntary retirees were the longest-serving members in the House. These careerists had served on average for just over 11.5 years, three years longer than people who ran and won in 1988 and 5.5 years longer than members who ran and lost. Voluntary retirees are also a much older group, leaving the House of Commons at an average age of 58. Those who lost were 7.5 years younger, and members who won were younger still, averaging just under 50 years of age.

The other indicators in Table 13.5 show that voluntary retirees and those re-elected have remarkably similar electoral histories, particularly when compared with incumbents who were defeated. There are three indicators here. First is the margin of victory each member achieved in 1984, the same indicator used in Table 13.3. Members who went down to electoral defeat in 1988 had an average 1984 margin of victory of 15.5 per cent, 7 points lower than winners and almost 8 points lower than retirees. It is true that party dominance in certain areas of the country helps to push up certain members' margins of victory; for example, the magnitude of the difference in victory margins drops slightly when Alberta Conservatives are excluded from this comparison. However, even with their exclusion a substantial difference remains between those defeated and those who either won or retired.

Members who lost in 1988 not only had smaller margins of victory in 1984, but achieved smaller overall vote totals in their last winning election than did their victorious and retiring counterparts. Winners and retirees won their ridings with an average of 53 per cent of the vote. By contrast, those defeated in 1988 had won their ridings with less than majority support in 1984: on average, 49 per cent. In terms of regional party support, retirees tended to come from regions of the country where their parties fared the best, receiving on average over 47 per cent of the vote. Those defeated came from areas where their parties were not as strong, receiving an average of 43.5 per cent of the vote.

In order to determine whether those who decided to sit out the 1988 election were influenced by more recent events, two measures of electoral support in 1987 are included in the table. The first indicator is the 'transposition of votes' produced by Elections Canada following the 1987 redistribution of seats. This document contains the 1984 poll-by-poll results for each new riding after the redistribution of seats, making it possible to determine how each member would have fared in 1984 under the new electoral boundaries. Once again, those members who were eventually defeated in 1988 come up short, with redistribution hypothetically dropping their 1984 winning totals almost two percentage points, from 49 per cent to 47.3 per cent. Redistribution had very little effect on victors and retirees.

The second and more immediate indicator is the support for each party by region shown in a December 1987 Angus Reid poll. Winners, losers, and retirees all hovered between 30.6 and 33.5 per cent of the popular support. There were no differences between any of the groups here. It seems, then, that recent events such as party support and redistribution should have had a minimal influence on those who chose to retire in 1988.

Finally, the truism that it is harder to defend a government than to oppose it appears to have been no less salient in 1988. Of the 64 defeated MPs, 50 were members of the Conservative caucus. Higher profiles also meant increased chances for re-election: MPs who at some point had been Cabinet ministers stood a greater chance of re-election than those who had never sat at the Cabinet table but had been members of a governing party. Once the effects of both leadership and parliamentary experience are combined, however, a much more striking picture emerges of who is and who is not electorally exposed. Leaders and veterans can hang onto their seats; amateurs and private members have a much more difficult time of it.

LOSERS AND LEAVERS
Who Are They?

Both voluntary retirees and defeated incumbents can be found, in varying numbers, in each of the six career categories outlined earlier in this chapter. So far, however, only factors common to all members, such as years served and status in the House, have been used to distinguish between those who choose to stay and those who choose to leave. Individual factors, though, are also undeniably at work. Different people lose or leave for different reasons, and after leaving they pursue different careers. What follows is a brief look at the individual political and post-political careers of some members of the 33rd Parliament.

Forty-three MPs who were first elected to the House in or after September 1984 were defeated in the 1988 general election. Of these, three were 'leader amateurs' and forty were 'private member amateurs'. Of the first group, one defeated amateur lost her re-election bid running as an independent: Suzanne Blais-Grenier spent just over one year in Cabinet, moving from the Environment portfolio to the ministry of state for Transport in August 1985 and resigning from the latter in December 1985. As Graham Fraser argues, 'although she resigned to protest the closing of an oil refinery in the east end of Montreal, she was widely believed to have jumped before she was pushed.'[32] Running as an independent Conservative, Ms Blais-Grenier finished a distant fourth.

A second 'leader amateur' who felt the wrath of the voters was Sault Ste Marie Conservative MP James Kelleher, who lost to New Democrat Steve Butland. Mr Kelleher's victory in 1984 was a close one: he enjoyed only a 7 per cent margin of victory, well below the average for rookie MPs. The rewards of defeat, however, were more bountiful for this party loyalist than they were for Ms Blais-Grenier. Mr Kelleher (previously minister for International Trade and Solicitor General of Canada) was rewarded not once but twice. Shortly after his defeat he was appointed to the FTA dispute-resolution panel, and later, in 1990, to the Senate.

A 'seasoned leader' who shared the same electoral fate as Mr Kelleher was Thomas McMillan, the former Environment minister from Prince Edward Island. First elected as part of the minority Conservative government in 1979, he served for nine years before being defeated. Like Mr Kelleher, Mr McMillan continued to serve his country after the election, accepting an appointment as Consul General in Boston.

One of the two defeated 'career leaders' was also called upon to continue to serve the public after his defeat. The Honourable Ray Hnatyshyn had served as the MP for Saskatoon West for fourteen years, including five years in the Cabinet, before his defeat in the 1988 election. Soon after, Mr Hnatyshyn was appointed governor general, replacing Jeanne Sauvé, another former member of Parliament and Cabinet minister.

By contrast, non-leader incumbents who lost re-election bids were less likely to receive patronage appointments (although some did). Other non-leaders who were defeated did not rule out a return to federal politics.

The largest group of individuals running unsuccessfully in 1988 were 'private member amateurs'. The majority of these forty private-member rookies were Conservatives who had come in on the crest of the Conservative wave in 1984 and rode the surf back out when the 1988 election reduced their party's majority. Some had managed to make a start up the leadership ladder, serving as parliamentary secretaries or committee chairs. For many of these Conservative newcomers, however, their brief political careers were spent entirely on the back bench.

Rookie opposition members were not immune to rejection by the voters. John Turner's Québec lieutenant Raymond Garneau, who had come to Parliament with provincial experience, was defeated after just one term; he moved to the private sector in Québec. Former Ottawa mayor Marion Dewar lost her first bid for re-election after winning a 1987 by-election to replace fellow New Democrat Ian Deans. A brief taste of federal politics was clearly not enough for Ms Dewar. After working as a private consultant for five years, Ms Dewar decided to run for federal office once again in 1993, this time unsuccessfully as the NDP candidate in Ottawa Centre.

Another New Democratic electoral victim in 1988, this one a member of the 'private member seasoned' cadre, also decided that federal politics was not sufficiently out of her blood. After winning the seat vacated by Bob Rae when he ascended to the leadership of the Ontario New Democratic Party in 1982, Lynn McDonald won re-election in 1984 with an 11 per cent margin of victory. Following her 1988 loss, she returned to her previous occupation as a professor, but later decided to fight the 1993 election, loosing a second time in her old riding of Toronto Broadview-Greenwood.

One of the few veteran women MPs, Aideen Nicholson, also went down to defeat in 1988. After redistribution had consolidated some of the smaller downtown Toronto ridings, the fourteen-year veteran found herself running against, and losing to, Cabinet minister Barbara McDougall in 1988. Following her defeat, Ms Nicholson was appointed to the Immigration and Refugee Determination Board, a federal appointment that comes under the Department of Immigration, Ms McDougall's portfolio at the time.

Among retirees—in particular, seasoned and career retirees—timing has clearly been one factor in the decision to leave office. In 1988 there were thirty-three retirees—both leaders and private members—who had served for more than one term. In 1984 they were still interested in pursuing a political career, but by 1988 they had changed their minds. As might be expected, their level of experience was quite high: they had served on average for over fourteen years, with seven serving for over twenty. The average age of entry to the House of Commons for these veteran retirees was just over 45; thus by 1988, when they were deciding to leave, their average age was roughly 60.

Members of Parliament are eligible for pensions after six years of service. Pensions reach their maximum after fifteen years of service, when members are eligible to receive 75 per cent of their salary.[33] This pension is no doubt a serious factor in the decisions of some of the more senior retirees. Like members of other professions, these individuals are opting for an attractive 'early retirement package'. Had they chosen to leave four years earlier, they would have suffered economically, and, leaving at an average age of 56, would have had to consider returning to their pre-political occupations or seeking new ones.

Amateurs, therefore, are excluded from the pension calculation. And, given that government appointments are not as forthcoming for these early quitters, their leaving may be the result of other factors: dissatisfaction with the role or requirements of an MP, or perhaps transgression of the acceptable codes of behaviour in Ottawa. For example, both 'leader amateurs' who chose not to run again, André Bissonette and Michel Côté, were involved in government scandals.[34] Neither received a patronage position.

Appointments for 'private member amateurs' who chose to leave after only one term were also noticeable by their absence. The only independent elected in 1984,

Tony Roman of Ontario, decided that four years as a lone member without a caucus were enough. He returned to municipal politics, gaining re-election as mayor of Markham, Ont., his political career before entering the federal arena. Another early retiree was Québec MP Michel Gravel, yet another Conservative touched with scandal who bowed out after only four years.

Unlike rookies who left by choice, veteran voluntary retirees were more likely to enjoy federal largesse. Both Pat Carney and David Crombie, 'seasoned leaders' who left by choice, continued in public life at the behest of the prime minister. Ms Carney went to the Senate in 1990, while Mr Crombie chaired a royal commission on the Toronto waterfront immediately upon his retirement from the House. While Ms Carney never had what was considered a safe seat (her margin of victory was 11 per cent in 1984), fear of losing was hardly a consideration for Mr Crombie. In the 1984 election he received 53 per cent of the vote, 24 per cent more than his closest opponent.

These were two of five Conservative ministers who gave up Cabinet positions with their 1988 retirement from office.[35] All left while at or near the top of their Cabinet careers. Some were careerists who had entered politics at an early age and were leaving to pursue other interests, such as former minister of Agriculture John Wise, who returned to his farm in southern Ontario. For one of these retiring ministers, the prospect of another four years at the hectic helm of a large portfolio was enough:

> I had to ask if I saw myself doing this for another four full years, knowing I was not going to move any further up [than my present cabinet post]. If I left then [in 1988] I could start a different type of career and do that for ten or so years. If I had stayed for another full term, I am not sure that would have been possible.

Such considerations reflect not only a concern with the 'threshold', but also the very real concern that an appointed position in government may be easier to obtain when your party still forms the government.

Not surprisingly, the veteran leaders who chose to leave in 1988 were older than the other cadres. Some, like George Hees and Alvin Hamilton, left after serving over a quarter of a century in the House of Commons. On full pension, they retired as most people do after at least twenty-five years in one career. Others, such as Bob Coates and Roch LaSalle, retired on a darker note, leaving a lifetime in politics under a cloud of scandal. It is possible that these two men would have sought office again if they had not been caught in politically embarrassing circumstances. Finally, there were three Conservative vacators who had served in the Clark Cabinet but were not called to the Cabinet table by Brian Mulroney. Had these MPs been members of the Mulroney executive, their career decisions in 1988 might well have been different. As it was, the diminished prospects of ever returning to Cabinet may have been enough to sway their decisions in favour of retirement.

Some left federal politics to seek leadership positions elsewhere. Prince Edward Island Conservative Mel Gass left Ottawa after nine years to head the PEI Conservative party; not finding a leadership position federally, he was successful in finding one at the sub-national level. Another nine-year private member who had not received a leadership position in Ottawa was Chris Speyer of southern Ontario, who accepted a judicial appointment within his community.

Finally, the 'private member careerists' who retired by choice in 1988 were all senior members of their parties who had carved out successful careers in Parliament. For members such as Lloyd Crouse, retirement from elected office was much the same as retirement from any other position after three decades of service. With the retirement of Mr Crouse and fellow Conservatives George Hees and Alvin Hamilton (these latter two with Cabinet experience), the House of Commons lost all but its last links to the Diefenbaker era. These three true careerists averaged over 31 years each as members of Parliament. The sole remaining MP who served during the Diefenbaker period, Herb Gray, is now Liberal House Leader.

These mini-portraits of political careers illustrate that there is not one door leading out of the House of Commons. Some careers, like Suzanne Blais-Grenier's, never really get started. Others, like Lloyd Crouse's, stand as exceptions to the conventional wisdom that there are no lifetime politicians in Canada. There are many stages to a political career, and each stage has its own exit. Even leaving by the same exit door does not guarantee that two MPs will find the same post-political opportunities.

Many exiting MPs receive appointments that help to ease or, in the case of the Senate, delay the return to private life. These appointments are not reserved exclusively for career leaders, or even for government members; redistribution may have forced Liberal Aideen Nicholson into running against a Cabinet minister, but it may also have helped her to find a post-political career. As a rule, however, former Cabinet ministers, whether they left by choice or force, were the most successful in terms of federal appointments.

Finally, people who run again, whether they win or lose, show a commitment to continue in public office. For some losers a five-year absence from the House of Commons is not long enough to weaken this commitment, as evidenced by their candidacies in the 1993 general election. These individuals hope that their first political exit is not their last. Such a commitment is not so common among the ranks of the voluntary vacators.[36] When individuals leave by choice, they are more reluctant to second-guess their actions.

CONCLUSION

Concern with the levels of turnover in the House of Commons has tended to focus on the total number of MPs exiting and the arrival of a large group of newcomers. Too little attention has been focused on who is leaving and why. Turnover is a function of two factors, electoral defeat and voluntary retirement.

The way a member of Parliament leaves the House is often linked to the type of career that he or she has experienced in Ottawa. The low number of amateur retirees suggests that few individuals are put off the job of federal representative soon after they take up the position. In 1988 fewer than 10 per cent of 'the amateurs' chose to leave just as they were finishing their apprenticeship period. And of these, three were directly involved in conflicts of interest. People who quit politics tend to do so only after they have passed through their apprenticeship period.

The most common mode of departure for amateurs is electoral defeat. Members elected for the first time have the lowest margins of victory of all MPs. They have very little personal vote to fall back on in the event of a popular swing against their party or leader. Amateurs who have achieved positions of leadership can offset this somewhat by building a more national profile, but they are not immune from the dictates of the voters. Nevertheless, three-quarters of all amateurs who run for re-election are successful.

As a member reaches the threshold point, the choice to stay or go becomes much more significant. Approximately 20 per cent of MPs, upon reaching their thresholds, decide not to make elected office a life-time responsibility, and bow out of office. Considerations that factor into the decision include age, ability to return to a previous career or start a new one, and perceived ability to win election should they choose to stay. Those who go take with them a healthy, but not full, pension, which is often supplemented by a government appointment. Those who decide to stay are not guaranteed a return ticket to Ottawa. One-quarter of private members who decided to stay beyond their career thresholds were defeated in 1988.

For MPs who successfully move beyond the threshold, fears of electoral defeat soon subside. Careerist MPs, both holders of leadership positions and private members, rarely lose elections. In 1988 only six of forty-one 'career members' lost their seats. This provides a simple explanation for the high number of retirees among career politicians. Career members leave politics by choice after a long and fruitful career. They leave with full (or close to full) pensions, and some even receive appointed positions.

Two final points may be briefly noted. First, despite concerns that Canadian elections are won and lost on party and leader popularity, it appears that some members do build a personal vote. While leaders with experience enjoyed the largest margin of victory in 1984, private members with more than one election under their belts also fared much better than rookie or one-term MPs. Given the opportunity to build a relationship with their constituents for more than one term, members of Parliament can turn this relationship into an electoral advantage.[37]

The success of political careerists may also be an indication, albeit indirect, that the Canadian people are more dissatisfied with politicians in the abstract than they are with their own members. Canadians may hold politicians in disrepute, but they also re-elect their own federal representatives quite regularly. The political longevity of some politicians should be taken as an encouraging reminder that good service does not go unrewarded by the public. The number of 'career private members' indicates that continual re-election is not the sole preserve of Cabinet ministers, who enjoy national profiles.

Second, if the way an organization loses its members tells us something about that organization, the exit patterns in Parliament should ease any fears held about amateurism and turnover. Canada is a long way from needing term limits. Neither, however, do we need to reform our legislature to attract and hold more of a certain type of leader. The relative balance between voluntary retirement and electoral defeat suggests that the Canadian House of Commons enjoys a healthy pattern of membership renewal. People choose to stay or go for different reasons, at different moments in their careers, and at any time the legislature holds a solid number of members in each career stage and at each level of leadership status.

NOTES

* With appologies to the Clash.

[1] 'Move to Limit Terms Gathers Steam After Winning in 14 States', *New York Times*, Thursday November 5, 1992. p. B16.

[2] According to Peter Dobell and Bryon Berry ('Anger at the System', *Parliamentary Government* 39, 1 [Jan./Feb. 1990]: 7), only advertising executives are considered to have lower ethical standards.

[3] See, for example, C.E.S. Franks, *The Parliament of Canada* (Toronto: University of Toronto Press, 1987).

[4] For analysis of the effects of term limits on turnover in state legislatures, see Gary F. Moncrief, Joel A. Thompson, Michael Haddon, and Robert Hoyer, 'For Whom the Bell Tolls: Term Limits and State Legislatures', *Legislative Studies Quarterly* XVII, 1 (Feb. 1992): 37-48.

[5] Unless otherwise noted the following analysis is based on data collected on members of the 33rd Parliament, 1984-1988 and from interviews with former MPs, the majority of whom were members of the 33rd Parliament. Data has been collected from *The Canadian Parliamentary Guide*.

[6] The analysis in this chapter is based on the 1988 general election. As the results of the more recent election in 1993 indicate, large national swings against the governing party do not spare even the most veteran cabinet ministers.

[7] Franks, *Parliament*, 72.

[8] Norman Ward, *The Canadian House of Commons: Representations* (Toronto: University of Toronto Press, 1950); John Porter, *The Vertical Mosaic* (Toronto: University of Toronto Press, 1965); Franks, *Parliament*.

[9] Franks, *Parliament*, 4-7.

[10] For a more thorough discussion of the different uses of the word 'amateur' in politics see Michael Atkinson and David Docherty, 'Moving Right Along: The Roots of Amateurism in the Canadian House of Commons', *Canadian Journal of Political Science* XXV, 2 (June 1992): 295-318. See also David Canon, *Actors, Athletes and Astronauts: Political Amateurs in the United States Congress* (Chicago: University of Chicago Press, 1990); also, James Q. Wilson, *The Amateur Democrat: Club Politics in Three Cities* (Chicago: University of Chicago Press, 1966).

[11] Peverill Squire, 'Career Opportunities and Membership Stability in Legislatures', *Legislative Studies Quarterly* XIII, 1 (Feb. 1988): 65-82. See also Wayne L. Francis and John R. Baker, 'Why Do U.S. State Legislators Vacate Their Seats?' *Legislative Studies Quarterly* XI, 1 (Feb. 1986) 119-26.

[12] V.S. Harder, 'Career Patterns and Political Parties', in Jean-Pierre Gadboury and Ross Harvey, eds, *The Canadian House of Commons Observed: The Parliamentary Internship Papers* (Ottawa: University of Ottawa Press, 1979), 327-45.

[13] Doreen Barrie and Roger Gibbins, 'Parliamentary Careers in the Canadian Federal State', *Canadian Journal of Political Science* XXII, 1 (March 1989): 141.

[14] Members of Parliament with provincial experience are more likely to come from the Atlantic provinces. See Ian Stewart, 'A Damn Queer Parliament', in Gary Levy and Graham White, eds, *Provincial and Territorial Legislatures in Canada* (Toronto: University of Toronto Press, 1989), 13-28.

[15] Ward, *House of Commons*, ch. 7.

[16] Robert Fleming, ed., *Canadian Legislatures 1992: Issues, Structures and Costs* (Scarborough, Ont.: Global Press, 1992), 160-1.

[17] Daniel J. Reagan and Donald Davidson, 'Ambition and Retirement from the U.S. House of Representatives, 1957-1984', paper delivered at the Annual Meeting of the American Political Science Association (Washington, DC, Sept. 1991), 4. See also John Hibbing, 'Voluntary Retirement from the U.S. House: The Costs of Congressional Service', *Legislative Studies Quarterly* 7 (Feb. 1982): 57-74. Joseph Cooper and William West, 'Voluntary Retirement, Incumbency and the Modern House', *Political Science Quarterly* 96, 2 (Summer 1981): 279-300.

[18] William Irvine, 'Does the Candidate Make a Difference: The Macro-Politics and Micro-Politics of Getting Elected', *Canadian Journal of Political Science* XV, 4 (Dec. 1982): 755-85. See also Michael Krashinsky, 'The Effect of Incumbency in the 1984 Federal and 1985 Ontario Elections', *Canadian Journal of Political Science* XIX, 2 (June 1986) 337-43.

[19] Franks, *Parliament*, 76.

[20] Atkinson and Docherty, 'Moving', 305. Not included in this total were twenty-one MPs who died while still serving.

[21] Ibid., 312.

[22] John R. Hibbing, *Congressional Careers: Contours of Life in the U.S. House of Representatives* (Chapel Hill: University of North Carolina Press, 1991). See chapters 1 and 2.

[23] Comments in quotations are taken from interviews with former members of Parliament.

[24] Porter, *Vertical Mosaic*, ch. 13.

[25] J.A.A. Lovink, 'Is Canadian Politics Too Competitive?' *Canadian Journal of Political Science* VI, 3 (Sept. 1973): 370; Franks, *Parliament*, 74.

[26] Sharon Sutherland, 'The Consequences of Electoral Volatility: Inexperienced Ministers 1949-90', in Herman Bakvis, ed., *Representation, Integration and Political Parties in Canada*, vol. 14 of the research studies of the Royal Commission on Electoral Reform and Party Financing (Toronto and Ottawa: Dundurn Press, 1992).

[27] This survey is part of a larger project by the author. MPs were asked the following question: 'Some members report that it took time to become comfortable with 'the formal and informal rules of the House of Commons. They have called this time an "apprenticeship period." How long did your "apprenticeship period" take?' The actual average was 1.487 years ($N = 85$).

[28] Franks, *Parliament*, 72.

[29] Peverill Squire, 'Member Career Opportunities and the Internal Organization of Legislatures', *Journal of Politics* 50: 726-44.

[30] See, for example, Harold Clarke, Jane Jenson, Lawrence Le Duc, and Jon H. Pammett, *Absent Mandate: Interpreting Change in Canadian Elections*. (Toronto: Gage, 1991). See also Graham Fraser, *Playing For Keeps: The Making of the Prime Minister* (Toronto: McClelland and Stewart, 1988), and, most recently, Richard Johnston, André Blais, Henry E. Brady, and Jean Crête, *Letting the People Decide: Dynamics of a Canadian Election* (Montreal: McGill-Queen's University Press, 1992).

[31] The small number of cases makes statistical comparisons across the six career typologies impossible.

[32] Fraser, *Playing for Keeps*, 35.

[33] The actual pension calculation is based on the average of the best consecutive six years of earnings. This may include the additional indemnities for parliamentary secretaries, ministers, and other such positions, if the MP chooses to contribute a portion of this additional indemnity. For a more detailed examination of federal and provincial representatives' pensions see Robert Fleming, ed., *Canadian Legislatures: 1992: Issues, Structures and Costs* (Toronto: Global Press, 1992), 90-100.

[34] For more detail on MPs who have left because of political corruption see Chapter 14 of this volume.

[35] As mentioned earlier, this analysis does not include mid-term vacancies; hence individuals such as Erik Nielsen, the veteran Yukon MP, are not included. Incumbents who lost their party nomination battle or whose nomination papers were not signed by their party leader were also not included in this analysis, as they were not considered to be 'voluntary vacators'.

[36] However, some individuals do leave by choice only to try to return to office. Former Liberal Cabinet minister Donald Johnston retired by choice in 1988. In the spring of 1993 he made a brief attempt at re-entering the House of Commons, seeking the nomination in a riding that, as a result of redistribution, overlapped with his former constituency. He withdrew his candidacy in the face of internal party opposition to his challenge of a sitting MP. It should also be noted that, one year after leaving elected office, Mr Johnston was elected President of the Liberal Party of Canada.

[37] For an examination of the relationship between MPs and their constituencies see Richard G. Price and Maureen Mancuso, 'Ties That Bind: Parliamentary Members and Their Constituencies', in Robert M. Krause and R.H. Wagenberg, eds, *Introductory Readings in Canadian Government and Politics* (Toronto: Copp Clark Pittman, 1991).

CHAPTER FOURTEEN

THE   POLITICS
OF   SHAME

Leaving   in   Disgrace

———■———

Maureen   Mancuso

The other chapters in this volume have discussed the attainment of a leadership role and the exercise of leadership once in position to do so. Both 'getting there' and 'being there' are studies in circumventing obstacles, overcoming frustration, and displaying grace under pressure. The same can be said of the final stage in the career of a leader: exiting from or relinquishing a leadership role.

Patterns of exit from leadership roles constitute an understudied field in political science. There is a burgeoning literature in the United States on the career patterns of legislators[1] and the reasons they give up leadership positions: electoral defeat and, for growing numbers of them, voluntary retirement. Atkinson and Docherty, in their work on amateurism in the Canadian House of Commons, have used two models— exhaustion and frustration—to account for the retirement of MPs.[2] But what about leaders who are not casualties of electoral volatility, and do not choose to leave, but are forced to leave because of scandal? In a world of 'honourable members', what happens to those who acquire the taint of dishonour?

Unplanned, scandal-tinged exits have been surprisingly common in recent cabinets.

Graham Moodie has defined 'scandals' as 'those complexes of deviant behaviour, revelation and public reaction that together make up a historical event'.[3] In this view, the term 'scandal' encapsulates an improper act, conveyed to the public, that elicits a sharply negative response. For the purpose of studying exit patterns, scandal becomes especially interesting when that response is so vigorous and so negative that some form of retribution is required. Politicians who arouse the ire and lose the respect of the electorate through improper behaviour may never face criminal charges, but may be expected to surrender the office and powers with which the public has entrusted them.

This chapter will examine the types of scandals over which political leaders in Canada have left office. The primary focus will be Cabinet ministers rather than all MPs, for several reasons. First, as ministers they have an elevated and sensitive position from which to fall: their every move is subject to intense scrutiny, and it is therefore easier to detect significant changes in status resulting from misbehaviour. Second, as members of the executive they have far more power and hence more opportunity to get into trouble. Most scandals involving backbench MPs revolve around relatively petty misuse of office budgets or expense padding; appropriately-placed ministers, on the other hand, can fiddle million-dollar contracts, threaten national security, or peddle truly valuable influence. Third, MPs, with only one recent exception, simply do not resign from the House over matters of ethics or morality, whereas character flaws and misconduct are still grounds for termination of a Cabinet career. To avoid fragmentation and questions of regional variance, the cases examined here will be limited to the federal Parliament.

Rather than explicate the mechanics of scandal—leaks, damage control, 'spin doctoring', and so on—this chapter will concentrate on the career effects that a scandal can have once it has come to light. These depend on several factors; most important, however, are the type and the perceived severity of the activity that triggered the scandal. An attempt will be made to categorize scandals according to their relative virulence. Also important in determining the ultimate dénouement is the way in which the leader responds to the scandal. Faced with allegations, a leader has a choice of strategies available for managing the scandal, some of which can be more successful than others. Such scandal management also involves planning for a potential recovery. Finally, the role of the prime minister in managing, resolving, and avoiding scandal will be examined through comparison of the experiences of Pierre Trudeau and Brian Mulroney. Illustrative cases will show the importance of effective management in mitigating the career effects of scandal, even if it can only delay an inevitable conclusion. With so many scandals affecting Parliament in recent years, it would seem that scandal-fighting is becoming an institutionalized part of the legislative process, instead of an exceptional and infrequent interruption.

SCANDAL—A SHOCKED RESPONSE

There is a definite distinction to be drawn between political scandal and political corruption. The study of corruption has from its inception been vexed by the problem of definition. What might be corrupt in the eyes of one citizen, scholar, or elected representative is just politics for another, and mere indiscretion for a third.[4] In the scholarly literature on political corruption, various definitions have been advanced and explored. Each definition has unique features, but most definitions do share a common element: the idea of intentional misuse of public office to achieve personal gain, usually of a financial nature.[5]

Accordingly, there is a difference between corruption—the abuse of public office for personal gain—and scandal—a 'hostile and shocked response'[6] to a given action. Studies that use scandal as an indicator of corruption run the risk of equating the two: assuming that only where there is scandal can there be corruption, that all corruption is scandalous, and that all scandal points to corruption. According to Graeme Moodie:

> Political scandals do not deal exclusively with corruption—they may well centre on inefficiency, incompetence, or mere carelessness, which owes little or nothing to pursuit of private gain or any other private purpose.[7]

A clear example of this distinction is the case of Alan Redway, who as minister of Housing, in 1991, made some facetious comments about a gun in his friend's luggage as he was passing through airport security. The subsequent scandal—the public was shocked that a person of such responsibility would behave so irresponsibly—cost him his Cabinet portfolio, yet clearly he made no private gain. On the other hand, in some countries, bribery of public officials has become institutionalized; this behaviour, clearly corrupt and flagrantly illegal, is grudgingly accepted without triggering scandal.

SCANDAL
Types and Temperatures

If scandal and corruption are not the same, then what types of activities lead to scandal? Sharon Sutherland has studied ministerial resignations since Confederation and grouped them into eleven explanatory categories;[8] four of these relate to scandal. The first, *misconduct in office*, occurs when a minister breaches a rule, guideline, or law. These offences can be placed on a continuum from 'hot' to 'cool', depending on the nature of the violation and the degree of political 'heat' generated by the resulting scandal (see Table 14.1). A typical 'cool' incident occurred in 1990 when Jean Charest, as minister of Fitness and Amateur Sport, telephoned a Québec judge who was about to rule on a case involving the Canadian Track and Field Association. Such contact was a clear violation of Cabinet rules—established by Pierre Trudeau in response to a series of similar incidents involving ministers John Munro and André Ouellet, and Senator Bud Drury—and Charest resigned after a brief flurry of public criticism, but few would deem his actions a threat to the public trust.

On the other hand, the case of Minister for Regional Industrial Expansion Sinclair Stevens, found by the Parker Commission in 1987 to have violated conflict-of-interest guidelines on at least 14 occasions, ignited far greater controversy. Like almost all 'hot' scandals, the Stevens case involved financial impropriety and the use

TABLE 14.1 TYPES AND TEMPERATURES OF SCANDALS
DISCUSSED IN THE TEXT

Type	Hot	Warm	Cool
Official Misconduct			
Financial	Michel Côté	André Bissonette	Marcel Masse
	Michel Gravel	Marc Lalonde	
	Richard Grisé	Bryce Mackasey	
	Roch LaSalle	John Munro (1980s)	
	Sinclair Stevens		
Judicial	Jean Charest		
	Bud Drury		
	John Munro (1978)		
	André Ouellet		
Security	Robert Coates		
Private misconduct	Robert Coates	Francis Fox	Bernard Valcourt
	Alan Redway	Roger Simmons	
Administrative error	John Fraser		
Political differences	Lucien Bouchard		
	Suzanne Blais-Grenier		

REMARKS: The *warm* financial misconduct scandals are those in which the allegations were eventually dropped or disproved, but only after an extended period of heated condemnation of the leaders involved. The Masse scandal qualifies as *cool* because it was so quickly resolved in his favour.

Fox, Simmons and Fraser are also listed as somewhat *warm*, Fox for the moral dimension of his offence, Simmons because money was involved (though not public money), and Fraser because of the extensive public outcry.

John Munro is listed twice for two different scandals, one involving contact with a judge, the other allegations of fraud and corruption.

Robert Coates is listed twice for the same scandal, as it appeared to contain elements of both personal and official misconduct.

of public office for private gain. As we will see, this type of scandal is the most difficult to recover from.

Official misconduct is the most common basis for scandal. Such misconduct reached a peak in the early years of the Mulroney government, when an unprecedented number of ministers resigned under allegations of impropriety. As Sutherland points out, this trend was not necessarily the result of the induction of particularly venal individuals into Parliament; it could as easily have reflected naïveté, inexperience, or ignorance on the part of those involved.[9] When a party comes to power after an extended period in opposition—as in the case of the Ontario NDP government elected in 1990—it must staff the Cabinet with many individuals who are unfamiliar with the level of responsibility inherent in executive positions. Misconduct may result not only from a calculated attempt to circumvent the rules, but also from an innocent mistake or misunderstanding.

Unfortunately, such misunderstandings are all too understandable. Unlike the United States, which has all-encompassing governmental ethics legislation (the Ethics in Government Act, 1978, and the Ethics Reform Act, 1989), Canada does not have any ethics statutes. Thus the major prohibitions regulating the ethical behaviour of parliamentarians are contained in the Criminal Code, the House of Commons and Senate Act, and the Standing Orders.[10] Cabinet ministers are expected to abide by an additional set of restrictions governing their financial holdings. Traditionally, these rules have taken the form of a letter from the prime minister to his Cabinet. The primary message of the letter, first sent by Lester Pearson, seems to be that 'formal adherence to the law is not enough; ministers "must act in a manner so scrupulous that it will bear closest public scrutiny".'[11] Each prime minister has made changes to the details of the letter—financial disclosure requirements have been extended in various ways—but reliance on an uncodified approach continues. Actual comprehensive conflict-of-interest legislation—covering not only ministers but all MPs and senators—has been working its way through the House since 1988, but it has yet to be enacted.

The second category, *private misconduct*, covers unacceptable activity in a non-official capacity; that is, the leader involved has not misused his office, but has nevertheless behaved in an unseemly or even illegal manner. These scandals usually arise from errors in judgement or moral lapses. Behaviour such as Alan Redway's, or that of Solicitor General Francis Fox, who forged the signature of his mistress's husband on an abortion document, suggests that the leader may not be the 'right sort' of person to be in a powerful public position. The 1984 case of Defence minister Robert Coates contained elements of both private and official misconduct. In deciding to visit a West German strip bar while on an official tour of NATO allies he not only made a poor personal choice but opened the Pandora's box of national security, by leaving himself vulnerable to blackmail. His ultimate departure from Cabinet was based on this official component of his misconduct.

The third type of scandal results from an *administrative error*, when a minister, without violating any rules, botches the responsibilities of his portfolio. Such mistakes rarely escalate to the level of scandal; the only recent example was the 'tainted tuna affair' (or 'Tunagate'), when Fisheries minister John Fraser overruled the decision of his bureaucrats and released for sale cans of tuna-fish that had been judged unfit for human consumption. While Fraser felt that his decision at the time was correct, it had such negative consequences that he had to give up his post.

The final category of scandals consists of those attributed to *political differences*. These occur when a minister publicly breaks with his Cabinet colleagues or the prime minister. While such a schism can come as a surprise to the public, and transgresses the principle of collective Cabinet responsibility, the shocked response is concentrated in the inner circle and almost always leads to political banishment. When Brian Mulroney's Québec lieutenant and Environment minister Lucien Bouchard, in the midst of the final Meech Lake push, publicly praised those who had fought for an independent Québec during the 1980 referendum, it was seen as both a public and personal betrayal of the prime minister. Bouchard quickly left Cabinet, and eventually twisted the knife (but at the same time insulated himself from further reprisals) by leaving the Conservative caucus to form the Bloc Québécois.

In general, scandals generated by political differences tend to remain quite 'hot', even if the heat is most intense within the Prime Minister's Office. Politicians tend to have long memories for breaches of solidarity. Administrative errors and private misconduct tend to be 'cooler' than the other two types, although the exact nature of the offence, any mitigating circumstances, and the favour of the party leadership all play large roles in the long-term career consequences of any scandal.

SCANDAL MANAGEMENT

Once embroiled in scandal, an implicated leader can attempt to manage the situation in four ways: denial, self-defence, blame-avoidance, or confession. These management strategies correspond to 'I didn't do it,' 'I did nothing wrong,' 'It wasn't my fault,' and 'I'm sorry.' As the scandal unfolds, the initial choice of strategy will affect the severity of punishment and future career impairment. A quick confession, followed almost always by a sincere apology and resignation of ministerial post, has an immediate soothing effect on the public, and can be crucial to the leader's chances for a full recovery. This tactic is useful, however, only when the underlying offence is of the 'cool' variety. For leaders caught with their hands in the public till, confession may be good for the soul, but little else.

Denial and blame-avoidance are more risky. An individual who is vindicated may suffer nothing more than a temporary loss of position while the case is being investigated; an example is Marcel Masse, who resigned as minister of Communications in September 1985, after being accused of electoral violations, but returned to the same portfolio two months later, after he was cleared. On the other hand, leaders found guilty — by jury, commission, or board of inquiry — after denying or avoiding blame are likely to see their careers permanently derailed, if not destroyed.

Self-defence is a common initial response, especially among leaders who sincerely believe their activities to be appropriate. As evidence mounts that the leader is isolated in this belief, the defence will often shift toward one of the other strategies. At the root of many scandals can be found such misunderstandings about standards of behaviour: in particular, failure to accurately assess public tolerance for questionable or 'grey-area' activities, especially conflict-of-interest situations. This problem is exacerbated by the relative scarcity of specific rules and regulations that might help leaders avoid unacceptable behaviour.[12]

This division into management strategies is somewhat arbitrary. Ultimately, each scandal develops at its own pace and follows its own logic. Often the best a leader can do is to try and ride out the storm. Whether they manage skilfully or not, the underlying motivation of almost all leaders caught in scandal is to salvage what they can of their political careers. Astute leaders will recognize that short-term pain can often lead to long-term gain.

THE MORNING AFTER
Short-Term Effects of Scandal

Once it is clear that a political 'situation' will not be effectively resolved by a nasty exchange in Question Period, but has grown into a scandal, the immediate aftermath for the political leader involved is transition, possibly temporary, to a non-leadership role. For ministers this means leaving Cabinet, either on their own initiative or at the behest of the prime minister. Ministers are expected to do the 'honourable' thing and tender their resignations, even if they maintain their innocence, so that an investigation does not besmirch the government's record. By resigning, a minister protects the government not only subjectively but also procedurally; an individual who is out of Cabinet is off-limits to opposition questions and accusations inside the House. In reality, the decision to resign is often aided by an unofficial signal from the PMO. Thus when ministers 'offer' their resignations, they are usually aware that the offer is required.

Some ministers have resigned quickly and without protest, such as Charest and Masse; others, notably Sinclair Stevens, have clung to their posts until the opposition or the media have hounded them from office, thereby forcing the prime minister's hand. Others have offered spontaneous resignations, which occasionally have been refused: Trudeau was not eager to accept resignations from his friends in Cabinet, such as those involved in the 'judges affair',[13] and some ministers, such as Michel Côté — who accepted a personal loan from a government contractor in clear violation of conflict-of-interest guidelines — have had to be fired.

The minister's departure from Cabinet takes much of the pressure off the government. Cases of official misconduct almost always involve misuse of an official position; removing the leader from that position assures the public that the offence cannot be compounded. This single degree of demotion, however, appears to be considered sufficient. Even those ministers later found guilty of violating rules or laws while in office have not been required to vacate their parliamentary seats. They continue, at least until the next general election, to enjoy the privileges of membership in Parliament and, as former ministers, in the Privy Council, despite their questionable status. Even the judiciary seems to consider loss of a Cabinet portfolio a significant punishment in its own right. A few months before Alan Redways's blunder, an ordinary citizen found guilty of the same foolish prank was sentenced to six months' probation and a $100 fine, and was required to make a formal apology to the airport security guard involved. Redway, by contrast, received an absolute discharge.[14]

Even ordinary backbenchers caught up in scandal are spared the indignity of expulsion from the Commons. There is no legal requirement that members give up their seats, even if found guilty under the Criminal Code. In recent years, the only MP who has left the House under the cloud of scandal is Richard Grisé, who resigned his seat in 1989, a week after pleading guilty to fraud (he had left the Tory caucus shortly after the November election, and then quit the party to sit as an independent after being charged in April). Grisé resigned only to avoid being ousted by the government, which was under great pressure to punish him. Despite his admitted guilt, he was technically eligible to run in the by-election that followed.

Parliament has the power to expel a member, but to do so requires a unanimous vote; the last time an expulsion was even sought was in 1947, when Fred Rose was thrown out of the House after being found guilty of espionage for the USSR.[15] Since then, the House has relied on dissolution to flush out tainted members. The fact is that the time required to lay charges, investigate, and exhaust all avenues of appeal is usually greater than that remaining in a mandate. Grisé was perhaps unlucky in that his malfeasance came to light so soon after his election. Others—such as MP Michel Gravel, who admitted taking $90,000 in bribes only after his case reached the Supreme Court, and after he had 'chosen' not to seek re-election in 1988—have been able to bide their time on the back benches until the dropping of an election writ has provided an honourable discharge. Almost all the ministers who resigned from Mulroney's first government followed a similar trajectory, although Sinclair Stevens thought he deserved a second chance, and had to endure the humiliation of the prime minister's refusal to sign his nomination papers.

Sometimes a scandal has lingered on long after a leader's political career has been extinguished. Accused of influence-peddling, Roch LaSalle resigned from the Public Works portfolio in 1987 and, after twenty years in politics, did not seek re-election in 1988. Despite continued allegations against him, including some voiced by former colleagues Michel Gravel and Suzanne Blais-Grenier, he was not formally charged until 1991, when Québec businessman Glen Kealey used an obscure provision of the Criminal Code to lay charges as a private citizen. Kealey had accused fifteen prominent Conservatives of fraud and corruption; the Crown threw out the charges against all but LaSalle.

Punishment for scandal is not necessarily straightforward. Bud Drury offered his resignation to Trudeau in the wake of the 'judges affair', but it was not accepted. Six months later, however, Drury was lifted out of Cabinet by an appointment to the National Capital Commission. Such 'horizontal restructuring' through patronage allowed Trudeau to remove a somewhat tainted minister from active participation without subjecting him to the humiliation of an explicit fall from grace.

PENANCE AND REHABILITATION
Recovering from Scandal

Although scandal rarely brings an abrupt end to a leader's political career, in effect it often sentences a leader to a slow demise, filing appeals or pleading innocence from the back benches, without hope of recovery. But scandal does not necessarily punctuate a career with a full stop; in some cases it is merely a comma—a pause or hiatus after which leaders can re-emerge to take another chance. In such cases, a leader will drop down to the back benches, concentrating on constituency work or committee assignments, maintaining a low profile, and keeping his or her nose clean. Time may not heal all wounds, but errors that are not too serious can eventually be forgiven.

The Possibility of Forgiveness

Whether a leader will be able to mount a comeback is strongly determined by the temperature of the scandal. The flames of 'hot' scandals—those involving public money, national security, or political differences—leave little more than ashes on which to rebuild a career. Sinclair Stevens had no shortage of drive to make a comeback, but he had also exhausted his supply of prime ministerial good will. Robert Coates, despite twenty-eight years in Parliament, was unable to restore his tainted image. Suzanne Blais-Grenier ignited a scandal in 1985 when she was demoted from minister of the Environment to minister of state for Transport following accusations of lavish spending habits. She then fanned the flames by publicly criticizing the government's economic strategy (this sent her to the back benches), and then, in 1988, accusing members of the Québec wing of the party of an elaborate kickback scheme (for which she was expelled from caucus). She sat as an independent until the 1988 election, but, deprived of party support, was defeated by the new Conservative candidate.

Other leaders have not been so self-destructive. Judicial interference seems to be an offence 'cool' enough to allow the possibility of forgiveness—all the ministers who have resigned after improperly contacting judges (including Ouellet, Munro, and Charest) have later returned to Cabinet, their careers none the worse off. Consumer and Corporate Affairs minister Bernard Valcourt, who crashed his motorcycle while under the influence of alcohol in 1989, was also able to return to Cabinet. Even admitted forger Francis Fox staged a comeback after a few years and two elections, although having fallen from the position of Solicitor General, he bounced back only as far as Communications.

On the other hand, Alan Redway, guilty of a rather minor, if particularly blatant, act of foolishness, has never returned from the wilderness. Unlike Charest and Valcourt, however, Redway was not considered a 'rising star' in his party, and unlike Fox, Munro, and Ouellet, he was not a personal friend or favourite of the prime minister. In the competitive struggle for Cabinet positions, Redway probably had only one chance to impress the party hierarchy, and he blew it.

Other leaders, of course, have survived potentially very 'hot' scandals for the simple reason that they were exonerated. Marcel Masse exhibited no ill effects following his two-month vacation from Cabinet. In 1989, MPs Terry Clifford and Bob Hicks were investigated by the RCMP for allegedly padding their payrolls by employing each other's daughters. After the charges were dropped, they resumed their parliamentary lives. But exoneration does not always restore a career: André Bissonette, who resigned as Transport minister in 1987 after the Oerlikon affair (he was alleged to have profited from a series of questionable land transactions), was eventually found not guilty, but did not run for re-election in 1988. John Munro, cleared of a battery of fraud and corruption charges in 1991, has claimed that the allegations cost him a seat in 1988; his plans to run in the 1993 election were reluctantly abandoned in the face of some local opposition. And Bryce Mackasey, a minister in Trudeau's Cabinet in the 1970s who had left the House to serve in the Québec National Assembly and then returned to Ottawa in 1980, was on the verge of a ministerial comeback when allegations of influence-peddling and improper lobbying erupted. He too was eventually cleared, but only after the window of opportunity for a Cabinet appointment had closed.

STRATEGIES FOR THE PENITENT
Managing the Rehabilitation Process

As in other facets of political life, savvy decision-making and sensitivity to the changing moods of those offended by scandal—the electorate, Cabinet colleagues, and especially the prime minister—can improve a leader's chances for rehabilitation after a damaging lapse. Just as the outbreak of scandal can be managed, so can the recovery process.

Those unjustly accused may feel that resignation would imply guilt, but a prompt departure from Cabinet helps in a number of ways. By stepping aside while under investigation, ministers can insulate the government from the media attention that will be lavished on them. Resignation also demonstrates political maturity and respect for the parliamentary process and procedures. Protestations of innocence are perfectly acceptable, but they should be short and simple: a leader must avoid whining or complaining. All these steps indicate the qualities of persistence and grace under pressure that are highly regarded in Cabinet selection. Even while their names are being dragged through the mud, leaders should provide subtle cues to remind their colleagues that they are deserving of trust and confidence.

Leaders who have been caught in authentic improprieties should follow the same course and take it a step further: they must not only resign their portfolios, but offer sincere public apologies. Again, the emphasis should be on taking responsibility for one's actions, and perhaps hinting that one's intentions at least were pure, and that a lesson has been learned. Once confession is complete, a period of penance and quiet reflection is required. While the 'innocent' Marcel Masse simply had to wait until his name was cleared, the 'guilty' Jean Charest had to do time and work his way back to the Cabinet table. A cool scandal such as his seems to require roughly a six-month sojourn in the parliamentary wilderness, and continued or re-established prime ministerial favour, before a repentant leader can return, chastened and wiser. Bernard Valcourt's political rehabilitation was rather a special case, as it coincided with his physical rehabilitation; the need to do penance for the private misconduct of impaired driving coincided with the need to recover from serious injuries. Nevertheless, Valcourt was also returned to Cabinet in approximately six months.

Charest's tactics serve as a particularly good example of how a leader can, with skill and some luck, sidestep the career damage that scandal can precipitate. Judicial expert Peter Russell described Charest's mistake as minor in comparison with previous incidents in which ministers improperly contacted judges, and suggested that simply by offering a full apology to the House, and enduring a public scolding by the prime minister, Charest might have legitimately remained in Cabinet.[16] Had he thus resisted calls for his resignation, however, he would have had to endure charges of failing to take responsibility for a transgression, and might have lost the respect of crucial party superiors. By leaving Cabinet promptly, he probably improved his long-term career prospects more than he could have if he had stayed on. His return to Cabinet—in a more senior post—six months later, and his strong campaign for the party leadership in 1993, indicate that the affair did not harm his future.

Rehabilitation of a scandal-tainted leader is not always complete. Sometimes, instead of returning to Cabinet, the leader escapes the obscurity of the back bench by moving into a different position. John Fraser, having decided to feed the electorate tainted tuna, might not have been able to re-achieve public acceptance in a portfolio where he would be responsible for policy, but he was easily elected to a position of great procedural importance and power as Speaker of the House of Commons. His election also indicated that he had retained or regained the respect of his colleagues in the House.

The case of Liberal Roger Simmons, brought into Cabinet as minister of Energy, Mines and Resources in 1983 only to resign for 'personal reasons' ten days later, may be one of rehabilitation in progress. After his resignation, the media pounced on Simmons, discovering tax problems that had been troubling him for years, and that eventually led to a conviction and fine for tax evasion. Simmons was defeated in the 1984 election, but later won a seat in the Newfoundland Legislature. In 1988 he returned to the House of Commons, apparently forgiven by the electorate, and he was re-elected in 1993. Although his scandal involved money—usually a key indicator of a 'hot' and unrecoverable scandal—the temperature may have been reduced by the fact that the money involved was not (directly) public.

THE ROLE OF THE PRIME MINISTER

A scandal involving any member of the government also involves at least one other person. Ultimately it is the prime minister who determines the temperature of a scandal and who decides what action must be taken. Almost every warm-to-hot scandal brings charges, from the media and especially the opposition, that the prime minister has also been 'tainted' by association, and that the scandal-causing minister's poor judgement calls into question the prime minister's ability to select appropriate advisers. In many official-misconduct scandals, the rule that has been violated stems from the prime minister, who sets the rules that govern his or her ministers' behaviour, especially those regarding conflict of interest and judicial contacts. If a scandal requires further investigation, the prime minister determines the form that the investigation will take. And finally, while unable to impose or stay criminal charges, the prime minister controls both the kind of political punishment to be levied and the chances of political rehabilitation.

Prime ministers manage all these facets of scandal in different ways. During his many years in office, Pierre Trudeau was not often subjected to scandal by his ministers; while a number of allegations surfaced, only a handful were eventually substantiated. Trudeau tended to try to ride out a scandal, especially 'cool' ones involving his closest Cabinet associates. The 'judges affair' implicated four of his top ministers—Chrétien, Drury, Lalonde, and Ouellet; Ouellet eventually resigned, Drury's resignation was refused, and the other two escaped unscathed. Trudeau also protected Lalonde from accusations in 1980 that he had been involved directly with Alistair Gillespie's attempts to lobby his former Cabinet colleagues. By contrast, Trudeau readily accepted the resignation of Cabinet neophyte Roger Simmons, saying, 'Well, Roger, that's a bit of bad luck for you and for us.'[17] The majority of resignations from his cabinets concerned policy differences, they were handled quietly and quickly forgotten. He seems to have managed the Cabinet selection process well, choosing ministers who for the most part gave him no grief.[18] Indeed, most of the negative publicity of the Trudeau years was focused on Trudeau himself.

Brian Mulroney also endured his share of public disapprobation, but in his case, a significant amount stemmed from the unprecedented frequency with which scandal plagued his Cabinet, especially during his first term. The barrage of accusations and resignations of ministers, many of them Mulroney's close friends, seemed to suggest a pattern. Over one-third of his first Cabinet (15 of 40) had little or no parliamentary experience. Of these almost half eventually left Cabinet under a cloud of scandal. Mulroney himself was one of the least politically experienced in the caucus. Unlike Trudeau, Mulroney was not fortunate in his Cabinet choices. After the first years of his administration, the pace of Cabinet resignations slowed, even though Conservative MPs continued to get into trouble. This may have been indicative of the increasing experience of his Cabinet pool, or of a more cautious approach to bringing in new talent.

Mulroney's scandal-management program was troubled right from the beginning. By campaigning loudly against patronage and promising a comprehensive public-sector ethics package, he invited the scrutiny of the Liberal 'Rat Pack'. The most difficult scandal for Mulroney to weather was undoubtedly the Stevens affair. Faced with intense partisan pressure and an accused minister who continued to defend his behaviour, Mulroney turned to the judiciary for resolution. The heat had already been turned up high by the resignations of Fraser, Coates, and Blais-Grenier. Adding Stevens to the fire made it imperative that the prime minister take action to protect both the legitimacy of his government and his own reputation. Appointing the Parker Commission of Inquiry to investigate Stevens[19] gave Mulroney the aura of impartiality he needed in order to maintain the confidence of the House and the electorate.

As ministers continued to resign in record numbers, Mulroney's management style deteriorated. After firing Michel Côté he expressed his frustration: 'I've worked like hell to make these things work. . . . I've read the riot act time and time again, both to my caucus and to my ministry. . . . to indicate that I'm displeased or disappointed today is the understatement of the year.'[20] Interestingly, it was only after he had reached this level of exasperation, and at the urging of Justice Parker, that Mulroney finally came forward with conflict-of-interest legislation.

This bill (C-114, introduced in 1988) would have formalized many of the prohibitions that are currently informally applicable only to ministers, and set up an ethics tribunal to adjudicate situations of conflict and offer advice. Opposition to the bill quickly mobilized, however, notably from the spouses of parliamentarians who did not wish to become subject to financial disclosure rules. The bill also had to be modified after it was revealed that Mulroney had been lent $324,000 by the Conservative party for renovation of 24 Sussex Drive; the unaltered legislation might have been used to deem this an improper act. Faced with these obstacles, the bill died on the Order Paper when the 1988 election was called. Reintroduced in late 1989 as Bill C-43, it continued to be tinkered with and watered down, most recently by a Special Joint Committee in March 1993.

In the meantime, scandals continued to cause trouble for the government. Two developments in particular suggest that the sheer frequency of scandal has become an effective force in moulding parliamentary procedure. The revelation in 1990 that as many as 15 MPs were under RCMP investigation led to the passage of Bill C-79, which requires that the House of Commons Board of Internal Economy be notified of and approve any search warrants for MPs' offices. At about the same time, the same board began offering financial assistance with the legal costs of MPs facing charges or criminal investigation, at least until their cases went to trial. These measures, designed to protect MPs from the nuisance of unjustified allegations and resultant scandals, would likely have been superfluous in an environment of more rigorously defined ethical regulation. Instead, a subculture of scandal-avoidance has perhaps been institutionalized as a part of the parliamentary process.

CONCLUSION

The 'shocked response' inherent in scandal is often rooted in the perception that, by inappropriate, illegal, or careless actions, a political leader has breached or betrayed the public trust that is the basis for the legitimacy of his or her power. This 'sacred' trust appears to be a fragile construct, easily shattered. The very righteousness of the rhetoric surrounding it, however, has perhaps led to an over-inflated assessment of its value, in that a leader's loss of public trust seems to be considered a serious punishment in itself. Career damage and loss of reputation often seem to be factored into the punishments meted out to politicians convicted of scandalous or even corrupt behaviour. While the termination of a promising career can of course be a devastating blow for anyone, for many politicians that career is a secondary one. And except in rare cases such as that of Richard Grisé — a victim of bad timing as much as political exasperation — career termination can usually be delayed for years.

Thus while scandal can easily cause a fall from prominence, it hardly ever shoves political leaders all the way off Parliament Hill. With respect to membership in Parliament, in most cases scandal only makes voluntary retirement more attractive. There remains an understood mode of response to scandal: when charged, a leader ought to withdraw from Cabinet; when convicted, the price is one's parliamentary seat. The cases show, however, that this final step is effectively avoided through tactical manoeuvering. As scandals continue to cast aspersions on the integrity of Parliament and its membership, it is perhaps time for the House to provide more formal ethical guidance. Members need help not only in avoiding situations that are potentially scandalous; they also need help in either recuperating from scandal or in making the decision to spare the institution of Parliament by terminating their careers.

NOTES

1 John Hibbing, *Congressional Careers: Contours of Life in the U.S. House of Representatives* (Chapel Hill: University of North Carolina Press, 1991); Wayne Francis and John Baker, 'Why Do U.S. State Legislators Vacate their Seats?' *Legislative Studies Quarterly* 11 (1986): 119-26; Hibbing, *Choosing to Leave* (Washington: University Press of America, 1982).

2 Michael M. Atkinson and David Docherty, 'Moving Right Along: The Roots of Amateurism in the Canadian House of Commons', *Canadian Journal of Political Science* xxv: 2 (June 1992): 295-318.

3 Graeme C. Moodie, 'On Political Scandal and Corruption', *Government and Opposition* 15, 2 (1980): 216.

4 John G. Peters and Susan Welch, 'Political Corruption in America: A Search of Definitions and a Theory, or If Political Corruption is in the Mainstream of American Politics, Why is it Not in the Mainstream of American Politics Research?', *American Political Science Review* 72 (1978): 974-84.

5 Robert Brooks, 'The Nature of Political Corruption', in Arnold J. Heidenheimer, ed., *Political Corruption: Readings in Comparative Analysis* (New Jersey: Holt, Rinehart and Winston, 1970).

6 Moodie, 'On Political Scandal', 219.

7 Ibid., 220.

8 Sharon L. Sutherland, 'The Consequences of Electoral Volatility: Inexperienced Ministers 1949-90', in Herman Bakvis, ed., *Representation, Integration and Political Parties in Canada*, Vol. 14 of the Research Studies of the Royal Commission on Electoral Reform and Party Financing (Toronto: Dundurn Press, 1991), 303; and Sutherland, 'Responsible Government and Ministerial Responsibility: Every Reform is its Own Problem', *Canadian Journal of Political Science*, 24 (1991): 91. Note that the category names used here differ slightly from Sutherland's.

9 Sutherland, 'Consequences of Electoral Volatility', *passim*.

10 Michael M. Atkinson and Maureen Mancuso, 'Do We Need A Code of Conduct for Politicians?', *Canadian Journal of Political Science* 18 (1985): 459.

11 Ian Greene, 'Conflict of Interest and the Canadian Constitution', *Canadian Journal of Political Science* 23 (1990): 246.

12 For an excellent discussion of ministerial guidelines, see ibid.

13 For an examination of the 'judges affair' and its implications, see Peter H. Russell, *The Judiciary in Canada: The Third Branch of Government* (Toronto: McGraw-Hill Ryerson, 1987).

14 *Ottawa Letter* xx: 13 (1 April 1991): 110.

15 *Ottawa Letter* xix: 22 (29 May 1989): 171.

16 'Charest wasn't first minister to contact a judge', *Montréal Gazette*, 25 Jan. 1990: A2.

17 'Two lowering shadows of doubt', *Vancouver Sun*, 29 Aug. 1983.

18 Sutherland, 'Consequences of Electoral Volatility', 328.

19 See Mr Justice W.D. Parker, *Report of the Commission of Inquiry into the Facts of Allegations of Conflict of Interest Concerning the Honourable Sinclair M. Stevens* (Ottawa: Supply and Services Canada, 1987).

20 'Côté Affair Enrages PM', *Vancouver Sun*, 3 Feb. 1988.